Extending and Embedding Perl

Extending and Embedding Perl

Tim Jenness
Simon Cozens

MANNING

Greenwich
(74° w. long.)

For online information and ordering of this and other Manning books,
go to www.manning.com. The publisher offers discounts on this book
when ordered in quantity. For more information, please contact:

Special Sales Department
Manning Publications Co.
209 Bruce Park Avenue   Fax: (203) 661-9018
Greenwich, CT 06830   email: orders@manning.com

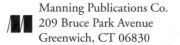

Manning Publications Co.   Copyeditor: Tiffany Taylor
209 Bruce Park Avenue   Typesetter: Dottie Marsico
Greenwich, CT 06830   Cover designer: Leslie Haimes

ISBN 1930110820
Printed in the United States of America
1 2 3 4 5 6 7 8 9 10 – VHG – 06 05 04 03 02

To the Perl open source community

contents

preface

Perl is a wonderful language. We, along with at least a million other programmers, love it dearly. It's great for all kinds of applications: text processing, network programming, system administration, and much more. But there are times when we need to go beyond the core of the language and do something not provided by Perl.

Sometimes we do this without noticing it: several modules that ship with Perl call out to C routines to get their work done, as do some of the most commonly used CPAN modules. Other times, we do it deliberately: the various modules for building graphical applications in Perl almost all, directly or indirectly, use external C libraries. Either way, writing extensions to Perl has historically been a bit of a black art. We don't believe this situation is fair, so we've written this book to attempt to demystify the process of relating Perl and C.

That's not to say we're fed up with writing modules in Perl. Both of us write many of our modules in Perl, and although sometimes it might be easier to interface to C, we've decided to stick with Perl. In fact, writing a module in Perl has a number of advantages over using other languages:

- It is far easier to write portable cross-platform code in Perl than in C. One of the successes of Perl has been its support of varied operating systems. It is unlikely that a module written in C could be as portable as a Perl version without much more effort on the part of the programmer, precisely because Perl strives to hide the complexities of differences between underlying operating systems from the programmer.

- Some problems do not need the speed gain that comes from using a compiled language or the added complexity of interfacing to another language. For many programmers who are proficient in Perl (and/or Java), writing a Perl module is much more efficient (in terms of programming effort) than writing the equivalent in C.

People program in Perl for a reason, and this fact should not be forgotten when it comes to deciding whether to use Perl for an extension module. These issues were addressed in the development of the standard `File::Temp` module (part of Perl 5.6.1). This module provides a standard interface for creating temporary files from Perl. The original intention was that this module would be written in C, but it quickly became apparent that a Perl implementation would be easier because of portability problems (it was to be a standard module, so it would have to work on all platforms supported by Perl); in addition, speed would not be an issue unless thousands of temporary files were required.

Having addressed why *not* to use a language other than Perl, we must now present two important reasons why another language *is* sometimes required:

- *Speed*—In some cases, Perl is simply too slow for a particular program. In this case, the choice is either to change the algorithm or to use a faster programming language. The Perl Data Language was created specifically to address the case of processing *N*-dimensional arrays, but there are times when another language is required. Similarly, Perl is definitely too slow for some tasks (for instance, the graphics manipulation functions provided by Imager and GD).

- *Functionality*—Many useful libraries have been written in other languages (especially C, and for numerical applications, Fortran). If new functionality is required that is present in an external library, then it is usually far better to provide a Perl interface to the library than to recode the library in Perl. For instance, the XML::Parser module provides a reasonably direct mapping onto the underlying functions of the expat library. Functionality is particularly an issue for things that simply *can't* be written in Perl, such as interfaces to certain system libraries (for instance, the Macintosh Carbon library) or to particular pieces of hardware.

As well as extending Perl by writing modules in C, sometimes it's advantageous to go the other way around: to add the flexibility of a Perl interpreter to an existing C program. Like extending, this process has a fearsome reputation, and so we provide two chapters on the topic. Chapter 8 introduces embedding Perl, and chapter 9 includes a full working example that explains Perl embedding.

We also realize that people want to know what's really going on under the hood, so we conclude our study of the interaction between C and Perl by examining the C sources of the perl interpreter itself, together with details of how to get involved in becoming a developer maintaining perl. Finally, we look ahead to Perl 6 and the Parrot project.

acknowledgments

The authors would like to thank the staff at Manning for their hard work, encouragement, and, where necessary, coercion. Susan Capparelle first approached us and got us to commit to the book; Marjan Bace oversaw the project. Ted Kennedy set up reviews and helped get some of the best people around to give us feedback on the book. Mary Piergies headed up production; Syd Brown and Dottie Marsico were the poor sods who had to deal with our awkward choice of markup and file formats. Tiffany Taylor was our eagle-eyed copy editor and Liz Welch our proofreader.

Our reviewers were wonderfully pedantic, catching every mistake from the unintentional slip to the outright lie. Martien Verbruggen headed up this exercise, and many thanks are also due to Alasdair Allan, Chuck Bailey, Clinton Pierce, Abhijit Menon-Sen, John Tobey, John Linderman, Norman Gray, Bennett Todd, Dan Sugalski, David Zempel, Doug MacEachern, Graham Barr, James Freeman, Spider Boardman, and Alex Gough.

The perl5-porters have been wonderfully helpful, answering obscure questions about the hidden corners of Perl. Particular thanks to Jarkko Hietaniemi, Gurusamy Sarathy, Nick Ing-Simmons, Hugo van der Sanden, Abhijit Menon-Sen, and Arthur Bergman. We hope that our explorations have been as beneficial to you as they have been intriguing to us.

TIM JENNESS   I would also like to thank Frossie for leading me onto the path to becoming a Perl hacker and for forcing me to write this book. Thanks to my brother, Matt, because he wanted to be thanked, and to the rabbits, Buns and Neo, for not eating *all* the draft versions of this book. Thanks to the Tuesday night movie gang for putting up with my terrible selections—the book can no longer be used as an excuse! Finally, thanks again to Frossie for expanding my horizons beyond measure and for being the center of my universe.

SIMON COZENS I would also like to thank the denizens of `#perl` and That Other IRC Channel, without whom this book would have been finished much earlier but would have been considerably more boring. Thanks to Ray, `pod`, and Aaron at Oxford University Computing Services, who have to put up with me on a daily basis and even seem to try not to mind; and to Oxford Go Club for providing welcome diversion and keeping me more or less sane. And thanks to Eiko, who has possibly been told "nearly finished now!" more times than the entirety of the Manning staff.

about this book

Guide to this book

This book is roughly divided into four sections. The first section covers the groundwork of dealing with C and the basics of XS, the extension language used to communicate between Perl and C:

- Chapter 1 provides an introduction to the C language from a Perl perspective. We explain the similarities and differences between the languages, and show how to write, compile, and run programs written in C.

- Chapter 2 presents the basics of the extension language, XS. By the end of this chapter, you will be able to create Perl modules that call simple C functions.

- Chapter 3 discusses more advanced features of the C language, such as strings, arrays, structures, and memory handling.

The next section explains XS in more detail:

- Chapter 4 describes how Perl values are stored internally: that is, how scalars, arrays, and hashes work. This concept is fundamental to doing any advanced work with XS, because you will be manipulating these types of values.

- Chapter 5 introduces the Perl API—the range of functions you have at your disposal as an XS programmer for manipulating values and interacting with the `perl` interpreter. As well as being a reference guide to the API, it contains many real-world examples of how the API functions are used in XS situations, including modules such as `Tk` and `DBI`, the `mod_perl` extension to the Apache web server, and the `perl` interpreter itself. In other words, it's intended to be a hands-on tutorial to using the API functions. (Note that appendix C provides an index of all Perl API references in the book.)

- Chapter 6 describes many more advanced uses of XS, such as how to create Perl arrays, hashes, and objects based on C structures; how to interface with Fortran; how to deal with files; how to call back from C to Perl; and much more. We believe this chapter represents, in a distilled format, the highest levels of XS magic, much of which has never been clearly written down before.

- Chapter 7 describes alternatives to XS that also help with C-Perl interaction: SWIG, `Inline`, and `PDL::PP`, among others.

The third section deals with embedding Perl in other projects:

- Chapter 8 describes embedding Perl in generic terms, including why and when you should consider embedding Perl in a C program, the fundamentals required to embed Perl, and how to call back from embedded Perl into C.

- Chapter 9 turns the description from chapter 8 into a working example, to help you understand the thought processes and programming involved in embedding Perl in a real-world application.

The fourth section deals with the internals of the `perl` interpreter:

- Chapter 10 provides an introduction to `perl` internals, including the path a Perl program takes from input to compilation to execution.

- Chapter 11 is a grab-bag of useful information on developing `perl`: how to debug the interpreter, how to contribute code back to the maintainers, and how the Perl development process works. We close by looking into the future at the Perl 6 development effort.

The final section consists of three appendices:

- Appendix A describes all of Perl's typemap entries used in the book.
- Appendix B lists further reading material.
- Appendix C provides an index of all Perl API references in the book.

Intended audience

We've worked hard to make this book the definitive tutorial and reference to all topics involved in the interaction of Perl and C. This means we've had to make some broad assumptions. Naturally, we assume you, the reader, are a competent Perl programmer.

We don't assume proficiency in C. Although we include an introduction to C at the beginning of this book, and it should be possible to gain a lot of benefit from this book without any prior exposure to C, this isn't intended to be a substitute for a good C tutorial—the idea is to whet your appetite regarding what can be done while extending Perl with C, and give you what you need to know to understand the majority of the examples provided. The book is also intended to inspire those who know the ground rules of C programming but find it hard to translate that knowledge into practical programs.

If you're an experienced C programmer, you'll naturally gain the most from this book, because you are likely to have practical ideas about how to apply the information in it. To avoid attacks of boredom, however, we recommend that the experienced C programmer skip chapters 1 and 3.

Source code downloads

The source code for all examples presented in this book is freely available from the publisher's web site, http://www.manning.com/jenness. Should errors be discovered after publication, all code updates will be made availabe via the Web.

Typographical conventions

In this book we use the following typographical conventions: example code, example output, variable names, variable types, and function names are all in `code` font. Examples that demonstrate user input use **`bold code`** font.

For instance, to demonstrate the output of a simple command we would have:

```
% perl -le 'print "hello"'
hello
%
```

The `%` indicates the shell or command prompt (on some systems this may be written as `>`), the emboldened text indicates what you would type, and the rest of the text is the output you would see.

Code annotations accompany many segments of code. Certain annotations are marked with chronologically ordered bullets such as ❶. These annotations have further explanations that follow the code.

author online

Purchase of *Extending and Embedding Perl* includes free access to a private web forum run by Manning Publications where you can make comments about the book, ask technical questions, and receive help from the authors and from other users. To access the forum and subscribe to it, point your web browser to http://www.manning.com/jenness. This page provides information on how to get on the forum once you are registered, what kind of help is available, and the rules of conduct on the forum.

Manning's commitment to our readers is to provide a venue where a meaningful dialog between individual readers and between readers and the authors can take place. It is not a commitment to any specific amount of participation on the part of the authors, whose contribution to the Author Online forum remains voluntary (and unpaid). We suggest you try asking the authors some challenging questions lest their interest stray!

The Author Online forum and the archives of previous discussions will be accessible from the publisher's web site as long as the book is in print.

about the cover illustration

The figure on the cover of *Extending and Embedding Perl* is a "Gauro o Larsi," a man from one of the many tribes that inhabited the mountainous and ethnically diverse region of the Indus River between Kashmir and Kabul. This illustration is taken from a Spanish compendium of regional dress customs first published in Madrid in 1799. The book's title page informs us:

> *Coleccion general de los Trages que usan actualmente todas las Nacionas del Mundo desubierto, dibujados y grabados con la mayor exactitud por R.M.V.A.R. Obra muy util y en special para los que tienen la del viajero universal*

which we loosely translate as:

> *General Collection of Costumes currently used in the Nations of the Known World, designed and printed with great exactitude by R.M.V.A.R. This work is very useful especially for those who hold themselves to be universal travelers.*

Although nothing is known of the designers, engravers, and artists who colored this illustration by hand, the "exactitude" of their execution is evident in this drawing. The Gauro o Larsi is just one of a colorful variety of figures in this collection which reminds us vividly of how distant and isolated from each other the world's towns and regions were just 200 years ago. Dress codes have changed since then and the diversity by region, so rich at the time, has faded away. It is now often hard to tell the inhabitant of one continent from another. Perhaps we have traded a cultural and visual diversity for a more varied personal life—certainly a more varied and interesting world of technology.

At a time when it can be hard to tell one computer book from another, Manning celebrates the inventiveness and initiative of the computer business with book covers based on the rich diversity of regional life of two centuries ago—brought back to life by the pictures from this collection.

C H A P T E R   1

C for Perl programmers

When using C and Perl together, the first thing you need to realize is that they are very different languages, requiring different styles and different thought patterns. Perl spoils programmers by doing much of the hard work for you; if you've never programmed in C, the language can feel very barren and empty. C is close to the machine—Perl is close to the user.

That said, Perl's syntax borrows heavily from C's, and so most of the elements of a C program should be familiar to a competent Perl programmer with a little thought and a little preparation.

1.1   HELLO, WORLD

The classic book on C programming is Brian Kernighan and Dennis Ritchie's *The C Programming Language*, which begins with a program a little like this:

```c
#include <stdio.h>

int main(int argc, char* argv[])
{
  printf("hello, world\n");
  return(0);
}
```

The classic book on Perl, on the other hand, is *Programming Perl*, by Larry Wall, Tom Christiansen, and Randal Schwartz. It begins with a similar program:

```
print "Howdy, world!\n";
```

Notice that Perl is much more compact: there's no waffle, no housekeeping. We want to print something, and we tell Perl to print it. C, on the other hand, requires more support from the programmer.

Let's first look at how to compile and run the C program, before we discuss how it's constructed.

1.2   THE C COMPILER

There's only one Perl, but a large variety of C compilers and implementations are available; they can have a graphical front-end, such as the Microsoft Visual Studio, or a simple command-line interface, such as the Free Software Foundation's Gnu C Compiler (GCC). We'll talk about GCC here, because it's the most popular free compiler.

The simplest way to call GCC is to give it the name of a C program to compile. GCC is particularly quiet; if all is well, it will give no output on the screen:

```
% gcc hello.c
%
```

This command produces an executable called a.out[1] in the current directory. If we run it like so

```
% ./a.out
hello, world!
```

we get our tired and worn greeting.

Sometimes we don't want our output called a.out, so we can tell GCC to give it another name with the -o option:

```
% gcc -o hello hello.c
```

Perl encourages programmers to turn on the -w flag for warnings; we encourage C programmers to turn on the -Wall flag for all warnings:[2]

```
% gcc -Wall -o hello hello.c
```

If we have a collection of C files that make up one program, we can list them all:

```
% gcc -Wall -o bigproject one.c two.c three.c four.c
```

---

[1]   It has this name for historical reasons; a.out was the name of a particular type of executable file format.

[2]   Of course, if you are not using GCC, the particular option will be different. Ironically, -Wall does not turn on all the warnings in GCC; it only turns on those the GCC programmers feel are important. See the GCC documentation for the full list of warnings. If you want to make sure your program will be ANSI compliant and you're not accidentally slipping in some GCC extensions, consider using the -ansi -pedantic option.

However, it's more popular to use GCC to convert each one to an *object file* (extension .o with GCC, equivalent to .obj files on Windows)—an intermediate stage in compilation—and then link all the object files together; doing so allows you to change individual files without needing to completely recompile everything. To tell GCC to produce an object file, use the -c flag:

```
% gcc -Wall -o one.o -c one.c
% gcc -Wall -o two.o -c two.c
% gcc -Wall -o three.o -c three.c
% gcc -Wall -o four.o -c four.c
```

Then, simply list the object files to link them together:

```
% gcc -Wall -o bigproject one.o two.o three.o four.o
```

There are more complicated ways to build large programs, using static and dynamic libraries, but we won't go into those in our examples.

1.3   HEADER FILES

The first line in the C "Hello world" program presented earlier in the chapter is an include directive: it is similar to Perl's require in that it instructs the language to go find a library file and read it in. However, whereas Perl's .pm and .pl library files contain real Perl code, C's .h files (*header* files) contain only the *promise* of code—they contain function prototypes, and just like Perl's subroutine prototypes, these prototypes allow the compiler to check your use of the functions while specifying that the real code will come later.

> **NOTE**   Header files can contain any code, but they're typically used for function prototypes that several C source files will need; they are also often used to declare constants (see section 1.9), enumerations (sets of related constants), and structures (see section 3.4).

But what function's prototype do we need, and where will the real code come from? The only function we use is printf, in line 5 of our example. Perl has a printf function, too, and the two functions are almost identical. However, all the Perl functions documented in perlfunc are built in to the language; C, on the other hand, has *no* built-in functions. Everything is provided by a library called the *standard C library*, which is included when any C program is compiled. The printf function comes from a section of the standard C library called the *standard IO library*, and to let the C compiler ensure that we are using it properly, we have it read the header file that contains the prototypes for the standard IO library, stdio.h.[3]

---

[3]   It's almost like use strict is always on—you can't use any function without telling C where it's coming from (or at least you shouldn't, because if you fail to declare the prototype, the compiler will make some assumptions that are unlikely to be correct).

1.4 THE MAIN FUNCTION

The Perl version of the "Hello world" program is much smaller because everything in C must be inside a function; if you have Perl code outside any subroutine, it will all be executed in order. C needs all this code in one place: the `main` function. When your program begins, C arranges for this function to be called.

NOTE   What you'd call a *subroutine* in Perl is called a *function* in C.

This function must have a prototype, and here it is again:[4]

```
int main(int argc, char* argv[]);
```

Perl's prototypes tell you only what type of data is coming into the function: `sub main($@)` tells you that the subroutine `main` takes a scalar and an array. The prototypes can also coerce values into a given type; for instance, `sub take_ref(\%)` will make the first element into a reference to a hash.

In C, you're not only told what's coming into the function, you're also told what variables it should be stored in, and also what type of data the function should return. C's prototypes do not coerce values to a type—instead, if you pass the wrong type, the C compiler will give an error.

In this case, we're returning an integer, and we're being given an integer called `argc` and something called `argv`. We'll look at what `char *` means later, but you might be able to guess that `argv` is similar to Perl's `@ARGV` and `[]` might denote an array—`argv` is an array of the command-line parameters. `argc` is the number of elements in the array—that is, the number of command-line parameters passed to the program (the argument count). One difference between Perl and C is that in C, `argv` contains the name of the command in element 0, whereas in Perl, `@ARGV` does not contain the command name (that can be retrieved using `$0`).

NOTE   `main` is a special C function in the sense that it can have multiple prototypes and you can decide which one to use. If you are not interested in using command-line arguments, you can use a much simpler prototype that has no arguments:

```
int main(void);
```

Some compilers also support a third argument to `main`:

```
int main(int argc, char *argv[], char **envp);
```

Here, `envp` provides access to the process environment. It is not part of `POSIX` or the ANSI C89 standard, so we won't mention it again.

---

[4] ISO standard C `main` is defined as being `int main(int argc, char** argv)`, but many programmers use the (roughly) equivalent `char* argv[]`. The difference is horribly subtle. We use `char* argv[]` here because it's easier to understand.

The `main` function almost always has the two-argument prototype given earlier: it should take two parameters that represent the command line and return an integer value to the operating system (the exit status). Additionally, just as in Perl, the program can end implicitly when there is no more code to execute, or explicitly when the `exit` function is called. We showed another explicit method in our first example, which returned a value to the operating system, ending the `main` function. We could also, theoretically, allow execution to fall off the end of the `main` function:

```
#include <stdio.h>

int main(int argc, char *argv[])
{
  printf("hello, world\n");
  /* No return, just falls off. */
}
```

TIP   This example includes the use of a C comment. Comments are made up of matched pairs of `/*` and `*/`.[5] Note that comments cannot be nested. This is legal:

```
/*
   Comment out some code:
   printf("This won't print\n");

   Now carry on with the program:
*/
```

But this isn't:

```
/*
   Comment out some code:
   printf("This won't print\n"); /* A comment */

   Now carry on with the program:
*/
```

The comment will be ended at the first `*/`—that is, after `A comment`—and the C compiler will try to compile `Now carry on...`.

Allowing execution to fall off the end of `main` is not recommended; doing so produces a warning to the effect that C expected your function to return a value, and it never did. Finally, we can call `exit` explicitly:

```
#include <stdio.h>

int main(int argc, char *argv[])
{
  printf("hello, world\n");
  exit(0);
}
```

---

[5] Many modern compilers (and the C99 standard) also implement C++-style `//` comments. These comments act just like Perl `#` comments.

The compiler makes a special exemption for `exit`, because it knows the function will not return.

1.5 VARIABLES AND FUNCTIONS

C forces you to define your variables, as well as define your function prototypes, just like the `use strict` mode of Perl. You can define four types of variables: function parameters, automatic variables, global variables, and static variables.

1.5.1 Function parameters

Function parameters are declared in the definition of a function.[6] Let's look at a very simple function:

```
int treble(int x)
{
    x *= 3;
    return(x);
}
```

Here we take an integer, x, multiply it by 3, and return its new value. Note that we don't strictly speaking need the parentheses around the `return` value, because `return` is not really a function; it's a keyword of the language. Unlike Perl subroutines, all functions in C require parentheses. However, we tend to place parentheses around the `return` value as a stylistic decision.

The Perl equivalent of the previous function looks like this:

```
sub treble {
    my $x = shift;
    $x *= 3;
    return $x;
}
```

And we'd call it like this:

```
print "Three times ten is ", treble(10), "\n";
```

We don't have a direct equivalent to `print` in C, but we can use `printf`:

```
#include <stdio.h>

int treble(int x) {
    x *= 3;
    return(x);
}

int main(int argc, char *argv[]) {
```

---

[6] In fact, because a function definition declares the input and output types as a function, most of the time you don't need a prototype—if you define your functions before they're used, the C compiler will know about their parameter signatures.

```
    printf("Three times ten is %d\n", treble(10));
    return(0);
}
```

The `printf` function is similar to the Perl version. The `%d` format is used to format a signed integer in both Perl and C.

As we mentioned earlier, function prototypes must appear before they are called, so the compiler can check the types: hence the definition of `treble` must appear before the `main` function calls it. Otherwise, C assumes that the return value will be `int`, and you will receive a warning from the compiler if warnings are turned on.

Function parameters act just like lexical variables in Perl (`my` variables); they have the same scope as their enclosing block (which is always the function) and they are private to that scope.

1.5.2 Automatic variables

Automatic variables have scoping properties similar to those of function parameters, but they can appear in any block. They are directly equivalent to Perl's lexical variables.

You declare an automatic variable by listing its type and its name; however, declaration of automatic variables *must* happen before any statements in the block. So, we can say this:

```
#include <stdio.h>

int main (int argc, char *argv[]) {
    int number;
    number = 4;

    printf("Hello world\n");
    return(0);
}
```

But we can't say this:

```
#include <stdio.h>

int main (int argc, char *argv[]) {
    printf("Hello world\n");

    int number;
    number = 4;

    return(0);
}
```

You can also initialize your automatic variables when you declare them, by saying, for instance `int number = 4;`. In addition, you can start a new block to declare an automatic variable:

```
int some_function(int parameter) {
    int one = 1;

    {
```

```
        int two = 2;
        printf("one = %d, two = %d\n", one, two);
    }

    /* "two" is out of scope here */
    return one;
}
```

Because of this property, it's likely that most of your temporary variables—in fact, most of the variables you use—will tend to be automatic variables. They are called automatic variables because C knows their scope and their type at compile time, so it can automatically allocate memory for them and free this memory at the end of the variable's scope.

Just as in Perl, if you have two lexical variables with the same name, only the most recently declared one is in scope. The newer definition "hides" the older one:

```
int main(int argc, char *argv[]) {
    int number = 10;
    {
        int number = 20;
        printf("%d", number); /* Will print "20" */
    }
    return number; /* Will return 10 */
}
```

However, unlike Perl in strict mode, many C compilers may not give you a warning in this case.

1.5.3   Global variables

If a variable is declared outside a function, it's available to all the functions in that file defined after that variable declaration:

```
#include <stdio.h>

int counter = 0;

void bump_it(void) {
    counter++;
}

int main(int argc, char *argv[]) {
    printf("The value of counter is %d\n", counter);
    bump_it();
    bump_it();
    printf("The value of counter is %d\n", counter);
    bump_it();
    printf("The value of counter is %d\n", counter);

    return(0);
}
```

The function bump_it modifies the global variable counter, which main reads. bump_it is declared to return type void—this just means it will not return anything (think of "void context" in Perl). This example has the following output when compiled and executed:

```
The value of counter is 0
The value of counter is 2
The value of counter is 3
```

It's also possible to share a global variable across multiple files by declaring it once in one file and then prefixing the declaration in other files with the extern keyword. For instance, suppose we have a file called count1.c that contains the earlier declaration and main function:

```
#include <stdio.h>

int counter = 0;

void bump_it(void);

int main(int argc, char *argv[]) {
    printf("The value of counter is %d\n", counter);
    bump_it();
    bump_it();
    printf("The value of counter is %d\n", counter);

    return(0);
}
```

(We still need to provide the prototype to bump_it, just as stdio.h provides the prototype for printf.) Suppose we also have a file called count2.c containing the bump_it function:

```
extern int counter;

void bump_it() {
    counter++;
}
```

We can now compile these files into object files and link them together, like this:

```
% gcc -Wall -o count1.o -c count1.c
% gcc -Wall -o count2.o -c count2.c
% gcc -Wall -o count count1.o count2.o
```

The function in count2.c knows that it should be able to access a global variable called counter, which is declared externally—somewhere else in the program. C finds the global declaration of counter in count1.c, and so the function can access the global variable.

1.5.4   Static variables

Static variables are the final type of variable available; these variables keep their value between calls to a function. One way to do something like this in Perl would be

```
{
    my $x;
    sub foo {
        return ++$x;
    }
}
```

or even to use a closure. But C does not allow you to declare bare blocks outside any function the same way you can in Perl. The C equivalent looks like this:

```
#include <stdio.h>

int foo (void) {
    static int x = 0;
    return ++x;
}

int main(int argc, char *argv[]) {
    int i;

    for (i=1; i<=10; i++)
        printf("%d\n",foo());

    return(0);
}
```

Notice the following few things here:

- To maintain a variable's state between calls, declare the variable `static`.
- There is no range operator, nor a special variable like $, nor a one-argument `foreach` loop to loop over an array; we only have the three-argument `for`.
- Calls to functions you declare must contain parentheses, even when they take no parameters; otherwise, you end up taking the address of the function! (See section 3.2.2.) (Leaving out the parentheses transforms &mysub into \&mysub.)
- If the code inside a `for` loop is only one statement, you do not need to enclose it in a block. If it's more than one statement, it must be enclosed in curly braces. This rule also applies to the other control structures, `if` and `while`. (see section 1.8).

C has no equivalent to Perl's dynamic scoping (variables with `local`); the Perl internals contain some scary hacks to implement their own dynamic scoping in C to get around this deficiency.

1.6 DATA TYPES

If `argc` is an integer and `argv` is an array of strings, what other data types do you have? Perl supports only three types of variables (ignoring globs for now): scalars for single data items, arrays for storing many scalars, and hashes for keyword/scalar pairs. A *scalar* is simply a *thing* that can be passed around and processed, but the type of the scalar is not important. In C, the compiler needs to know whether you are using a number or a character and the type of number you are using (integer, floating-point number, or double-precision floating-point number). C supports a variety of data types, and the implementation of most of these types can vary from machine to machine; the Perl internals define some special types that give you a machine-independent environment.

1.6.1 C types

First, let's look at the basic C types. We assume that you are familiar with bitwise arithmetic, such as the Perl ^, |, ~, and & operators, and also with how computers store numbers. (If you're a little hazy, the Perl manual page `perlnumber` has a good summary.)

The int type

The `int` type represents positive or negative integer values. The C standard defines the various data types in terms of minimum acceptable versions of their maximum and minimum values—an `int` is *at least* the range -32767 to 32767, but can be (and almost certainly, on modern machines, will be) larger.

For example, an `int` on my machine is represented using 32 bits of memory. One of these bits is used as a *sign bit* to determine whether the value is positive or negative, and the other 31 bits are used to store the number; thus it has a range from -2147483647 to 2147483647. You can tell C to not use a sign bit and have all 32 bits available for storage by declaring an `unsigned int`, giving you a range from 0 to 4294967295.

I say "on my machine" because the size of these types is not guaranteed, nor is it defined by the C language; a compiler for a 64-bit processor may choose to use 64 bits to represent an `int`, or it may not. Although the C standard specifies the minimum size, it doesn't guarantee the actual size. (This is why the Perl internals define their own types, to guarantee sizes.) There are a number of ways to determine the limits. The easiest is to set all the bits in an unsigned variable to 1 and examine the number produced. Just as in Perl, you can set all the bits to 1 using the bitwise NOT operator (~):

```
#include <stdio.h>

int main (int argc, char *argv[]) {
    unsigned int i = ~0;

    printf("i is %u\n", i);
    return(0);
}
```

(Note that we use %u as the `printf` format specifier for an unsigned integer—this is the same as in Perl.)

Running this program will tell us that the highest unsigned integer is 4294967295, so the highest signed integer must be 1 less than half of 1+4294967295.

Because this method will only work for unsigned types, we use another method to determine the limits of a built-in type; this approach is slightly more complex, but more flexible. The header file limits.h defines some constants (see section 1.9 for an explanation of how this happens) that tell us the limits of the various sizes. For example, the code

```
#include <stdio.h>
#include <limits.h>

int main (int argc, char *argv[]) {
    printf("The maximum signed integer is %d\n", INT_MAX);
    printf("The minimum signed integer is %d\n", INT_MIN);
    printf("The maximum unsigned integer is %u\n", UINT_MAX);
    /* UINT_MIN is not declared because it's obviously 0! */
    return(0);
}
```

produces the following output:

```
The maximum signed integer is 2147483647
The minimum signed integer is -2147483648
The maximum unsigned integer is 4294967295
```

You should note that the POSIX module in Perl can also define these constants (and notice how similar Perl with use POSIX can be to C!):

```
use POSIX;
printf("The maximum signed integer is %d\n", INT_MAX);
printf("The minimum signed integer is %d\n", INT_MIN);
printf("The maximum unsigned integer is %u\n", UINT_MAX);
```

The char type

Characters are nothing more than numbers. To C, a character is merely an integer of at least 8 bits; depending on your architecture and compiler, it may be signed or unsigned. Because you're used to thinking of characters running from character 0 to character 255, you can use unsigned chars to get that range.

Because characters are just numbers, a single-quoted character in C acts like the ord operator in Perl—it produces an integer representing the character set codepoint of that character (but note that there is a big difference between '*' and "*" in C; we'll discuss this difference further in section 3.3). The following is equivalent to Perl's print ord("*"),"\n":

```
#include <stdio.h>

int main(int argc, char *argv[]) {
    printf("%d\n", '*');
    return(0);
}
```

Similarly, you can turn numbers into characters with the printf format specifier %c, just as in Perl:

```
#include <stdio.h>

int main(int argc, char *argv[]) {
    unsigned char c;

    /* print "Character $_ is ", chr($_), "\n" for 0..255; */
    for (c=0; c < 255; c++)
        printf("Character %d is %c\n", c, c);

    return(0);
}
```

We say c < 255 instead of c <= 255 because of the way c is stored; it must be between 0 and 255, so our termination clause is useless. When a C value overflows the storage of its variable, it *wraps around*—the higher bits are truncated. For instance, see figure 1.1.

```
              |87654321| - 8 bits of an unsigned char
              | Binary |
c = 254       |11111110|
c++           |11111111|
c = 255       |11111111|
c++          1|00000000| - Overflow
c = 0         |00000000| - Truncation
```

Figure 1.1 Variables wrap around when storage is overflowed.

So, for an unsigned char, 255+1 = 0, and because 0 is less than or equal to 255, our program will never terminate. This analysis, of course, assumes we have an 8-bit variable (use the CHAR_BIT macro defined in limits.h to find out how many bits are used to represent a char on your system). In general, you should not rely on overflow behavior in your C programs because the behavior for signed types is not defined as part of the C standard.

With the push toward Unicode, people gradually realized that having 8 bits to represent characters is not enough, and so wide characters were introduced: the wchar type. Perl does not use wide characters.

The short type

Sometimes an int stores more bits than you need, so you may want to use a smaller type. A short (or short int) is usually half the size of an int: the limits SHRT_MAX and SHRT_MIN tell you the size:

```
printf("The maximum short is %d\n", SHRT_MAX);
printf("The minimum short is %d\n", SHRT_MIN);
```

You can run this code in either C or Perl.

Shorts are available in signed and unsigned flavors, but are only rarely used.

The long type

To represent larger numbers, you can use longs (long ints). On some machines, these are twice the width of an int; however, on many machines longs and ints are equivalent. The new C standard, C99, also allows long long ints, which are twice as wide again. Both types are available as unsigned variants.

The float type

The world is not made up purely of integers; there are also floating-point values, and these require a separate data type. (Perl is happy to have you put strings, integers, and floating-point values in the same scalar, but C forces you to split them up.)

Floating-point types are always signed in C, and a floating-point value is represented by two numbers: the *exponent* (e) and the *mantissa* (m), such that the value to be stored is $n=m2^e$. The choice of the number of bits for exponent and mantissa determines the accuracy and the range of the type. It is important to remember that a floating-point number cannot represent every number with complete accuracy. Some numbers (for example, 1/3 and 1/7) can never be represented perfectly, regardless of the number of bits in the float; you must carefully consider this fact if accuracy of numerical calculations is important to you.

You must also carefully consider the difference between floating-point operations and integer operations. Look at the following program:

```
#include <stdio.h>

int main (int argc, char *argv[]) {
    float fraction1 = 1 / 4;
    float fraction2 = 1 / 4.0;
    printf("%f %f\n", fraction1, fraction2);

    return 0;
}
```

When you run this program, you may be surprised to get the following output:

```
0.000000 0.250000
```

Here, fraction2 correctly has a value of 0.25, but fraction1 has a value of 0.00. This seeming inconsistency is a product of the compiler; when the compiler sees literal numbers, it must assign a type to them. Because there is no indication to the contrary, numbers that look like integers are assigned to integer types, and numbers that look like floating-point numbers are assigned to floating-point types. Thus the compiler translated the previous assignments to

```
float fraction1 = (int)1 / (int)4;
float fraction2 = (int)1 / (float)4.0;
```

When an arithmetic operation takes place between two variables of different types, the compiler converts the variables to the highest type using the rules given in section 1.7. In this case, an integer is converted to a `float` when combined with another `float`:

```
float fraction1 = (int)1 / (int) 4;
float fraction2 = (float)1.0 / (float)4.0;
```

Now for the trick: the division operator performs integer division (that is, effectively, `int(1/4)`) when both of its operands are integers, and floating-point division when its operands are floats. Hence, the value that's stored into `fraction1` is the result of *integer* division of `1` and `4`; the value that's stored into `fraction2` is the result of floating-point division, which keeps the fractional part.

The moral of the story is: if you want a floating-point result from your code, make sure that at least one of your operands is a `float`.

The double type

`double`s are, very simply, high-precision `float`s; they contain a larger exponent, and the C standard requires them to be able to hold `1e-37` up to `1e+37`. As usual, most systems provide much larger storage—on my system, `double`s can range from `2.2250738585072e-308` all the way up to `1.79769313486232e+308` (that's 10 bits of exponent and 53 bits of mantissa).

On some systems, `long double`s may be available, for even more bits.

The void type

`void` is a special data type that is used, as you saw in our earlier global variable example, to indicate that a function has no return value and should be called in void context. As you'll see in chapter 3, the `void` type can also used as a generic type for a pointer, to enable data of any type to be passed to and from a function.

1.6.2   Types defined in Perl

To get around the implementation-specific nature of the limits of the basic C types, Perl defines a number of types that are guaranteed to have certain properties. Perl also defines a number of far more complex types, which let you represent Perl scalars, hashes, and so on. We will look at these in chapter 4. For now, we'll examine the simple types from which almost all Perl variables are formed. For guaranteed portability, you should use these types when your code interfaces with Perl, rather than the types described earlier.

The I8, I16, and I32 types

These types are used for different sizes of integers and are guaranteed to hold *at least* the number of bits their name implies: an `I8` will definitely hold 8 bits (and might hold more) and so can be used to store values from `-128` to `127`. An `I8` is almost always equivalent to a `char`.

Each of these types has a corresponding unsigned type: U8, U16, and U32. On 64-bit machines, I64 and U64 are also available.

C has a special convention for defining types: the typedef operator, which lets you provide aliases for type names. Here is our earlier char example reimplemented using typedef and U8:

```
#include <stdio.h>

typedef unsigned char U8;

int main(int argc, char *argv[]) {
    U8 i;

    for (i=0; i < 255; i++)
        printf("Character %d is %c\n", i, i);

    return 0;
}
```

The IV and UV types

IV and its unsigned counterpart UV are the types used to represent integers used in a Perl program. When you say $a = 123456;, the 123456 is stored in an IV or UV. Perl uses an IV rather than any of the guaranteed-size types in the previous section because IV provides another guarantee: it's big enough to be used to store a *pointer*, which is the C equivalent of a reference. (We'll look at pointers in more detail in chapter 3 and see how they relate to Perl references in chapter 4.)

The NV type

The NV type is used to represent floating-point numbers in a Perl program; once again, this type is guaranteed to be able to store a pointer, although it's hardly ever used to do so. This type is at least a double.

The STRLEN type

Finally, in our tour of types, STRLEN is an unsigned integer type that tells you how big something is in bytes; it's generally used to represent the size of a string.

1.7   CASTING

C uses simple rules to convert values between types. Data is converted when it moves from a "smaller" type to a "bigger" type, such as from an int to a float; but when converting back down, only the portion of the representation that "fits" in the smaller type is retained. (This process may or may not trigger a warning from the compiler about information being lost.) For instance, the code

```
int x = INT_MAX;
short int y;
y = x;
```

will leave y equal to -1, because all the bits in the smaller type will be set.[7]

The conversion happens implicitly when two differently typed values are the operands to the arithmetic operators, or when one assigns a value to a variable of a different type; it also happens when the type of a value passed as a function parameter is different than the function's prototype says it should be.

You can also force the explicit conversion to a particular type by using the *cast* operator; simply put the target type in parentheses before the expression you wish to cast. This technique is rarely used for real values, but you'll see that it is extremely important when we examine pointers and structures.

1.8 CONTROL CONSTRUCTS

Because Perl borrowed its syntax heavily from C, C's control constructs should be familiar to you. We have `if (...) {...}`, `while (...) {...}`, `do { ... }`, `while (...)` and `for(;;)`, and they all work the same way they do in Perl.

1.8.1 Statements and blocks

However, in C, one difference is that you can omit the braces from a block under a control construct if that block contains only one statement. For instance, we can write

```
if (a > b) {
    max = a;
} else {
    max = b;
}
```

as

```
if (a > b)
    max = a;
else
    max = b;
```

A control construct counts as only one statement, so we can also write such things as this program, to count the number of printable characters in the character set:

```
#include <stdio.h>
#include <ctype.h>

int main(int argc, char *argv[])
{
    unsigned char i;
    int printables = 0;

    for (i=0; i<255; i++)
        if (isprint(i))
            printables++;
```

---

[7] Probably. This is another area that isn't guaranteed by the standard.

```
        printf("%i printable characters\n", printables);
        return(0);
}
```

The function isprint, whose prototype is in ctype.h, tells us whether a character in the range 0 to 255 is printable.

When you're using nested control structures without braces like this, it's important to be aware of the *dangling else* problem. For example, in the following code, which if does the else belong to?

```
if (utf)
    if (!haslen)
        len = getlength(string);
else
    len = 1;
```

The indentation shows what we *mean*—we want len to be 1 if utf is not set—but that's not how the compiler sees it. What really happens looks like this:

```
if (utf)
    if (!haslen)
        len = getlength(string);
    else
        len = 1;
```

Editors such as Emacs will automatically indent code to the correct column when you press Tab, but it's best to use braces in such cases to reduce confusion.

1.8.2 The break and continue statements

Perl's last control statement is spelled break in C. Here's a function that cuts off a string after the first space character:

```
int token (char s[]) {
    unsigned int len = strlen(s);
    int i;

    for (i=0; i < len; i++)
        if (isspace(s[i]))
            break;

    s[i] = '\0';
    return i;
}
```

When a whitespace character (space, tab, new line, and so forth) is found, the break statement makes C immediately leave the for loop, and makes that character the end of the string. We return the character offset as the new length of the string. (In chapter 3, we'll explain how you can use this return value to get at the rest of the string.)

Similarly, next is replaced by continue; this fragment of code (modified from sv.c in the Perl core) processes only non-zero elements in an array:

```
for (i=0; i > oldsize; i++) {
    if (!ary[i])
        continue;
    curentp = ary + oldsize;
    ...
}
```

There is no equivalent to Perl's redo. If you really need it, you can use goto and labels just as in Perl; but, just as in Perl, 10 times out of 10, you don't.

1.8.3 The switch statement

One control structure that Perl doesn't have[8] is the switch statement. This statement allows you to test an integral expression against multiple (constant) values. It's much easier than using else if over and over again. Here's an example from the Perl core, when Perl has seen one of the -X file test functions and is trying to figure out which one you mean. It has the next character in tmp, and is choosing from a number of constants to set the value of ftst:

```
switch (tmp) {
   case 'r':
            ftst = OP_FTEREAD;
            break;

   case 'w':
            ftst = OP_FTEWRITE;
            break;

   case 'x':
            ftst = OP_FTEEXEC;
            break;

   case 'o':
            ftst = OP_FTEOWNED;
            break;
   ...
}
```

Notice that we break after every case, because switch is, in fact, a glorified computed goto. If we don't break, the program control will fall through to the next case:

```
int i = 0;

switch (i) {
   case 0:
            printf("It's 0\n");
   case 1:
            printf("It's 1\n");
   case 2:
            printf("It's 2\n");
}
```

---

[8] Although Damian Conway's Switch module provides an implementation.

This code will execute *all three* print statements. Sometimes this result really is what you want, but you should take care to mark the fall-through if you're likely to forget it. Here's an example of how falling through could be useful. Note that we're falling through the cases that have no statements, as well; if the character is 1, then we fall through cases 2, 3, ..., 7:

```
switch (c) { /* "c" is some character"
   case '0': case '1': case '2': case '3':
   case '4': case '5': case '6': case '7':
           could_be_octal = 1;
           /* Fall through */

   case '8': case '9':
           could_be_dec = 1;
           /* Fall through */

   case 'A':
   case 'B':
           /* This is actually fall through, too */
   case 'C':
   case 'D':
   case 'E':
   case 'F':
           could_be_hex = 1;
}
```

1.9   MACROS AND THE C PREPROCESSOR

Before your C code reaches the compiler, it goes through an intermediary program: the *preprocessor*. We've already said that header files such as stdio.h and ctype.h contain function prototypes; the preprocessor is responsible for inserting the content of those files into the current program. It does so with the `#include` preprocessor directive:

```
#include "header.h"
```

This directive will insert the contents of the file header.h from the current directory into the copy of your source code that is passed to the compiler.

NOTE   Why did we have this

```
#include "header.h"
```

but previously this?

```
#include <stdio.h>
```

By using quotes, we tell the preprocessor that the file `header.h` is in our current directory but `stdio.h` is somewhere in the system, and the preprocessor should go look for it. The preprocessor has a built-in search path that includes the locations of the headers for the standard library.

Header files may themselves use `#include` directives to pull in other files; if you looked at the preprocessed output to our "Hello, world" example at the beginning of the chapter, you would see that many different header files have been included:

```
# 1 "/usr/include/stdio.h" 1 3
# 1 "/usr/include/features.h" 1 3
# 142 "/usr/include/features.h" 3
# 208 "/usr/include/features.h" 3
# 1 "/usr/include/sys/cdefs.h" 1 3
# 65 "/usr/include/sys/cdefs.h" 3
# 283 "/usr/include/features.h" 2 3

# 1 "/usr/include/gnu/stubs.h" 1 3

# 311 "/usr/include/features.h" 2 3

# 27 "/usr/include/stdio.h" 2 3
...
```

As well as include header files, you can use the preprocessor to define *macros*: pieces of text that are substituted in your source. The syntax for a macro is

```
#define text replacement
```

For instance, you can use macros to give meaningful names to particular constants:

```
#define MAX_RECURSE  64
#define FAILURE       -1

int recursive ( ... ) {
    static level=0;

    if (++level > MAX_RECURSE) {
        printf("! Maximum recursion level reached!\n");
        level--;
        return FAILURE;
    }

    /* Do something here */

    return level--;
}
```

As you saw in section 1.6, the standard C header files define many constants you can use to simplify programs and make them more portable. ANSI C also defines constants you can use to specify the exit status without using naked numbers. For instance, we could have written the first example of this chapter as

```
#include <stdlib.h>
#include <stdio.h>

int main(int argc, char* argv[])
{
  printf("hello, world\n");
  return(EXIT_SUCCESS);
}
```

The EXIT_SUCCESS macro is defined in stdlib.h.[9] It is generally a better idea to use constants such as these rather than naked numbers.

Macros can also be given arguments, so they appear to be like functions; for instance, the isspace we used in our break example is typically defined as a macro, like this:

```
#define isspace(c)   ((c) == ' ' || (c) == '\t' || (c) == '\n' || \
                      (c) =='\r' || (c) == '\f')
```

The replacement text will be placed into our program wherever we use isspace, and the c will be replaced by whatever argument we gave to it. Thus, when our example reaches the compiler, it probably looks more like this:

```
int token (char s[]) {
    unsigned int len = strlen(s);
    int i;

    for (i=0; i < len; i++)
        if (((s[i]) == ' ' || (s[i]) == '\t' || (s[i]) == '\n' ||
            (s[i]) =='\r' || (s[i]) == '\f'))
            break;

    s[i] = '\0';
    return i;
}
```

NOTE Because the text is literally replaced, you must be very careful about calling macros (or things you suspect to be macros) when you're using side effects such as post-increment. If we'd said, for instance,

```
while (i < len)
    if (isspace(s[i++]))
        break;
```

the compiler would have seen

```
while (i < len)
    if (((s[i++]) == ' '   ||
        (s[i++]) == '\t' ||
        (s[i++]) == '\n' ||
        (s[i++]) == '\r' ||
        (s[i++]) == '\f'))
        break;
```

and i would have been incremented rather a lot faster than we wanted.

As you saw earlier, in the preprocessor you can use backslash (\) characters to break up a long code line over several lines; when the preprocessor sees a backslash at the end of a line, the backslash is removed and the next line is concatenated. Hence, we could also define isspace as follows:

---

[9] If you want to exit with bad status, you can use EXIT_FAILURE.

```
#define isspace(c)    ((c) == ' '  || \
                       (c) == '\t' || \
                       (c) == '\n' || \
                       (c) == '\r' || \
                       (c) == '\f')
```

Perl makes heavy use of macros internally.

1.10   LIBRARY FUNCTIONS

As we've already mentioned, C provides a standard library of useful functions and macros—things like `printf` and `isspace`. However, some aspects of the behavior of these library functions are left undefined by the C standard, and Perl needs greater control over what's going on. For instance, Perl reimplements the memory allocation functions for greater efficiency; functions like `printf` are extended to take Perl-specific arguments; string manipulation functions are reimplemented to have guaranteed behavior on both ASCII and EBCDIC systems; and so on.

The file `pod/perlclib.pod` in distributions after 5.6.0 and 5.7.0[10] contains a table of equivalents among the kinds of functions you'd expect to see in an ordinary C program, and the functions that should be used in XS, embedding, and the Perl internals (which you'll see in later chapters).

1.11   SUMMARY

This chapter has given you an introduction to the C language from a Perl programmer's point of view. The most important things you should take from this chapter are:

- In C, everything is a function (even the `main` body of your program), and all functions should have prototypes before they are called.
- C has four types of variables: parameter, automatic, global, and static. All variables *must* be declared before being used.
- C is a *strongly typed* language (compared to Perl); it has a number of data types, and each variable can have one and only one type.
- C has no built-in functions, but it does provide a standard library of functions; however, as you'll see in later chapters, when using Perl and C, you're likely to use Perl's reimplementations of the standard functions.
- C's syntax is very similar to Perl's, but is more austere: it has no statement modifiers, no `foreach`, and no `redo`, but it does have a `switch`.
- C programs are automatically run through a preprocessor, which can be used to give meanings to tokens and create inline functions.

---

[10] See section 11.1.1 for details of the Perl versioning scheme. 5.7.0 was indeed released prior to version 5.6.1.

C H A P T E R   2

Extending Perl: an introduction

This chapter will introduce the fundamentals of interfacing Perl to the C programming language; we assume you have a basic understanding of C, as described in chapter 1. Before we can describe how to do this, we must first explain how Perl modules work and how they are created.

2.1   PERL MODULES

This section describes the anatomy of a Perl module distribution. If you are already familiar with how to create pure Perl modules, then you can safely skip to the next section. In essence, a Perl module is simply a file containing Perl code (usually in its own namespace, using the `package` keyword) with a file extension of `.pm`. When you use a module, `perl` searches through a series of directories (specified by the `@INC` array) looking for a file with the correct name. Once found, the file is parsed and the routines are made available to the main program. This mechanism allows code to be shared and re-used and is the reason behind the success of the Comprehensive Perl Archive Network (CPAN; http://www.cpan.org/).

To maximize the reusability of your modules, you should write them in such a way that they do not interfere with other parts of Perl or other modules. If you don't, your modules may clash with other modules or with the main program—and this behavior is undesirable. You can do so in three primary ways:

- You should assign a namespace to each module. This namespace is usually the same as the module name but does not have to be. As long as another part of your program does not choose the identical namespace, the module will interact with the caller only through its defined interface.

- Your modules should export subroutines by request rather than by default. If all the subroutines provided by a module are exported, then it is possible that they will clash with other subroutines already in use. Exporting subroutines by request is particularly important if you add new subroutines to a module after writing the main program, because you may add a routine that will overwrite a previous definition. Doing so is not relevant when you define object-oriented classes, because they never export subroutines explicitly.

- You should use lexical variables (those declared with my) in modules wherever possible to limit access from outside the namespace and to make it easier for the module to become thread-safe.[1] Globals should be used only when absolutely necessary; in many cases you can limit them to $VERSION for version numbering, $DEBUG for switching debugging state, and the Exporter globals (in other words, globals that are not modified during program execution).

Here is an example of a minimalist module that shows how you can implement these constraints:

```
package Example;

use 5.006;
use strict;

use base qw/Exporter/;

our $VERSION = '1.00';

our @EXPORT_OK = qw/ myfunc /;

# Code
sub myfunc { my $arg = shift; return $arg; }

1;
```

---

[1] We will not attempt to cover thread safety here. All you need to know for this book is that global variables and static memory hinder the use of threads, because you must make sure parallel threads do not change the information in a variable while another thread is using the value. If you only use Perl lexical variables (limited to subroutine scope rather than file scope) and C automatic variables, you will be fine.

The first line is the namespace declaration. All code in this file is visible only in this namespace unless explicitly referred to from outside or until another package statement is encountered.

The next line makes sure that the Perl version used by this module is at least version 5.6.0 (we use the old numbering style of 5.006 to ensure that older versions of Perl will be able to understand the version). This check is necessary because the module uses the our variable declaration, which was introduced in this version of Perl.

All Perl modules should have strict checking. Among other things, this pragma instructs Perl to tell you about any undeclared variables it comes across; it's an excellent way to avoid many bugs in code.

Next, we inherit methods from the Exporter class in order to enable exporting of subroutines and variables to the namespace that uses this module.

The following line defines the version number of the module. It is used by CPAN for indexing and enables Perl to check that the correct version of a module is available.

The @EXPORT_OK array contains a list of all the subroutines that can be exported by this routine. They will not be exported unless explicitly requested. The @EXPORT array can be used to always export a function, but that functionality is not desirable in most cases.

The code on the next-to-last line implements the module functionality. The actual code for the module goes here.

Finally, all modules that are read into Perl must finish with a true value (in this case 1) so that Perl can determine whether the module was read without error.

If we name this file Example.pm, we can load it with

```
use Example qw/ myfunc /;
```

in order to import the named function into the current namespace. Alternatively, if we load it as

```
use Example;
```

the function myfunc will not be imported but can still be accessed as Example::myfunc(). You can find more information about Perl modules in the perlmod man page that comes with Perl.

2.1.1 Module distributions

With a single Perl-only module, installation could consist simply of copying the file to a location that Perl searches in, or changing the PERL5LIB environment variable so that it contains the relevant directory. For anything more complex, or if the module is to be distributed to other sites (for example, via CPAN), Perl provides a framework you can use to automate installation. In order to use this framework, you need to create a number of files in addition to the module (see figure 2.1).

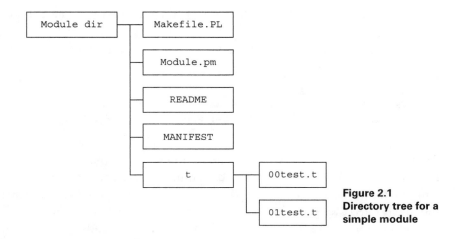

Figure 2.1
Directory tree for a simple module

The README file

This file provides a short description of the module, tells how to install it, and gives any additional information the author wants to add. The file is not required by Perl but is useful to have; it is required for any module submitted to CPAN.

The Makefile.PL file

Along with the module itself, this is the most important file that should be supplied to help build a module. It is a Perl program that generates a make file (called Makefile) when run.[2] This make file is used to build, test, and install the module. A Perl module installation usually consists of the following four lines:

```
% perl Makefile.PL
% make
% make test
% make install
```

The first line generates make file. The second line uses make file to build the module. The third line runs any included tests, and the last line installs the module into the standard location.

The Makefile.PL program is useful because it deals with all the platform-specific options required to build modules. This system guarantees that modules are built using the same parameters used to build Perl itself. This platform configuration information is installed, when Perl itself is configured and installed, as the Config module.

---

[2] A *make file* is a list of rules used by the make program to determine what action to take. make is a standard program on most Unix distributions. On Microsoft Windows and other operating systems that lack compilers as standard, you'll need to install a version of make.

At its simplest, Makefile.PL is a very short program that runs one subroutine:

```
use ExtUtils::MakeMaker;
# See lib/ExtUtils/MakeMaker.pm for details of how to influence
# the contents of the Makefile that is written.
WriteMakefile(
    'NAME'          => 'Example',
    'VERSION_FROM'  => 'Example.pm', # finds $VERSION
    'PREREQ_PM'     => {}, # e.g., Module::Name => 1.1
);
```

All the system-dependent functionality is provided by the ExtUtils::Make-Maker module. The WriteMakefile routine accepts a hash that controls the contents of the make file. In the previous example, NAME specifies the name of the module, VERSION_FROM indicates that the version number for the module should be read from the VERSION variable in the module, and PREREQ_PM lists the dependencies for this module (the CPAN module uses it to determine which other modules should be installed; in this example there are no additional module dependencies, so this isn't really required). Additional options will be described in later sections; you can find a full description in the documentation for ExtUtils::MakeMaker.

The MANIFEST file

This file contains a list of all files that are meant to be part of the distribution. When the Makefile.PL program is run, it checks this file to make sure all the required files are available. This file is not required, but is recommended in order to test the integrity of the distribution and to create a distribution file when using make dist.

The test.pl file and the t directory

Although it isn't a requirement, all module distributions should include a test suite. Test files are important for testing the integrity of the module. They can be used to ensure that the module works now, that it works after improvements are made, and that it works on platforms that may not be accessible to the module author. When ExtUtils::MakeMaker sees a test.pl file in the current directory, the resulting Makefile includes a test target that will run this file and check the results.

A good test suite uses all the functionality of the module in strange ways. A bad test suite simply loads the module and exits; a module with no test suite is even worse.

Perl provides two means of testing a module. The test.pl file is the simplest, but a more extensible approach is to create a test directory (called simply t) containing multiple tests. The convention is that tests in the t directory have a file suffix of .t and are named after the functionality they are testing (for example, loading.t or ftp.t).

Test programs are written using the framework provided by the Test module (or the new Test::Simple and Test::More modules). A simple example, based on this Example module, could be as shown in listing 2.1.

Listing 2.1   Simple test program

```
use strict;
use Test;

BEGIN { plan tests => 2 }

use Example qw/ myfunc /;
ok(1);

my $result = myfunc(1);
ok( $result, 1 );
```

The second line loads the testing framework. Then, the program informs the test framework to expect two test results.

The next line loads the module that is being tested and imports the required routines. The ok subroutine takes the supplied argument and checks to see whether it is true or false. In this case, the argument is always true, so an ok message is printed whenever the module has been loaded correctly.

In the last line, the ok routine accepts two arguments: the result from the current test and the expected result. An ok message is printed if the two arguments are equal; a not ok message is printed if they are different.

You can create templates for these files using the h2xs program that comes as part of Perl. When used with the -X option, it creates a basic set of files:

```
% h2xs -X Example
Writing Example/Example.pm
Writing Example/Makefile.PL
Writing Example/README
Writing Example/test.pl
Writing Example/Changes
Writing Example/MANIFEST
```

In addition to the files described here, h2xs generates a file called Changes that you can use to track changes made to the module during its lifetime. This information is useful for checking what has happened to the module; some editors (such as Emacs) provide an easy means of adding to these files as the code evolves.

NOTE   If you want to learn more about building module distributions, we suggest you take a look at the perlnewmod, perlmodlib, and perlmodstyle Perl manual pages.

2.2 INTERFACING TO ANOTHER LANGUAGE: C FROM XS

Now that we have discussed how to create a module and determined that you need to create an interface to other languages, this section will describe the basics of how to combine C code with Perl. We begin with C because it is the simplest (Perl itself is written in C). Additionally, this section will only describe how to interface to C using facilities that are available in every Perl distribution. We'll describe interfacing to C using other techniques (such as SWIG and the `Inline` module) in chapter 7. If you are familiar with the basics, more advanced XS topics are covered in chapter 6.

Perl provides a system called XS (for eXternal Subroutines) that can be used to link it to other languages. XS is a glue language that is used to indicate to Perl the types of variables to be passed into functions and the variables to be returned. The XS file is translated by the XS compiler (xsubpp) into C code that the rest of the Perl internals can understand. In addition to the XS file, the compiler requires a file that knows how to deal with specific variable types (for input and output). This file is called a *typemap* and, for example, contains information about how to turn a Perl scalar variable into a C integer.

This section will begin by describing the changes that must be made to a standard Perl module in order to use XS. We'll then present an example of how to provide simple C routines to Perl.

2.2.1 The Perl module

As a first example, we will construct a Perl module that provides access to some of the examples from chapter 1. The first thing we need to do is to generate the standard module infrastructure described in section 2.1 using h2xs, but this time without the -X option to indicate that we are writing an XS extension. The module can be called `Example`:

```
% h2xs -A -n Example
Writing Example/Example.pm
Writing Example/Example.xs
Writing Example/Makefile.PL
Writing Example/README
Writing Example/test.pl
Writing Example/Changes
Writing Example/MANIFEST
```

The -A option indicates to h2xs that constant autoloading is not required (more on that topic later; see section 2.3.3). The -n option specifies the name of the module in the absence of a C header file. Besides the creation of the Example.xs file, the only difference from the previously discussed pure Perl module generation is a change to the module itself (the .pm file) so that it will load the compiled C code. The module created by h2xs has many features that are not important for this discussion, so we will begin from the minimalist module described in section 2.1 and modify it to support shared libraries:

```
package Example;

use 5.006;
use strict;

use base qw/Exporter DynaLoader/;

our $VERSION = '0.01';
our @EXPORT_OK = qw/ print_hello /;

bootstrap Example $VERSION;
1;
```

There are only two changes (highlighted in the code). The first is that the module now inherits from the DynaLoader module as well as the Exporter module. The DynaLoader module provides the code necessary to load shared libraries into Perl. The shared libraries are created from the XS code on systems that support dynamic loading of shared libraries.[3] The second change is the line added just before the end of the module. The bootstrap function does all the work of loading the dynamic library with the name Example, making sure its version matches $VERSION. The bootstrap function is technically a method that is inherited from the DynaLoader class and is the equivalent of

```
Example->bootstrap($VERSION);
```

2.2.2   The XS file

Now that the preliminaries are taken care of, the XS file must be examined and edited. The first part of any XS file is written as if you are writing a C program, and the contents are copied to the output C file without modification. This section should always begin by including the standard Perl include files so that the Perl internal functions are available:

```
#include "EXTERN.h"
#include "perl.h"
#include "XSUB.h"
```

These lines must always be here and are not automatically added by the xsub compiler (although h2xs includes them) when it generates the C file. Any other C functions or definitions may be included in the first section of the file.

As a first example of interfacing Perl to C, we will try to extend Perl to include functions described in chapter 1. These must be added to the .xs file directly or included from either a specially built library or a separate file in the distribution. For

---

[3] On other systems, it is still possible to use DynaLoader; however, the module must be statically linked into the Perl binary by using make perl rather than just make for the second stage.

simplicity, we will begin by adding the code from sections 1.1 and 1.5.1 directly to the .xs file:

```
#include <stdio.h>

void print_hello (void)
{
   printf("hello, world\n");
}

int treble(int x)
{
   x *= 3;
   return x;
}
```

On the first line we have replaced the name of the main function from section 1.1 with a new name. XS modules do not define a main, because all functions are supposed to be called from somewhere else.

The XS part of the file is indicated by using the MODULE keyword. It declares the module namespace and defines the name of the shared library that is created. Anything after this line must be in the XS language. The name of the Perl namespace to be used for subroutines is also defined on this line, thus allowing multiple namespaces to be defined within a single module:

```
MODULE = Example  PACKAGE = Example
```

Once the module and package name have been declared, the XS functions can be added.

2.2.3   Example: "Hello, world"

As a first example, we will call the print_hello function declared at the start of the file. It has the advantage of being the simplest type of function to call from XS because it takes no arguments and has no return values. The XS code to call it is therefore very simple:

```
void
print_hello()
```

We begin by specifying the type of value returned to Perl from this function. In this case nothing is returned, so the value is void. We then give the name of the function as seen from Perl and the arguments to be passed in.

An XS function (also known as an XSUB) consists of a definition of the type of variable to be returned to Perl, the name of the function with its arguments, and then a series of optional blocks that further define the function. The print_hello function is very simple, so XS needs no extra information to work out how to interface Perl to the function.

IMPORTANT Unlike a C prototype, XS must have the return type (in this case, `void`) by itself on the first line of the declaration. The function name and arguments appear on the next line.

Our XS file now contains the following:

```
#include "EXTERN.h"
#include "perl.h"
#include "XSUB.h"

#include <stdio.h>

void print_hello (void)
{
   printf("hello, world\n");
}

int treble(int x)
{
   x *= 3;
   return x;
}

MODULE = Example  PACKAGE = Example

void
print_hello()
```

If we save this file as `Example.xs`, we can build the module in the *normal* way (don't forget to add this file to the `MANIFEST` if it is not there already). Listing 2.2 shows the output from Perl 5.6.0 (with some lines wrapped to fit on the page).

Listing 2.2   Output from the build of our first XS example

```
% perl Makefile.PL
Checking if your kit is complete...    ❶
Looks good
Writing Makefile for Example
% make
mkdir blib    ❷
mkdir blib/lib
mkdir blib/arch
mkdir blib/arch/auto
mkdir blib/arch/auto/Example
mkdir blib/lib/auto
mkdir blib/lib/auto/Example
cp Example.pm blib/lib/Example.pm    ❸
/usr/bin/perl -I/usr/lib/perl5/5.6.0/i386-linux
  -I/usr/lib/perl5/5.6.0
  /usr/lib/perl5/5.6.0/ExtUtils/xsubpp
  -typemap /usr/lib/perl5/5.6.0/ExtUtils/typemap Example.xs
  > Example.xsc    ❹
  && mv Example.xsc Example.c
Please specify prototyping behavior for Example.xs
```

```
(see perlxs manual)    ❺
gcc -c  -fno-strict-aliasing -O2  -DVERSION=\"0.01\"    ❻
  -DXS_VERSION=\"0.01\" -fPIC -I/usr/lib/perl5/5.6.0/i386-linux/CORE
   Example.c
Running Mkbootstrap for Example ()
chmod 644 Example.bs
LD_RUN_PATH="" gcc -o blib/arch/auto/Example/Example.so    ❼
  -shared -L/usr/local/lib Example.o
chmod 755 blib/arch/auto/Example/Example.so
cp Example.bs blib/arch/auto/Example/Example.bs
chmod 644 blib/arch/auto/Example/Example.bs
```

❶ This line checks that all the relevant parts of the distribution are present by comparing the contents of the directory with the contents listed in the MANIFEST file.

❷ We create the directory structure that will receive the module files as the build proceeds. This directory is called blib (for "build library").

❸ This line copies all the Perl files to the architecture-independent directory.

❹ We run the XS compiler, which translates the XS file to C code. The compiled file is written to a temporary file and then moved to Example.c rather than being written straight to the C file. This is done to prevent partially translated files from being mistaken for valid C code.

❺ This warning can be ignored. It informs us that we defined some XS functions without specifying a Perl prototype. You can remove this warning either by using PROTO-TYPES: DISABLE in the XS file after the MODULE declaration or by specifying a prototype for each XS function by including a PROTOTYPE: in each definition.

❻ The C file generated by xsubpp is now compiled. The compiler and compiler options are the same as those used to compile Perl itself. The values can be retrieved from the Config module. Additional arguments can be specified in Makefile.PL.

❼ The final step in library creation is to combine all the object files (there can be more than one if additional code is required) and generate the shared library. Again, the process is platform dependent, and the methods are retrieved from the Config module.

When we run Makefile.PL, it now finds an .xs file in the directory and modifies the resulting Makefile to process that file in addition to the Perl module. The build procedure therefore adjusts to the presence of the .xs file. The additional steps in the procedure are illustrated in figure 2.2.

We don't yet have an explicit test program (if you started with h2xs, you have the outline of a test program, but it will only test whether the module will load correctly). However, we can test the newly built module from the command line to see what happens:

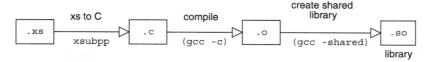

Figure 2.2 Flow diagram demonstrating the steps involved in transforming an .xs file to a shared library. The bracketed commands and the suffixes for object code and shared libraries will vary depending on the operating system used.

```
% perl -Mblib -MExample -e 'Example::print_hello'
Using /examples/Example/blib
hello, world
```

As expected, we now see the "hello, world" message. The command-line options are standard Perl but may require further explanation if you are not familiar with using Perl this way. This example uses the -M option to ask Perl to load the external modules blib and Example and then execute the string Example::print_hello. The full package name is required for the subroutine name because Perl will not import it into the main namespace by default. The blib module simply configures Perl to use a build tree to search for new modules. It is required because the Example module has not yet been installed.

Running tests like this is not efficient or scalable, so the next step in the creation of this module is to write a test program (or modify that generated by h2xs). The testing framework provided by the Test module[4] makes this easy. Here the test program from listing 2.1 has been modified to test our Example module:

```
use strict;
use Test;
BEGIN { plan tests => 2 }
use Example;

ok(1);
Example::print_hello();
ok(1);
```

If this program is saved to a file named test.pl, we can then use the make program to run the test:[5]

```
% make test
PERL_DL_NONLAZY=1 /usr/bin/perl -Iblib/arch -Iblib/lib
 -I/usr/lib/perl5/5.6.0/i386-linux -I/usr/lib/perl5/5.6.0 test.pl
1..1
```

---

[4] Prior to versions 5.6.1 of Perl, the test program created by h2xs does not use the Test module and is therefore more complicated than necessary.

[5] It may be necessary to rerun the make-file creation phase if the test program is created after the make file has been created. This is the case because ExtUtils::MakeMaker adjusts the contents of the make file depending on what is present in the module distribution.

```
ok 1
hello, world
ok 2
```

The problem with this simple test is that it is not really testing the `print_hello` subroutine but simply whether (a) the module has loaded and (b) the `print_hello` subroutine runs without crashing. Although these are useful tests, they do not tell us anything about the subroutine. This is the case because the testing system can only test variables, and the `print_hello` routine does not return anything to the caller to indicate that everything is OK. In the next section, we will fix this situation by adding a return value to the function.

2.2.4 Return values

Adding a simple return value to an XS routine (that is, a single scalar, not a list) involves telling Perl the type of return value to expect. Our `print_hello` C function does not have a return value (it returns `void`), so it must be modified. We can do so by adding the function in listing 2.3 to the top of our XS file.

> **Listing 2.3   "Hello, world" with a return value**

```
int print_hello_retval (void)
{
    return printf("hello, world\n");
}
```

We have added a new function with a slightly different name to indicate that we are now returning an integer value. This function makes use of the fact that `printf` returns the number of characters that have been printed.

We can now add a new function to our XS code to take the return value into account:

```
int
print_hello_retval()
```

The function is identical to the XS code for `print_hello`, but the `void` declaration has been changed to an `int`. Once we've saved, we can rebuild it by typing make as before. If we modify the test script to add

```
my $retval = Example::print_hello_retval();
ok( $retval, 13 );
```

and change the planned number of tests to three, we can now test that the routine returns the correct value (in this case, the number of printed characters should be 13):

```
% make test
PERL_DL_NONLAZY=1 /usr/bin/perl -Iblib/arch -Iblib/lib
-I/usr/lib/perl5/5.6.0/i386-linux -I/usr/lib/perl5/5.6.0 test.pl
```

```
1..3
ok 1
hello, world
ok 2
hello, world
ok 3
```

If the return value did not agree with the value we were expecting, the test script would have told us there was a problem:

```
% make test
PERL_DL_NONLAZY=1 /usr/bin/perl -Iblib/arch -Iblib/lib -I/usr/lib/perl5/
5.6.0/i386-linux -I/usr/lib/perl5/5.6.0 test.pl
1..3
ok 1
hello, world
ok 2
hello, world
not ok 3
# Test 3 got: '13' (test.pl at line 11)
#    Expected: '12'
```

However, it won't tell us whether there is a problem with our XS code or a bad assumption in our test script!

2.2.5   Arguments and return values

Our `treble` function from section 1.5.1 takes an integer argument and returns an integer. This function would be represented in XS as shown in listing 2.4.

Listing 2.4   XS for the treble function

```
int
treble( x )
  int x
```

The first line returns an integer. The next is the signature of the command as it will be visible to Perl; there is now an input argument. All the arguments listed in the second line are then typed in the third and successive lines. For simple C types, Perl knows the translation without having to be told.

The example from section 1.5.1 could now be written as

```
use Example;
print "Three times ten is ", Example::treble(10), "\n";
```

with the following output:

```
% perl -Mblib treble.pl
Three times ten is 30
```

2.3   *XS AND C: TAKING THINGS FURTHER*

So far, we have shown you how to use XS to provide wrappers to simple C functions with simple arguments where you want the signature of the Perl subroutine to match the signature of the C function. In many cases, this approach is too simplistic, and extra code must be supplied in the XS layer. The XS wrapper lets you provide C code as part of the subroutine definition using the CODE keyword. XS keywords occur after the initial XSUB declaration and are followed by a colon. Here are listings 2.3 and 2.4 coded entirely in XS without going through an extra function:

```
int
print_hello_retval ()
 CODE:
    RETVAL = printf("hello, world\n");
 OUTPUT:
    RETVAL

int
treble( x )
  int x
 CODE:
   RETVAL = 3*x;
 OUTPUT:
   RETVAL
```

The CODE keyword indicates that the following lines will contain C code. The RETVAL variable is created automatically by the XSUB compiler and is used to store the return value for the function; it is guaranteed to be the same type as the declared return type of the XSUB (integer in both these examples). One complication is that RETVAL is not automatically configured as a return value; xsubpp needs to be told explicitly that it should be returned, and this is done with the help of the OUTPUT keyword.

2.3.1   Modifying input variables

In some cases, input arguments are modified rather than (or as well as) providing a return value. In that case, XS needs to be told which arguments are solely for input and which are for output. You use the OUTPUT keyword for this purpose. Here we modify the `treble` function so that the argument is modified instead of providing the result as a return value:

```
void
treble_inplace( x )
  int x
 CODE:
  x *=3;
 OUTPUT:
  x
```

This code is equivalent to the following Perl subroutine:

```
sub treble_inplace {
  $_[0] *= 3;
  return;
}
```

Or, more pedantically:

```
sub treble_inplace {
  my $x = int($_[0]);
  $x *= 3;
  $_[0] = int($x);
  return;
}
```

It suffers from the same problem: the input argument must be a variable, not a constant, in order to be modified. If a constant is passed in (for example, a straight number, as in our previous example), Perl will generate a "Modification of a read-only value attempted" runtime error. The OUTPUT keyword forces the value of the variable at the end of the XSUB to be copied back into the Perl variable that was passed in.

2.3.2 Output arguments

In many C functions, some arguments are only returned (that is, the value of the argument on entry is irrelevant and is set by the function itself). In these cases, the XSUB must specify not only which arguments in the list are to be returned but which are to be ignored on input.

> **NOTE** To be pedantic, all arguments in C are passed in by value; however, some arguments are thought of as return values because they are passed in a pointer to some memory and that memory is modified by the function. The pointer itself is not affected. Here we will use a non-pointer XS example, because XS can be used to copy the results into the correct variable. More detailed examples explicitly involving pointers can be found in chapter 6.

For example, if we wanted our `treble` function to return the result into a second argument

```
&treble(5, $out);
```

we would have to write XS code like this:

```
void
treble(in, out)
  int in
  int out = NO_INIT
 CODE:
  out = 3 * in;
 OUTPUT:
  out
```

The NO_INIT flag tells the XS compiler that we don't care what the value of the second argument is when the function is called—only that the result is stored in it when we leave. This code is functionally equivalent to the following Perl code:

```perl
sub treble {
  $_[1] = 3 * $_[0];
  return;
}
```

Of course, this approach preserves a C-style calling signature and forces it onto Perl. In some cases, this calling signature is desirable (maybe for familiarity with existing library interfaces), but in other cases it isn't. This brings us to the question of interface design, which is addressed in section 2.5.

2.3.3 Compiler constants

Providing access to functions is only part of the problem when interfacing to external libraries. Many libraries define constants (usually in the form of preprocessor defines) that are useful to Perl programmers as well as C programmers. h2xs automatically provides the code necessary to import preprocessor constants, unless it is invoked with the -c or -A option. The approach taken by h2xs uses the AutoLoader module to determine the value of constants on demand at runtime rather than import every constant when the program starts.

> **NOTE** An extreme example is the standard POSIX module. It defines more than 350 compiler constants, and creating this many subroutines during loading would impose a large overhead.

The autoloading is implemented in two parts. First, an AUTOLOAD subroutine is added to the .pm file. For versions of Perl before 5.8.0, the code will look something like this:

```perl
use strict;                              Checks for explicit values of
use Errno;        ◄─────────┐            the errno variable
use AutoLoader;   ①
use Carp;         ◄────────┐ Loads the Carp module, which
                           │ imports the croak function
sub AUTOLOAD {    ②
    my $sub = $AUTOLOAD;           ③
    (my $constname = $sub) =~ s/.*:://;       ④
    my $val = constant($constname);       ⑤
    if ($! != 0) {    ⑥
        if ($! =~ /Invalid/ || $!{EINVAL}) {          ⑦
            $AutoLoader::AUTOLOAD = $sub;
            goto &AutoLoader::AUTOLOAD;
        } else {
            croak "Your vendor has not defined constant $constname";       ⑧
        }
    }
    {
```

```
        no strict 'refs';
        *$sub = sub () { $val };      9
    }
    goto &$sub;      10
}
```

● This line loads the `AutoLoader` module. It is required only if we want to dynamically load additional functions from their corresponding files.

● The subroutine must be called `AUTOLOAD` so that Perl will call it automatically when it cannot find a definition for the subroutine in this package.

● The `$AUTOLOAD` package variable contains the name of the subroutine that is being requested. Here we copy that value to a lexical variable for convenience.

● This line strips the package name (and associated colons) from the requested function name, leaving just the name of the function in the current namespace.

● Next, we run the `constant` function that returns the value of the required constant. This routine is an XS function that is created by the h2xs command (more on that later). The `AUTOLOAD` code generated by h2xs passes a second argument to this routine (`$_[0]`), but for simple constants it can usually be removed from the routine.

● This line checks the error status from the `constant` function. In C, a common way of setting status is for the function to set a global variable `errno` and for the caller of the function to check `errno` when control is returned to it. In Perl, this behavior is implemented by the `$!` variable. `$!` is tied to the C `errno` variable so that Perl can check the value after system calls. Here, the `constant` function sets `errno` if the requested constant cannot be located.

● We now check to see if `errno` is set to a value that indicates the constant does not exist. In that case, control passes to `AutoLoader`, so it can check whether the required subroutines are to be autoloaded from .al files. These checks are required only if autoloaded routines are expected; otherwise this is an extra overhead for the program.

● If the constant should be available but was not defined, this line stops the program. The `croak` function is used rather than `die` so that the line number in the caller's code is printed in the error message rather than the line number in the `AUTOLOAD` subroutine.

● At this point in the routine, the value of the constant has been determined and, in principle, could be returned to the caller. Although it is valid to do so, in practice the constant will probably be called more than once. If the value is returned immediately, then the `AUTOLOAD` subroutine will be called every time the constant is requested—very inefficient. To overcome this inefficiency, the `AUTOLOAD` subroutine creates a new subroutine in this package that simply returns the constant value. In the example, this is done by creating an anonymous subroutine and storing it in a glob (see section 4.6 for more details of how this process works). The name of the glob is stored in $sub and therefore requires that soft references be allowed; the no strict 'refs' turns off strict checking to allow them. If you are uncomfortable with glob assignments, you can achieve the same effect by using a string eval:

```
eval "sub $sub () { $val }";
```

⑩ Finally, Perl is instructed to jump to the newly created subroutine and resume execution there. Using goto allows the program to run as if AUTOLOAD were never called.

The second part of the solution generated by h2xs lies in the constant function in the .xs file. Here is a simple yet functional form of the code generated by h2xs for some of the file constants that are available from the Fcntl module:

```
static IV    ❶
constant(char *name)          Sets to "no error";
{                             value checked on exit
  errno = 0;    ◄──────────── from function
  switch (*name) {    ❷       Executes if the constant
  case 'S':            ◄────── name begins with S
      if (strEQ(name, "S_ISGID"))  ◄──  Compares the
#ifdef S_ISGID                ❸        requested name with
          return S_ISGID;              the string S_ISGID
#else
          goto not_there;
#endif
          break;
  case 'O':
      if (strEQ(name, "O_RDONLY"))
#ifdef O_RDONLY
          return O_RDONLY;
#else
          goto not_there;
#endif
      if (strEQ(name, "O_RDWR"))
#ifdef O_RDWR
          return O_RDWR;
#else
          goto not_there;
#endif
      break;    ❹
      }
      errno = EINVAL;    ❺
      return 0;

not_there:    ❻
      errno = ENOENT;
      return 0;
```

```
}
MODULE = Fcntl_demo PACKAGE = Fcntl_demo   ◁⎯⎯⎯┐  **Defines the start of**
                                                  **the XS part of the file**
IV  ❼
constant(name)
    char * name
```

❶ This line indicates the return type of the function. In this case, the return type is forced to be the Perl integer type (see section 1.6.2).

❷ This line denotes the start of a block that will switch on the first character of the requested constant name.

❸ This block does all the work for the S_ISGID constant. The C preprocessor is used to determine the code that is passed to the compiler. If the symbol is defined, its value is returned; if it is not defined, the code branches to the not_there label.

❹ If the constant cannot be found even though it started with the letter O, the switch is exited; it isn't possible for any of the remaining case statements to match.

❺ If the constant name did not match anything in the switch block, errno is set to EINVAL ("Invalid argument") and the function returns 0.

❻ If the requested name was valid and present in the switch but was not available (maybe because the constant was not defined on this operating system), the function sets errno to ENOENT (literally, "No such file or directory") and returns.

❼ The XSUB definition for constant is simple; it has a single string argument and a return type of IV (integer value).

It is important to realize that this example only deals with numeric constants (the constants are assumed to be integers). String constants must be handled differently— especially if a mixture of numeric and string constants is required.

ExtUtils::Constant

A new ExtUtils::Constant module has been added from Perl 5.8.0; it simplifies the handling of constants. With this module, the XS and C code required to deal with the compiler constants is generated automatically when Makefile.PL is executed. This approach has a number of advantages over the current scheme:

- You can make improvements in the constant-handling code without having to touch every module that uses constants.

- The XS files are much simpler. Files are no longer dominated by long, repetitive lists of constants and C preprocessor directives.

- The new system allows compiler constants to have different types. An integer constant is treated differently than a floating-point constant.

2.4   WHAT ABOUT MAKEFILE.PL?

So far, we have not addressed the contents of the file that is instrumental in configuring the build process. When you're building simple Perl modules, Makefile.PL is almost empty; it just provides the name of the module and a means for determining the location to install the module (see section 2.1.1). The Makefile.PL program is much more important when you're building XS extensions, because the make file that is generated must include information about how to translate the XS code to C, how to run the C compiler, and how to generate shared libraries. In all the examples presented so far, this process has been handled automatically by the WriteMakefile function because it detects the presence of an XS file and sets up the appropriate make file targets. However, this detection works only if the module can be built without additional configurations above and beyond those used to build Perl originally.

So far, the examples have not required anything more than standard include files and libraries. What happens if you build a wrapper around a library that is not included by default? Let's add the following code to the XS example to find out. It will print out the version of the XPM library on our system. The include directive goes after the Perl includes and the XS declaration in the XS section. A minimum XS file looks something like this:

```
#include "EXTERN.h"
#include "perl.h"
#include "XSUB.h"

#include <X11/xpm.h>

MODULE = Example PACKAGE = Example

int
XpmLibraryVersion()
```

If we add this XPM code to our example file and build, we get the following:

```
% perl Makefile.PL
Checking if your kit is complete...
Looks good
Writing Makefile for Example
% make
mkdir blib
mkdir blib/lib
mkdir blib/arch
mkdir blib/arch/auto
mkdir blib/arch/auto/Example
mkdir blib/lib/auto
mkdir blib/lib/auto/Example
cp Example.pm blib/lib/Example.pm
/usr/bin/perl -I/usr/lib/perl5/5.6.0/i386-linux
    -I/usr/lib/perl5/5.6.0
    /usr/lib/perl5/5.6.0/ExtUtils/xsubpp
    -typemap /usr/lib/perl5/5.6.0/ExtUtils/typemap Example.xs
```

```
    > Example.xsc && mv Example.xsc Example.c
Please specify prototyping behavior for Example.xs
(see perlxs manual)
gcc -c  -fno-strict-aliasing -O2 -march=i386
    -mcpu=i686 -DVERSION=\"0.01\"
    -DXS_VERSION=\"0.01\" -fPIC
    -I/usr/lib/perl5/5.6.0/i386-linux/CORE  Example.c
Running Mkbootstrap for Example ()
chmod 644 Example.bs
LD_RUN_PATH="" gcc -o blib/arch/auto/Example/Example.so  -shared
    -L/usr/local/lib Example.o
chmod 755 blib/arch/auto/Example/Example.so
cp Example.bs blib/arch/auto/Example/Example.bs
chmod 644 blib/arch/auto/Example/Example.bs
```

It looks like everything worked fine. Let's try it:

```
% perl -Mblib -MExample -e 'Example::print_hello'
Using ..../Example/blib
hello, world
```

```
% perl -Mblib -MExample -e 'print Example::XpmLibraryVersion'
Using ..../Example/blib
perl: error while loading shared libraries:
    /path/to/library/Example/blib/arch/auto/Example/Example.so:
    undefined symbol: XpmLibraryVersion
```

The output indicates that the earlier routines (such as print_hello) still work, but the new routine doesn't. The error message says that Perl could not find XpmLibraryVersion in any of the libraries it has already loaded. This is not surprising, because Perl is not linked against graphics libraries during a standard build. To overcome this problem, we can use Makefile.PL to provide the information necessary to locate the correct libraries. The Makefile.PL file generated by h2xs looks something like this:

```
use ExtUtils::MakeMaker;
# See lib/ExtUtils/MakeMaker.pm for details of how to influence
# the contents of the Makefile that is written.
WriteMakefile(
    'NAME'         => 'Example',
    'VERSION_FROM' => 'Example.pm', # finds $VERSION
    'PREREQ_PM'    => {}, # e.g., Module::Name => 1.1
    'LIBS'         => [' '], # e.g., '-lm'
    'DEFINE'       => ' ', # e.g., '-DHAVE_SOMETHING'
    'INC'          => ' ', # e.g., '-I/usr/include/other'
);
```

The hash provided to WriteMakefile can contain many different keys, but the ones that are usually modified for simple XS projects are LIBS and INC. You can use the LIBS key to specify additional libraries that are needed to build the module. The string must be in the form expected by the linker on your system. Usually this means a format of -L/dir/path -lmylib, where -L indicates additional search directories and -l indicates the name of actual libraries.[6] WriteMakefile expects the LIBS argument to be either a simple scalar or a reference to an array. In most cases, a scalar is all that is required; but the array allows multiple sets of library combinations to be provided, and MakeMaker will use the first that refers to a library that can be found on disk.

In order to fix our example, we must change the LIBS entry so that the Xpm library (and associated X11 library) will be included:

```
'LIBS'  => '-L/usr/X11R6/lib -lX11 -lXpm',
```

Rebuilding the module now gives the following:

```
% perl Makefile.PL
Writing Makefile for Example
% make
gcc -c  -fno-strict-aliasing -O2 -march=i386 -mcpu=i686
    -DVERSION=\"0.01\"
    -DXS_VERSION=\"0.01\" -fPIC
    -I/usr/lib/perl5/5.6.0/i386-linux/CORE
    Example.c
Running Mkbootstrap for Example ()
chmod 644 Example.bs
LD_RUN_PATH="/usr/X11R6/lib" gcc
    -o blib/arch/auto/Example/Example.so
    -shared -L/usr/local/lib Example.o
    -L/usr/X11R6/lib -lX11 -lXpm
chmod 755 blib/arch/auto/Example/Example.so
cp Example.bs blib/arch/auto/Example/Example.bs
chmod 644 blib/arch/auto/Example/Example.bs
```

The value specified for LIBS is highlighted.

The test runs as expected:

```
% perl -Mblib -MExample -e 'print Example::XpmLibraryVersion'
Using ..../Example/blib
30411
```

Similarly, you can add extra include paths using the INC key if you are using include files that are not in the standard locations. This value is always a scalar and contains a list of directories to search for include files, in the format expected by your compiler. This list is usually of the form

```
INC => '-I/some/dir -I/some/other/dir'
```

---

[6] On Unix systems, -lmylib refers to a file on disk called libmylib.a or libmylib.so. The former is a static library, and the latter is a shared library that is loaded at runtime.

2.4.1 It really is a Perl program

It is important to remember that Makefile.PL is a normal Perl program. All that matters is that `WriteMakefile` is called with the correct arguments to generate the make file. You can write arbitrarily complex code to generate those arguments, you can prompt the user for information (as, for example, the Makefile.PL file for the `libnet` package does), or you can even dynamically generate the Perl module itself!

As an example, suppose we wanted to build an interface to a Gnome library.[7] Most Gnome libraries come with configuration scripts that can be used to determine the required libraries and include directories, and you must use these in `Makefile.PL` rather than hard-wiring the location of the Gnome system into the program.[8] To support doing this, the Makefile.PL file may look something like this:

```
use ExtUtils::MakeMaker;

# Use gnome-config to determine libs
my $libs = qx/ gnome-config --libs gnome /;

# Use gnome-config to determine include path
my $incs = qx/ gnome-config --cflags gnome /;

# Remove newlines
chomp($libs);
chomp($incs);

# Might want to exit with an error if the $libs or $incs
# variables are empty

# See lib/ExtUtils/MakeMaker.pm for details of how to influence
# the contents of the Makefile that is written.
WriteMakefile(
    'NAME'         => 'Gnome',
    'VERSION_FROM' => 'Gnome.pm', # finds $VERSION
    'PREREQ_PM'    => {}, # e.g., Module::Name => 1.1
    'LIBS'         => $libs, # all X11 programs require -lX11
    'DEFINE'       => ' ', # e.g., '-DHAVE_SOMETHING'
    'INC'          => $incs, # e.g., '-I/usr/include/other'
);
```

2.5 INTERFACE DESIGN: PART 1

Now that you have seen how to create Perl interfaces to simple C functions and library routines, this section will provide some advice about how these C routines should behave in a Perl world. When you're interfacing Perl to another language, it is important to take a step back and design the Perl interface so that a Perl programmer would be comfortable with it rather than a C programmer.

---

[7] Modules for many Gnome libraries are already on CPAN.

[8] Gnome is usually installed into /usr on Linux but /opt/gnome on Solaris.

2.5.1   Status and multiple return arguments

In C, although all arguments are passed by value, arguments can act as input arguments, return arguments, or both, and there is no way to distinguish this behavior from the prototype (knowing you are using a pointer cannot tell you whether the data will change).[9] In Perl, input arguments are supplied and return arguments are returned. A C function such as

```
int compute(int factor, double *result);
```

that may take an input integer, store a value into a `double` (the asterisk indicates a pointer in C; we will talk about those in chapter 3), and return an integer status is almost always better written in Perl as

```
($status, $result) = compute( $factor );
```

rather than

```
$status = compute( $factor, $result );
```

In versions of xsubpp prior to v1.9508 (the version shipped with Perl 5.6.1), the only way to return multiple arguments is to manipulate the argument stack by hand (as described in chapter 6). In newer versions of xsubpp, you can indicate that some arguments are to be returned differently using modifiers when declaring the function signature:

```
REQUIRE: 1.9508

int
compute( factor, OUTLIST result )
  int factor
  double result
```

The first line makes sure we are using a version of `xsubpp` that is new enough. The `OUTLIST` keyword indicates that the argument is a return value that should be placed on the output list. In fact, if the status is only telling us whether something worked or failed, we should consider removing it

```
$result = compute( $factor );
```

and returning `undef` if an error occurs. We'll show how to do this in section 6.9.

2.5.2   Don't supply what is already known

Do not ask the Perl programmer to provide information that Perl already has. For example, a C function might need to know the size of a buffer being passed in.

---

[9] In C, the `const` modifier can be used to indicate that a variable will not change. Unfortunately, many libraries still do not use it consistently. It is therefore almost impossible for automatic tools like xsubpp to infer that a variable is an output argument, simply because it lacks `const` in the declaration.

Because the length of Perl strings is already known, it is redundant and error-prone to ask the programmer to provide that information explicitly.

2.5.3 Don't export everything

When interfacing to a library, do not blindly import every function into Perl. Many of the functions may be support functions needed by the C interface but irrelevant to Perl. Additionally, many of the constants may not be needed.

2.5.4 Use namespaces

Use Perl namespaces. Many C libraries use the library name as a prefix to every function (for example, many function names in the Gnome library begin with gnome_, and function names in the XPM library begin with Xpm), so use the package name to indicate that information and strip the common prefix. The PREFIX keyword can be used to do so:

```
MODULE = Xpm  PACKAGE = Xpm  PREFIX = Xpm

int
XpmLibraryVersion()
```

This XS segment indicates that the function should appear to Perl as Xpm::LibraryVersion rather than the more verbose and repetitive Xpm::XpmLibraryVersion.

2.5.5 Use double precision

If a library provides a single- and double-precision interface, consider using just the double-precision interface unless there is a major performance penalty if you do. All Perl floating-point variables are already double precision, and there is little point in converting precision when transferring data between Perl and the library. If you need to preserve the function names in Perl (but, as noted in a previous comment, it may be better to adopt a more unified interface on the Perl side), you can export both the single- and double-precision names but only use the double-precision function from the library. XS provides a way to do this using the ALIAS keyword. For example:

```
double
CalcDouble( arg )
   double arg
 ALIAS:
   CalcFloat = 1
 CODE:
   printf("# ix = %d\n", ix );
   RETVAL = CalcDouble( arg );
 OUTPUT:
   RETVAL
```

Here, CalcFloat is set up as an alias for CalcDouble. The ix variable is provided automatically and can be used to determine how the function was called. In this example, if the function is called as CalcDouble, ix will have a value of 0; if the function is called as `CalcFloat`, `ix` will have a value of `1`. Any integer value can be used for the `ALIAS`; there is nothing special about the use of `1` as the first alias.

2.6   FURTHER READING

More information on Perl modules and XS can be found at the following locations:

- *ExtUtils::MakeMaker*—This man page describes `Makefile.PL` options and `MakeMaker`.
- *Managing Projects with make (2nd ed.)*—This book by Andrew Oram and Steve Talbott (O'Reilly and Associates, Inc.; ISBN 0937175900) is an introduction to the `make` command.
- *perlmod, perlmodlib*—These are the standard Perl manual pages on module creation.
- *perlxstut, perlxs*—These man pages are the standard XS tutorial and documentation that come with Perl. They cover everything about Perl and XS but they rapidly move on to advanced topics.

2.7   SUMMARY

In this chapter, you have learned the following:

- How to build a simple Perl module
- How to extend Perl using XS, first using C functions that take arguments and then with functions that can return values
- How to import constants from C header files into Perl

Finally, we discussed some of the issues of interface design.

CHAPTER 3

Advanced C

So far, we have given a simple introduction to the C programming language and used that knowledge to provide Perl interfaces to simple C functions. Before we can progress to a description of the Perl internals—and the implementation of Perl variables in particular—we need to introduce some more advanced C programming concepts. In this chapter, we will show how to use arrays and data structures and how to deal with memory management.

3.1 ARRAYS

In Perl, arrays are collections of scalars. Perl knows how many elements are in the array and allocates memory for new elements as required. In C, arrays are contiguous blocks of memory that can only store variables of a specific type; for instance, an array of integers can only contain integers. Listing 3.1 shows how you can create and access arrays of a known size in C along with the Perl equivalent. The use of square brackets is identical to the usage in Perl.

51

Listing 3.1   Array handling in C

```c
#include <stdio.h>              ①
#include <stdlib.h>

int main(void) {
  int i;
  int iarr[5] = { 10,20,30,40,50 };    ②
  double darr[10];    ③

  for (i=0; i<10; i++) {
    darr[i] = i/100.0;    ◄── Assigns values to each
  }                              element in the double-
                                 precision array
  for (i=0; i<5; i++) {
    printf("%d %d %f\n", i, iarr[i], darr[i]);    ◄── Prints the contents of
  }                                                    the first five elements
                                                       of iarr and darr
  return EXIT_SUCCESS;
}

#!/usr/bin/perl

@iarr = ( 10, 20, 30, 40, 50 );

for (0..9) {
  $darr[$_] = $_/100.0;
}

for (0..4) {
  printf("%d %d %f\n", $_, $iarr[$_], $darr[$_]);
}
```

① These are the standard include files, which provide the prototype for `printf` and the definition of `EXIT_SUCCESS`.

② This line declares an integer array with five elements and then assigns the elements using a comma-separated list. (Note the use of the `{ x, y, z }` initializer in C, whereas in Perl you use `( x, y, z )`).

③ This line creates an array that can hold 10 double-precision numbers (although it is not initialized at this point).

Arrays in C are more complex than their Perl equivalents because they don't automatically grow when the programmer needs more space than was originally allocated (see section 3.6.2 to find out how to work with dynamic arrays). The C compiler allocates only the memory it knows you will need, and not the memory you *might* need. To make things worse, C will not stop you from "walking off the end" of the array by assigning to an element you have not allocated memory for. For instance, some compilers will let you get away with

```c
int array[10];

array[20] = 1234;
```

However, this code is not legal. It will almost certainly cause annoying problems that are occasionally difficult to detect, because you will be writing either into unallocated memory (possibly causing a segmentation fault) or, worse, into another variable's allocated storage.

Similarly, be careful about creating arrays without initializing them; the `darr` array in point 3 earlier may be filled with zeros when it is declared—or it may be filled with garbage. Be sure to initialize before expecting sensible values in it.

A multidimensional array can be declared in much the same way as a one-dimensional array:

```
int array[3][2];
```

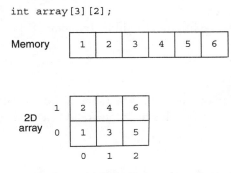

Figure 3.1 **A two-dimensional array is implemented as a single chunk of memory.**

This line declares a two-dimensional integer array containing six elements. The elements are stored in a contiguous block of memory, as shown in figure 3.1, with individual elements addressed using `array[0][0]`, `array[0][1]`, and so forth. Use of a single block of memory is possible because the compiler knows exactly how many bytes are used to represent each element.

3.2 POINTERS

In C, all arguments are passed to functions by value. So, if you have a C function such as

```
int findsum(int in1, int in2);
```

the subroutine will retrieve the values of `in1` and `in2` but will not be able to modify those variables directly. This is analogous to the Perl subroutine

```
sub findsum {
  my $in1 = shift;
  my $in2 = shift;
  return ($in1 + $in2);
}
```

where the arguments are read from the stack and then used in the subroutine. C has no analogue to the variable-aliasing trick available in Perl (where @_ can be modified in place); in order to modify a variable, the memory address of the variable must be passed to the function. Once the memory address is available, it can be used to modify the value *pointed* to by this address. Given this definition, it is not surprising that a variable containing a memory address is called a *pointer*.

Pointers are associated with a particular variable type (much like a reference to a Perl hash is different from a reference to a Perl scalar), although, unlike in Perl, they can be converted to other types by using type-casting. Thus a pointer to an integer is not the same as a pointer to a character (although in this particular case, you can force it to be treated as such[1]). In order to dereference a C pointer and modify the value of the variable, * notation is used; it is reflected in the declaration of a pointer:

```
char *str;
int  *x;
double *y;
```

This notation indicates that because, for example, *x is an integer, x itself must be a pointer to an integer. An alternative reading is to think of x as a variable of type int *, which is a pointer to an integer.

A function that multiplies a variable by three could be implemented as follows:

```
void treble ( int * value ) {
    *value *= 3;
}
```

Here the input variable is declared as a pointer, and the value in the variable is multiplied by three by dereferencing the pointer. This function could be called as follows:

```
int number = 5;
treble( &number );
```

We use an ampersand (&) to indicate that we want to take the memory address of number and pass it to the function, rather than simply passing in the value. The Perl equivalents would be

```
$number = 5;
&treble( \$number );

sub treble {
  my $value = shift;
  $$value *= 3;
}
```

To summarize, &variable is used to retrieve the memory address, and *variable is used to find the thing pointed to by the memory address stored in the variable.

There are some important differences between Perl references and C pointers. In Perl, the reference can only be dereferenced; once dereferenced, it behaves like the original Perl data type. Generally, in C, the memory address can be examined and modified. Modifying pointers can lead to errors, though, because bad things can happen if the pointer does not point to a valid location in memory. Additionally, a C pointer usually contains a memory address, and it is not possible to determine just

---

[1] Strictly speaking, you cannot just cast any pointer type to any other pointer type. A pointer to void may be converted to and from any other pointer type, and any pointer type can be converted to a pointer to char. If you use the converted pointer, it is your responsibility to make sure the data you are now pointing to makes sense for the type you're using.

from that pointer whether it points to a single variable or, as described in the next section, an array of variables.

A special type of pointer is a pointer to a void (a void *). It simply indicates to the compiler that the contents are a pointer, but that you do not care what type it points to. This type of pointer is useful when you're designing data structures that are designed to be extensible or that contain data of a type that is not known until the program is run.

3.2.1 Pointers and arrays

In Perl, when you need to pass an array into a subroutine, you usually do it by taking a reference to the array and storing it in a Perl scalar variable. Once the reference is stored in a scalar, it must be dereferenced in order to retrieve the original variable:

```
&foo( \@bar, \%baz );

sub foo {
  my ($refArr, $refHash) = @_;
  $refArr->[3] = "foo";
  $refHash->{"bar"} = "foo";
}
```

In C, the equivalent of this reference is a pointer. When an array is used in a context that expects a pointer, the pointer to the first element is used automatically. This process is shown in listing 3.2: an array is declared normally, but it is passed to another function as a pointer and is also treated as a pointer by printf.

Listing 3.2 Equivalence of arrays and pointers

```
#include <stdlib.h>
#include <stdio.h>

void foo_as_array ( int array[] ) {      ❶
  array[0] = 1;
}

void foo_as_pntr ( int * array ) {       ❷
  array[1] = 2;
}

int main (void) {
  int array[5];        ◄── Declares an integer array
                           with five elements, but
                           does not populate it

  foo_as_array( array );     ❸
  foo_as_pntr( array );

  printf("First  element is %d\n", array[0]);     ◄── Prints the value of
  printf("Second element is %d\n", *(array+1) );  ❹     the first array
                                                        element using
  return EXIT_SUCCESS;                                  standard array syntax
}
```

❶ This function has a single argument that is declared explicitly as an integer array. The empty square brackets indicate that the size of the array is not known. Note that, despite the notation with the square brackets, in C it is impossible to pass a real array to a function. Array variable names always decay to a pointer to the first element, and both of these functions are equivalent.

❷ This function has a single argument that is declared simply as a pointer to an integer. Note that this declaration does not distinguish between a pointer to a single integer and a pointer from an actual array (and the compiler doesn't care).

❸ Both routines are called with the same syntax, regardless of whether the function is expecting a pointer or an array.

❹ Now we print the value of the second element. Here we use pointer syntax to retrieve the second value. In fact, the method we used first to retrieve element n from an array, `array[n]`, is by definition identical to incrementing the pointer to the start of the array by n and dereferencing the result: `*(array+n)`. This code works because the compiler knows the size of each type, so it also knows how many bytes to increment the pointer.

A key difference between a real C array and a pointer to it is that the C compiler knows exactly how large an array is but does not know the amount of memory a pointer refers to. This fact is demonstrated in the following code:

```
#include <stdlib.h>
#include <stdio.h>

int main () {
  int array[5];
  int *pntr;

  printf("Size of array: %d bytes\n",sizeof(array));
  printf("Size of array: %d elements\n",sizeof(array)/sizeof(int));

  pntr = array;
  printf("Size of pointer: %d bytes\n", sizeof(pntr));

  return EXIT_SUCCESS;
}
```

This example gives the following output:

```
Size of array: 20 bytes
Size of array: 5 elements
Size of pointer: 4 bytes
```

In general, though, this ability to determine the size of an array using `sizeof` is not particularly useful, because you only use arrays of unknown size when they have been created dynamically (in which case `sizeof` is irrelevant). (Section 3.6 contains more details about how to allocate memory for arrays.)

3.2.2 Pointers to functions

Although C doesn't support "subroutine references" in the Perl sense, it is possible to get a pointer to a function. Doing so is particularly useful when you're creating callbacks or stashing a function inside a Perl value. Taking a pointer to a function is straightforward—you just use the function's name without parentheses:

```
pntr = some_function;
```

Two points are slightly tricky: declaring `pntr` and knowing what to do with the pointer once you've got it.

You declare a pointer to a function just as though you were declaring the function, but you replace the function's name with *(*pntr)*. You need not specify the names of the parameters. So, for instance, we can take pointers to the functions we've defined in this section:

```
int (*findsum_pntr)(int, int);
void (*treble_pntr)(int *);
void (*foo_as_array_pntr)(int foo[]);
void (*foo_as_pntr_pntr)(int foo[]);
```

> **TIP** If you get stuck with these or any other declarations, the `cdecl` utility can help you:
>
> ```
> cdecl> declare findsum_pntr as pointer to
>                function (int, int) returning int
> int (*findsum_pntr)(int , int )
> cdecl> explain void (*fn)(void*);
> declare fn as pointer to function (pointer to void) returning
>                void
> ```

You might guess from the way we defined the pointer to a function that calling a pointer to a function is just like calling a function, except you surround the pointer's name with " (*" and ") ":

```
sum = (*findsum_pntr)(a, b);
```

This approach will work; but, luckily, the C standard allows you to simply use a function pointer as if it was a function. So, all you really need to do is

```
sum = findsum_pntr(a, b);
```

Casting things into a pointer to a function is also a little tricky; essentially, you take the declaration of the pointer to a function, surround it in brackets, and remove the pointer's name. Hence this

```
int (*findsum_pntr)(int, int)
```

becomes this

```
(int (*)(int, int))data
```

We'll look at function pointers again in the section, "Casting pointers to integers (and back)," page 158.

3.3 STRINGS

As we mentioned previously, a string in C is treated as an array of characters. Most commonly, a `char` is a single character and a `char *` is a pointer to an array of characters.[2] Because a C compiler does not know how many characters are contained in a piece of memory that is being referenced, the convention in C is that a special character value is used to indicate the end of a string.[3] This string-termination character is character `\0` (the character with value 0 in the character set [`chr(0)` in Perl], not the number zero [`ord(0)` in Perl]) and is known as the NUL character.

Figure 3.2 shows a simple example of string manipulation using a pointer. The Perl equivalent is somewhat contrived, because Perl manipulates strings as a whole instead of character by character:

```
$a = "hello";
$b = \$a;
substr($$b, 0, 1) = 'm';
substr($$b, 3, 1) = 'd';
$a = substr($$b, 0,4);
```

This example shows that in Perl, a dereferenced reference is no different than the original (the example would be identical if `$$b` was replaced with `$a` throughout); it also demonstrates that a string in Perl is a single entity, whereas in C it is a group of characters.

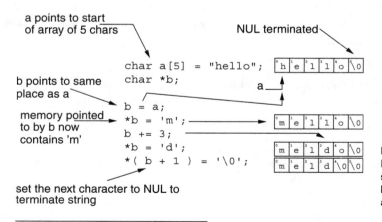

**Figure 3.2
Example of how a C string can be manipulated one character at a time, using pointers**

---

[2] A character is not necessarily a single byte. This is true in ASCII, but not in Unicode.

[3] Problems can occur when you link Perl via C to languages that do not use this particular convention. Fortran is a popular example of a compiler that does know how long each string is and therefore does not need a special string-termination character.

When you're using characters and strings in C, it is important to realize that there is a distinction between single-quoted and double-quoted characters. As discussed in "The char type," page 12, `'*'` is treated by the compiler as the equivalent of the Perl code snippet `ord("*")` and returns a variable of type `char`. When double quotes are used, `"*"`, the compiler treats it as a string literal, allocating two bytes of static memory (including one for the NUL) and returning a pointer to that memory. Thus the following code example is fine

```
char c = '*';
char *string = "*";
```

but this version will cause compiler errors:

```
char c = "*";
char *string = '*';
```

The errors will be similar to these:

```
warning: initialization makes integer from pointer without a cast
warning: initialization makes pointer from integer without a cast
```

3.3.1   Arrays of strings

Unlike multidimensional numeric arrays, which are contiguous blocks of memory (because a single number is always represented by a fixed number of bytes; see figure 3.1), arrays of strings are actually arrays of *pointers* to strings. The strings themselves can be in completely unrelated areas of memory. The pointer to the first element of an array of `char` pointers is represented by the type `char**`. If the variable `x` is a `char**`, then `*x` is a pointer to a string and `**x` is the single character at the beginning of the string (see the graphical representation in figure 3.3).

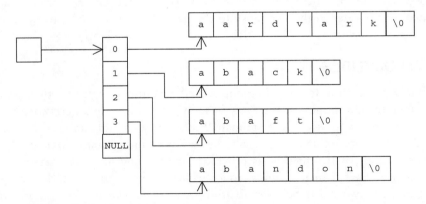

Figure 3.3   The memory organization of an array of strings. On the left is a simple pointer. This pointer (a `char**`) points to the first element in an array of pointers (shown in the middle). These pointers are of type `char*` and point to the first character in each string. We use the NULL at the end of the pointer array to tell us where the end of the array is.

As a simple example of using a `char**`, we can use the Unix environment. The environment is available to programmers as an array of strings. For example, if we wanted to write a small program to print our current environment (similar to the `printenv` shell command), we could do something like this:

```c
#include <stdio.h>

extern char** environ;        ❶

int main (void) {
  int i;
  char **array = environ;     ❷

  while (*array) {      ❸
    printf("%s\n", *array);
    array++;
  }

  return(0);
}
```

❶ `environ` is a special variable provided by the system and populated when the process starts. The `extern` declaration tells the compiler that we are using a variable declared in some other file.

❷ Here we declare a new `char**` and copy the pointer from the environment array. We do this so that we can manipulate the pointer without affecting the base pointer.

❸ This `while` loop continues until `*array` evaluates to `false`. Because `*array` is itself a pointer, this happens only when `*array` is NULL. Each time around the loop, we print out the string associated with the current pointer value and then increment the pointer so that we move to the next element in the array. When we reach the end of the array, we hit the NULL and terminate the loop.

3.4   STRUCTURES

In many cases, it is desirable to group related data into a single unit that can be passed easily into subroutines. In Perl, you do so by using a hash or an array, which can contain references to any of the standard Perl data types and can even be blessed into classes and treated as objects. In C, arrays can only contain variables of the same type;[4] an alternative method is provided for grouping data into structures that can contain named elements, similar to a Perl hash. These structures, declared using the `struct` keyword, can be given an arbitrary type and can also include any other variable type:

---

[4]   Although, in principle, you could have an array of pointers to items of different types, in practice it is difficult to keep track of which element points to which data.

```
struct person {
   double income; /* A double precision number */
   int    age;    /* An integer */
   char*  name;   /* Pointer to a character string */
};

struct survey {
   struct person* respondent; /* Pointer to a person structure */
   float length;           /* Floating point number */
   int* answers;           /* Pointer to an array of integers */
};
```

Once a structure has been declared, variables of that type can be defined in the normal way:

```
/* define mystruct as a variable of type person */
struct person mystruct;
/* define mypoint as a pointer to a struct of type survey */
struct survey* mypoint;
```

A common trick is to instruct the compiler to use an alias, rather than type `struct person` all the time. The `typedef` command (see section 1.6.2) allows any variable type to be aliased to another:

```
/* define myint to be identical to an int declaration */
typedef int myint;
/* define PERSON as an alias for struct person */
typedef struct person PERSON;

struct person mystruct; /* mystruct declared as a struct person */
PERSON mystruct;        /* Same as previous line */
```

This technique is used a lot in the Perl source code, where you rarely see an explicit struct. All struct accesses are done with aliases (and even more commonly done with C preprocessor macros).

Accessing the members of a structure depends on whether you have a pointer to it or have declared a variable of the structure type directly. The following example shows C struct accessors with a corresponding Perl hash accessor:

```
mystruct.age = 5; /* Set member 'age' to 5 */
$mystruct{'age'} = 5;  # perl

mypoint->length = 5.234; /* Set member y by dereferencing pointer */
$mypoint->{'length'} = 5.234; # Perl dereference

(*mypoint).length = 5.234; /* Same as previous */
$$mypoint{'length'} = 5.234; # Alternative form of dereferencing
```

The main difference between a struct and a hash is that all the members of a struct must be declared beforehand and no extra members can be created as the program executes. This is the case because a struct, like an array, is a contiguous block of memory of a fixed size. Even if a particular element of a struct is not initialized, it will take up the same amount of memory as a fully initialized struct. Our struct person declared earlier consists of a `double`, an `int`, and a pointer to a string. On a normal 32-bit system, this struct will probably take up 8+4+4=16 bytes of memory; the standard `sizeof` function can be used to determine how much memory the structure actually uses (in some cases, a compiler will pad the structure with extra bytes to make it align nicely on fixed-size boundaries for the underlying architecture). Structures must be well defined like this so that the compiler can decide how much memory to allocate to each one and also can statically reference elements in advance (and hence discard the element names in favor of offsets). This is all different from a Perl hash, where keys can be added at any time and the memory requirement is not fixed. (Details about how hashes are implemented in C to overcome any restriction of this kind can be found in section 4.5.[5])

In a similar manner to arrays, you can initialize a structure in one statement:

```
struct example {
  double a;
  float b;
  int c;
};

struct example eg = { 52.8 , 65.4, 40 };
```

This approach provides a useful shorthand way of configuring structures without having to address each member by name. The curly brackets effectively pack the data into a single block of memory; the result is the same as using the Perl `pack` function:[6]

```
$packed = pack("dfi", 52.8,65.4,40);
```

3.5   FILE I/O

In C, just as in Perl,[7] there are two approaches to handling input from and output to external files:[8] stream-based I/O and file descriptors.

Stream-based I/O offers a high-level interface, specifically providing buffering facilities and the ability to move forward and backward within a file. Buffered I/O is important for performance reasons (when writing to real hardware it is usually more efficient to accumulate writes to a disk into large chunks rather than sending a byte at a time). Perl filehandles use buffered streams, and the special variable `$|` controls whether the output buffer is flushed after every print or only when the buffer is full

---

[5] Additionally, because a structure is represented by a single contiguous block of memory (just like an array), it is possible to simply step the required number of bytes into a structure to extract information. However, this technique is not recommended and can lead to confusion and difficulty in porting the code to other platforms; you should always use the standard accessor techniques.

[6] With the exception of the padding we described earlier

[7] Simply because Perl provides interfaces to both types of I/O in the standard C library

[8] This includes sockets and devices. On Unix, all devices are treated as files.

(the default is to disable autoflush, leading to much confusion the first time someone writes a CGI script!). In C, a stream is represented by a `FILE*` (a pointer to a `FILE`). This is an opaque structure because you never look inside it—that is left to the low-level implementation in the C library. To open a stream, you can use `fopen`

```
FILE *fopen(const char *path, const char *mode);
```

and to print to a file you can use `fprintf`:

```
int fprintf(FILE *stream, const char *format, ...);
```

To close it, you use (predictably) `fclose`:

```
int fclose(FILE *stream);
```

These are similar to the corresponding Perl routines: `open`, `printf`, and `close`.

A lower level approach to I/O (at least on Unix-like systems) is to use *file descriptors*. These are simple integers (you can get the file descriptor from a Perl filehandle using the `fileno` function). File descriptors can be used for non-buffered I/O and are especially useful for socket communication. The C functions `open`, `close`, `read`, and `write` provide what you would expect from the Perl functions `sysopen`, `close`, `sysread`, and `syswrite`. Just as in Perl, you should not mix stream-based I/O with file descriptor I/O on the same filehandle.

In general, all the Perl file I/O operations have analogues in C, either as stream-based functions or functions using file descriptors (the `perlfunc` documentation is careful to distinguish between the two).

3.6 MEMORY MANAGEMENT

We have explained the different variable types and made sure our programs specified the amount of memory required to use them. In listing 3.1, we specified the number of elements for each array. The memory for these variables is allocated by the compiler, which works out the total amount of memory required by the program. Unfortunately, sometimes you cannot know at compile time how much memory your program will need. For example, if you are writing image-processing software, you may not know how big an image you will need to process. One solution—required if you use a language such as Fortran77[9]—is to make an inspired guess of the maximum image size you wish to process and hard-wire the dimensions into your program. This approach will work, but it has two problems:

- If you need to process larger images, you must recompile your program (presumably doing so is easy, because you have specified the dimensions in a header file).

---

[9] However, most modern implementations of Fortran77 provide the means for dynamic memory management, outside of the scope of the language definition.

- Even if you are processing small images, the program will require the same amount of memory it uses for large images.

Clearly, an alternative approach is required. We want to determine the image size we are intending to process and then allocate that memory when the program is running.

3.6.1 Allocating memory at runtime

The main C function for *dynamically* allocating memory is `malloc`:

```
void * malloc(size_t size);
```

The argument specifies the number of bytes required, and the function returns a pointer to the newly allocated memory. Recall that if you declare a pointer variable, you must make sure it points to some allocated memory. So far, we have done this by obtaining the pointer from some other variable. For example:

```
char * pointer_to_char;
char a_string[4];
int an_integer;
int * pointer_to_int;

pointer_to_char = a_string;
pointer_to_int = &an_integer;
```

With dynamic memory allocation, we can do the following (the prototype for `malloc` can be found in `stdlib.h`):

```
#include <stdlib.h>
char * pointer_to_char;

pointer_to_char = malloc(4);
```

Here we have requested 4 bytes of memory and stored the pointer returned by `malloc` in the variable `pointer_to_char`. It is important to realize that the memory has been allocated but not necessarily initialized (the contents will be undefined). We are responsible for storing information in that memory.

The downside of dynamic memory allocation in C is that the programmer is responsible for giving the memory back when it is no longer required. If you keep on requesting memory but never give it back, you will rapidly run out of resources; this problem is known as a *memory leak*. C provides the `free` function to allow you to return memory to the system:

```
void free(void * ptr);
```

This function takes a single pointer argument and will free the memory at that address. This memory must have been allocated by a call to `malloc` (or the related functions `calloc` and `realloc`), and you should take care not to call it twice with the same pointer value (strange things can happen, because the system may have already given that memory to something else!).

Memory management is one of the hardest things to get right in C. If your program is large and contains many dynamic memory allocations, it is difficult to guarantee that the memory will be freed correctly in all cases. One of the key advantages of Perl, Java, and other languages is that they handle all the memory allocation and freeing, allowing the programmer to focus on the core functionality of the program.

3.6.2 Altering the size of memory

Occasionally you may realize that the memory you requested is not enough for the task at hand: maybe you want to extend an array so that it can hold more elements, or perhaps you want to extend a string. The obvious approach is to allocate a new block of memory of the correct size, copy the contents from the first block, and then free the memory associated with it. This technique is painful, but luckily the standard C library comes with a function that will do it for you:

```
void * realloc(void * ptr, size_t bytes);
```

This function will resize the available memory pointed to by `ptr`. The original contents of the memory will be retained, and any new memory will be uninitialized. If `bytes` is less than the previous size, then the additional memory will be freed. `realloc` returns a new pointer, which will not necessarily be the same as that stored in `ptr`. You should always use the return value rather than assume you will be getting memory at the same location.

NOTE Recall that arguments in C are passed by value. Because the content of `ptr` is passed in as a memory address, the function will not be able to modify the contents of `ptr` in the calling routine. This issue could have been overcome by passing in a pointer to the pointer (!), but the designers of the interface wanted to make sure the original pointer was still available in case the `realloc` failed:

```
newptr = realloc( ptr, nbytes );
```

As with all memory allocation routines, do not forget to check the returned pointer to make sure it is non-NULL. All these routines return NULL pointers if the memory cannot be allocated. Remember that if this routine fails, the memory associated with `ptr` will not have been freed; so, it's possible to try again by asking for less memory.

3.6.3 Manipulating memory

Now that you have allocated your memory, what can you do with it? If you want to copy it to another variable (for example, to copy the contents of a structure before it is reused), you can use memcpy (use memmove if the memory destination lies within the chunk of data that is being copied):

```
#include <stdlib.h>
#include <stdio.h>
#include <string.h>
```
Declares the prototypes for `malloc`, `printf`, `memcpy`, and `strcpy`

```c
typedef struct {              ◄──── Creates an anonymous
    double income;                   structure and
    int    age;                      simultaneously typedefs
    char*  name;                     it to a person
} person;

int main (void) {  ❶
    char name[6] = "fred";
    person someone = { 20000.0, 5, NULL };   ❷
    person *other;

    someone.name = name;

    other = malloc(sizeof(*other));   ❸
    memcpy(other, &someone, sizeof(*other));   ❹              Prints out the
                                                             contents of the
    other->income = 0.0;   ◄─── Sets income in other to 0    original structure
    printf("Someone: %d, %6.0f, %s\n", someone.age, someone.income,   ◄──
           someone.name);
                                          Sets the name in the original
                                          structure to "wilma"
    strcpy(someone.name, "wilma");   ◄──┘
    printf("Other:   %d, %6.0f, %s\n", other->age, other->income   ◄──
           other->name);
                                                     Prints out the
                                                     contents of the copy
    free(other);   ◄─── Frees dynamically allocated memory
    return(EXIT_SUCCESS);
}
```

❶ This is the standard C `main` routine; we do not declare any arguments, because we are not interested in them.

❷ These are variable declarations. We allocate a string, initialize a person structure, and declare a pointer to a `person`. The `someone.name` field is set to NULL initially and is pointed to the string name later, because standard C89 and many compilers don't allow initialization from non-constant values.

❸ This line allocates memory for a new structure. We determine the number of bytes required by using `sizeof`. Note that we calculate the size of `*other` rather than `person`. Either approach will work, but using the variable name rather than the type will allow for simpler editing if we change the type in a later version of the code.

WARNING   You should always, always check the return value from `malloc`. We're omitting the check for the sake of brevity in our examples.

❹ We use `memcpy` to copy the contents of `someone` to the memory indicated by `other`. We must supply the size of the structure in bytes.

When we run this program, we get the following output:

```
% gcc -Wall memcpy.c -o memcpy
% ./memcpy
Someone: 5,  20000, fred
Other:   5,      0, wilma
```

So, modifying the income of `other` did not affect the contents of `someone`, but modifying the name of `someone` did affect `other`. What is going on? The answer lies in the struct declaration. When the structure is copied, everything is copied exactly to the destination. The first two entries are simply numbers and are copied as such. If they are modified, the bytes change as we would expect without affecting anything else. The third member is a pointer; the pointer is identical in both structures, and if that memory is modified, both structures "see" the change.

To initialize an array with a default value, you can use the `memset` function (or you can allocate the array using the `calloc` function, which allocates the memory and then sets all bits to zero):

```
#include <stdlib.h>    │  Declares the prototypes
#include <stdio.h>      │  for malloc, printf,
#include <string.h>     │  and memset

#define NELEM 10    ❶

int main (void) {   ❷

  int i;              │  Declares array as a
  int * array;    ◁──┘  pointer to an integer
  array = malloc( NELEM * sizeof(*array) );    ❸  │  Sets each byte in the
  memset(array, 0, NELEM * sizeof(*array) );  ◁──┘  new array to 0

  for (i=0; i<NELEM; i++) {
    printf("Index %d element %d\n",i, array[i]);  ◁┐
  }                                                 │  Loops through each
                                                    │  element of the array,
  free(array);  ◁─┐ Frees the                       │  printing it to the screen
  return(0);       │ memory
}
```

❶ We declare the size of the array in a single place so we don't need to rely on a bare number in the code. Remember that C pointers do not know the number of elements they have been allocated.

❷ As in the previous example, this is the standard C `main` routine, but we do not declare any arguments because we are not interested in them.

❸ Next we allocate `NELEM` integers. We multiply the number of elements by the number of bytes in each integer to determine the total number of bytes required.

In some architectures, setting all bytes to 0 does not initialize all values to 0 (because a number is represented by multiple bytes). To be absolutely sure you are initializing the memory correctly, an explicit loop is the safest solution.

3.6.4   Memory manipulation and Perl

Having said all this, we must advise you that in the Perl source code you will never use any of the functions for memory allocation and manipulation we have described.

In the interests of cross-platform portability and debugging support, Perl uses private definitions of these functions by providing C preprocessor macros. For example, the Perl memory allocator, New, may eventually translate to a malloc, but it doesn't have to. If you are attempting to check for memory leaks, you may want to redefine New so that it keeps track of the allocations and corresponding frees—and a macro makes this process extremely simple. The full suite of Perl functions dealing with memory manipulation is described in section 5.5.1.

3.7 C TRAPS FOR THE PERL PROGRAMMER

A number of pitfalls await the unwary Perl programmer writing C. In this section, we list some of the common ones:

- Functions all need parentheses (unlike in Perl). If you don't supply parentheses, you end up taking a pointer to a function!
- Initialization of values is very important. If you don't initialize variables before using them, they may be set to 0—or they may contain garbage.
- "x" and 'x' are not the same. "x" creates a constant string, whereas 'x' acts like the Perl ord operator.
- Memory management is not automatic. If you don't allocate memory before using it, you'll end up writing on memory that's in use; if you don't free memory after using it, you'll end up leaking memory.
- You cannot return a pointer to an automatic variable (one you have declared at the top of a block). In this respect, automatic variables are unlike Perl's lexical variables declared with my. Automatic variables' storage is assigned as part of the call stack, and once you've finished with the current function, the call stack frame is released and automatic variables are freed. In short, don't expect closures to work, because C doesn't support them!
- Writing into read-only strings is not supported. Constants in C really are constant. If you're going to modify a string, chances are you can't start by saying

  ```
  char* s = "My string";
  ```

  because doing so creates a constant. Use strcpy or memcpy instead, and be sure you write only to non-constant memory.
- Make sure you've recompiled all the object files you need to recompile before linking them together. There's nothing more annoying than fixing a bug, recompiling, and still seeing the old behavior because you haven't compiled the right files (or, in extreme cases, you've forgotten to recompile). A good Make-file will help immensely.
- Variable declarations can only be placed at the start of blocks. This isn't strictly true any more, because the C99 standard allows you to put variable declarations wherever you want them; but not all compilers are C99-compliant yet.

3.8 FURTHER READING

- *C*—Many books on the C programming language are available, and we cannot recommend all of them. The standard reference works are *The C Programming Language* by Brian Kernighan and Dennis Ritchie and *C: A Reference Manual* by Samuel Harbison and Guy Steele.

- *Library functions*—All the library functions described in this chapter have corresponding manual pages on most systems. The comp.lang.c FAQ (http://www.eskimo.com/~scs/C-faq/faq.html) is also useful.

- *Perl wrappers*—The Perl wrappers for standard C functions are described in the `perlclib` documentation that comes with Perl.

3.9 SUMMARY

In this chapter, you have learned the following:

- Arguments to C functions are passed by value. In order to modify a variable in a function, you must use a pointer to the variable.

- Arrays in C are contiguous blocks of memory. They cannot be resized without allocating more memory; when dynamically allocated, they do not know how long they are. C strings are just arrays of characters, terminated by a NUL character.

- File I/O can either be buffered, using streams, or unbuffered, using file descriptors.

- C has no native hashes, only fixed-size structures.

- C will not automatically allocate more memory as you need it. You must explicitly ask for more memory, and you must make sure you give it back to the system when it is no longer required.

CHAPTER 4

Perl's variable types

Before we can delve deeper into the secrets of XS and Perl embedding, we need to describe how variables exist in Perl. This chapter will explain how Perl variables (scalars, arrays, hashes, and globs) are represented within Perl. Starting from the various scalar types ($x in Perl), we will then continue to discuss magic (for example, ties), the more complex data types, and the organization of namespaces and lexical ("my") variables.

This will be our first detailed look inside Perl, and we'll use our knowledge of the types of variables used in C and how C data structures are implemented. This chapter assumes no more familiarity with C than that presented in chapters 1 and 3, although it can get a little scary. If this is your first look at the insides of Perl, feel free to skip this chapter and come back to it later.

4.1   GENERAL CONCEPTS

We'll begin our discussion of Perl variables by examining some general issues before covering the specifics of each variable type. A Perl variable is much more clever than a simple C variable. Perl knows how many characters the variable needs, how to convert it from a number to a string, and how many other variables know about it (so that Perl can tidy up after itself). Perl does this by using a C data structure (a *struct*) rather than a simple variable or array. As explained in chapter 3, a C struct is a block of memory that can contain any number of variables of any type. Each entry in the struct can be accessed by name and is functionally equivalent to a simplified Perl hash.

The different types of Perl variables use slightly different structures but share a core functionality. The Perl internals can determine what type of variable is being used from its type code. The internal names of the common variable types along with their corresponding type codes and structure names (all of which are defined in the Perl include files) can be found in table 4.1.

Table 4.1 Internal Perl variable types and their corresponding C structure names

Name	Variable type	C structure	Perl function
SvNULL	SVt_NULL	None	undef
SvIV	SVt_IV	xpviv	Integer
SvNV	SVt_NV	xpvnv	Floating-point number
SvRV	SVt_RV	xrv	Reference or undef
SvPV	SVt_PV	xpv	String
SvPVIV	SVt_PVIV	xpviv or xpvuv	String and/or number
SvPVNV	SVt_PVNV	xpvnv	Float, string, and/or integer
SvPVMG	SVt_PVMG	xpvmg	Magic
SvPVAV	SVt_PVAV	xpvav	Array
SvPVHV	SVt_PVHV	xpvhv	Hash
SvPVCV	SVt_PVCV	xpvcv	Code block
SvPVGV	SVt_PVGV	xpvgv	Glob

4.1.1 Reference counting

Reference counting is a key concept in Perl, because Perl decides whether the memory associated with a variable can be recycled on the basis of reference counting. When a variable is created, it has a reference count of 1. Whenever a reference of that variable is stored somewhere, the reference count is increased by 1; whenever a reference is no longer required, the reference count is decreased by 1. If the reference count becomes 0, Perl can no longer use the variable, and the memory associated with it is freed. Forgetting to increment or decrement the reference count at the correct times is a common way to cause a memory leak when you're using XS or the Perl internals. In order to find out the reference count of a particular variable from Perl, you need to be able to look inside it. We describe how to do this in the next section.

4.1.2 Looking inside: Devel::Peek

When you are developing Perl extensions (or are simply interested in what is happening to a variable), it is useful to be able to examine the internal structure of a Perl variable (known as an SV or scalar value; we'll talk more about the structure of an SV in section 4.2) from a Perl program. The Devel::Peek module is available as part of the standard Perl distribution and provides this functionality. You can use it to list the current state of a variable in detail.

In the following example, the Perl code is on the left and the corresponding output from each line is on the right:

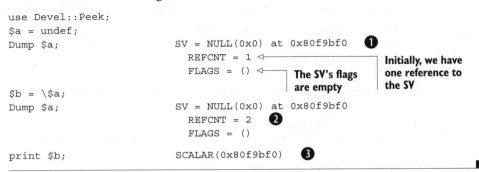

```
use Devel::Peek;
$a = undef;
Dump $a;                    SV = NULL(0x0) at 0x80f9bf0    ❶
                               REFCNT = 1
                               FLAGS = ()

$b = \$a;
Dump $a;                    SV = NULL(0x0) at 0x80f9bf0
                               REFCNT = 2    ❷
                               FLAGS = ()

print $b;                   SCALAR(0x80f9bf0)    ❸
```

❶ Devel::Peek shows us that we have an SvNULL structure, and it tells us the memory address of that structure: 0x80f9bf0 in this instance (expect your output to show a different location). The address in brackets (0x0) tells us where the ANY field in the SV's structure is pointing—in the case of an SvNULL, this address is 0; but in more complicated SVs, it will point to another structure in memory. We'll talk more about the SvNULL type in section 4.2.1

❷ When we create a new reference to the SV, its reference count increases by 1.

❸ When the reference is printed (the contents of $b), note that the stringified reference Perl generates includes the memory address.

4.1.3 The flag system

Much of the state information for a Perl variable is contained in the FLAGS field; so, before describing the structures used to construct Perl variables, we will explain how the flag system works. All computer data is stored in terms of binary digits (bits). A particular bit can either be set (a value of 1) or unset (0), and you can check the state of a bit by comparing it with a bitmask using binary logic (a bitwise AND can be used to determine if a bit is set; a bitwise OR can be used to set a bit). The following example compares a 4-bit number with a bitmask to determine whether the specific flag is set (that is, both the bit in the number to be checked and the bit in the bitmask are set):

```
            Binary      Decimal
Bit number  3 2 1 0

FLAG        0 1 1 0        6
BITMASK     0 0 1 0        2
            -------
AND         0 0 1 0        2
```

The flag has a decimal value of 6 (0b0110 in binary); when a bitwise AND operation is performed with the bit mask, the result is non-zero and indicates that the bit set in the bit mask is also set in the flag. If the result of the operation was zero, it would mean the flag was not set.

In this example, four independent states can be stored, because we are using a 4-bit number. In Perl, the FLAGS field is stored in the first 24 bits of a 32-bit integer, so it is possible to record 24 different states. The other 8 bits are used for type information (see figure 4.1 and table 4.1). The size of the flag variable and the bit number associated with each state are irrelevant because those values are set with C macros, hiding the details. All that really matters is that Perl provides C routines that you can use to query an SV for a particular state.

For example, in order to see whether an SV is read-only, you can use the SvREAD-ONLY macro:

```
if ( SvREADONLY( sv ) )
    printf("SV is readonly\n");
```

Similar macros exist for all the allowed states. The following example shows how a Perl implementation of the READONLY flag we just used might look. This Perl implementation is similar to that found in the Perl C include files:

```
use 5.006;  # binary 0b0010 notation needs perl 5.6
use constant SVf_READONLY => 0b0010; # Set the mask bit

sub SvREADONLY { $_[0] & SVf_READONLY } # Test the mask bit
sub SvREADONLY_on { $_[0] |= SVf_READONLY } # Set the READONLY bit
sub SvREADONLY_off { $_[0] &= ~SVf_READONLY } # Unset READONLY bit

# Set the flag
$flag = 0;
SvREADONLY_on( $flag );

# Test for the flag
print "Flag is readonly\n" if SvREADONLY( $flag );
```

The important point is that in this example, we only use the SvREADONLY subroutines and never need to use the SVf_READONLY value directly (or even care what its value is).

NOTE Perl-level access to the READONLY flag is available via Graham Barr's List::Util module, which has been a standard part of Perl since version 5.8.0.

When you use the Devel::Peek module, it lists all the flags that are currently set in the variable:

```
% perl -MDevel::Peek -e 'Dump( my $a )'
SV = NULL(0x0) at 0x80e58c8
  REFCNT = 1
  FLAGS = (PADBUSY, PADMY)
```

Here the PADMY flag is set, indicating that $a is a lexical variable (the PADBUSY flag is set for the same reason; see section 4.8). We'll discuss the important flags in this chapter as we examine the relevant variable types.

4.2 SCALAR VARIABLES

The simplest Perl variable type is a scalar (such as $xyz); it's represented in Perl as a C structure of type SV.[1] In this section, we will describe how the different scalar types are implemented in Perl.

4.2.1 The SvNULL type

The basic implementation of an SV, from which all Perl variables are derived, is the SvNULL (type SVt_NULL in sv.h). This type is represented as a simple C structure with three elements:

```
struct sv {
    void* sv_any;
    U32   sv_refcnt;
    U32   sv_flags;
}
```

The first line creates a new structure named sv. The next is simply a pointer of any allowed type. On the last two lines are unsigned integers that must be at least 4 bytes (32 bits) long.

Using Perl hash syntax and adding some initialization, this code would become

```
$sv = {
        sv_any => undef,
        sv_refcnt => 1,
        sv_flags  => 0
      };
```

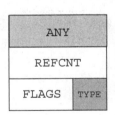

Figure 4.1
SvNULL structure

You can access the actual fields (sv_any, sv_refcnt, and sv_flags) using the C macros (defined in the sv.h include file) SvANY, SvREFCNT, and SvFLAGS, respectively (they also match the output provided by the Devel::Peek module). From now on, the structure fields will be named after the macro (without the leading Sv string) rather than the actual name used to define the structure, because all programs written using the internals go through the provided macros rather than directly to the structure. Figure 4.1 is a diagram representing an SvNULL using this notation.

---

[1] In Perl, the SV type is a typedef (or alias) for a structure of type sv (a struct sv) defined in the sv.h include file.

The ANY field points to an additional structure that contains the specific state of the variable; it can be changed depending on whether the variable is an integer (IV), double-precision floating-point number (NV), or character string (PV; stands for *pointer value* rather than *string value* because SV is already taken, and because a string in C is defined by using a pointer to the memory location of the first character). Why does Perl have to use different structures? Recall that a C structure must be defined as a fixed size at compilation time. If you wanted to define a structure that included support for all of Perl's variable types, it would be extremely large—and a simple undefined variable would use the same amount of memory as the most complex Perl variable! This design is not acceptable, even if you have access to huge amounts of memory; so, an alternative was developed.

The SvNULL represents a structure that contains just the information that all Perl variables need. If you need more information, tack a different structure onto the ANY field. If you have an SV containing a string and you then request the numeric form, the structure will be upgraded in a manner that is transparent to the programmer.[2] (The different structures and their relative hierarchy are described in subsequent sections and listed in table 4.1.) In terms of memory, this design is a very efficient solution, even though it sometimes requires a few extra pointer dereferences.

> **NOTE** This similarity extends much further than the top-level structure. As you read this chapter, you will see that the structures attached to ANY share the same organization at the beginning even if some of the fields are unused. Although this sharing leads to a small increase in required memory, it allows the code to make assumptions about relative positions of fields in similar structures for increased performance.

For an SvNULL, the ANY field does not point to anything (it contains a NULL pointer[3]); this structure represents a scalar with a value of undef. The REFCNT field contains the current reference count for the variable (see section 4.1.1) and the FLAGS field contains bit flags that you can use to determine the behavior of certain fields and the current state of the variable (for example, whether the variable is a package variable or a lexical variable, or whether the variable contains a valid integer). Currently, 24 bits are allocated with these flags; the other 8 bits are used to indicate the type of structure attached to the ANY field. You can use the SvTYPE macro to determine the variable type. As an example, here is an excerpt of the logic from a switch statement in Perl_sv_upgrade in sv.c of the Perl source:

```
switch (SvTYPE(sv)) {
case SVt_NULL:
    ...
case SVt_IV:
```

---

[2] It is not possible to *downgrade* an SV, because doing so might throw away information.

[3] NULL is the C equivalent of undef.

```
    . . .
case SVt_NV:
    . . .
```

The type of the variable to be upgraded is returned and compared against the known types, beginning with the most basic type: SVt_NULL.

4.2.2 SvRV: references

The simplest Perl variable that contains data is the SvRV subtype. It is used to contain references to other SVs. An SvRV is an SV whose ANY field points to a simple structure (named xrv) containing a single field that is a pointer to another SV (an SV*):

```
struct xrv {
    SV *         xrv_rv;          /* pointer to another SV */
};
```

A simple reference of $b=\$a would be represented diagrammatically as shown in figure 4.2.

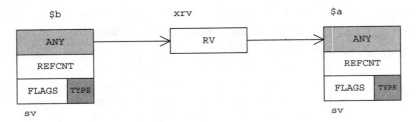

Figure 4.2   The SvRV subtype

Or, using Devel::Peek, the reference would be organized as follows:

```
SV = RV(0x80fbabc) at 0x80f9c3c   <———— SV of type SvRV
   REFCNT = 1   <
   FLAGS = (ROK)      ❶          Reference has a ref
   RV = 0x80ef888                count of l—that is, $b
   SV = NULL(0x0) at 0x80ef888   <
      REFCNT = 2   ❷             This is the SV being referred
      FLAGS = ()                 to (the SV stored in $a)
```

❶ The ROK (reference OK) flag bit is set to true to indicate that the reference is valid (if ROK is false, the variable contains the undefined value).

❷ We see that this SV has two references: the value itself, in $a; and the reference to it, in $b.

4.2.3 SvPV: string values

Perl variables that contain just a string representation are type SvPV (they simply contain a PV). They are represented by an SV whose ANY field points to a structure

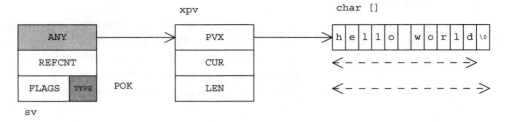

Figure 4.3   The SvPV subtype

containing a pointer to a string (a `char *` named PVX) and two length fields (the CUR and LEN fields); see figure 4.3.[4]

The PVX field contains a pointer to the start of the string representation of the SV. The CUR field is an integer containing the length of the Perl string, and the LEN field is an integer containing the number of bytes allocated to the string. Additionally, the byte at position (PVX + CUR) must be a \0 (recall from chapter 3 that C uses a NUL byte to indicate the end of a string) so other C functions that receive this string will handle it correctly. Thus LEN must be at least one more than the value of CUR. Perl's memory management is such that, for efficiency, it will not deallocate memory for the string once it has been allocated, if the string is made smaller. It is much more efficient to change the value of CUR than it is to free the unused memory when a string becomes shorter:

```
use Devel::Peek;

$a = "hello world";
Dump $a;              SV = PV(0x80e5b04) at 0x80f9d98
                          REFCNT = 1
                          FLAGS = (POK,pPOK)
                          PV = 0x80e9660 "hello world"\0
                          CUR = 11
                          LEN = 12

$a = "hello";         SV = PV(0x80e5b04) at 0x80f9d98
Dump $a;                  REFCNT = 1
                          FLAGS = (POK,pPOK)
                          PV = 0x80e9660 "hello"\0
                          CUR = 5
                          LEN = 12
```

The POK flag indicates that the PV stored in the variable is valid and can be used. The pPOK flag is related to the POK, but it is an internal flag to indicate to the magic system (see section 4.3) that the PV is valid.

---

[4]   The actual name of the SvPV struct in the Perl include files is xpv (similarly, an SvPVIV uses a struct named xpviv). For the rest of this chapter, we won't explicitly state the struct names, but they are all listed in table 4.1.

4.2.4 SvPVIV: integers

In C, it is not possible to store a number or a string in a variable interchangeably. Perl overcomes this restriction by using a data structure that contains both a string part and an integer part, using flags to indicate which part of the structure contains valid data. The name SvPVIV indicates that the structure contains a string (PV) and an integer (IV) and is simply an SvPV with an extra integer field; see figure 4.4.

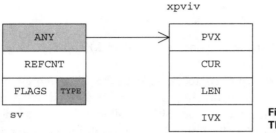

Figure 4.4
The SvPVIV subtype

This structure introduces three flags: the IOK and pIOK flags indicate that the IVX field is valid (the same way POK and pPOK indicate that the string part is valid), and the IsUV flag indicates that the integer part is unsigned (a UV) rather than signed (an IV)[5]. This last flag is useful in cases where a large positive integer is required (such as inside loops), because a UV has twice the positive range of a signed integer and is the default state when a new variable is created that contains a positive integer.

When you request a string value (using the SvPV function; see chapter 5), the integer is converted to a string representation and stored in the PVX field, and the POK and pPOK flags are set to true to prevent the conversion happening every time a string is requested. The following example shows how the variable contents change during a simple operation:

```
use Devel::Peek;

$a = 5;
Dump $a;                           SV = IV(0x80f0b28) at 0x80f9d0c
                                     REFCNT = 1
                                     FLAGS = (IOK,pIOK,IsUV)      ❶
                                     UV = 5

# string comparison
print "yes" if $a eq "hello";
Dump $a;                           SV = PVIV(0x80e5f50) at 0x80f9d0c
                                     REFCNT = 1
                                     FLAGS = (IOK,POK,pIOK,pPOK,IsUV)  ❷
                                     UV = 5
                                     PV = 0x80e9660 "5"\0
```

---

[5] Whether you get IsUV in your dump output depends critically on the Perl version you are using. The logic concerning whether an SV should be a signed or unsigned integer was overhauled by Nicholas Clark during the development of Perl 5.8.0.

```
                                              CUR = 1
# Copy in a new string                        LEN = 2
$a = "hello";
Dump $a;                              SV = PVIV(0x80e5f50) at 0x80f9d0c
                                         REFCNT = 1
                                         FLAGS = (POK,pPOK)              ❸
                                         IV = 5
                                         PV = 0x80e9660 "hello"\0
                                         CUR = 5
                                         LEN = 6
```

❶ Initially, the SV contains a UV and a flag indicating that the integer part of the SV is OK.

❷ The string comparison forces the SV to be stringified. This action results in an upgrade to a PVIV; the POK flag is set to true in addition to the IOK flag, and a string representation of the number is stored in the PV slot.

❸ The string part is modified so the integer part is now invalid. The IOK flag is unset, but the IV retains its value.

4.2.5   SvPVNV: floating-point numbers

For the same reason a C variable cannot contain a string and an integer, it cannot contain a floating-point value. You can overcome this limitation by adding a floating-point field to an SvPVIV; see figure 4.5.

As with the other types, previous settings for the string and integer parts are retained as the variable evolves, even if they are no longer valid:

```
use Devel::Peek;
$a = "hello world";
$a = 5;
$a += 0.5;
Dump $a;
```

gives

```
SV = PVNV(0x80e65c0) at 0x80f9c00
 REFCNT = 1
 FLAGS = (NOK,pNOK)
```

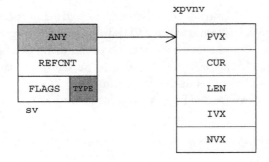

Figure 4.5
The SvPVNV structure

```
IV = 5
NV = 5.5
PV = 0x80e9660 "hello world"\0
CUR = 11
LEN = 12
```

where the IV and PV parts retain their old values but the NV part is the only value that is currently valid (as shown by the flags).

4.2.6   SvIV and SvNV

You may be wondering why we haven't discussed the SvIV and SvNV types. Table 4.1 indicates that SvIV and SvNV are implemented using the same structures as SvPVIV and SvPVNV; in fact, they only look like that on the surface. In reality, unless Perl is built to check memory violations,[6] these types are implemented with a single integer or double-precision number; however, they return a pointer as if it was a pointer to an xpviv or xpvnv structure rather than a pointer to the number (see figure 4.6). In other words: allocate memory for the single number, retrieve the pointer to the number, subtract the number of bytes that precede that number in the corresponding structure, and return the new pointer. This pointer no longer points to a valid area of memory, but that's OK because Perl will always add the offset back on when retrieving the value. This technique is a good optimization of memory usage even if it's not strictly legal, and it can clearly be considered a great hack!

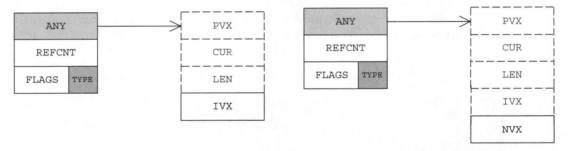

Figure 4.6   The SvIV and SvNV subtypes are implemented with a single integer or floating-point number but act as if they are part of a structure.

4.2.7   SvOOK: offset strings

To improve the speed of character removal from the front of a string, a special flag is provided (OOK—offset OK) that lets you use the IVX part of the SV to represent an offset in the string rather than as an integer representation of the string; see figure 4.7.

It is not possible for the IOK flag and the OOK flag to be set at the same time, because the IVX cannot be both an offset and a valid number.

The use of this flag is best demonstrated by example; see listing 4.1.

---

[6] In which case Perl plays by the rules and always allocates a xpviv or xpvnv structure

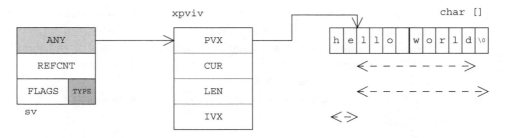

Figure 4.7 The SvOOK structure

Listing 4.1 SvOOK example

```
% perl -MDevel::Peek \
    -e '$a="Hello world"; Dump($a); $a=~s/..//; Dump($a)'
SV = PV(0x80f89ac) at 0x8109b94
  REFCNT = 1                     Standard flags
  FLAGS = (POK,pPOK)             for a PV
  PV = 0x8109f88 "Hello world"\0    String stored
  CUR = 11        ❶                 in the PV
  LEN = 12
SV = PVIV(0x80f8df8) at 0x8109b94
  REFCNT = 1
  FLAGS = (POK,OOK,pPOK)    ❷
  IV = 2  (OFFSET)    ❸
  PV = 0x8109f8a ( "He" . ) "llo world"\0    ❹
  CUR = 9     Length information is now
  LEN = 10    relative to the offset
```

---

❶ These lines specify the length of the string and the size of the buffer allocated for storage.

❷ After processing, the PV has an additional flag (OOK) indicating that offsetting is in effect.

❸ This line indicates the real start of the string. Devel::Peek indicates that this is an offset.

❹ This line shows the string split into two parts: the piece that is ignored at the start and the current value.

4.3   MAGIC VARIABLES: SvPVMG

In Perl, a *magic* variable is one in which extra functions are invoked when the variable is accessed rather than the PV, IV, or NV part of the SV. Examples are tied variables where the FETCH and STORE routines (plus others) are supplied by the programmer, the %SIG hash where a signal handler is set on assignment, and the $! variable where the C level errno variable is read directly. Additionally, objects use magic when they are blessed into a class.

An SvPVMG magic variable is just like an SvPVNV variable, except that two extra fields are present (the structure attached to the ANY field is of type xpvmg). The MAGIC field points to an additional structure of type magic, and the STASH field points to a namespace symbol table relating to the object (stashes are described later, in section 4.7); see figure 4.8.

When the STASH field is set (that is, the SV is blessed into a class), the OBJECT flag is set:

```
use Devel::Peek;
$a="bar";
$obj = bless( \$a, "Foo::Bar");
Dump $obj;
SV = RV(0x80fb704) at 0x80f9d44
  REFCNT = 1
  FLAGS = (ROK)
  RV = 0x80f9d98
  SV = PVMG(0x8102450) at 0x80f9d98
    REFCNT = 2
    FLAGS = (OBJECT,POK,pPOK)
    IV = 0
    NV = 0
    PV = 0x80e9660 "bar"\0
    CUR = 3
    LEN = 4
    STASH = 0x80f9ce4    "Foo::Bar"
```

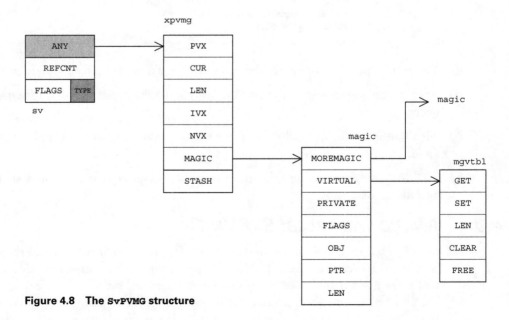

Figure 4.8   The SvPVMG structure

CHAPTER 4   PERL'S VARIABLE TYPES

The important entries in the magic structure (defined in `mg.h`) are the following:

- *moremagic*—A pointer to a linked list of additional `MAGIC` structures. Multiple `MAGIC` structures can be associated with each variable.

- *virtual*—A pointer to an array of functions. Functions can be present for retrieving the value (`get`), setting the value (`set`), determining the length of the value (`len`), clearing the variable (`clear`), and freeing the memory associated with the variable (`free`). In Perl, this array of functions is equivalent to

```
$virtual = {
    "get"   => \&get,
    "set"   => \&set,
    "len"   => \&len,
    "clear" => \&clear,
    "free"  => \&free
    };
```

- *obj*—A pointer to anything important for the type of magic being implemented. For a tie, it will be an `SV` of the tied object.

- *type*—A single character denoting the type of magic implemented. A value of `P` indicates that the magic is a tied array or hash, and `q` indicates a tied scalar or filehandle. A value of `~` or `U` indicates that the functions in the virtual table have been supplied by the programmer. An extensive list of the different types can be found in the `perlguts` documentation.

At least one of the magic flags will be set. The important flags are `GMAGICAL` (the `SV` contains a magic `get` or `len` method), `SMAGICAL` (the `SV` contains a magic `set` method), and `RMAGICAL` (the `SV` contains some other form of *random* magic).

Let's investigate the properties of magic by seeing what happens when we tie a class to a Perl variable. The following class can be used to tie a scalar such that the contents of the blessed variable increment each time its value is retrieved:

```
package Tie::Foo;           ◁──┐ Declares the name of
                               │ the current package
sub TIESCALAR {  ❶       ❷
  my $obj="foo1";
  return bless(\$obj,"Tie::Foo");  ◁──┐ Blesses the reference to
}                                     │ the scalar variable into
sub FETCH {   ❸                       │ the Tie::Foo class
  ${ $_[0] }++;   ❹
}
1;   ❺
```

❶ This is a special method name reserved by the tie system. It is invoked automatically whenever someone tries to tie a scalar variable to this class.

❷ We create a variable to act as the object and initialize it with a value. It must be a lexical to allow other, independent, variables to be tied.

❸ This is a special method name reserved by the tie system. Perl invokes this method on the object each time the value is required.

❹ We return the current value of the object and store the next value in the object. Doing so guarantees that the value first stored in the object (by the constructor) is the first value retrieved.

❺ If this is a standalone module (as opposed to being some code at the end of a program), we need to return true to indicate to Perl that the module has been read successfully.

If we now use this class, we can dump the contents of the tied variable and see how it is organized and how it changes as the tie is used. This code ties a variable to class Tie::Foo and dumps the results:

```
use Devel::Peek;
use Tie::Foo;
tie $a, 'Tie::Foo';

print "Initial state:\n";
Dump $a;

print "\nFirst value: $a\n\n";
print "State after a FETCH:\n";
Dump $a;
```

Listing 4.2 shows the output of the program used to investigate how the state of a magic variable changes when a tied variable is accessed. The changes in the structure after the first run are highlighted in bold.

Listing 4.2   Program output showing how the magic variable changes

```
Initial state:
SV = PVMG(0x81171f8) at 0x8107b14   ⟵── SV is of type SvPVMG
  REFCNT = 1
  FLAGS = (GMG,SMG,RMG)
  IV = 0
  NV = 0
  PV = 0
  MAGIC = 0x81000b8
    MG_VIRTUAL = &PL_vtbl_packelem
    MG_TYPE = 'q'   ⟵┐ The magic type is q to indicate
    MG_FLAGS = 0x02    │ that we have a tied scalar
      REFCOUNTED
    MG_OBJ = 0x80f8ae0
    SV = RV(0x810f220) at 0x80f8ae0   ⟵┐ Reference to the scalar that is
      REFCNT = 1                        │ being used as the object
      FLAGS = (ROK)
      RV = 0x81197b4
      SV = PVMG(0x81171d8) at 0x81197b4   ⟵── Actual scalar ($obj)
        REFCNT = 1
        FLAGS = (PADBUSY,PADMY,OBJECT,POK,pPOK)   ❶
        IV = 0
```

```
              NV = 0
              PV = 0x8107820 "foo1"\0
              CUR = 4
              LEN = 5
              STASH = 0x811976c      "Tie::Foo"  ⟵┐ Symbol table associated
                                                   │  with this object
     First value: foo1   ❷

     State after a FETCH:
     SV = PVMG(0x81171f8) at 0x8107b14
       REFCNT = 1
       FLAGS = (GMG,SMG,RMG,pPOK)   ❸
       IV = 0
       NV = 0
       PV = 0x81000f8 "foo1"\0   ⟵┐ Current value for
       CUR = 4                     │ the tied variable
       LEN = 5
       MAGIC = 0x81000b8
         MG_VIRTUAL = &PL_vtbl_packelem
         MG_TYPE = 'q'
         MG_FLAGS = 0x02
           REFCOUNTED
         MG_OBJ = 0x80f8ae0
         SV = RV(0x810f220) at 0x80f8ae0
           REFCNT = 1
           FLAGS = (ROK)
           RV = 0x81197b4
           SV = PVMG(0x81171d8) at 0x81197b4
             REFCNT = 1
             FLAGS = (PADBUSY,PADMY,OBJECT,POK,pPOK)
             IV = 0
             NV = 0                     Current value of the string
             PV = 0x8107820 "foo2"\0  ⟵┐ stored in the object itself
             CUR = 4
             LEN = 5
             STASH = 0x811976c      "Tie::Foo"
```

❶ The flags indicate that this is a lexical variable being used as an object; it contains a valid string.

❷ The first value retrieved from $a is the initial value stored by the object constructor.

❸ In addition to the flags indicating magic, the pPOK flag is now set to indicate that a cached value is available (even though it will be overwritten each time the FETCH is invoked).

4.4   ARRAY VARIABLES

A Perl array is an array of scalar variables; and at the C level, an array value (AV) is fundamentally an array of SVs. You implement an AV using a structure the same as that used for an SvPVMG (defined in av.h as type xpvav), except that three additional fields are present:

- *ALLOC*—Points to an array of SVs (in fact, because this is C, it points to an array of pointers to SV structures [an SV**]).
- *ARYLEN*—Points to a magic SV that is responsible for dealing with the $#array Perl construct.
- *Flag*—An extra array flag variable that controls whether the elements' reference counter should be decremented when the variable is removed from the array. Reference counts are usually decremented but the @_ array is an example where this does not happen.

In addition, the first three fields of the structure have different names: PVX becomes ARRAY, CUR becomes FILL, and LEN becomes MAX; see figure 4.9.

Note that the ARRAY field points to the first valid element of the Perl array, but the ALLOC field points to the first element of the C array. Usually ARRAY and ALLOC point to the same thing; but, similar to the OOK trick described earlier (section 4.2.7), you can use the ARRAY field to efficiently shift elements off the array without adjusting memory requirements; to do so, you simply increment the pointer (and decrement FILL and MAX). Similarly, you can pop elements off the top of the array by decrementing FILL. Listing 4.3 demonstrates how a simple array is organized.

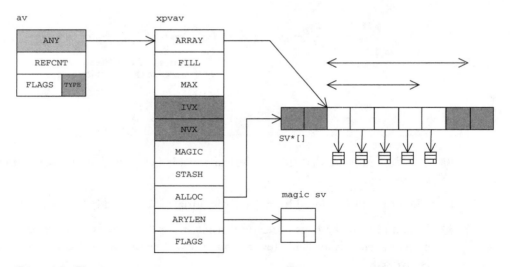

Figure 4.9   The AV structure

Listing 4.3   Devel::Peek of @a

```
% perl -MDevel::Peek -e '@a=qw/a b/;Dump(\@a)'
SV = RV(0x80fb6f8) at 0x80e5910
  REFCNT = 1
  FLAGS = (TEMP,ROK)    ❶
  RV = 0x80f9c90
  SV = PVAV(0x80fcba0) at 0x80f9c90
    REFCNT = 2    ❷
    FLAGS = ()
    IV = 0
    NV = 0
    ARRAY = 0x80ec048         ┌── Index of the highest entry
    FILL = 1  ◁───────────────┤  Highest index that can be stored
    MAX = 3   ◁───────────────┘  without allocating more memory
    ARYLEN = 0x0  ◁─┐  Pointer is null until $#
    FLAGS = (REAL)  │  is used for this array
    Elt No. 0
    SV = PV(0x80e5b04) at 0x80e5838  ◁─┐  First element: an SvPV
      REFCNT = 1                        │  containing the letter a
      FLAGS = (POK,pPOK)
      PV = 0x80faaa8 "a"\0
      CUR = 1
      LEN = 2
    Elt No. 1
    SV = PV(0x80e5b28) at 0x80e58c8  ◁─┐  Second element: an SvPV
      REFCNT = 1                        │  containing the letter b
      FLAGS = (POK,pPOK)
      PV = 0x80f4820 "b"\0
      CUR = 1
      LEN = 2
```

❶ These flags indicate that the SV passed to the Dump function is a reference to another SV and that it is temporary.

❷ The reference count is 2 because there is one reference from @a and one from the reference passed to Dump.

4.5   HASHES

Hashes (HVs) are the most complex data structure in Perl and are used by many parts of the internals. There is no equivalent to an associative array in C, so a Perl hash is implemented as a hash table—an array of linked lists. In principle a simple associative array could be arranged as an array where alternating elements are the key and the value, and this is one way of populating a hash in Perl:

```
%hash = ( 'key1', 'value1', 'key2', 'value2');
```

The problem with this approach is that value retrieval is inefficient for large associative arrays, because the entire array must be searched in order to find the correct key:

```
for ($i=0; $i<= $#arr; $i+=2) {
  return $arr[$i+1] if $arr[$i] eq $key;
}
```

A more efficient approach is to translate the key into an array index, which results in a hash lookup that is almost as fast as an array lookup. The number generated from the key is called a *hash*, and it gives the data structure its name. In Perl 5.6, a hash number is generated for each key using the following algorithm (the specific algorithm is modified slightly as Perl versions change):

```
use integer;
$hash = 0;
foreach my $i ( 0..(length($key)-1)) {
    $hash = $hash * 33 + ord( substr($key,$i,1) );
}
$hash += ( $hash >> 5 );
```

Of course, the Perl internals version is written in C.

In general, this hash number is very large. It's translated into an index by calculating the bitwise AND of the hash number and the index of the largest entry of the array (the size of the array minus one, because the index begins counting at zero):

```
$index = $hash & $#array;
```

The array sizes used for hashes are always a number 2^N (a binary number containing all 1s, the maximum index is therefore 2^N-1), which guarantees the index will be between 0 and the maximum allowed value. Unfortunately, this technique does *not* guarantee that the index will be unique for a given hash number, because only some of the bits from the hash number are used in the comparison. You can overcome this problem by chaining together hash entries with the same index such that each one has a data field containing a reference to the next field in the list. When searching for a specific key, you modify the algorithm slightly so that it first determines the index from the hash and then goes through the chain (known as a *linked list*) until it finds the correct key; this process is much faster than searching every entry because the search is reduced to those entries with a shared index. This technique is called *collisional hashing*, for the "collision" that occurs when two different keys result in the same array index.

Each hash entry (HE) is represented by the following structure (denoted in Perl hash syntax here and visually in figure 4.10):

```
$HE = {
    NEXT => $HE_next,        ◁──┐   Pointer to the next
    HEK  => {      ❶            │   hash entry in the list
              HASH => $hash,
              LEN  => length($key),
              KEY  => $key,
```

```
        }
VAL  => $SV,        ◁─┐  Contains the actual
};                     │  value of the hash entry
```

❶ The hash entry key (HEK) structure is purely a function of the hash key and therefore
does not change across hashes.

The RITER and EITER fields are used to keep track of position when you're looping
through the hash (for example, with the each or keys function). EITER contains a
pointer to the current hash entry, and RITER contains the array index of that entry.
The next hash entry is determined by first looking in the HE for the next entry in the
linked list and then, if that is not defined, incrementing RITER and looking into the
array until another hash entry is found.

Because a particular hash key *always* translates to the same hash number, if the
SHAREKEYS flag is set, Perl uses an internal table (called PL_strtab) to store every
hash key (HEK structure) currently in use. The key is removed from the table only
when the last reference to it is removed. This feature is especially useful when you're
using object-oriented programming, because each instance of a hash object will use a
single set of keys.

In a perfect hash, the number of hash entries matches the size of the array, and none
of them point to other hash entries. If the number of elements in the list exceeds the
size of the array, the assumption is that too many elements are in linked lists, where
key searches will take too long, rather than evenly spread throughout the array. When
this occurs, the size of the array is doubled and the index of every hash entry is

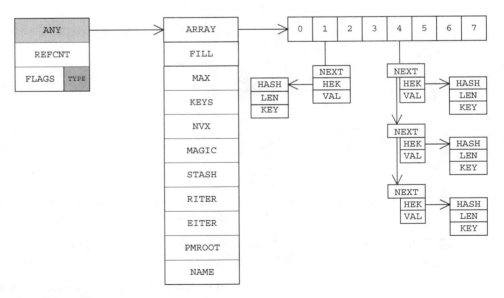

Figure 4.10   The HV structure

recalculated. This process does not involve recalculating the hash number for each element (because that simply involves the key)—only recalculating the index, which is the bitwise AND of the hash number and the new array size. If you will be inserting large numbers of keys into a hash, it is usually more efficient to preallocate the array; doing so prevents many reorganizations as the array increases in size. From Perl, you can do this using the `keys` function:

```
keys %h = 1000;
```

In the following dump, the keys have different hash numbers but translate to the same index (when the maximum size of the array is 8):

```
% perl -MDevel::Peek -e 'Dump({AF=>"hello",a=>52})'
SV = RV(0x80fbab8) at 0x80e5748
  REFCNT = 1
  FLAGS = (TEMP,ROK)
  RV = 0x80e5838
  SV = PVHV(0x80fd540) at 0x80e5838
    REFCNT = 2
    FLAGS = (SHAREKEYS)          ❶
    IV = 2
    NV = 0
    ARRAY = 0x80eba08  (0:7, 2:1)    ❷
    hash quality = 75.0%    ❸
    KEYS = 2   ⟵⎯⎯ Total number of keys stored in the hash
    FILL = 1   ⟵⎯┐
    MAX = 7    ❹   │ Number of slots filled in the array
    RITER = -1
    EITER = 0x0
    Elt "a" HASH = 0x64    ❺
    SV = IV(0x80f0b98) at 0x80e594c
      REFCNT = 1
      FLAGS = (IOK,pIOK,IsUV)
      UV = 52
    Elt "AF" HASH = 0x8ec    ❻
    SV = PV(0x80e5b04) at 0x80e5904
      REFCNT = 1
      FLAGS = (POK,pPOK)
      PV = 0x80faa98 "hello"\0
      CUR = 5
      LEN = 6
```

❶ This flag indicates that the keys (the HEK structures) should be stored in the shared string table, PL_strtab, which makes them available to all hashes.

❷ The bracketed numbers indicate how the hash is populated. In this example, there are seven slots in the array with zero hash entries and one slot with two entries.

❸ This number is a measure of the hash efficiency. It attempts to reflect how well filled the hash is. If many hash entries share the same slot, this number is less than 100%.

④ MAX is the index of the last element of the array, which, as usual, is one less than the size of the array.

⑤ This is a description of the SV stored using the key a. The hash value is 0x64 in hexadecimal; it translates to slot 4 when MAX is 7.

⑥ This is a description of the SV stored using key AF. The hash value is 0x8ec in hex, which translates to slot 4 when MAX is 7.

4.6   GLOBS

In Perl, a *glob* provides a way of accessing package variables that share the same name. Whereas globs were important in earlier versions, the design of Perl 5 has strongly reduced the need for them—at least for *normal* tasks. In fact, as of Perl version 5.6.0, you no longer even need to know that filehandles are globs.[7] However, knowledge of globs is required in order to understand the internal representation of variables. This section describes what they are and how they are implemented.

A glob variable (shown in figure 4.11) is based on the structure of a magic variable (see section 4.3), with the addition of fields for storing the name of the glob (NAME and NAMELEN), the namespace of the glob (GvSTASH), and the shared glob information (GP):

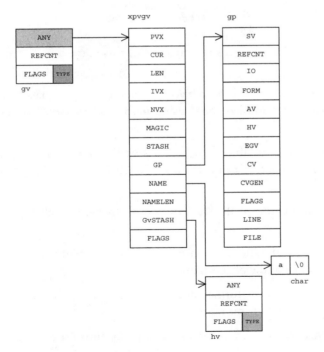

Figure 4.11
The structure of a glob variable

---

7   From Perl v5.6.0, you can say open my $fh, $file and treat $fh as a normal scalar variable.

```
% perl -MDevel::Peek -e 'Dump(*a)'
SV = PVGV(0x8111678) at 0x810cd34          ◁──── A glob structure is
  REFCNT = 2                                      called a PVGV
  FLAGS = (GMG,SMG)    ◁───── Flags indicate that set and
  IV = 0                      get magic are available
  NV = 0
  MAGIC = 0x81116e8                          Name of the table containing
    MG_VIRTUAL = &PL_vtbl_glob   ◁───┘       the glob get/set functions
    MG_TYPE = '*'   ◁────── Type of magic is *, indicating
    MG_OBJ = 0x810cd34            that this is a glob
  NAME = "a"   ❶
  NAMELEN = 1
  GvSTASH = 0x81004f4   "main"   ❷
  GP = 0x81116b0   ❸
    SV = 0x810cce0   ◁────── Contains a reference to
    REFCNT = 1   ❹           the SV stored in $a
    IO = 0x0   ❺
    FORM = 0x0   ❻
    AV = 0x0   ❼
    HV = 0x0   ❽
    CV = 0x0   ❾
    CVGEN = 0x0
    GPFLAGS = 0x0        LINE is the line number of the
    LINE = 1   ◁──────   file where the glob first occurred
    FILE = "-e"   ◁──────────── FILE is the name of the
    FLAGS = 0x0                 file that declared the glob
    EGV = 0x810cd34   "a"   ❿
```

❶ This is the name of the glob. All package variables of this name will be contained in this glob.

❷ This is the namespace to which this glob belongs. Each namespace has its own set of globs. Package variables are implemented using globs and stashes. Stashes are discussed in section 4.7.

❸ This structure contains the variable information specific to a particular glob. They are separate so that multiple GVs can share a single GP in order to implement variable aliasing.

❹ REFCNT is the reference count of the GP structure. It increases each time a variable is aliased.

❺ IO contains a reference to the filehandle stored in a. It is currently set to 0x0, indicating that there is no filehandle of this name.

❻ FORM contains a reference to the format stored in a. It is currently set to 0x0, indicating that there is no format of this name.

❼ AV contains a reference to the array stored in @a. It is currently set to 0x0, indicating that there is no array of this name.

⑧ HV contains a reference to the hash stored in `%a`. It is currently set to `0x0`, indicating that there is no hash of this name.

⑨ CV contains a reference to the subroutine stored in `&a`. It is currently set to `0x0`, indicating that there is no subroutine of this name.

⑩ EGV is the name and reference of the glob that created this GP structure. It is used to keep track of the original variable name after aliasing.

Listings 4.4 and 4.5 further illustrate how globs work by showing how aliasing affects the glob structure. Listing 4.4 is a Perl program, and Listing 4.5 shows the corresponding output of that program.

Listing 4.4 Glob aliasing demonstration program

```
use Devel::Peek;
open(A,"/dev/null");
$A = 5;
@A = (2,3,4);
sub A { 1; }
*b = *A;
Dump(*b);
```

Uses the variable A to store different Perl types

*b = *A; ◄——— Makes b an alias of A

Listing 4.5 Output of glob aliasing demonstration program

```
SV = PVGV(0x81082b0) at 0x811a0d8
  REFCNT = 3        ❶
  FLAGS = (GMG,SMG,MULTI)    ❷
  IV = 0
  NV = 0
  MAGIC = 0x8108718
    MG_VIRTUAL = &PL_vtbl_glob
    MG_TYPE = '*'
    MG_OBJ = 0x811a0d8  ◄——┘  to the parent GV
    MG_LEN = 1
    MG_PTR = 0x8108738 "b"  ◄——┘  with the magic structure
  NAME = "b"  ◄——————
  NAMELEN = 1
  GvSTASH = 0x80f8608    "main"
  GP = 0x810a350
    SV = 0x81099d0
    REFCNT = 2    ❸
    IO = 0x8104664    ❹
    FORM = 0x0
    AV = 0x8109a30
    HV = 0x0
    CV = 0x811a0f0
    CVGEN = 0x0
    GPFLAGS = 0x0
    LINE = 2
```

MG_OBJ points back to the parent GV

Name of the glob associated with the magic structure

Name of the GV that is being listed

```
FILE = "glob.pl"
FLAGS = 0x2
EGV = 0x8104598    "A"  ⟵⎯┘
```
Name of the first GV to use this GP—in this case, A

❶ This is the reference count of the GV *b and is distinct from the GV *A. There are three references to it: one in the main program, one from the argument passed to Dump, and one from itself via MG_OBJ.

❷ In addition to the flags described previously, an additional flag, MULTI, indicates that more than one variable is stored in the glob.

❸ REFCNT is the reference count of this GP structure. In this case, it is being used by *A and *b, so the reference count is 2.

❹ These are pointers to the variables created using this package name. A scalar, a file-handle, an array, and a subroutine all share a name.

4.7 NAMESPACES AND STASHES

Perl uses namespaces to separate global variables into groups. Each global variable used by Perl belongs to a namespace. The default namespace is main:: [8] (compare this naming convention with the main in C), and all globals belong to this namespace unless the package keyword has been used or unless a namespace is explicitly specified:

```
$bar = "hello";    ⟵⎯⎯ Sets $main::bar
$Foo::bar = 3;
                   Sets $Foo::bar
package Foo;
$bar = 2;
```

Internally, namespaces are stored in *symbol table hashes* (always abbreviated to *stashes*). They are implemented exactly as the name suggests. Each namespace (or symbol table) is made up of a hash; the keys of the hash are the variable names present in the namespace, and the values are GVs containing all the variables that share that name. Stashes can also contain references to stashes in related namespaces by using the hash entry in the GV to point to another stash; Perl assumes that any stash key ending in :: indicates a reference to another stash. The root symbol table is called defstash and contains main::. In order to look up variable $a in package Foo::Bar, the following occurs:

1 Starting from defstash, look up Foo:: in the main:: stash. This entry points to the Foo:: glob.

2 Look up the HV entry in the glob. This entry points to the Foo:: stash.

---

[8] In all cases, the main:: namespace can be abbreviated simply to ::.

CHAPTER 4   PERL'S VARIABLE TYPES

3 Look up Bar:: in this stash to retrieve the GV containing the hash for this stash.

4 Look up a in the Bar:: hash to get the glob.

5 Dereference the required SV.

As you can see, finding package variables in nested namespaces has a large overhead! One final thing to note about hashes is that Perl does not hide the implementation details. The symbol table hashes can be listed just like any other Perl hash:

```
% perl -e '$Foo::bar = 2; print $Foo::{bar},"\n"'
*Foo::bar
```

Here the bar entry in the hash %Foo:: is a glob named Foo::bar that contains the scalar variable that has a value of 2. This fact can be proven by aliasing this hash to another glob:

```
% perl -e '$Foo::bar = 2; *x = $Foo::{bar}; print "$x\n"'
2
```

4.8   LEXICAL "MY" VARIABLES

Lexical variables are associated with code blocks rather than namespaces, so they are implemented in a very different way than globals. Each code block (a CV; see section 4.9) contains a reference to an array (an AV) of scratch pads. This array is called a *padlist*. The first entry in this padlist is a scratch pad (also an AV) that lists all the lexical variables used by the block (not just those that were declared in the block). The names contain the full variable type ($, %, @) so that $a and @a have different entries. The second scratch pad is an array that contains the values for each of these variables. The main complication occurs with recursion. Each time a block of code calls itself recursively, you need to make sure the variables available to the block cannot affect variables in the block that called this one. In order that each recursive call does not trash the previous contents of the variables in the scratch pads for that block, a new entry in the padlist is created for each level of recursion.

This layout means that at least three AVs are required to implement lexical variables in each code block: one to hold the variable names (the first scratch pad), one to hold the first set of values (the second scratch pad), and one to hold both these arrays and subsequent ones (the padlist). Figure 4.12 shows an example of four lexical variables and one level of recursion. Lexical variables are faster than local variables because the scratch pads are created at compile time (because Perl knows which variables are to be associated with each block at that point) and can be accessed directly.

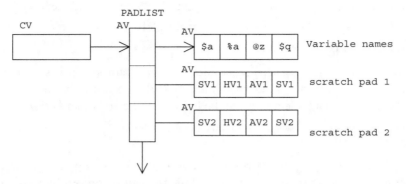

Figure 4.12   Lexical variables in scratch pads

4.9   CODE BLOCKS

You can think of subroutines or code blocks in Perl the same way as other Perl variables. A code value (CV) contains information about Perl subroutines. The layout (shown in figure 4.13) is similar to the structure of other variables, with additional fields dealing with issues such as namespaces (section 4.7), padlists (section 4.8), and opcodes (section 10.4):

```
% perl -MDevel::Peek -e 'sub foo {}; Dump(\&foo)'
SV = RV(0x8111408) at 0x80f86e0
  REFCNT = 1
  FLAGS = (TEMP,ROK)
  RV = 0x8109b7c
  SV = PVCV(0x811b524) at 0x8109b7c   <─── Structure is of type PVCV
    REFCNT = 2
    FLAGS = ()
    IV = 0
    NV = 0
    COMP_STASH = 0x80f8608     "main"   ❶
    START = 0x8108aa0 ===> 655   ❷
    ROOT = 0x810b020
    XSUB = 0x0   ❸
    XSUBANY = 0
    GVGV::GV = 0x8109ae0        "main" :: "foo"   ❹
    FILE = "-e"   ❺
    DEPTH = 0   ❻
    FLAGS = 0x0   ❼
    PADLIST = 0x8109b28   ❽
    OUTSIDE = 0x80f8818 (MAIN)
```

❶ This line indicates the location and name of the symbol table hash that is in effect when this subroutine executes. In this example, no packages are declared and the `main::` stash is in scope.

② These items refer to the opcodes that are used to implement the subroutine; they are explained in section 3.2.2.

③ When this subroutine represents an external C function, these fields contain a pointer to that function and other related information. See chapters 2 and 6 for more information on XSUBs.

④ GVGV is a pointer to the GV that contains this subroutine. Recall that a glob can contain references to all the Perl variable types; in this case, the GV is named *main::foo.

⑤ FILE is the name of the file that defined the subroutine. This subroutine was created on the command line.

⑥ DEPTH contains the recursion depth of the subroutine. This number increments for each level of recursion, allowing the correct entries in the padlist to be retrieved.

⑦ FLAGS is the actual value of the flags field that is expanded in words at the top of the dump.

⑧ This is a reference to the padlist containing all the lexical variables required by this subroutine.

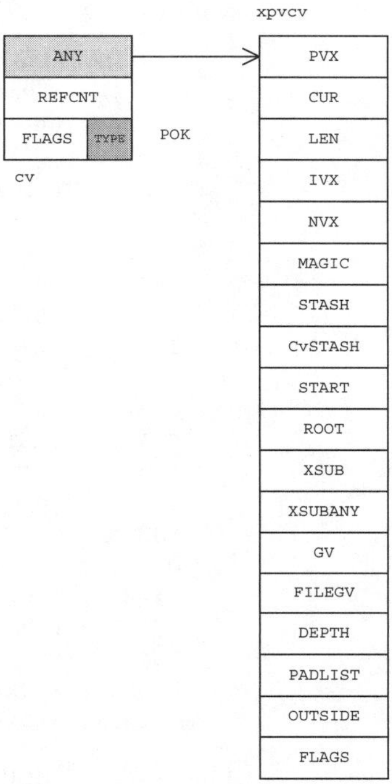

Figure 4.13
The structure of a CV

4.9.1 Important CV flags

The following flags are of particular interest when you're examining CVs.

The ANON flag indicates that the subroutine is anonymous (for example, $x = sub { 1; };). When this flag is set, the GV associated with the CV is meaningless, because the subroutine is not present in any stash.

The LVALUE flag indicates that the subroutine can be used as an lvalue. For example,

```
use Devel::Peek;
$x = 1;
sub foo :lvalue {
  $x;
}
print foo,"\n";
foo = 5;
print foo,"\n";

Dump(\&foo);
```

would show

```
1    <--- Shows the initial state of $x
5    <--- $x now has a value of 5
SV = RV(0x8109998) at 0x8100dec
  REFCNT = 1
  FLAGS = (TEMP,ROK)
  RV = 0x810d4f8
  SV = PVCV(0x8109044) at 0x810d4f8
    REFCNT = 2
    FLAGS = (LVALUE)          <--- LVALUE flag is now set,
    IV = 0                         confirming that the subroutine
    NV = 0                         can be used as an lvalue
    COMP_STASH = 0x8100d14    "main"
    START = 0x8113490 ===> 1178
    ROOT = 0x8130d48
    XSUB = 0x0
    XSUBANY = 0
    GVGV::GV = 0x810d4d4         "main" :: "foo"
    FILE = "lvexample.pl"     <--- The example was stored in a
    DEPTH = 0                      file, so now the FILE field
    FLAGS = 0x100                  contains a proper filename
    PADLIST = 0x810d528
    OUTSIDE = 0x8109e34 (MAIN)
```

The CONST flag indicates that the subroutine returns a constant value and is eligible
for in-lining at compile time:

```
% perl -MDevel::Peek -e 'sub foo () { 123; }; Dump(\&foo)'
SV = RV(0x8125e50) at 0x810fc94
  REFCNT = 1
  FLAGS = (TEMP,ROK)
  RV = 0x810fd54
  SV = PVCV(0x812ffc8) at 0x810fd54
    REFCNT = 2
    FLAGS = (POK,pPOK,CONST)
    IV = 0
    NV = 0
    PROTOTYPE = ""
    COMP_STASH = 0x0
    ROOT = 0x0
    XSUB = 0x80881dc
    XSUBANY = 135377308
    GVGV::GV = 0x811b190"main" :: "foo"
    FILE = "op.c"
    DEPTH = 0
    FLAGS = 0x200
    PADLIST = 0x0
    OUTSIDE = 0x0 (null)
```

This optimization occurs only if a subroutine has been declared with an empty
prototype.

The METHOD flag indicates that the CV has been marked as a method. This flag is currently used in conjunction with the LOCKED attribute to determine whether the subroutine itself should be locked or only the object when Perl is running with multiple threads:[9]

```
sub foo : method locked {
   ...
}
```

If the LOCKED flag is set, the subroutine will lock itself on entry when Perl is running with multiple threads. If the METHOD attribute is also set, the object will be locked rather than the subroutine:

```
sub foo : locked {
   ...
}
```

4.10   FURTHER READING

More detailed information on the structure of Perl's internal data structures can be found at the following locations:

- *perlguts*, *perlapi*—The main source of Perl internals documentation is the perlguts and perlapi man pages that come with the Perl distribution.
- *illguts*—*Perl Guts Illustrated* by Gisle Aas (http://gisle.aas.no/perl/illguts/) provides an alternative illustrated explanation of the internal implementation of Perl variable types.
- *sv.h, av.h, hv.h, mg.h, cv.h*—These C include files define all the structures and flags. If you really want to know the details of what is happening, read these files; they come with the Perl source.

4.11   SUMMARY

In this chapter we've shown how variables are implemented inside Perl. We've covered the implementation of simple scalars and how the different scalar types relate to each other. We've also shown you how Perl hashes and arrays are realized and talked a little about the organization of namespaces and lexical variables.

---

[9] The LOCKED and METHOD flags are only really used with the original Perl threads implementation. The new interpreter threads (ithreads) implementation in Perl 5.8.0 will not need these flags.

The Perl 5 API

The Perl 5 API is the interface by which your C code is allowed to talk to Perl; it provides functions for manipulating variables, for executing Perl code and regular expressions, for file handling, for memory management, and so on.

The API is used inside the Perl core as a set of utility functions to manipulate the environment that the Perl interpreter provides. It also provides the building blocks out of which you will create extensions and by which you will drive an embedded Perl interpreter from C—hence, the functions and macros you learn about here will form the basis of the rest of the book.

This chapter is a reference to the Perl 5 API, so the example code for many functions will contain uses of other functions not yet explained. You are encouraged to jump around the chapter, following references to later functions and jumping back to see how they're used in real code.

As much as possible, we've made the example code real, rather than contrived; we've taken the code from XS modules and, where possible, from the Perl sources or extension modules inside the Perl core. However, development doesn't stop, so don't be surprised if you look at the sources and find that some things are slightly different.

NOTE   The index in appendix C lists all Perl API references in this book.

5.1 SAMPLE ENTRY

Here is the format we will use when introducing functions:

something (the name of the function)

```
char * something(int parameter);
```

A brief explanation of what the function does.

> **Listing 5.1   Using something**

```
if (testing)
    result = something(whatsit);   ◁────┐  An explanation of how the
                                          function is used in the example
```

5.2 SV FUNCTIONS

As you know from chapter 4, scalar values (SVs) are the internal representation of Perl's scalars. Although XS lets you get away without necessarily doing anything with SVs, any sophisticated XS module will need to create, destroy, and manipulate scalars. These functions allow you to do this.

5.2.1 Special SVs

Before we look at the functions for manipulating SVs, let's examine certain special values that Perl defines.

PL_sv_undef

This is the undefined value; you should use it when, for instance, you want to return undef rather than an empty list or a false value. Note that PL_sv_undef is the SV structure itself—because you'll usually want a pointer to an SV, you should use this as &PL_sv_undef whenever anything needs an SV*.

Example   This example is taken from the Apache module mod_perl, which embeds a Perl interpreter inside the Apache web server. We'll look at an entire function that takes a request for a file, opens the file, reads it all into an SV, and returns a reference to it. In Perl, we'd write it like this:

```
sub mod_perl_slurp_filename {
    my ($request) = @_;
    my $sv;

    local $/ = undef;
    open FP, $request->{name};
    $sv = <FP>;
    close FP;

    return \$sv;
}
```

Now, listing 5.2 shows how we'd write it in C.

TIP Because this is our first example, we haven't yet introduced any of the other functions in the Perl API. Don't worry; we'll provide a commentary about what's going on, and you're encouraged to jump around to the entries for other functions so you know what they do. We'll also skim over some things that will be covered in future chapters; these topics are peripheral to the points we're making.

Listing 5.2 $/ = undef in C

```
SV *mod_perl_slurp_filename(request_rec *r)
{
    dTHR;
    PerlIO *fp;
    SV *insv;

    ENTER;
    save_item(PL_rs);          ❶
    sv_setsv(PL_rs, &PL_sv_undef);   ◄────  Sets this SV equal to undef using
                                             the function sv_setsv (see
    fp = PerlIO_open(r->filename, "r");  ❷    "sv_setsv," page 124)
    insv = newSV(r->finfo.st_size);  ❸
    sv_gets(insv, fp, 0); /*slurp*/  ❹
    PerlIO_close(fp);          ◄──────  Closes the
    LEAVE;                              filehandle with
    return newRV_noinc(insv);  ❺        PerlIO_close
}
```

❶ PL_rs is the record separator, and save_item is the equivalent to local; it will save a copy of the variable away and restore it at the end of the current *XS block*—the code delimited by ENTER and LEAVE.

❷ PerlIO_open opens a file. The first parameter is the filename, which we extract from the request structure r, and the second parameter is the mode: we're opening the file for reading. This function will give us back a filehandle, just like the open function in Perl.

❸ We use newSV (see "newSV and NEWSV," page 104) to create a new SV to receive the file contents. We pass the size of the file as a parameter to newSV so that Perl can grow the string to the appropriate length in advance.

❹ sv_gets is equivalent to the readline (<>) operator in Perl—it reads a line from the specified filehandle into the SV. Because we've set the record separator to undef, calling this function has the effect of slurping the entire file into the SV.

❺ Finally, we use newRV_noinc (see "newRV and newRV_noinc," page 129) to create a reference to the SV without increasing its reference count, and we return the new reference.

See also: "PL_sv_yes and PL_sv_no," page 103.

PL_sv_yes and PL_sv_no

These SVs represent true and false values; you can use them as boolean return values from your functions. Just like PL_sv_undef earlier, these are the actual SV structures, rather than pointers to them; so, you should use &PL_sv_yes and &PL_sv_no in your code.

Example The looks_like_number function in sv.c in the Perl core takes an SV and decides whether it's a valid numeric value. In the DBI module, a wrapper around the function allows it to take a list of items and return a list of true or false values. Listing 5.3 shows the meat of that function.

Listing 5.3 Is it a number?

```
for(i=0; i < items ; ++i) {
    SV *sv = ST (i);    ❶
    if (!SvOK(sv) || (SvPOK(sv) && SvCUR(sv)==0))   ◁── If the SV isn't
        PUSHs(&PL_sv_undef);                             available, or if it's a
    else if ( looks_like_number(sv) )   ❷               string and has no
        PUSHs(&PL_sv_yes);                               length, we put undef
    else                                                 onto the stack
        PUSHs(&PL_sv_no);
}
```

❶ We loop over the arguments to the function. ST is a special macro that gets the numbered SV from the list of arguments Perl keeps on the argument stack. Having taken all the arguments off the stack, we'll fill it back up with the return values.

❷ We call the function in sv.c, and if that returns true, we put the true value (&PL_sv_yes) on the stack. If the function returns false, we put &PL_sv_no on the stack instead.

See also: "SvTRUE," page 110.

5.2.2 Creating SVs

Other than the SVs that Perl passes to you or sets in special variables, you can get SVs in two major ways: you can fetch the SV representing a Perl variable, or you can create your own.

get_sv

```
SV* get_sv(char* name, bool create);
```

This function returns the SV that represents the Perl-side variable *name*; if this SV doesn't currently exist in the Perl symbol table, it will be created if *create* has a true value; otherwise you get back a null pointer. This function is the usual way to communicate with options provided by the user as Perl package variables. It should be called as merely get_sv, but you may also see it as perl_get_sv in older code.

The most common use of get_sv is to read parameters set by the user in Perl space. For instance, $YourModule::DEBUG could be set to true to turn on debugging information. This is exactly what the Storable module does. Listing 5.4 shows how it sets up its debugging mode.

Listing 5.4   Debugging XS modules

```
#ifdef DEBUGME      ❶
#define TRACEME(x)   do {                                          \
    if (SvTRUE(perl_get_sv("Storable::DEBUGME", TRUE)))  \    ❷
        { PerlIO_stdoutf x; PerlIO_stdoutf ("\n"); }      \    ❸
} while (0)    ❹
#else
#define TRACEME(x)
#endif

...

TRACEME(("small integer stored as %d", siv));
```

---

❶ The module must be compiled with -DDEBUGME before any debugging can take place: if it is not, TRACEME() simply expands to nothing—that is, it is optimized away.

❷ We get a handle on the Perl-side variable $Storable::DEBUGME, creating it if it doesn't already exist. We then call SvTRUE (see "SvTRUE," page 110) to test whether the variable is set to a true value.

❸ If it is, the debugging message is formatted and printed to standard output using PerlIO_stdoutf, followed by a new line.

❹ The do { ... } while (0) is a preprocessor trick to make sure the code consists of one statement, so that it can be used like this:

```
if (broken)
    TRACEME(("Something is wrong!"));
```

Without the do-while trick this code would require braces, because it would be more than one statement.

See also: "get_av," page 132, and "get_hv," page 145.

newSV and NEWSV

```
SV* newSV(STRLEN length);
SV* NEWSV(IV id, STRLEN length);
```

There are many ways to create a new SV in Perl; the most basic are newSV and NEWSV. Both take a parameter length—if it is more than 0, the SV will be an SVPV and the pointer value (PV) will be pre-extended to the given length. If it is 0, you'll get an SVNULL back. The NEWSV macro also takes an id parameter; it was intended to be used to track where SVs were allocated from in case of memory leaks, but it's never really used—you can use a unique identifier for this parameter value if you think it will be used again, or 0 if you aren't bothered. To be honest, it's not likely that the leak detection code will be used again and so it doesn't really matter which one you use.

Example When you execute `eval $string`, Perl has to store the code you're evaluating. In fact, Perl splits it into separate lines, so that it can return error messages like this:

```
syntax error at (eval 1) line 3, at EOF
```

As you can see, Perl has split the string and returns an error message based on the line number. It does so by putting the code into an array, using the internal S_save_lines function in pp_ctl.c of the Perl sources (see listing 5.5).

Listing 5.5   Saving eval'd code

```
S_save_lines(pTHX_ AV *array, SV *sv)
{
    register char *s = SvPVX(sv);           ❶
    register char *send = SvPVX(sv) + SvCUR(sv);
    register char *t;
    register I32 line = 1;

    while (s && s < send) {
        SV *tmpstr = NEWSV(85,0);           ❷

        sv_upgrade(tmpstr, SVt_PVMG);       ❸
        t = strchr(s, '\n');                ❹
        if (t)
            t++;
        else
            t = send;

        sv_setpvn(tmpstr, s, t - s);        ❺
        av_store(array, line++, tmpstr);    ❻
        s = t;
    }
}
```

---

❶ The string s contains the text in the SV—that is, the text of the Perl code we're splitting; send represents the end of the string.

❷ For each line, before we reach the end of the string, we create a new SV using NEWSV; we give it the leak ID 85 and do not give a length, because we don't know how long or how short our line will be.

❸ We upgrade the new SV to a PVMG (string plus magic) so the Perl debugger can use the magic structure.

❹ The next few lines find the next newline character and set t to the start of the next line. If there are no more newline characters, we set t to the end of the string.

❺ We now have a string running from s to t-1, which is our line; we use sv_setpvn (see "sv_setpv and sv_setpvn," page 121) to store that string into our temporary SV.

❻ Finally, we store the SV as the next element in the array we're building up and set our string point to t, the start of the next line. Notice that we start at array element 1, rather than zero—we do so because although arrays are zero-based, files start from line 1. Hence, we skip the 0th element of the array.

See also: "newAV," page 133, "newHV," page 145, and "get_sv," page 103.

Creating SVs with values

```
SV* newSViv ( IV i );
SV* newSVuv ( UV u );
SV* newSVnv ( NV n );
SV* newSVpv ( char* string , STRLEN len );
SV* newSVpvn ( char* string , STRLEN len );
```

These functions all create a new SV with some particular value. You will probably use these functions the most when you're creating SVs to return from your XS routines. The names are pretty much self-explanatory: newSViv creates a new SV from a given integer value, newSVuv creates a new SV from an unsigned integer, newSVnv creates a new SV from a floating-point value, and newSVpv creates a new SV from a given string. (newSVpvn is equivalent, but newSVpv will compute the length for you if you pass in a length of 0.)

This example is taken from Unicode::Normalize in recent Perl distributions. The function getCanon gets either the canonical or compatibility decomposition of a Unicode character. For instance, if fed à, it returns a`, where ` is character 0x300, "COMBINING GRAVE ACCENT". The heavy lifting is done by a C function, but listing 5.6 shows the XS glue that returns the string.

Listing 5.6 Returning a string

```
rstr = ix ? dec_compat(uv) : dec_canonical(uv);      ❶
if(!rstr) XSRETURN_UNDEF;      ❷
RETVAL = newSVpvn((char *)rstr, strlen((char *)rstr));      ❸
```

---

❶ This line performs the decomposition of the character uv, storing the result in the string rstr.

❷ If rstr is empty, we return undef.

❸ Otherwise, we return a new scalar from the string rstr.

See also: "newSV and NEWSV," page 104, "newSVsv," on this page, and "newRV and newRV_noinc," page 129.

newSVsv

```
SV* newSVsv ( SV* old );
```

As its name implies, this function creates a new SV from an existing SV. It's conceptually equivalent to performing a NEWSV and an sv_setsv. You'd do this mainly to dissociate a new SV from its ancestor—the new SV will not have any references to the ancestor and can be modified without perturbing anything else in the program.

Example A *statement handle* object in the Perl DBI module (usually called $sth) knows a number of things about the SQL statement it's executing; one of these things is the name of the fields. However, the DBI module doesn't guarantee the case of the field names, and because some databases are case-sensitive, this can cause problems. So, instead of using

```
$sth->{NAME}
```

you're encouraged to use

```
$sth->{NAME_lc} or $sth->{NAME_uc}
```

to get a lower- or uppercase version of the array of field names. This array is generated on demand by the code in listing 5.7.

Listing 5.7   Case-folding an array

```
    int up = (key[5] == 'u');      ❶
    AV *av = newAV();   ←                      We need a new array
    i = DBIc_NUM_FIELDS(imp_sth);   ❷          to hold the results
    assert(i == AvFILL(name)+1);
    while(--i >= 0) {
        sv = newSVsv(AvARRAY(name)[i]);  ❸
        for (p = SvPV(sv,lna); p && *p; ++p) {  ❹
#ifdef toUPPER_LC
            *p = (up) ? toUPPER_LC(*p) : toLOWER_LC(*p);   ❺
#else
            *p = (up) ? toUPPER(*p) : toLOWER(*p);
#endif
        }
        av_store(av, i, sv);   ←   Stores the appropriately modified
    }                              SV into the result array
```

---

❶ We determine whether we're uppercasing or lowercasing depending on whether we've seen NAME_uc or NAME_lc.

❷ We use some DBI magic to get the number of fields, and we make sure it's the same as the number of names in the names array. If so, we can walk the array from the highest-numbered element down to zero.

❸ We extract each element from the array and make a copy of it with newSVsv. Notice we don't use av_fetch (see "av_fetch," page 136), because we know the array will contain the correct number of elements and can be accessed directly.

❹ We use the pointer p to walk over each string. lna is just DBI-speak for PL_na, the "don't bother giving me a length" variable.

❺ We either upper- or lowercase, depending on the value of up; if locale-aware macros are available, we use them. This step replaces each character in the string with the appropriately cased version. Because we made a copy of the SV, we're not affecting the original names array.

See also: "sv_setsv," page 124.

sv_newmortal and sv_mortalcopy

```
SV* sv_newmortal (void);
SV* sv_mortalcopy ( SV* oldsv );
```

Like newSV, sv_newmortal creates a new SV. However, the returned SV is marked as mortal, meaning that it will go away at the next close of scope. It is difficult to know precisely when you need to make an SV mortal; see "Returning a hash reference," page 179, for more discussion.

sv_mortalcopy is the "mortalized" equivalent of newSVsv.

See also: "sv_2mortal," page 123, "newSV and NEWSV," page 104, and "Creating SVs with values," page 106.

newSVpvf

```
SV* newSVpvf ( const char* pat , ... );
```

The final method of creating SVs uses *format strings*, in a similar vein to sprintf. Perl's pvf functions support all the usual sprintf patterns, plus the additional, undocumented pattern %_, which formats another SV. This pattern is particularly useful for constructing error messages, as our example shows.

Example   Sometimes in your XS programming, you'll want to return the value of various constants defined in C headers. The ExtUtils::Constant module helps create an AUTOLOAD subroutine that calls an XS function to retrieve constants. This XS routine is backed by a C function to do the actual work, while the XS routine takes care of manipulating the Perl stack and dealing with constants that are either undefined on the current machine or not known to the C headers. Listing 5.8 shows an extract of the front-end routine from the core POSIX module.

Listing 5.8   Undefined and unknown constants

```
type = int_macro_int(s, len, &iv);      ❶
/* Return 1 or 2 items. First is error message, or undef if no
   error. Second, if present, is found value */
switch (type) {                          If the status code is "not found",
case PERL_constant_NOTFOUND:  ◄──┘ returns an error
  sv = sv_2mortal(newSVpvf("%s is not a valid POSIX macro", s));   ❷
  EXTEND(SP, 1);      ❸
  PUSHs(&PL_sv_undef);
  PUSHs(sv);
  break;
case PERL_constant_NOTDEF:   ❹
  sv = sv_2mortal(newSVpvf(
    "Your vendor has not defined POSIX macro %s, used", s));
  EXTEND(SP, 1);
  PUSHs(&PL_sv_undef);
  PUSHs(sv);
  break;
case PERL_constant_ISIV:     ❺
  PUSHi(iv);
  break;                      If it isn't an IV, we weren't
default:                      expecting that result, and we need
  sv = sv_2mortal(newSVpvf(  ◄──┘ to format another error message
    "Unexpected return type %d processing POSIX macro %s, used",
        type, s));
  EXTEND(SP, 1);
  PUSHs(&PL_sv_undef);
  PUSHs(sv);
}
```

❶ We call the back-end int_macro_int C function to get the value of the macro. It returns a status code expressing the type of value returned, and it modifies the iv parameter to reflect the value of the macro.

❷ We use newSVpvf to format a new SV with the error message reflecting the original parameter.

❸ Now we return the error message and undef to Perl. (See "Returning a list," page 181, for more about the PUSHs macro.)

❹ Similarly, for cases where we know about the macro in question but it isn't defined on the current system, we return an error message and undef.

❺ If the return type is an integer value (IV)—the only type we're expecting from the macros in the POSIX module—then we push the IV onto the stack to return it to Perl.

See also: "sv_setpvf," page 122, and "sv_catpv, sv_catpvn, and sv_catpvf," page 127.

5.2.3 Accessing data

Now that you have seen how to create an SV, in this section we will look at the functions that help you get the value of the SV and test its properties.

SvOK

```
bool SvOK ( SV* sv );
```

This macro tests whether *sv* contains a valid SV.

Example   The encode_base64 function from the MIME::Base64 module takes a string to encode and an optional end-of-line character to add to each line. If this character is not present, MIME::Base64 will default to using "\n" as the newline character. Listing 5.9 shows how it sets up the optional parameter in XS.

Listing 5.9   An optional parameter

```
if (items > 1 && SvOK(ST(1))) {        ❶
    eol = SvPV(ST(1), eollen);    ◄────  Extracts its string value
} else {                                using SvPV and stores
    eol = "\n";        ❷                 that value in eol and
    eollen = 1;                          its length in eollen
}
```

---

❶ If we have more than one parameter to this XS function (items is automatically set up to be the number of parameters) and the second parameter looks like a decent SV, then we can use it.

❷ If we have only one parameter we use the default "\n", which is one character long.

SvTRUE

```
bool SvTRUE ( SV* sv );
```

SvTRUE, as its name implies, determines whether the SV contains a true value. Truth is determined by Perl's normal rules (does not evaluate to the null string "", 0, or "0").

Example   Tk is an event-driven environment, so it deals a lot with callbacks. After executing each callback, it runs the lines shown in listing 5.10 (Tk/Event/Event.xs).

Listing 5.10   Checking $@

```
err = ERRSV;
if (SvTRUE(err))
 {
  croak("%s",SvPV(err,na));
 }
```

ERRSV is the XS equivalent of $@; if it contains a true value, then we die with that value. na is the old-fashioned way of writing PL_na, an identifier specifying that we don't care about the length.

SvIOK and friends

```
bool SvIOK ( SV* sv );
bool SvNOK ( SV* sv );
bool SvPOK ( SV* sv );
```

These macros provide access to the OK flags described in chapter 4; you can use them to determine whether a given SV has a valid integer, number, or string value. perl also provides _on and _off forms of these macros to allow you to manually validate or invalidate the relevant values. For instance,

```
SvIVX(sv) = 123;
SvIOK_on(sv);
```

sets the raw IV slot of this SV to 123 (see section "SvIV and friends," page 112) and then tells perl that the IV slot is usable.

This isn't necessarily a wise thing to do, particularly if other values are already marked as OK and don't contain something like 123. If you want to say that one value is valid and turn off all other OK flags, use the _only form:

```
SvIVX(sv) = 123;
SvIOK_only(sv);
```

Now all other values stored in the SV will be invalidated.

Example   Experienced Perl programmers know that the magic built-in variable $! can be used as a string to get an error message, or in numeric context to get an error number. Scalar::Util provides a means of creating your own dual-valued scalars; listing 5.11 shows a cut-down version of its dualvar function.

Listing 5.11   Dual-valued scalars

```
void
dualvar(num,str)
    SV *        num
    SV *        str
PROTOTYPE: $$
CODE:
{
    STRLEN len;
    char *ptr = SvPV(str,len);        ◄── Extracts the string
    ST(0) = sv_newmortal();      ❶          buffer and length
    (void)SvUPGRADE(ST(0),SVt_PVNV);  ❷     from the "string"
    sv_setpvn(ST(0),ptr,len);    ◄──        value passed
    if(SvNOK(num) || SvPOK(num) || SvMAGICAL(num)) {   ❸
        SvNVX(ST(0)) = SvNV(num);    ❹
        SvNOK_on(ST(0));         ❺
```

Calls **sv_setpvn** ("sv_setpv and sv_setpvn," page 121) to set its string value

```
    }
    else {
        SvIVX(ST(0)) = SvIV(num);      ❻
        SvIOK_on(ST(0));
    }
    if(PL_tainting && (SvTAINTED(num) || SvTAINTED(str)))   ❼
        SvTAINTED_on(ST(0));
    XSRETURN(1);     ❽
}
```

❶ Now we create a new scalar on top of the Perl stack to hold the dual value.

❷ We call SvUPGRADE to ensure that this new scalar is a type of SV that can hold both strings and numbers: SVt_PVNV.

❸ If the parameter which is to be the numeric part of our dual-valued scalar has a floating-point or string value, or it's a magical value, we treat it as floating point.

❹ We extract the floating-point value with SvNV (see "SvIV and friends," page 112) and set the raw NV slot of the destination SV to be this value. Because we've upgraded, we know it's safe to use SvNVX, which doesn't affect the POK flag that was set by sv_setpvn.

❺ We also set the NOK flag, meaning that we have a dual-valued scalar with both string and floating-point slots OK.

❻ Similarly for non-floating-point values, we take the IV value and assign it to our destination SV.

❼ If we're in taint mode, and one of the two sources of our dual-valued scalar was tainted (see "Tainting functions," page 119), then we also mark the newly created SV as tainted.

❽ Finally, we tell Perl that our XS function is returning one value: the scalar at the top of the stack.

SvIV and friends

```
IV SvIV ( SV* sv );
NV SvNV ( SV* sv );
PV SvPV ( SV* sv , STRLEN len );
```

These functions extract values from an SV, coercing the SV into the relevant type if required. For instance, if the SV is currently marked with the POK (string OK) flag only, then SvIV will internally call sv_2iv to coerce the string into an integer, set the IOK flag, and return the IV slot of the SV.

Similarly, if the SV currently contains a valid double-precision floating-point number (NV) and we call SvPV, then sv_2pv will be called to stringify the value, and the

PV will be returned; as a side effect, `len` is set to the string's length. If you don't want the length, use either the dummy variable `PL_na` or the variant function `SvPV_nolen`.

TIP   If you know for sure that the value you want is OK, you can use the macros `SvIVX`, `SvPVX`, and so forth for direct access to the appropriate slot. These X macros can be used as lvalues, so you can assign to `SvPVX(sv)`. This is a common technique.

Because these are such fundamental macros, we'll present a number of examples. Listing 5.12 shows a simple yet breathtaking use of `SvPV` from `Apache::PerlRunXS`.

Listing 5.12   Change to server directory

```
#define ApachePerlRun_chdir_scwd() \
    chdir(SvPV(perl_get_sv("Apache::Server::CWD", TRUE),na))
```

In one stroke, this macro gets the `SV` referring to `$Apache::Server::CWD`, extracts the PV while discarding the length, and then changes to that directory.

Example   Listing 5.13 shows a modified version of `List::Util`'s `min` function[1] that returns the minimum of a list of values. The implementation is straightforward.

Listing 5.13   Finding the minimum of a list of values

```
void
min(...)
PROTOTYPE: @
CODE:
{
    int index;
    NV retval;
    SV *retsv;
    if (!items) {               If there are no
        XSRETURN_UNDEF;         items in the list,
    }                           we return undef
    retsv = ST(0);          ❶
    retval = SvNV(retsv);                              Iterates over the list;
    for(index = 1 ; index < items ; index++) {  ◄──   we've already
        SV *stacksv = ST(index);    Keeps track of the processed element 0,
        NV val = SvNV(stacksv);     current entry in the so we begin at 1
        if (val < retval) {     ❷  list and its value
            retsv = stacksv;
            retval = val;
        }
```

---

[1]   The original function implements `min` and `max` in the same code, using the magic variable `ix` to know which name it was invoked as. Our example is less hairy.

```
    }
    ST(0) = retsv;          ❸
    XSRETURN(1);
}
```

❶ `retsv` will be the SV that we return—the minimum entry in the list. We start with the first item in the list and swap smaller items into `retsv` as we find them. In order to do comparisons, however, we need to track the NV of this SV, so `retval` begins life as the value of the first item.

❷ If this entry's value is lower than our current candidate minimum, we make this one our minimum and keep track of the SV.

❸ Now that we've been through them all and have found the real minimum, we set the top element in the stack to be the SV we found and declare that we're returning one value.

Example The B module's `ppaddr` function returns strings of the form `PL_ppaddr [OP_something]`, where *something* is the name of a Perl internal operation. Getting the name is easy, but we want to return it in uppercase. Listing 5.14 shows how.

Listing 5.14 Uppercasing a string in place

```
sv_setpvn(sv, "PL_ppaddr[OP_", 13);    ❶
sv_catpv(sv, PL_op_name[o->op_type]);   ❷
for (i=13; i<SvCUR(sv); ++i)       ❸
    SvPVX(sv)[i] = toUPPER(SvPVX(sv)[i]);    ❹
sv_catpv(sv, "]");    ❺
```
---

❶ We write the constant 13 characters `PL_ppaddr[OP_` to the SV.

❷ We look up the name of this operation in our table of names, `PL_op_name`, and then use `sv_catpv` (see "sv_catpv, sv_catpvn, and sv_catpvf," page 127) to append the name to the end of the SV.

❸ Now we uppercase what we've just appended. We do so by walking over the string, starting at the thirteenth character, to the end of the string. (`sv_catpv` updates SvCUR with the new current length of the string.)

❹ We know we have a string, so it's safe to use SvPVX. Because it returns a string, we can use the array element syntax to get each character in turn. Hence, (`SvPVX(sv)`)`[i]` gets the *i*th character of the string. We pass this character to `toUPPER` (see "toLOWER and toUPPER," page 161) to uppercase it before assigning it back to where we found it.

❺ Finally, we add the closing bracket to the end of the SV.

SvCUR and SvLEN

```
STRLEN SvCUR ( SV* sv );
STRLEN SvLEN ( SV* sv );
```

These macros provide "raw" access to the CUR and LEN slots of an SV. (See section 4.2.3.) Because they're macros that simply access parts of the SV structure, you can assign to them (if you're sure the PV buffer has the appropriate number of bytes of memory available...). You can also use SvCUR_set(sv, len) to set the current length, but similarly you need to ensure the PV buffer is large enough.

The example in listing 5.15 shows a wealth of techniques for dealing with SV strings. Taken from Data::Dumper, it is the meat of the sv_x function; this function repeats a given C string a number of times, adding it to the end of an SV.

Listing 5.15   Concatenating repeatedly

```
SvGROW(sv, len*n + SvCUR(sv) + 1);     ❶
if (len == 1) {
    char *start = SvPVX(sv) + SvCUR(sv);     ❷
    SvCUR(sv) += n;          Tells Perl that the string
    start[n] = '\0';    ❸   will be n characters
    while (n > 0)       ❹   longer than it currently is
        start[--n] = str[0];
}
else
    while (n > 0) {     ❺
        sv_catpvn(sv, str, len);
        --n;
    }
```

❶ We need to ensure that the string is long enough to take what we're about to append. We use SvGROW to grow the SV to its current length (SvCUR(sv)) plus the size of the repeated string (length times number of repetitions) plus a final byte for the null character at the end.

❷ The "start" of where we're appending is actually the end of the current buffer. We take the address of the PV (the start of the buffer) and add the current length to it to get the end of the buffer.

❸ We put a null byte at the end. (Confirm for yourself that this is the end of the now-expanded PV.)

❹ Now, we can fill the remaining part backward to the start of our additions with the character we're repeating.

❺ If we're repeating more than one character, we call upon sv_catpv (see "sv_catpv, sv_catpvn, and sv_catpvf," page 127) to do the heavy work.

SvTYPE

```
SvTYPE (SV* sv);
```

SvTYPE looks at an SV's type field to determine if it's an ordinary SV (and if so, what sort of SV) or an array value (AV), hash (HV), or one of the more complex types. The values it can return for a given SV range in complexity as follows:

```
SVt_NULL,    /* 0 - Null SV */
SVt_IV,      /* 1 - IV only */
SVt_NV,      /* 2 - NV only */
SVt_RV,      /* 3 - RV only */
SVt_PV,      /* 4 - PV only*/
SVt_PVIV,    /* 5 - PV and IV*/
SVt_PVNV,    /* 6 - PV, IV and NV */
SVt_PVMG,    /* 7 - PV and magical structure */
SVt_PVBM,    /* 8 - PV and optimized Boyer-Moore search data */
SVt_PVLV,    /* 9 - PV and lvalue structure */
SVt_PVAV,    /* 10 - Array */
SVt_PVHV,    /* 11 - Hash */
SVt_PVCV,    /* 12 - Code value (subroutine) */
SVt_PVGV,    /* 13 - Glob */
SVt_PVFM,    /* 14 - Format */
SVt_PVIO     /* 15 - IO stream*/
```

Example   Data::Dumper is usually used to dump the value of a variable; however, if you also pass it an array reference of variable names, it can be used to dump out assignment statements to re-create variables. For instance:

```
% perl -MData::Dumper -e '$hashref = {a =>
123, b => 456}; print Data::Dumper->Dump([ $hashref ], [q($myref)])'
$myref = {
            'a' => 123,
            'b' => 456
          };
```

However, just as in Perl, if you decide to assign a hash reference to a glob (*myref in this example), Data::Dumper interprets this action as assigning to the hash with that name:

```
% perl -le '*myref = {a => 123}; print $myref{a}'
123
%  % perl -MData::Dumper -e '$hashref = {a => 123, b => 456};
     print Data::Dumper->Dump([ $hashref ], [q(*myref)])'
%myref = (
            'a' => 123,
            'b' => 456
          );
```

Hence, Data::Dumper must look at the type of the reference it's being asked to dump and determine the appropriate sigil ($, %, @, etc.) to assign to (see listing 5.16).

Listing 5.16 Qualifying a Perl variable

```
if (SvOK(name)) {                                    ❶
    if ((SvPVX(name))[0] == '*') {                   ❷
        if (SvROK(val)) {                            ❸
            switch (SvTYPE(SvRV(val))) {             ❹
                case SVt_PVAV:
                    (SvPVX(name))[0] = '@';        ◀── ┐ If it's an array reference,
                    break;                             ┘ we replace the * with a @
                case SVt_PVHV:
                    (SvPVX(name))[0] = '%';        ◀── ┐ If it's a hash reference,
                    break;                             ┘ we use %
                case SVt_PVCV:
                    (SvPVX(name))[0] = '*';          ❺
                    break;
                default:
                    (SvPVX(name))[0] = '$';        ◀── ┐ Otherwise, we'll use $ to
                    break;                             ┘ represent this reference
            }
        }                                     ┌ If it's not a reference, it's
    }                                         │ an ordinary scalar; so,
    else                                      │ we'll also use $
        (SvPVX(name))[0] = '$';        ◀──────┘
}
```

❶ First, we check to see whether we have a second parameter: a name.

❷ If this name begins with *, then we need to do something tricky and qualify the name by looking at the type of the value.

❸ If we're dealing with a reference, we need to see what type of reference it is.

❹ This line is not much different than the Perl ref operator.

❺ If it's a subroutine reference, we use *. (&mysub = sub { ... } doesn't work in Perl 5.[2])

sv_isa and sv_derived_from

```
int sv_isa ( SV* obj , const char* class );
int sv_derived_from ( SV* obj , const char* class );
```

Both these functions check whether an object belongs to a given class. Unlike the UNIVERSAL::isa method, sv_isa only checks whether the object is blessed into the named class. The method that implements UNIVERSAL::isa is sv_derived_from, which also checks the inheritance tree to determine whether the object is blessed into a superclass of the given class.

---

[2] sub AUTOLOAD :lvalue { *{$AUTOLOAD} } is considered harmful.

Some functions make sure they're called with objects of the appropriate class; IPC::Semaphore::stat::unpack, from the IPC::SysV package, is one of them (see listing 5.17).

Listing 5.17   Should you be here?

```
void
unpack(obj,ds)
    SV * obj
    SV * ds
PPCODE:
{
#ifdef HAS_SEM
    STRLEN len;
    AV *list = (AV*)SvRV(obj);
    struct semid_ds *data = (struct semid_ds *)SvPV(ds,len);
    if(!sv_isa(obj, "IPC::Semaphore::stat"))      ❶
        croak("method %s not called a %s object",    ❷
              "unpack","IPC::Semaphore::stat");
    ...
```

❶ If the object the function has been called with isn't an IPC::Semaphore::Stat object (subclassed objects will not do!) …

❷ … then the function needs to die, complaining that it's been called with the wrong sort of object.

sv_len

```
STRLEN sv_len ( SV* sv );
```

sv_len is a "safe" way to get the length of a Perl scalar; it's equivalent to the length keyword in Perl. Normally, in XS programming, you request a Perl string with SvPV, which also returns the length.

To get the length of a string alone, the SvCUR macro is used to extract the CUR slot in the SvPV structure. (See section 4.2.3). However, this data is not always available—for magical variables, for instance, or values that are not currently POK. sv_len handles these cases correctly, and hence should be used unless you know what the SV you're dealing with will be.

Example   The example in listing 5.18 is taken from jpl/JNI/JNI.xs in the Perl distribution. JPL is the Java Perl Lingo, an interface between Java and Perl. At this point in the program, we've been asked to create a Java byte array containing the contents of a Perl scalar.

Listing 5.18 Storing a Perl scalar in a Java byte array

```
jsize len = sv_len(sv) / sizeof(jbyte);      ❶

jbyteArray ja = (*env)->NewByteArray(env, len);      ❷
(*env)->SetByteArrayRegion(env, ja, 0, len,
                           (jbyte*)SvPV(sv,n_a));      ❸
```

❶ We work out how big the array needs to be. The size is the length of the scalar in bytes, divided by the size of a jbyte (which we hope is 1—but the world is funny sometimes).

❷ We call upon our Java environment to create a byte array of that length.

❸ We use the JNI SetByteArrayRegion interface to store the contents of the scalar into the byte array.

See also: "SvCUR and SvLEN," page 115, and "sv_len_utf8," page 157.

5.2.4   Manipulating data

You've seen the functions that let you create scalars and access their contents; the functions in this section allow you to change the values or properties of SVs.

Tainting functions

```
void SvTAINT ( SV* sv );
void SvTAINTED_on ( SV* sv );
bool SvTAINTED ( SV* sv );
TAINT(void);
```

These functions control tainting. When your XS routines read in data from external sources, you should be sure to call SvTAINT on the SV containing the foreign data to protect the user against any unsafe operations they may perform on it.

SvTAINTED tells you whether a given SV is tainted. SvTAINTED_on is like SvTAINT, but you should probably use the latter because SvTAINT actually checks whether Perl is running in -T mode.

Finally, TAINT tells Perl that you've seen tainted data somewhere—it speeds up the runtime by allowing Perl to skip SvTAINTED checks unless TAINT is set. The opposite of TAINT is TAINT_NOT; it tells Perl that things are OK so far.

Example   Listing 5.19 shows our next example. When File::Glob performs a glob, the data that comes back is found by looking at the filesystem, which is full of data external to Perl and hence can't be trusted in tainted mode. So, after we pick up data from the glob system call and put it into SVs, we must make sure we taint the SVs before returning them to Perl.

Listing 5.19   Globbing paths

```
retval = bsd_glob(pattern, flags, errfunc, &pglob);      ❶
GLOB_ERROR = retval;
                                               Ensures that the stack has
/* return any matches found */                 enough space on it to
EXTEND(sp, pglob.gl_pathc);    ◁───┘           store gl_pathc elements
for (i = 0; i < pglob.gl_pathc; i++) {
    tmp = sv_2mortal(newSVpvn(pglob.gl_pathv[i],     ◁───┐
                strlen(pglob.gl_pathv[i])));           │ Stores each element
    TAINT;       ❷                                       │ in the array in a
    SvTAINT(tmp);       ❸                                │ temporary SV
    PUSHs(tmp);       ❹
}
```

❶ We perform the glob (bsd_glob is an alias for the system's glob function, because the function we're interfacing is also called glob) and store the results in pglob. This is a glob_t structure, and the interesting elements are gl_pathc (a count of the number of files found by the glob) and gl_pathv (an array of filenames).

❷ We call TAINT to tell Perl we've come across some tainted data.

❸ Now we call SvTAINT on the SV we've just created, to taint the data.

❹ Properly protected, we can put the SV onto the stack.

> **NOTE**   Given SvTAINTED_on and the general way that Perl handles flags, you might wonder whether there's an SvTAINTED_off. There is, but the function is extremely dangerous, not to mention naughty. You should undo tainting with regular expression backreferences, instead of blindly attacking it at the XS level.

sv_setiv, sv_setnv, and sv_setuv

```
void sv_setiv ( SV* sv , IV num );
void sv_setnv ( SV* sv , NV num );
void sv_setuv ( SV* sv , UV num );
```

These functions set an SV to the given numeric value, invalidating any other kinds of data stored in the SV.

Example   The IO::Poll module interfaces to the Unix poll call, which takes an array of filehandles and returns information about "events" that have occurred on those filehandles. Listing 5.20 gives the essence of _poll, the back-end XS interface to this module, found in IO.xs.

Listing 5.20   Polling several filehandles

```
for(i=1, j=0  ; j < nfd ; j++) {
    fds[j].fd = SvIV(ST(i));
    i++;
    fds[j].events = SvIV(ST(i));           ❶
    i++;
    fds[j].revents = 0;
}
if((ret = poll(fds,nfd,timeout)) >= 0) {   ❷
    for(i=1, j=0 ; j < nfd ; j++) {
        sv_setiv(ST(i), fds[j].fd); i++;       ❸
        sv_setiv(ST(i), fds[j].revents); i++;
    }
}
```

❶ We need to set up the array of `pollfd` structures[3] by taking pairs of file descriptors and bitmasks (to specify the events we're interested in) from the Perl stack.

❷ We perform the call to `poll`, which will repopulate these arrays with descriptions of the events that have occurred.

❸ Accordingly, we want to repopulate the Perl list by using `sv_setiv` to write the file descriptor and the event mask back to each SV in turn.

See also: "sv_setpv and av_setpvn," below.

sv_setpv and sv_setpvn

```
void sv_setpv ( SV* sv , const char* ptr );
void sv_setpvn ( SV* sv , const char* ptr , STRLEN len );
```

These functions set the string value of an SV. If *len* is 0, or `sv_setpv` is used rather than `sv_setpvn`, Perl will use `strlen` to compute the length. Don't forget to use SvUTF8_on (see "SvUTF8," page 155) if your string is UTF8-encoded.

Listing 5.21 shows the guts of the `inet_aton` function provided in the `Socket` core module.

Listing 5.21   inet_aton: writing an IP address to an SV

```
struct in_addr ip_address;
struct hostent * phe;

int ok =
    (host != NULL) &&
    (*host != '\0') &&
    inet_aton(host, &ip_address);       ❶
```

---

[3] See the manual page for the Unix system call `poll(2)`.

```
    if (!ok && (phe = gethostbyname(host))) {   ②
        Copy( phe->h_addr, &ip_address, phe->h_length, char );
        ok = 1;
    }
    ST(0) = sv_newmortal();   ③
    if (ok)
        sv_setpvn( ST(0), (char *)&ip_address, sizeof ip_address );   ④
```

❶ We attempt to use `inet_aton` to convert the name into an IP address; ok will be true if that step succeeds.

❷ If it doesn't succeed, we try again, this time using `gethostbyname` to do a full lookup of the host. If that works, we copy the IP address portion of the hostent structure into our buffer.

❸ Now we create a new SV (see "sv_newmortal and sv_mortalcopy," page 108) to hold the result. If we still haven't got a valid IP address, the SV will remain undefined.

❹ If we have obtained an IP address, we set our new SV's string buffer to contain the machine-readable IP address we cast to a string. Notice that `sv_setpvn` takes care of upgrading the new SV to be able to contain strings.

sv_setpvf

```
void sv_setpvf ( SV* sv , const char* pat , ... );
```

Similar to `newSVpvf` and `sv_catpvf`,[4] this function sets an SV's string value according to the pattern of a format string.

Example Listing 5.22 is part of the `size_string` function in `Apache::Util`, which converts the size of a file in bytes into a human-readable string.

Listing 5.22   Reporting a file's size

```
SV *sv = newSVpv("    -", 5);      ⟵  Makes a new SV with
if (size == (size_t)-1) {              newSVpv ("Creating SVs
/**/                                   with values," page 106)
}
else if (!size) {
    sv_setpv(sv, "   0k");         ⟵  For the easy cases, we use
}                                      sv_setpv to write a
else if (size < 1024) {                constant string into the SV
    sv_setpv(sv, "   1k");
}
```

---

[4] If you dig deep enough into sv.c, you'll find that `sv_setpvf` is implemented in terms of `sv_setpvn` and `sv_catpvf`.

```
else if (size < 1048576) {
    sv_setpvf(sv, "%4dk", (size + 512) / 1024);
}
else if (size < 103809024) {
    sv_setpvf(sv, "%4.1fM", size / 1048576.0);
}
else {
    sv_setpvf(sv, "%4dM", (size + 524288) / 1048576);
}
```

When we need formatted information, we use `sv_setpvf` just like `sprintf`

See also: "newSVpvf," page 108, and "sv_catpv, sv_catpvn, and sv_catpvf," page 127.

sv_2mortal

```
SV* sv_2mortal ( SV* sv );
```

This function *mortalizes* an SV. See "Returning a hash reference," page 179, for a discussion of when you need to use it.

See also: "sv_newmortal and sv_mortalcopy," page 108.

sv_inc and sv_dec

```
void sv_inc ( SV* sv );
void sv_dec ( SV* sv );
```

These functions provide *magic* increments and decrements on a scalar; that's to say, they perform just like `$var++` and `$var--` in Perl. String values will be autoincremented as described in `perlop.pod`.

However, if the variable has been used only in string contexts since it was set, and it has a value that is not the empty string and matches the pattern `/^[a-zA-Z]*[0-9]*\z/`, the increment is done as a string, preserving each character within its range, with carry:

```
print ++($foo = '99');    # prints '100'
print ++($foo = 'a0');    # prints 'a1'
print ++($foo = 'Az');    # prints 'Ba'
print ++($foo = 'zz');    # prints 'aaa'
```

SvSetSV

```
void SvSetSV ( SV* dsv , SV* ssv );
```

`SvSetSV` is a conditional version of `sv_setsv`. It compares the source and destination to see if they're pointing at the same SV; if they're not, then it calls `sv_setsv` to perform the assignment.

See also: "sv_setsv," page 124.

sv_setsv

```
void sv_setsv ( SV* dsv , SV* ssv );
```

sv_setsv is the ordinary way to assign one SV to another. Obviously, you can't just say dsv = ssv; because doing so will copy the pointers and not the underlying data. sv_setsv copies the data and all the flags, duplicating an SV completely.

Example   The code fragment in listing 5.23, from the DBI module, shows the use of sv_setsv in conjunction with AvARRAY to duplicate each SV in an array in turn.

> **Listing 5.23   Copying an array**

```
for(i=0; i < num_fields; ++i) {      /* copy over the row    */  ❶
    sv_setsv(AvARRAY(dst_av)[i], AvARRAY(src_av)[i]);      ❷
}
ST(0) = sv_2mortal(newRV((SV*)dst_av));      ❸
```

❶ We'll loop over the arrays in the two AVs (having checked, of course, that they're the same size). We happen to have the number of elements in num_fields.

❷ AvARRAY turns an AV into a C array of SVs; we can hence get each element of each AV and use sv_setsv to copy the value from the source array to the destination.

❸ We return a reference to this destination array by calling newRV and putting the result at the top of the stack. We mortalize the result to make sure the reference doesn't hang around longer than it should.

5.2.5   String functions

Much of the work you'll perform on SVs will probably involve some form of string manipulation. Accordingly, perl provides several useful functions for dealing with strings.

sv_chop

```
void sv_chop ( SV* sv , char* ptr );
```

sv_chop uses the offset hack (section 4.2.7) to efficiently remove a number of characters from the beginning of a string. ptr must be a pointer to somewhere inside SvPVX(sv), or you can expect unpleasant results.

Example   The very brief example in listing 5.24, from op.c in the Perl sources, shows you how to remove a substring from the beginning of an SV.

> **Listing 5.24   s/main:://**

```
if (SvCUR(n)>6 && strnEQ(SvPVX(n),"main::",6))      ❶
    sv_chop(n, SvPVX(n)+6);      ❷
```

❶ If the SV n is more than six characters long, and the first six characters are equal to main:: ...

❷ ... then we chop the string so that it starts after the sixth character, deleting the main::.

See also: section 4.2.7.

form

```
char * form(const char * format, ...);
```

Quite often in C, you'll want to use sprintf to make a temporary value to pass to another function. It's a lot of work—not to mention inefficient—to allocate a temporary buffer, fill it using sprintf, call your function, and then free it again. Perl provides a neater way to do this: form acts like sprintf but hands you a shared string pointer that will be valid until the next call to form. It's perfect for one-off string concatenation and formatting. And, because it's based on the Perl sv_catpvf functions, you get the use of the %_ hack for SVs.

Example When the embedded Perl handler for Apache (mod_perl) starts up, it wants to add its own version number. That is, instead of just seeing:

```
Server: Apache/1.3.22 (Darwin)
```

you see

```
Server: Apache/1.3.22 (Darwin) mod_perl/1.26
```

And, optionally, if the $Apache::Server::AddPerlVersion variable is set, you see the version of Perl as well:

```
Server: Apache/1.3.22 (Darwin) mod_perl/1.26 Perl/v5.6.0
```

Listing 5.25 shows where mod_perl does this.

Listing 5.25   Starting mod_perl

```
void perl_module_init(server_rec *s, pool *p)
{
    ap_add_version_component(MOD_PERL_STRING_VERSION);     ❶
    if(PERL_RUNNING()) {
#ifdef PERL_IS_5_6
    char *version = form("Perl/v%vd", PL_patchlevel);      ❷
#else
    char *version = form("Perl/%_", perl_get_sv("]", TRUE));    ❸
#endif
    if(perl_get_sv("Apache::Server::AddPerlVersion", FALSE)) {    ❹
        ap_add_version_component(version);
    }
    }
    perl_startup(s, p);
}
```

❶ We call `ap_add_version_component`, which is an Apache API function that adds strings to the `Version` header. We pass it the constant `mod_perl` version, as `#define`'d on the command line while building the `mod_perl` library.

❷ If Perl is version 5.6 or above, we do the equivalent of

```
$version = sprintf("Perl/v%vd", $^V);
```

and get the Perl version number as a new-fangled *v-string*.

❸ If the Perl version is before 5.6, we look at the `$]` SV, using `form` to catenate its string value to the end of `Perl/`.

❹ Now, if we can retrieve `$Apache::Server::AddPerlVersion` from the symbol table without specially creating it, we add the string we `form`ed to the Apache version number. Note the subtlety here—we're only checking whether `$Apache::Server::AddPerlVersion` exists in the symbol table, not whether it's true. If we wanted to do that, we'd have to say something like

```
if(SvTRUE(perl_get_sv("Apache::Server::AddPerlVersion", TRUE))) {
```

In other words, it's a hack, but it works in non-pathological cases.

Also note that we don't have to do anything particular with `version` once we're done. In fact, freeing it would be harmful, because it's a shared string that may be used by Perl later.

See also: "sv_catpv, sv_catpvn, and sv_catpvf," page 127.

savepv and savepvn

```
char* savepv ( const char* string );
char* savepvn ( const char* string , I32 len );
```

These functions are a quick way to create a new copy of a string. They're the Perl equivalents of `strcpy` and `strncpy`; but despite the reference to PVs, they act purely on C strings, not on SVs. Use savepvn if you're worried about strings with embedded nulls.

The `savepv` function is a great way to return a string from a function, leaving the caller responsible for freeing the string afterward.[5] For instance, `find_script` in the Perl core returns a string value like this:

```
return (scriptname ? savepv(scriptname) : Nullch);
```

This allows you to safely return strings that are declared as automatic variables. (`Nullch` is a NULL char*.)

---

[5] If you wanted to be really clever, you could try using SAVEFREEPV(string) to have Perl free the string at the end of the current scope, but doing so isn't recommended. Either way, your XS interface should document who is responsible for cleaning up memory.

SvGROW

```
char * SvGROW ( SV* sv , STRLEN len );
```

This macro ensures that the SV's string buffer (PV) is at least len characters long and returns a pointer to the PV's character buffer. If more memory is required, the SvGROW macro calls the function sv_grow to resize the buffer, using Renew (see "Renew," page 153).

sv_grow does not "pre-emptively" extend the string to longer than the requested size, so if you think you may be growing the string again in the future, you should ask for more memory than you need right now.

For example, see "SvCUR and SvLEN," page 115.

sv_catpv, sv_catpvn, and sv_catpvf

```
void sv_catpv ( SV* sv , const char* pv );
void sv_catpvn ( SV* sv , const char* pv , STRLEN len );
void sv_catpvf ( SV* sv , const char* pat , ... );
```

These functions provide mechanisms for catenating a string onto the end of an existing SV. They take care of ensuring that the SV in question is forced into having a string value, and then add the char* data to the end of the current SV's string buffer.

The basic function is sv_catpv, which determines the length of the incoming string automatically; if you want to force perl to only add a given number of characters, use sv_catpvn. The most complex function is sv_catpvf, which uses a format string just like sv_newSVpvf (see "newSVpvf," page 108).

Example A lot of Perl's usefulness as a tool for "one-liners" comes from the -l, -a, -n, -p, and other command-line switches. The fragment of code in listing 5.26, taken from toke.c in the Perl core, shows how some of these flags are implemented.

Listing 5.26 What really happens when you say perl -lane

```
if (PL_minus_n || PL_minus_p) {                    ❶
    sv_catpv(PL_linestr, "LINE: while (<>) {");     ❷
    if (PL_minus_l)
        sv_catpv(PL_linestr,"chomp;");     ◁─┐ If –1 has been given, we add a
    if (PL_minus_a) {                        └─ chomp to deal with the input
        if (PL_minus_F) {
            if (strchr("/'\"", *PL_splitstr)    ❸
                && strchr(PL_splitstr + 1, *PL_splitstr))
                Perl_sv_catpvf(aTHX_ PL_linestr,
                    "our @F=split(%s);", PL_splitstr);     ❹
...
```

❶ If -p or -n has been specified on the command line, the PL_minusn and PL_minusp variables will be set accordingly.

❷ `PL_linestr` is an `SV` containing the current piece of Perl code being compiled. This snippet occurs just after Perl has examined the "shebang" (`#!`) line and before any other Perl code has been parsed. Hence, when `-p` or `-n` is present, we add the `while` loop into the current program using `sv_catpv`.

❸ If both `-a` and `-F` (alternate delimiter for autosplit) are present, this line determines whether the delimiter has already been sufficiently quoted. It looks to see if the first character of `PL_splitstr` is one of `/`, `'`, or `"` and if that character occurs again in the string.

❹ If it does, we add to the `@F` array the code that does the autosplit. It uses the already-quoted string, simply passing it to `split`.

See also: "sv_setpvf," page 122, and "newSVpvf," page 108.

sv_catsv

```
void sv_catsv ( SV* dest_sv , SV* source_sv );
```

`sv_catsv` simply catenates the string value of `source_sv` onto the end of `dest_sv`.

Example   As of Perl 5.6.1, `Data::Dumper` has elementary object freezing and thawing capability. Let's look at what happens when `Data::Dumper` is writing the output code that, when `eval`ed, will restore an object. In listing 5.27 we've currently emitted `bless` and a description of the reference to be blessed, and we're just about to emit the classname and the method call to the *toaster* method responsible for re-creating the object.

Listing 5.27   Reviving frozen objects with Data::Dumper

```
sv_catpvn(retval, ", '", 3);                              ❶
sv_catpvn(retval, realpack, strlen(realpack));
sv_catpvn(retval, "' )", 3);
if (toaster && SvPOK(toaster) && SvCUR(toaster)) {        ❷
    sv_catpvn(retval, "->", 2);            ❸
    sv_catsv(retval, toaster);
    sv_catpvn(retval, "()", 2);
}
```

❶ Given that we've already output `bless ( { ... }`, the next stage is to add to the return value `, 'classname' )`, which is precisely what these three statements do.

❷ If the `toaster` variable is set and looks like a decent string ...

❸ ... we add the three components `->`, the name of the toaster function, and `()`, to form a method call. We'll eventually end up with something like this in `retval`:

```
bless ( { some => "data" }, 'Whatever::Class' )->restore()
```

See also: "sv_catpv, sv_catpvn, and sv_catpvf," page 127.

5.2.6   References

Finally, you can also take a reference to a Perl value with the newRV functions, and dereference the references again.

newRV and newRV_noinc

```
SV* newRV(SV* referent);
SV* newRV_noinc(SV* referent);
```

newRV is the C side of the Perl \ (reference) operator. It returns an SvRV structure as described in section 4.2.2 and increases the reference count of the referent. Although we say the referent is an SV*, this function applies to any type of SV, including AVs and HVs.

The variant function newRV_noinc takes a reference and returns an SvRV, but it does not increase the reference count of its referent. Because this can cause problems if the referent goes out of scope while you still have a reference to it, you should use this function with caution.

Example   An *anonymous hash reference* ({ } in Perl) is a reference to a hash that has nothing else referring to it—that is, its reference count is 1. To create an anonymous hash, you create a hash and take a reference to it. Unfortunately, when a hash is created, its reference count is already 1. If you take a reference to it with newRV, its reference count will increase. The correct solution is seen in Apache mod_perl, in modules/perl/perl_config.c, as shown in listing 5.28.

Listing 5.28   return bless {}, $class in C

```
if(!SvTRUE(*sv)) {             ❶
    *sv = newRV_noinc((SV*)newHV());     ❷
    return sv_bless(*sv, pclass);     ❸
}
```

---

❶ We're about to return a value from a constructor; if we don't have a sensible (that is, true) return value already, we need to make one.

❷ The comment in the C source at this point is /* return bless {}, $class */, which tells you what we're trying to do. We create a hash with newHV (see "newHV," page 145) and then take a reference to it without increasing its reference count. Notice that because newRV_noinc expects an SV*, we need to use a cast. Doing so isn't a problem, because the sv_type field of the SV structure tells newRV what sort of reference it's taking.

❸ Now that we have our anonymous hash reference, we use sv_bless to bless it into the class specified in the string pclass.

SvRV

```
SV* SvRV(SV* rv);
```

Given a reference rv, SvRV dereferences the SV. Note that, as with newRV, this SV can be an SV, AV, HV, or even another RV. You can use the SvTYPE function to work out what sort of value to expect back after dereferencing.

Example Listing 5.29 shows some debugging code in the middle of the DBI module; DBI functions, like all XS functions, return values through the stack. This debugging code prints out a copy of the stack in a readable format, dealing with array and hash references as well as ordinary SVs. This code can be found in DBI.xs.

Listing 5.29   Dumping the return values

```
for(i=0; i < outitems; ++i) {        | Loops over the stack storing
    SV *s = ST(i);                   | each value returned in s
    if ( SvROK(s) && SvTYPE(SvRV(s))==SVt_PVAV) {      ❶
        AV *av = (AV*)SvRV(s);   ←──┐ Dereferences the array using
        int avi;                     │ SvRV, and casts it into an AV
        PerlIO_printf(logfp, " [");
        for(avi=0; avi <= AvFILL(av); ++avi)                    ❷
            PerlIO_printf(logfp, " %s",
                            neatsvpv(AvARRAY(av)[avi],0));
        PerlIO_printf(logfp, " ]");
    }
    else {
        PerlIO_printf(logfp, " %s",  neatsvpv(s,0));
        if ( SvROK(s) && SvTYPE(SvRV(s))==SVt_PVHV &&
             !SvOBJECT(SvRV(s)) )     ❸
            PerlIO_printf(logfp, "%ldkeys", HvKEYS(SvRV(s)));    ❹
    }
}
```

❶ If it's a reference, and the type of the referred value is an array, then we'll display all the elements in the array.

❷ Now we call neatsvpv (a DBI utility function) on each value of the array, giving us a cleaned-up version of that SV's string value. We print this out with printf.

❸ If, on the other hand, this is a reference to a hash, and also if it's not an object ...

❹ ... then we dereference the hash and print out its number of keys.

SvROK

```
bool SvROK ( SV* sv );
void SvROK_on ( SV* sv );
void SvROK_off ( SV* sv );
```

SvROK is the ordinary way to find out whether an SV is a reference. It's similar to the Perl-side ref function, except it doesn't give you any information about whether the scalar is blessed (see "sv_isobject," below) or what type of reference it is (see "SvTYPE," page 116).

You hardly need to use the low-level SvRV_on and SvRV_off functions; they turn on and off the underlying flag that Perl uses to detect whether something's a reference. If you inadvertently turn this flag on when it shouldn't be, bad things can happen.

sv_isobject

```
bool sv_isobject ( SV* sv );
```

This function tests whether the given SV is an object (a blessed reference).

Example   The addcolors method in the Imager module adds palette colors to a paletted image. It takes a variable number of arguments, but after the first argument (conceptually, $self) all the others need to be color objects in the Imager::Color class. Listing 5.30 shows how Imager enforces this requirement.

Listing 5.30   Adding colors

```
for (i=0; i < items-1; ++i) {         ❶
  if (sv_isobject(ST(i+1))            ❷
      && sv_derived_from(ST(i+1), "Imager::Color")) {    ❸
    IV tmp = SvIV((SV *)SvRV(ST(i+1)));        ❹
    colors[i] = *INT2PTR(i_color *, tmp);      ❺
  }
  else {
    myfree(colors);
    croak("i_plin: pixels must be Imager::Color objects");
  }
}
```

❶ We loop over the parameters passed to the subroutine.

❷ If this is an object (notice that we say i+1 because the first parameter will always be $self) ...

❸ ... and the object *is-a* Imager::Color ...

❹ ... then we treat the object as a reference to a scalar, and find the integer component of the referent.

❺ The integer is actually a memory address. We convert it back into a pointer with INT2PTR and then cast it to the appropriate type, i_color *. This is the usual way of caching C pointers in Perl objects (see "Casting pointers to integers (and back)," page 158).

sv_bless

```
SV* sv_bless ( SV* rv , HV* stash );
```

This function is the C-level equivalent of Perl's `bless` keyword. It takes a reference and a stash and blesses the reference. It modifies the original reference and returns it as a convenience.

The stash is most commonly retrieved with `gv_stashpv`, which turns a string into a pointer to an HV.

Example Listing 5.31 shows a simple object constructor, taken from `XML::Parser`.

Listing 5.31 A simple constructor

```
HV * hash = newHV();          ❶
SV * obj = newRV_noinc((SV *) hash);     ❷

sv_bless(obj, gv_stashpv("XML::Parser::ContentModel", 1));     ❸
```

❶ We create a new anonymous hash.

❷ We take a reference to the hash, but we don't increase its reference count, because we want it to be anonymous—that is, we want the object to be the only thing that refers to it.

❸ Now we fetch the stash for `XML::Parser::ContentModel`—the second argument 1 means to create the stash if it's not currently found—and then bless our anonymous hash into that stash.

5.3   AV FUNCTIONS

As you know, `AV`s are Perl arrays; this section describes the functions you can perform on those arrays.

5.3.1   Creation and destruction

As with `SV`s, there are two ways to get a pointer to a Perl array; however, unlike `SV`s, the interface to `AV`s is much simpler. In this section, we describe how to create or get hold of `AV`s, and also how to clear and undefined them once you're finished with them.

get_av

```
AV* get_av(char* name, bool create);
```

This function returns the AV variable from the Perl-side array name: for instance, `get_av("main::lines", FALSE)` will return a pointer to the AV that represents `@main::lines` in Perl space. If the boolean `create` is true, a new AV will be created if the Perl-side array hasn't been created yet; if it is false, the function will return a null pointer if the Perl-side array hasn't been created.

In the core DynaLoader module, the XS function dl_unload_all_files calls a Perl subroutine DynaLoader::dl_unload_file on all the elements of the @DynaLoader::dl_librefs array. Listing 5.32 (from $CORE/ext/Dyna-Loader/dlutils.c:39) shows how it does this.

Listing 5.32 Popping a Perl array from C

```
if ((sub = get_cv("DynaLoader::dl_unload_file", FALSE))
        != NULL) {          ❶
    dl_librefs = get_av("DynaLoader::dl_librefs", FALSE);    ❷
    while ((dl_libref = av_pop(dl_librefs)) != &PL_sv_undef) {    ❸
        dSP;
        ENTER;
        SAVETMPS;
        PUSHMARK(SP);
        XPUSHs(sv_2mortal(dl_libref));
        PUTBACK;
        call_sv((SV*)sub, G_DISCARD | G_NODEBUG);
        FREETMPS;
        LEAVE;
    }
}
```

❶ We call get_cv (see "get_cv," page 159) to attempt to fetch the subroutine.

❷ If that subroutine exists, we call get_av to retrieve the AV for the Perl-side array @DynaLoader::dl_librefs.

❸ This block is equivalent to this piece of Perl:

```
while (defined($dl_libref = pop @dl_librefs)) {
    DynaLoader::dl_unload_file($dl_libref)
}
```

We call av_pop (see "av_pop and av_shift," page 139) in a while loop to pop SVs off the array and store them in dl_libref. The following lines then set up a call-back to call the subroutine (see section 6.7.1).

See also: "get_hv," page 145, "get_sv," page 103, and "get_cv," page 159.

newAV

```
AV* newAV(void);
```

This function creates a brand-new array in C space, completely unconnected to the Perl symbol table and thus inaccessible from Perl. You'll generally use this function if you don't need any Perl code to see your array. (See "get_av," page 132, if you want Perl to see it.)

Example   Perl has several special named blocks of code: BEGIN, END, DESTROY, and so on. The perlmod documentation tells you that an END subroutine is executed as late as possible—that is, after `perl` has finished running the program and just before the interpreter is being exited, even if it is exiting as a result of a `die` function. You may have multiple END blocks within a file; they will execute in reverse order of definition (last in, first out [LIFO]).

If you can have multiple blocks, what better to store them in than an array? In fact, this is exactly what Perl does with op.c, line 4769. In listing 5.33 we're in the middle of a function called `newATTRSUB`, which is called to set up one of the special blocks.

Listing 5.33   Storing END blocks

```
else if (strEQ(s, "END") && !PL_error_count) {       ①
    if (!PL_endav)
        PL_endav = newAV();       ②
    DEBUG_x( dump_sub(gv) );
    av_unshift(PL_endav, 1);       ③
    av_store(PL_endav, 0, (SV*)cv);
    GvCV(gv) = 0;                          /* cv has been hijacked */
}
```

① `s` contains the name of the block. If this name is END and we haven't had any errors compiling it, we have a valid END block, which we'll store in the array `PL_endav`.

② First, though, we check to see if that array exists yet. If the `PL_endav` pointer is NULL, it hasn't been initialized; so, we create a new array using the `newAV` function.

③ Because END blocks are processed in LIFO order, we put each successive END block at the beginning of the array. We call `av_unshift` (see "av_push and av_unshift," page 140) to move all the elements up, and then `av_store` (see "av_store," page 138) to store the code for this block (the CV) at the first element of the array.

See also: "newSV and NEWSV," page 104, and "newHV," page 145.

av_make

```
AV* av_make(I32 length, SV** svp);
```

`av_make` is a little-used function that turns a C array of SVs into a new AV. The parameters are the number of elements in the array and a pointer to the C array.

Example   As listing 5.34 shows, `mod_perl` makes an ingenious use of this function to copy an array.

Listing 5.34   Copying an array

```
#define av_copy_array(av) av_make(av_len(av)+1, AvARRAY(av))
```

`AvARRAY(av)` points to the first element of the C array held in `av`; `av_len` (see "av_len," page 143) returns the highest element in the array, so the total number of elements is one more than that. Passing these two values to av_make produces a new array with the same elements.

av_clear

```
av_clear(AV* av);
```

av_clear simply removes all the elements from an array, decreasing the reference count of all the SVs in it.

Example One of the things the Tk module has to do is marshal data between Tcl and Perl. For instance, if you want to assign from Tcl to a Perl value, you must first get the Perl value into an appropriate state. If you're doing a scalar assignment, you need to make sure your SV is a scalar. Listing 5.35 shows how Tk does it.

Listing 5.35 Emptying an array

```
static SV *
ForceScalarLvalue(SV *sv)
{
 if (SvTYPE(sv) == SVt_PVAV)     ❶
  {
   AV *av = (AV *) sv;
   SV *nsv = newSVpv("",0);      ⟵──  Creates a new empty SV
   av_clear(av);   ❷                  to receive the assignment
   av_store(av,0,nsv);  ⟵
   return nsv;                   Stores the recipient SV
  }                              into the first element of
 else                           the newly emptied array
  {
   return sv;
  }
 ...
```

❶ The SV that we're handed may be a real scalar, or it may be an array. We use SvTYPE (see "SvTYPE," page 116) to determine its type. If it's just a scalar, we can simply return it. If it's an array, though, we have to deal with it.

❷ We get rid of everything in the array: we're effectively doing @PerlArray = $TclValue, which obviously will have to get rid of what was in the array before.

See also: "hv_clear," page 146.

av_undef

```
av_undef(AV* av);
```

As its name suggests, av_undef(array) is not dissimilar to undef @array. It is used to completely destroy an array prior to freeing the memory the array uses. It is obviously not used often in XS; the usual idiom is to let the reference count fall to zero and have Perl automatically garbage-collect unwanted values.

Example Here is one example of destroying an array: the `Storable` module must clean up any memory it uses before it dies in the event of an error. Let's say we're using `Storable` to retrieve an array from a file, and something goes wrong. As part of dying, `Storable` calls `clean_context`, which detects that we're in the middle of a retrieve and then calls `clean_retrieve_context`. That's where the code in listing 5.36 appears.

Listing 5.36 Removing and freeing an old array

```
if (cxt->aseen) {                      ❶
    AV *aseen = cxt->aseen;       ❷
    cxt->aseen = 0;
    av_undef(aseen);    ◄──
    sv_free((SV *) aseen);   ❸
}
```

Calls `av_undef` to shut down the Perl array structure

❶ `Storable` uses a structure `stcxt_t` in which to store its state. If it's dealing with an array, it will attach the array it's constructing to the `aseen` entry in the structure. So, if this pointer's valid, there's a Perl `AV` on the end of it—and that's what we want to destroy.

❷ We take a copy of that `AV` pointer and set the value of the pointer to 0, disconnecting the Perl `AV` from the `Storable` context structure.

❸ Once this is done, we can free the structure, gracefully destroying the array we were in the process of building.

5.3.2 Manipulating elements

API functions are available to do everything you can do to an array Perl-side; here are the functions for manipulating elements of an array.

av_fetch

```
SV** av_fetch(AV* array, I32 index, bool lvalue);
```

This function retrieves an `SV` from an array. It is the C-side equivalent of

```
$array[$index]
```

The `lvalue` parameter should be set if you're about to store something in the specified index: if the array is not big enough, or nothing has been stored in the array index yet, Perl will extend the array, make a new `SV` for you, store it in the specified index, and return it for you to manipulate.

The `Storable` module implements persistency by storing and retrieving Perl data structures in disk files. Listing 5.37 shows an abridged form of the function for storing arrays.

Listing 5.37   Storing an array in a file

```
static int store_array(stcxt_t *cxt, AV *av)
{
    SV **sav;
    I32 len = av_len(av) + 1;    ❶
    I32 i;
    int ret;

    PUTMARK(SX_ARRAY);           ❷
    WLEN(len);

    for (i = 0; i < len; i++) {  ❸
        sav = av_fetch(av, i, 0);
        if (!sav) {
            STORE_UNDEF();
            continue;
        }
        if (ret = store(cxt, *sav))  ❹
            return ret;
    }

    return 0;
}
```

❶ Because we're going to iterate over all the elements in the array, we need to know how many elements Perl thinks there are: we can't use the usual C trick of continuing until `av_fetch` returns null, because there could be a hole in the middle of the array where elements haven't been used. (See the example for "av_extend and av_fill," page 142.) So, we call `av_len` (see "av_len," page 143) to find the highest-numbered element, and add 1 to get the number of elements.

❷ These two lines are internal `Storable` macros that write a header to the file saying the next thing stored is an array.

❸ We iterate over the elements of the array, calling `av_fetch` on each element. Note that `av_fetch` returns `SV**`—a pointer to an `SV*`—because there's a difference between storing the null `SV` in an array and not storing an `SV` at all. If the return value of `av_fetch` is `NULL`, then no `SV` is stored in that element, and `Storable` stores `undef`.

❹ If we do find a scalar in a particular element, we call `store` to write it out to the file; note that we need to dereference the `SV**` when passing it to `store`, because `store` expects an `SV`.

See also: "av_store," page 138, and "hv_store and hv_store_ent," page 148.

av_store

```
SV** av_store(AV* array, I32 index, SV* value);
```

This function stores an SV in an array. It is equivalent to the Perl code

```
$array[$index] = $value;
```

Example The core `Threads` module manages Perl threads; it uses an array for each thread to hold the thread's return status. In the (slightly abridged) extract from `threadstart` in listing 5.38, we look at what happens when a thread terminates and sets up its return values ($CORE/ext/Thread/Thread.xs line130).

Listing 5.38   Storing return values in an array

```
av = newAV();           ❶
if (SvCUR(thr->errsv)) {      ❷
    MUTEX_LOCK(&thr->mutex);
    thr->flags |= THRf_DID_DIE;
    MUTEX_UNLOCK(&thr->mutex);
    av_store(av, 0, &PL_sv_no);      ❸
    av_store(av, 1, newSVsv(thr->errsv));
}
else {
    av_store(av, 0, &PL_sv_yes);      ❹
    for (i = 1; i <= retval; i++, SP++)
        sv_setsv(*av_fetch(av, i, TRUE), SvREFCNT_inc(*SP));      ❺
}
```

❶ We create a new array to hold the return values; because this array does not need to be accessible in the Perl symbol table, we use `newAV`.

❷ If the thread exited with an error message, we need to update the thread's status flags to report that it died an unnatural death. (The `MUTEX` business on either side of the flag manipulation just makes sure that no other threads try to interfere while we're doing this.)

❸ We use `av_store` to store the return status in our array: the first element, element 0, will contain a `false` value (see "PL_sv_yes and PL_sv_no," page 103) to denote failure. We call `newSVsv` to copy the error message into a new SV, and then use `av_store` once more to store our copy in element 1 of our return array.

❹ If everything succeeded, on the other hand, we store a `true` value (see "PL_sv_yes and PL_sv_no," page 103) as the first element of the array.

❺ Here you see another way to store an SV in an array: we use the `av_fetch` function with the *lvalue* parameter set to `true` to create the array element and return a pointer to the new SV; we then dereference that pointer and call `sv_setsv` ("sv_setsv," page 124) to set it to what we want. Because we're storing the same SV in multiple places without taking a copy of it, we must increase the reference count of what we're storing.

WARNING *Sometimes the core isn't the best example ...* In the example, we don't check the return values from `av_fetch` and `av_store`—we assume the operations will succeed. This is usually a safe assumption, but it's not the best thing to do: if, for instance, `av_fetch` failed for some reason, we'd attempt to dereference 0, which would cause the program to crash. Furthermore, you should check that `av_store` completed successfully if you are storing the same SV in multiple places—you are responsible for increasing the reference count of the SV before calling `av_store`, and if `av_store` returns 0, you are responsible for decreasing the reference count again.

See also: "av_fetch," page 136, and "hv_store and hv_store_ent," page 148.

av_pop and av_shift

```
SV* av_pop(AV* array);
SV* av_shift(AV* array);
```

`av_pop` is just like the Perl function `pop`; it removes the highest element from an array and returns it. You've already seen an example in "get_av," page 132. If the array is empty, then `&PL_sv_undef` is returned.

Similarly, `av_shift` does the same thing as the Perl function `shift`. In fact, the Perl `shift` function is implemented in terms of `av_shift`.

Example In this example we'll dive into Perl's push pop (PP) code; this part of Perl implements the fundamental operations. Listing 5.39 is the `pp_shift` function in `pp.c`. PP code is extremely macro-laden, but don't worry—we'll examine every line in detail.

Listing 5.39 Implementing shift

```
PP(pp_shift)              ❶
{
    dSP;                  ❷
    AV *av = (AV*)POPs;      ◄——— Pops an array off the
                                   top of the stack and
                                   stores it in av
    SV *sv = av_shift(av);   ◄———
    EXTEND(SP, 1);        ❸         Uses av_shift to
    if (!sv)                        remove the first
        RETPUSHUNDEF;  ❹            element from that array
    if (AvREAL(av))
        (void)sv_2mortal(sv);  ❺   Pushes the SV that we
                                   shifted off the array
    PUSHs(sv);            ◄———      back onto Perl's stack
    RETURN;    ◄——— Returns to the next operation
}
```

---

❶ The macro PP is used to define a push-pop routine, which implements a Perl fundamental operation.

❷ This declares the variable SP to be a local copy of the stack pointer, so we can access arguments on Perl's stack.

❸ EXTEND extends the stack by one place, so we can be sure that the return value from unshift will fit on the stack.[6]

❹ If the SV was null—that is, if there was no element to shift off the array—then we return undef.

❺ If the array was "real" and its contents are reference counted, we need to make the SV return mortal so the reference count is not disturbed.

av_push and av_unshift

```
av_push(AV* array, SV* value);
av_unshift(AV* array, SV* value);
```

av_push and av_unshift, just like av_pop and av_shift ("av_pop and av_shift," page 139), are similar to their Perl equivalents for manipulating an array. They implement the Perl push and unshift built-in functions in XS.

Example   Here's an interesting question: How do you specify that an all-XS class inherits from another class? In Perl, you'd say something like this:

```
package Apache::SubRequest;
use base qw/Apache/;
```

or even

```
package Apache::SubRequest;
@Apache::SubRequest::ISA = qw(Apache);
```

But what if no Perl is involved? No problem—just do the equivalent in XS (see listing 5.40).

Listing 5.40   Inheritance in XS

```
MODULE = Apache   PACKAGE = Apache::SubRequest

BOOT:
    av_push(perl_get_av("Apache::SubRequest::ISA",TRUE),
      newSVpv("Apache",6));
```

---

[6] This step is redundant, because we popped an array off the stack; hence at least one element must be free there.

We use the BOOT section of the XS just like a Perl BEGIN block. We get a handle on the @Apache::SubRequest::ISA variable, creating it if necessary, and push onto the end of it the string "Apache".

av_delete

```
SV* av_delete(AV* array, I32 element, I32 flags);
```

This function is the XS equivalent of $x = delete $array[$element]. It deletes the element from the array and returns the deleted element.

See also: "av_exists," page 141.

av_exists

```
bool av_exists(AV* array, I32 element);
```

This function is similar to the Perl-side exists $array[$element].

See also: "av_delete", above.

sortsv

```
void sortsv ( SV ** array , size_t num_elts , SVCOMPARE_t cmp );
```

Although not strictly an array manipulation function, because it doesn't deal with Perl AVs, sortsv is used to sort a C array of SVs. It takes the array, the number of elements, and a comparison function. Generally, you'll use either Perl_sv_cmp (the ordinary lexicographical sort routine) or Perl_sv_cmp_locale (the locale-aware variant). sortsv sorts the SVs in place in the array, rather than returning a sorted array.

Example Data::Dumper supports the sortkeys option to sort the keys of a hash. If this option is set to a subroutine reference, the subroutine is supposed to get the keys in the right order; if it's set to true, the keys are sorted lexicographically, as in listing 5.41.

Listing 5.41   sort keys %hash

```
    if (sortkeys == &PL_sv_yes) {
        keys = newAV();          ❶
        (void)hv_iterinit((HV*)ival);          ❷
        while (entry = hv_iternext((HV*)ival)) {
            sv = hv_iterkeysv(entry);
            SvREFCNT_inc(sv);
            av_push(keys, sv);
        }
#ifdef USE_LOCALE_NUMERIC
        sortsv(AvARRAY(keys),          ❸
                av_len(keys)+1,
                IN_LOCALE ? Perl_sv_cmp_locale : Perl_sv_cmp);
#else
```

```
        sortsv(AvARRAY(keys),
               av_len(keys)+1,
               Perl_sv_cmp);
#endif
    }
```

If we aren't in a locale-aware situation, we use `Perl_sv_cmp`

❶ We create a new array to store the keys in. Remember that in an AV, AvARRAY is a C array of SVs.

❷ We iterate over the keys of the hash we're dealing with (curiously named ival), pushing the keys onto the new array. This is a slightly different way of iterating a hash than the one described in "Iterating a hash," page 149, because it returns just the keys, rather than the keys and values.

❸ If we're in a locale-aware situation, we need to sort the array using `Perl_sv_cmp_locale` inside the scope of use `locale`. Doing so will sort the keys array in place.

5.3.3 Testing and changing array size

Finally, let's look at functions for manipulating the size of an array. Notice that arrays can only be grown, never shrunk.

av_extend and av_fill

```
av_extend(AV* array, IV index);
av_fill(AV* array, IV index);
```

av_extend and av_fill do similar jobs; they ensure that an array has a given number of elements. However, their operation is slightly different. av_extend makes sure the array has *at least* index elements, whereas av_fill makes sure it has exactly index elements. You can think of av_fill as the XS equivalent of $#array = $index.

Example   When you assign to an array slice in Perl, it's possible you'll be assigning to elements that don't exist yet. For instance, in this code

```
@array = (1,2,3,4);

@array[10, 30] = qw( hi there );
```

we have only four elements in our array, and we're about to store to elements 10 and 30. If we used av_store, Perl would have to extend the array twice: once to accommodate element 10, and once to accommodate element 30. Instead, Perl looks over the slice, finds the maximum element it's going to assign to (in this case, 30), and calls av_extend to pre-extend the array (pp.c, line 3339); see listing 5.42.

Listing 5.42   Assigning to an array slice

```
I32 max = -1;
for (svp = MARK + 1; svp <= SP; svp++) {      ❶
    elem = SvIVx(*svp);      ❷
    if (elem > max)
        max = elem;
}
if (max > AvMAX(av))      ❸
    av_extend(av, max);
```

❶ Perl ensures that the elements of our slice (10 and 30) are placed on a stack, starting from MARK + 1 and ending at SP. We look at each element in turn.

❷ These elements are pointers to SV*s, and to find the numerical value, we dereference the pointer and call SvIVx on the SV to examine its IV. We compare each one against our stored maximum and, if necessary, update the maximum value.

❸ Now that we know the highest element we'll be assigning to, we check to see whether it is higher than the current size of the array. If so, we need to call av_extend to increase the array's size.

av_len

```
I32 av_len(AV* av);
```

av_len is the ordinary way of returning the highest index of an array. It's directly equivalent to the Perl-side $#array. The idiom av_len(av) + 1 is commonly used in XS for counting the number of elements in an array.

Example   Here's another example taken from the Tk module. The Tk::Substitute function takes three references: a set of callbacks, a source subroutine, and a destination subroutine. The set of callbacks is stored in a Perl array. We'll look through the array; if it contains the source subroutine, we'll take that out and replace it with the destination subroutine. Listing 5.43 shows the implementation, from Tk.xs.

Listing 5.43   Substituting elements in an array

```
AV *av = newAV();         ◁          Creates a new array to store
int n = av_len((AV *) cb);  ◁          the results of our substitution

int i;                                Finds out the highest element
int match = 0;                        in the array of callbacks, cb
for (i=0; i <= n; i++)
  {
  SV **svp = av_fetch((AV *) cb,i,0);     ❶
  if (svp)
    {
```

```
        if (SvROK(*svp) && SvRV(*svp) == src)
          {
           av_store(av, i, SvREFCNT_inc(dst));
           match++;
          }
        else
          {
           av_store(av, i, SvREFCNT_inc(*svp));
          }
      }
    }
  if (match)
    {
     ST(0) = sv_2mortal(sv_bless(
              MakeReference((SV *)av),SvSTASH(cb)
           ));
    }
  else
    {
     SvREFCNT_dec(av);
    }
```

❶ As we iterate over the area, we use `av_fetch` ("av_fetch," page 136) to get a pointer to each element, and then check that the pointer is valid.

❷ If this element is a reference, and it's equal to the source subroutine reference we were given, then we store a new reference to our destination subroutine in that location of our output array, `av`. We also flag the fact that we've done a substitution, so we'll have to return this new array instead of being able to simply return the input array.

❸ If the reference in this element doesn't match the one we were given, we instead store a new reference to the original element.

❹ If we have done any substitutions, we need to use the new output array; we bless it into the stash of the original callback array, and put it at the top of the stack.

❺ If we haven't done any substitutions, we get rid of the new array by decreasing its reference count to 0. As this destroys it, Perl will take care of decreasing the references to the subroutines referred to by the array elements.

5.4 *HV FUNCTIONS*

Hashes are, as you might expect, similar to arrays, and the interface to HVs has a lot in common with the interface to AVs.

5.4.1 Creation and destruction

As usual, we'll begin our investigation by looking at the ways of getting a handle on HVs and how to sweep them away once you're finished with them.

get_hv

```
HV* get_hv ( const char* name , I32 create );
```

Similar to get_av and get_sv, this function lets you get a handle on a Perl-space variable—this time, predictably, a hash.

Example As an event-driven environment, Tk deals with a lot of callbacks. However, Tk needs to have control over what happens during these callbacks. If a callback is called inside an eval and the user has installed a __DIE__ handler, anything could happen. Tk must install its own __DIE__ handler to achieve finer-grained control over what happens to an exception. Hence, when setting up a call to a callback, we see the code from listing 5.44 in Event/pTkCallback.c.

Listing 5.44 Installing our own die handler

```
if (flags & G_EVAL)   ❶
 {
  CV *cv  = perl_get_cv("Tk::__DIE__", FALSE);   ❷
  if (cv)
   {
    HV *sig  = perl_get_hv("SIG",TRUE);                 Grabs the %SIG hash and
    SV **old = hv_fetch(sig, "__DIE__", 7, TRUE);       fetches the __DIE__
    save_svref(old);    ◁                               entry from it
    hv_store(sig,"__DIE__",7,newRV((SV *) cv),0);   ❸   Saves the user's
   }                                                    old die handler
 }                                                      for later
```

❶ We only care about the cases where the code is being called inside an eval, because in other cases a die will exit the program, as it should.

❷ We grab our own die handler, using the get_cv function to get a Perl-side CV—that is, a subroutine reference. We're doing the equivalent of $cv = \&Tk::DIE.

❸ Finally, we install our own handler by storing the CV we retrieved earlier into $SIG{__DIE__}.

See also: "get_sv," page 103, and "get_av," page 132.

newHV

```
HV* newHV(void);
```

As you might expect, this function creates a new HV. As you're about to see, it's particularly useful for returning a hash from an XS routine.

Example The POSIX module provides a Perl interface to a variety of system functions; one of them is the locale subsystem. The C function localeconv returns a host of information about the current locale—the decimal point, how to group numbers, the currency symbol, and so on. It stores this information in a C struct lconv. We make that structure useful for the Perl programmer as shown in listing 5.45.

Listing 5.45   Converting a structure to a hash

```
HV *
localeconv()
    CODE:
        struct lconv *lcbuf;
        RETVAL = newHV();     ❶
        if ((lcbuf = localeconv())) {     ❷
            if (lcbuf->decimal_point && *lcbuf->decimal_point)
                hv_store(RETVAL, "decimal_point", 13,     ❸
                    newSVpv(lcbuf->decimal_point, 0), 0);
            if (lcbuf->thousands_sep && *lcbuf->thousands_sep)
                hv_store(RETVAL, "thousands_sep", 13,
                    newSVpv(lcbuf->thousands_sep, 0), 0);
            ....
```

❶ We initialize the return hash first; we'll fill it with entries in a few moments.

❷ We fill the lcbuf structure with the results of our locale information.

❸ Now we can store the entries of this structure into the hash using hv_store. Notice how we use newSVpv to create SVs to store the strings in the locale structure.

See also: "newAV," page 133, and "newSV and NEWSV," page 104.

hv_clear

```
void hv_clear ( HV* hash );
```

hv_clear is an uninteresting function that empties a hash.
   See also: "av_clear," page 135.

hv_undef

```
void hv_undef(HV* hash);
```

This function is the XS equivalent of undef %hash.
   See also: "av_undef," page 135.

5.4.2   Manipulating elements

There's not much you can do with hashes—fetch and store values, delete keys, and see if a key exists. You can also iterate over a hash in the style of the Perl keys function.

hv_delete and hv_delete_ent

```
SV* hv_delete ( HV* hash , const char* key , I32 klen , I32 flags );
SV* hv_delete_ent ( HV* hash , SV* key , I32 flags ,
                    U32 hash_value );
```

These functions are the XS equivalent of delete $hash{$key}. As usual, you can specify the key either as a C string using hv_delete or as an SV using hv_delete_ent. The flags parameter can be set to G_DISCARD to execute the delete in a void context—that is, to return NULL instead of the deleted SV. hash_value in hv_delete_ent should be set to the hash value of the key if known, or to 0 to have Perl compute the hash value.

See also: "av_delete," page 141.

hv_exists_ent

```
bool hv_exists_ent ( HV* hash , SV* key , U32 hash_value );
```

hv_exists_ent is similar to exists $hash{$key}—it tells you whether a given key exists in an HV. You can use the additional parameter hash_value if you know the hash value for the key, or it can be 0 if you want Perl to compute the hash value for you.

Example When you use a Perl module, it gets put in a hash called %INC, linking its relative filename (for instance, IO/File.pm) to its absolute pathname (/System/Library/Perl/darwin/IO/File.pm). So, if we want to know whether IO::File has been loaded, we simply turn it into a filename and look it up in %INC. As listing 5.46 shows, mod_perl does this in the perl_module _is_loaded function of perl_util.c.

Listing 5.46 Is a module loaded?

```
I32 perl_module_is_loaded(char *name)
{
    I32 retval = FALSE;
    SV *key = perl_module2file (name);      ❶
    if((key && hv_exists_ent(GvHV(incgv), key, FALSE)))   ❷
        retval = TRUE;
    if(key)
        SvREFCNT_dec(key);  ◁─  Gets rid of the SV we
    return retval;              created by decreasing
}                               its reference count
```

---

❶ We call perl_module2file, another function in perl_util.c, to turn the string containing the module name into an SV containing the associated filename.

❷ If we get something other than a null SV, we can look up the key in the %INC hash. incgv is the glob *INC, and GvHV extracts the hash part of that glob.

See also: "av_exists," page 141.

hv_fetch and hv_fetch_ent

```
SV** hv_fetch ( HV* hash , const char* key , I32 klen , I32 lval );
HE* hv_fetch_ent ( HV* hash , SV* key , I32 lval , U32 hash_value );
```

These two functions both fetch values from a hash. hv_fetch requires you to specify the key as a C string, whereas hv_fetch_ent is more useful if you have an SV; on the other hand, hv_fetch returns a pointer to an SV or null if the entry was not found, whereas hv_fetch_ent returns a hash entry (HE) structure (see section 4.5) requiring you to extract the value with HeVAL(he).

In both cases, lval can be set to true to tell Perl to create the key if it doesn't exist, returning an SV that can be set. hash_value is the key's hash value or 0, if you want Perl to compute the value; you can also set the key length (klen) to 0 in hv_fetch, and Perl will call strlen on the key string.

Example   A hash is a common way of passing options to a subroutine in Perl, like this:

```
process( data => $data,
         force => 1,
         separator => ":",
         transform => \&invert ... );

sub process {
    my %options = @_;
    my $force = $options{force};
    ...
}
```

Data::Dumper takes options in a similar way; listing 5.47 shows how this is done in XS.

Listing 5.47   Getting options

```
if ((svp = hv_fetch(hv, "indent", 6, FALSE)))     ❶
     indent = SvIV(*svp);     ❷
if ((svp = hv_fetch(hv, "purity", 6, FALSE)))
     purity = SvIV(*svp);
if ((svp = hv_fetch(hv, "terse", 5, FALSE)))
     terse = SvTRUE(*svp);
```

---

❶ We call hv_fetch, storing the result in svp. If this pointer is true, then the entry exists in the hash.

❷ We can dereference the pointer to get a real SV, and then call SvIV on it to find the integer value for the indent parameter.

See also: "hv_store and hv_store_ent," page 148.

hv_store and hv_store_ent

```
SV** hv_store ( HV* hash , const char* key , I32 klen ,
                SV* val , U32 hashval );
SV** hv_store_ent ( HV* hash , SV* key , SV* val , U32 hashval );
```

hv_store is the ordinary way of storing a value in a hash with a constant key. If you already have the key as an SV, consider using hv_store_ent instead. If you specify 0 for the *hashval* parameter, perl will compute the hash for you.

See "newHV," page 145 for an example; see also: "hv_fetch and hv_fetch_ent," page 147.

Iterating a hash

```
I32 hv_iterinit ( HV* hash );
SV* hv_iternextsv ( HV* hash , char** key , I32* keylen );
```

There are several ways to iterate over a hash's keys and values in the Perl API; we'll show you the simplest and most immediately useful. After performing an hv_iterinit, each call to hv_iternextsv will return the next value and store the key and its length in the memory pointed to by *key* and *keylen*, respectively.

Example Listing 5.48 shows a slightly simplified example from mod_perl. When mod_perl starts up, it wants to remove anything that might be dangerous from the environment it has inherited, saving only selected environment entries. It does so by iterating over %ENV.

Listing 5.48 Cleaning the environment

```
void perl_clear_env(void)
{
    char *key;
    I32 klen;
    SV *val;
    HV *hv = (HV*)GvHV(envgv);          ❶     Initializes the hash
                                               for iteration
    (void)hv_iterinit(hv);          ◀──────┘
    while ((val = hv_iternextsv(hv, (char **) &key, &klen))) {   ❷
        if((*key == 'G') && strEQ(key, "GATEWAY_INTERFACE"))
            continue;
        else if((*key == 'M') && strnEQ(key, "MOD_PERL", 8))
            continue;
        else if((*key == 'T') && strnEQ(key, "TZ", 2))
            continue;
        else if((*key == 'P') && strEQ(key, "PATH"))
            continue;
        }
        delete_env(key, klen);          ❸
    }
}
```

❶ envgv is the glob representing *ENV; we extract the hash value from this glob, giving us %ENV in hv.

❷ We iterate over the hash, storing the value in `val`, the key in `key`, and the key's length in `keylen`. Notice that we finish iterating when `hv_iterkeysv` returns NULL.

❸ After allowing some elements that we don't mind having in the environment, we delete the entry by calling the macro `delete_env`; this macro is specific to mod_perl and deletes the entry from the environment.

5.5 MISCELLANEOUS FUNCTIONS

Some of the functions in the Perl API aren't about manipulating Perl values directly; they're either low-level functions for memory and string handling, or just basically miscellaneous.

5.5.1 Memory management

Perl provides its own memory-management library and a set of handy macros to make it easier to handle memory in C.

New

```
void New(int id, void* ptr, int nitems, type );
void Newz(int id, void* ptr, int nitems, type );
void Newc(int id, void* ptr, int nitems, type , cast );
```

New is the XS writer's interface to `malloc`, for allocating new memory. Because Perl can opt to use its own memory-management system, you should always use New rather than `malloc`.

Newz is similar to New, but it also ensures that the returned memory is filled with zero bytes. Newc is the same as New, but it also allows for a cast to a different type.

Example DBM databases are files storing key-value relationships, the same way hashes do. In fact, it's common practice in Perl to use a DBM database to store a hash so that its data can be saved and restored between calls to a Perl program. There are several flavors of DBM, and one of them ("old DBM") stores its data in two files: a database called `birthdays` would be stored on disk as birthdays.dir and birthdays.pag. That's to say, the code responsible for opening the directory must catenate `.dir` and `.pag` onto the filename. Listing 5.49 shows how this is done; it's from ext/ODBM_File/ODBM_File.xs in the Perl sources.

Listing 5.49   Opening a DBM database

```
New(0, tmpbuf, strlen(filename) + 5, char);      ❶
SAVEFREEPV(tmpbuf);      ❷
sprintf(tmpbuf,"%s.dir",filename);      ❸      │ Tests to see if
if (stat(tmpbuf, &PL_statbuf) < 0) {  ◄───────┘   the file exists
```

❶ We must allocate memory for a temporary buffer to hold the filename plus the extension. It's five characters longer than the filename itself, and each element of the array is of type `char`. (Why five characters? " `.dir`" is four, and we add the trailing zero to end a string.)

❷ `SAVEFREEPV` is a wonderful way to not have to worry about freeing memory once we've used it. Perl has a *save stack* that holds values to be freed at the end of the current scope—for instance, Perl `local` SVs or subroutine return values. The save stack can therefore be used to process any actions that must be done at the end of scope. Here it's being used to hold a string pointer (a PV) that will be freed at the end of scope. If you use `SAVEFREEPV` on your strings, Perl will clean them up for you.

❸ We copy the filename followed by " `.dir`" into this new buffer to get the filename as it would be on disk.

See also: "Renew," page 153, and "Safefree," page 153.

Copy

```
void Copy(void* src, void* dest, int items, type);
```

`Copy` is the XS version of the standard C `memcpy`. It copies an area of memory from a source to a destination. Use `Move` if the areas may overlap.

Example When you write to the elements of `%ENV`, Perl modifies the process's environment. It does so by setting up a string of the form `key=value` and then handing this string to the operating system's way of modifying the environment. Normally, you'd use `sprintf(buffer, "%s=%s", key, value)` to achieve this result, but Perl defines a macro to help it do things a little faster (see listing 5.50, from util.c).

Listing 5.50 Beating sprintf

```
#define my_setenv_format(s, nam, nlen, val, vlen) \
    Copy(nam, s, nlen, char); \        ❶
    *(s+nlen) = '='; \                 ❷
    Copy(val, s+(nlen+1), vlen, char); \   ❸
    *(s+(nlen+1+vlen)) = '\0'          ❹
```

❶ We copy *nlen* characters from the key string into the beginning of our buffer s.

❷ We set the next character to be =.

❸ We copy *vlen* characters of the value to the end of the buffer.

❹ Finally, we add our null terminator.

See also: "Move," page 152.

Move

```
void Move ( void* src , void* dest , int nitems , type );
```

Move is the XS writer's interface to memmove; that is, it moves a chunk of memory from a source src to a destination dest. When using Move, you specify how many (*nitems*) of what type (type) of thing you want to move.

Example   You heard about the offset hack in section 4.2.7; what happens when you need to do something that doesn't know about that hack? At some point, you must really move the memory around instead of faking it. The sv_backoff function does this, and it can be found in sv.c in the Perl sources; see listing 5.51.

Listing 5.51   Backing off offset strings

```
int
Perl_sv_backoff(pTHX_ register SV *sv)
{
    assert(SvOOK(sv));              ❶
    if (SvIVX(sv)) {
        char *s = SvPVX(sv);        ❷
        SvLEN(sv) += SvIVX(sv);     ❸
        SvPVX(sv) -= SvIVX(sv);
        SvIV_set(sv, 0);           ❹
        Move(s, SvPVX(sv), SvCUR(sv)+1, char);    ❺
    }
    SvFLAGS(sv) &= ~SVf_OOK;    ← Turns off the
    return 0;                        offset flag
}
```

---

❶ The code checks that it's being called with an offset string; if not, there's a logic bug somewhere else in Perl.

❷ We take a copy of the start of the string as stored in the PVX slot of the SV. This isn't the real start of the string, because some characters are obscured by the offset hack.

❸ We undo the effects of the offsetting by declaring the available length of the string to be slightly larger (due to the offset) and moving the string stored in PVX to be the actual start of the string.

❹ Now we can set the offset to 0. Remember that s still holds the string starting from the visible portion, whereas SvPVX now includes some characters that have been deleted.

❺ Hence, we need to move things around so that the visible portion coincides with the real start of the string. That is, we must move the SvCUR(sv) characters of the string (plus one for the null terminator) starting at s back to what Perl thinks is the start of the string, SvPVX(sv). The Move call does this.

See also: "Copy," page 151.

Renew

```
void Renew ( void* ptr , int nitems , type );
void Renewc ( void* ptr , int nitems , type , cast );
```

Renew is the XS version of `realloc`—it tries to extend the size of an allocated area of memory, obtained with New.

Renewc is supposed to be "renew with cast," but we could find only one occurrence of it in real code. A lot of code uses `saferealloc`, which is another interface to `realloc`.

Example Devel::DProf is a Perl profiler; it keeps track of which subroutines call other subroutines, the most often called routines, and so on. It keeps its own call stack, and to avoid extending the call stack for every subroutine call, it ensures it always has room for at least five extra calls; see listing 5.52.

Listing 5.52   Keeping the stack big enough

```
if (g_SAVE_STACK) {                                         ❶
    if (g_profstack_ix + 5 > g_profstack_max) {
            g_profstack_max = g_profstack_max * 3 / 2;      ❷
            Renew(g_profstack, g_profstack_max, PROFANY);   ❸
    }
}
```
---

❶ If we're keeping our own call stack, and five more subroutines would take us over the maximum our stack has allocated, we need to make more room for subroutine call information.

❷ We increase the depth of our stack by half as much again, to give us plenty of leeway.

❸ We call Renew to allocate that many PROFANY structures.

See also: "New," page 150.

Safefree

```
void Safefree ( void* ptr );
```

The XS writer should use Safefree instead of `free`, because Perl can be compiled with its own memory allocation functions, and Safefree knows which one to use.

Example POSIX-compliant operating systems can use the `getppid` function to find a process's parent. What about non-POSIX-compliant OSs, such as OS/2? In these cases, Perl includes functions that implement the same job. The function `ppidOf` from OS2::Process calls the OS/2 system call `get_sysinfo` to get information about the process (see listing 5.53). This function allocates and returns a buffer, which we need to clean up.

Listing 5.53   Parent Process ID on OS/2

```
int
ppidOf(int pid)
{
  PQTOPLEVEL psi;
  int ppid;

  if (!pid)
      return -1;
  psi = get_sysinfo(pid, QSS_PROCESS);        ◁─┐  get_sysinfo returns
  if (!psi)                                       a structure representing
      return -1;                                  the process information
  ppid = psi->procdata->ppid;    ◁─┐  Extracts the ppid slot of the
  Safefree(psi);   ◁── Frees the buffer  process information table
  return ppid;
}
```

See also: "New," page 150.

Zero

```
void Zero ( void* dest , int nitems , type);
```

Zero is the Perlish way of saying bzero—that is, filling a chunk of memory with zeros. It's useful for clearing out assigned memory after a New (although you can use Newz to do the same thing) in case the system doesn't set it to zero for you, or in case you want to reuse some memory and erase its old contents.

Example   The Opcode module lets you turn on and off some of Perl's internal operations. It keeps the collection of disallowed ops in a bitmask it calls an *opset*. When you begin using the module, you want the opset to be empty, so Opcode initializes a new opset as shown in listing 5.54.

Listing 5.54   Emptying a bitmask

```
opset = NEWSV(1156, opset_len);        ❶
Zero(SvPVX(opset), opset_len + 1, char);        ❷
SvCUR_set(opset, opset_len);        ❸
(void)SvPOK_only(opset);        ❹
```

❶ We make a new SV with a string buffer of at least opset_len. This is a static variable initialized when the module boots up. (That's a slight simplification, because the details are pretty hairy, but it's close enough.)

❷ We ensure that all the characters in the buffer are set to 0: one for each operation in our opset, plus one at the end to be the "real" null terminator.

③ We tell Perl that the string part of this SV is exactly one opset long.

④ We also tell Perl that the string buffer is the only part worth looking at.

See also: "New," page 150.

5.5.2   Unicode data handling

Perl 5.6 added support for Unicode strings; the interface to these strings is still not developed and is changing fairly rapidly, so we'll only document the more stable functions. For more information on Perl's Unicode support and how to use the Unicode functions in your XS routines, see NetThink's "Perl and Unicode" training course (http://www.netthink.co.uk/downloads/unicode.pdf).

SvUTF8

```
bool SvUTF8 ( SV* sv );
void SvUTF8_on ( SV* sv );
void SvUTF8_off ( SV* sv );
```

The UTF8 flag on an SV determines whether Perl expects to treat the string data in the SV as UTF-8 encoded. Looking at it the other way, the flag tells your XS function whether you need to treat the string data as UTF-8 encoded.

If you're writing string data into an SV, you should use SvUTF8_on and SvUTF8_off to tell the rest of Perl how your data is encoded.

Because UTF8-ness is indicated by a flag in the SV, not in the PV, when you're copying strings, you need to remember to copy around the UTF8-ness information too. Listing 5.55 shows the correct way to copy a string portion, taken from S_sublex_start in toke.c in the Perl core.

Listing 5.55   Copying an SV's string portion

```
STRLEN len;
char *p;
SV *nsv;

p = SvPV(sv, len);          ←┐ Gets the string value
nsv = newSVpvn(p, len);   ❶   into p and the
if (SvUTF8(sv))           ←    length into len
                               If the old SV was
    SvUTF8_on(nsv);       ←┐   UTF-8 encoded ...
SvREFCNT_dec(sv);         ❷   ... then this SV should
                               be UTF-8 encoded, too.
```

❶ We create a new SV with that string value and length. See "Creating SVs with values," page 106.

❷ Because we're using the new SV in place of sv, we decrement sv's reference count to indicate that we're not using it any more.

is_utf8_char and is_utf8_string

```
STRLEN is_utf8_char ( U8* s );
bool is_utf8_string ( U8* s , STRLEN len );
```

These functions test whether a given C string contains valid UTF-8 encoded characters. is_utf8_char is a once-off test, checking whether the first character of the string is a valid UTF8-encoded character. If so, it returns the length of the character in bytes. is_utf8_string, on the other hand, checks the validity of *len* bytes of the string.

Now that regular expressions can understand UTF-8 encoded matches as well as non-UTF-8 encoded matches, we need to be more careful when dealing with the magical variables related to regular expressions. For instance, a captured variable such as $1 may be represented by 5 bytes of the match, but this may be only two UTF-8 characters. Given that these variables do not have their own SVs but are derived magically, as if they were tied, the function that implements length on them (mg_length in mg.c) has to be a little clever; see listing 5.56.

Listing 5.56   length($1)

```
    i = t1 - s1;
getlen:
    if (i > 0 && PL_reg_match_utf8) {        ❶
        char *s    = rx->subbeg + s1;
        char *send = rx->subbeg + t1;

        if (is_utf8_string((U8*)s, i))
            i = Perl_utf8_length(aTHX_ (U8*)s, (U8*)send);
    }
```

> If the captured substring really is UTF-8 encoded ...

> ... we must use utf8_length to get its real length in characters instead of in bytes

---

❶ If we're currently matching things in a UTF-8-aware manner (reg_match_utf8), then we recalculate the start and end of the substring so we can check its length.

uvchr_to_utf8

```
U8* uvchr_to_utf8 (U8* dest , UV uv );
```

In many of the examples we've looked at, the standard way to write a character to a given location has been

```
*string = 'a';
```

Hence, to fill a 12-byte string with as, you'd say

```
int i = 12;
while (i-- != 0)
    *(string++) = 'a';
```

This is fine for non-UTF8 strings. Unfortunately, in the Unicode world, characters can be more than one byte long, and so this idiom breaks down for wider characters.

To counter this situation, `perl` provides `uvchr_to_utf8`:

```
int i;
UV mywchar = 0x0388; /* GREEK CAPITAL LETTER EPSILON WITH TONOS */
for (i=0; i++; i<12)
    string = uvchr_to_utf8(string, mywchar);
```

`uvchr_to_utf8` returns the new position in the string after inserting the given character.

sv_len_utf8

```
STRLEN sv_len_utf8 ( SV* sv );
```

This function is similar to `sv_len`, except that it returns the length in characters, not in bytes—wide characters in a UTF-8 encoded string are counted as a single character.

See also: "sv_len," page 118, and "utf8_length," below.

bytes_to_utf8 and utf8_to_bytes

```
U8* bytes_to_utf8 (U8* original , STRLEN* len );
U8* utf8_to_bytes (U8* original , STRLEN* len );
```

These functions convert a string between UTF-8 encoding and byte encoding.

WARNING   The memory behavior of these two functions is subtly different, so you must be careful to avoid memory leaks. Specifically, `utf8_to_bytes` (given that it is guaranteed to return a string either the same size as or smaller than the original string) will overwrite the original string in memory.

Because `bytes_to_utf8` will always return a string that is the same size or larger than the original string, it creates a new string and returns a pointer to the newly created string.

Both functions update `len` with the new length of the string.

utf8_length

```
STRLEN utf8_length ( U8* s , U8* e );
```

This function counts the number of UTF-8 encoded characters between `s` and `e`; UTF-8 characters are of variable width, so this function must be used to determine the length of a UTF-8 string.

See "is_utf8_char and is_utf8_string," page 156 for an example; see also "sv_len_utf8," above, which is implemented in terms of `utf8_length`.

Unicode Case Modification

```
UV to_utf8_upper ( U8* src , U8* dest , STRLEN* length );
UV to_utf8_lower ( U8* src , U8* dest , STRLEN* length );
UV to_utf8_title ( U8* src , U8* dest , STRLEN* length );
UV to_utf8_fold ( U8* src , U8* dest , STRLEN* length );
```

These functions perform case folding of a UTF-8 encoded character as per the rules specified by the Unicode tables. They take a character from `src` and place the folded version in `dest`, which must have enough room for the result; "safe" values are provided in `UTF8_MAXLEN_UCLC` for upper- and lowercase transformation and in `UTF8_MAXLEN_FOLD` for titlecase and foldcasing.[7]

5.5.3   Everything else

Finally, let's examine a grab-bag of API functions that don't fit nicely anywhere else.

Casting pointers to integers (and back)

```
IV PTR2IV(pointer);
INT2PTR ( type , IV integer );
NV PTR2NV(pointer);
UV PTR2UV(pointer);
```

The ability to cast functions into pointers becomes exceptionally useful in XS programming, because it provides a way to store a pointer in an `SV`. Expanding slightly on this reason, it gives you a way to store any C structure as a Perl value that other parts of your XS library can retrieve and manipulate later. Indeed, it's the standard way of wrapping up a C structure as a Perl object.

However, simply converting a pointer to an integer is an operation that is not portable across compilers and architectures. To assist you, `perl` provides the `PTR2IV` macro to turn a pointer into an integer safely, and the `INT2PTR` macro to turn it back.

Our example shows an example of this technique, but with a subtle twist—instead of storing a C structure in an `SV`, we're storing a C *function*. In this book we primarily discuss providing an interface from C to Perl via XS; however, some modules go a little further. One such module is `Time::HiRes`, which also provides an interface for other XS modules to use. This interface is provided via the `PL_modglobal` hash, a dumping ground that XS modules can use to share information. `Time::HiRes` stores a pointer to its `myNVtime` function for other XS modules to retrieve later.

Here's the code that stores the pointer:

```
hv_store(PL_modglobal, "Time::NVtime", 12,
        newSViv(PTR2IV(myNVtime)), 0);
```

As you can see, the code takes a pointer to `myNVTIME` and then converts it to an integer. This integer is passed to `newSViv` (see "Creating SVs with values," page 106) to produce an `SV`, which can be stored in the `PL_modglobal` hash.

Listing 5.57 shows some code (provided in the `Time::HiRes` documentation as an example) that accesses that function pointer.

---

[7]   Foldcasing and the rules used to convert cases are explained in Unicode Technical Report 21 (http://www.unicode.org/unicode/reports/tr21/).

Listing 5.57 Providing an interface for other XS writers

```
double (*myNVtime)();          ❶
SV **svp = hv_fetch(PL_modglobal, "Time::NVtime", 12, 0);    ❷
if (!svp)          croak("Time::HiRes is required");    ❸
if (!SvIOK(*svp))
    croak("Time::NVtime isn't a function pointer");    ❹
myNVtime = INT2PTR(double(*)(), SvIV(*svp));    ❺
printf("The current time is: %f\n", (*myNVtime)());    ❻
```

❶ We declare the variable that will receive the function pointer; this is a pointer to a function of type `double` with no arguments.

❷ We attempt to fetch the previously cached `Time::NVtime` key from the `PL_modglobal` hash.

❸ If we don't get anything back, then `Time::HiRes` hasn't had a chance to store the key yet.

❹ If what we get back isn't an integer (that is, a function pointer masquerading as an integer), then something has gone horribly wrong.

❺ We can use `INT2PTR` to cast this integer back into being a function pointer.

❻ Finally, we have a function we can call to give us the time of day. Remember that because it's a function pointer, we need to say `*myNVtime` to get the actual function.

get_cv

```
CV* get_cv ( const char* name , I32 create );
```

Like the related `get_sv`, `get_av`, and `get_hv`, this function is responsible for looking up a name in the symbol table. This time, you look for a subroutine called *name*, creating it if *create* is set.

Example The Perl core contains a number of hooks for the debugger; one is triggered when control flow jumps around with a `goto`, triggering the debugger subroutine `DB::goto`. This process is implemented in pp_ctl.c as shown in listing 5.58.

Listing 5.58 Debugging goto

```
if ( PERLDB_GOTO          ❶
    && (gotocv = get_cv("DB::goto", FALSE)) ) {    ❷
    PUSHMARK( PL_stack_sp );    ❸
    call_sv((SV*)gotocv, G_SCALAR | G_NODEBUG);    ❹
    PL_stack_sp--;    ❺
}
```

❶ If we're currently debugging calls to `goto` …

❷ … and we can find a subroutine called `DB::goto`, we store it into `gotocv`.

❸ We add a mark onto the stack so we remember where we are …

❹ … call the `DB::goto` subroutine, making sure to turn off debugging for the time being …

❺ … and pop the mark off the stack when we return.

See also: "get_sv," page 103, "get_av," page 132, and "get_hv," page 145.

GIMME

```
U32 GIMME (void);
U32 GIMME_V (void);
```

These macros are the equivalent of the Perl `wantarray`. `GIMME_V` is preferred over `GIMME`, because the latter doesn't understand void contexts. `GIMME_V` will return one of the constants `G_SCALAR`, `G_ARRAY`, or `G_VOID`; `GIMME` will return one of the first two, returning `G_SCALAR` in void context.

Example Apache's tables are a little like Perl's hashes, except they can be multi-valued—several entries can be filed under a single key. The `Apache::Table` module provides an interface to Apache tables, and

```
$table->get("some key")
```

will return either a single value in scalar context or all values for a key in list context; see listing 5.59.

Listing 5.59 Context-sensitive hash fetches

```
if(GIMME == G_SCALAR) {                                            ❶
    const char *val = table_get(self->utable, key);               ❷
    if (val) XPUSHs(sv_2mortal(newSVpv((char*)val,0)));           ❸
    else XSRETURN_UNDEF;
}
else {
    int i;
    array_header *arr  = table_elts(self->utable);
    table_entry *elts = (table_entry *)arr->elts;
    for (i = 1; i < arr->nelts; ++i) {    ◁─────────────
        if (!elts[i].key ||
            strcasecmp(elts[i].key, key)) continue;      ❹
XPUSHs(sv_2mortal(newSVpv(elts[i].val,0)));   ◁──────────
    }
}
```

Extracts the number of elements from the table and begins to loop over each element

❹ Adds the element's value onto the Perl stack as a new SV

---

① If we're in scalar context …

② … we call upon the Apache function `table_get` to do the work for us.

③ If this function returns a string, we ship it to the user as a new SV; if not, we put `undef` onto the stack.

④ If this element's key is empty or isn't the same as the key we're looking for,[8] then we skip to the next element.

toLOWER and toUPPER

```
char toLOWER ( char ch );
char toUPPER ( char ch );
```

These are simply Perl replacements for the `tolower` and `toupper` functions. They are deliberately *not* locale aware, as opposed to the system's `tolower` and `toupper` functions, which may be.

String comparison functions

```
bool strEQ ( char* s1 , char* s2 );
bool strNE ( char* s1 , char* s2 );
bool strnEQ ( char* s1 , char* s2 , STRLEN length );
bool strnNE ( char* s1 , char* s2 , STRLEN length );
```

The standard C way of comparing strings, `strcmp`, can be confusing sometimes. The problem is that it returns 0 when the strings are identical, acting like the Perl `cmp` operator. Hence, to do something if two strings are the same, you need to say

```
if (!strcmp(a,b))
```

which is weird at best. Perl tries to get around this situation by defining more Perl-like string comparison macros. It allows you to replace the previous code with

```
if (strEQ(a,b))
```

The n forms of these functions test for equality or inequality for the first *length* characters.

As well as `strEQ` and `strNE`, Perl also provides `strLT`, `strLE`, `strGT`, and `strGE`, which operate like their Perl-side equivalents. These functions do not have n forms.

isALNUM and friends

```
bool isALNUM ( char ch );
bool isALPHA ( char ch );
```

---

8 Remember that string comparison functions in C return 0 for equality, so if `strcasecmp` returns a true value, the strings differ.

```
bool isDIGIT ( char ch );
bool isLOWER ( char ch );
bool isSPACE ( char ch );
bool isUPPER ( char ch );
```

Like toLOWER, these functions are locale-insensitive replacements for the ordinary ctype character-type functions. Only hard-core XS hackers use them.

See also: "toLOWER and toUPPER," page 161.

5.6 SUMMARY

In this chapter we've covered a lot of the API used within Perl. You've seen how to extract information from variables, learned how to manipulate hashes and arrays, and examined some general helper functions. In the following chapters, we'll use these functions to delve into the details of extending and embedding Perl. If you ever come across a function you are not sure about, recall that we have put a full API index in appendix C to make it easier to track down related examples.

#### CHAPTER 6

Advanced XS programming

Gluing simple C functions to Perl is fairly straightforward and requires no special knowledge of the Perl internals. Chapter 2 covers the basics of XS and how to pass in and return values associated with simple C scalar types. Unfortunately, many functions and libraries have more complicated signatures and require additional work to implement a Perl interface.

This chapter discusses a more advanced use of XS and deals with topics such as structures, arrays, and callbacks. This chapter builds on chapter 2 and also refers to functions used in the Perl internals and described in chapter 5.

IMPORTANT Many of the examples in this chapter (in particular, those related to Perl references and arrays) work only with Perl version 5.8.0 or newer. The typemap file distributed with older versions of Perl has problems that make it unusable in some cases. In principle, all you need is the new typemap file. You can copy the typemap file from a Perl 5.8.0 distribution and use it in conjunction with Perl 5.6 if you want.

6.1 POINTERS AND THINGS

Now that you know about pointers and dynamic memory allocation and how the Perl API deals with them, you can begin doing more interesting things with XS. To demonstrate some of these issues, let's use the following function, which concatenates two strings to a third and returns the total length of the final string:[1]

```
#include <string.h>

STRLEN strconcat (char* str1, char* str2, char* outstr) {
    strcpy( outstr, (const char*)str1 );
    strcat( outstr, (const char*)str2 );
    return strlen( outstr );
}
```

We will now write an XS interface to mirror the C calling interface. The C signature

```
STRLEN strconcat(char *str1, char *str2, char *outstr);
```

will then translate to the Perl signature

```
$len = strconcat($str1, $str2, $outstr);
```

In this case, we could write the XS interface as follows:

```
STRLEN
strconcat( str1, str2, outstr )
  char* str1
  char* str2
  char* outstr = NO_INIT
 OUTPUT:
  outstr
  RETVAL
```

The NO_INIT keyword tells the compiler not to care about the input value of out-str. Remember that we have to tell xsubpp that we want to use the return value, even though we have specified a return type.

Unfortunately, this code will not work, because our simple strconcat function assumes the output string has enough space to hold the concatenated string. In our XS segment, outstr is typed as a pointer to a string but is not actually pointing to anything! We must fix this by using a CODE block that allocates the memory for a string of the required size:[2]

---

[1] However, why you would want to use this function rather than the standard strcat function or sv_catpv from the Perl API is a mystery!

[2] The alternative is to preallocate the memory within Perl by passing in a string as the third argument (and removing the NO_INIT declaration). The contents of the string will then be overwritten by strconcat. This approach will work but can generate core dumps if the string is not large enough to receive the result string. Not recommended!

```
STRLEN
strconcat( str1, str2, outstr )
  char* str1
  char* str2
  char* outstr = NO_INIT
 PREINIT:  ◁─────────────────
  STRLEN length;
 CODE:
  length = strlen( str1 ) + strlen( str2 ) + 1;  ◁──
  New(0, outstr, length, char );  ❶
  RETVAL = strconcat( str1, str2, outstr );
 OUTPUT:
  outstr
  RETVAL
```

PREINIT is used to declare additional variables

Calculates the size of the required string. Don't forget the extra space for the null character!

❶ We use New rather than malloc to allocate the memory, because this is the standard Perl interface to memory allocation and the Perl macros are available from within the XS environment. See "New," page 150, for more details about this function.

Now this routine is becoming complicated! The PREINIT block initializes additional variables that are required for the CODE section. PREINIT guarantees that the variable declaration will occur as soon as possible after entering the function, because some compilers do not like declarations after code sections have started; it provides a nice way to separate variable declarations from code. Even worse, although our XS interface will now work, there is still a problem: each time the routine is entered, memory is allocated to outstr—but it is never freed. XS provides a means to tidy up after ourselves by using the CLEANUP keyword. The cleanup code is guaranteed to run just before the C code returns control to Perl. Our XS function should now work without memory leaks:

```
STRLEN
strconcat( str1, str2, outstr )
  char* str1
  char* str2
  char* outstr = NO_INIT
 PREINIT:
  STRLEN length;
 CODE:
  length = strlen( str1 ) + strlen( str2 ) + 1;
  New(0, outstr, length, char );
  RETVAL = strconcat( str1, str2, outstr );
 OUTPUT:
  outstr
  RETVAL
 CLEANUP:
  Safefree( outstr );
```

This example shows how to deal with pointer types (in this case a simple string) and how to allocate and free memory using XS. It also demonstrates the wrong way to approach interface design—in a real application, the string would be a return value (without the length) and would not be returned via the argument list. The code might look something like this:

```
char *
strconcat( str1, str2 )
  char* str1
  char* str2
 PREINIT:
  STRLEN length;
 CODE:
  length = strlen( str1 ) + strlen( str2 ) + 1;
  New(0, RETVAL, length, char );
  length = strconcat( str1, str2, RETVAL );
 OUTPUT:
  RETVAL
 CLEANUP:
  Safefree( outstr );
```

6.2   FILEHANDLES

Sometimes an external library needs to print to a user-supplied filehandle or open a file and return a filehandle to the user. If the library uses C input/output streams, then it is easy to pass the C stream to and from Perl with XS—by default, XS knows how to deal with a FILE*, converting it to and from a Perl filehandle. The following example could be used to provide an XS interface to one of the Gnu readline functions:[3]

```
int
rl_getc( file )
  FILE * file
```

This example shows that a FILE* can be treated like any other simple type. In this case, the filehandle is an input argument

```
$retval = rl_getc(FH);
```

but it is just as easy to import a stream into Perl.

If your external library requires a file descriptor (see section 3.5), then you will have to use the fileno function to extract the file descriptor from the filehandle or stream (by using the fileno function in either Perl or C). Similarly, if you are importing a file descriptor into Perl, you need to convert it to a filehandle either by using the fdopen C function (if you are comfortable with XS and C) or by importing the descriptor into Perl as an integer and then using Perl's open command[4] to translate it:

---

[3] The Term::ReadLine::Gnu module has a full implementation.

[4] Or even IO::Handle->new_from_fd()

```
$fd = some_xs_function();
open(FH, "<&=$fd");
```

As of version 5.7.1 of Perl, the I/O subsystem is completely self contained and no longer relies on the underlying operating system for implementation. Perl uses a `PerlIO*` rather than a `FILE*` for all I/O operations (in some cases a `PerlIO*` can be the same as a `FILE*`, but you can't rely on it). If you are using I/O in your XS code but you are not using an external library, then you should be using `PerlIO*` in preference to a `FILE*`. Of course, XS automatically recognizes both `PerlIO*` and `FILE*`.

6.3   TYPEMAPS

When a variable is passed from Perl to C (or from C to Perl), it must be translated from a Perl scalar variable (chapter 4) to the correct type expected by the C function. So far, we've implicitly assumed that this translation is something that "just happens"; but before we can move further into XS, we must explain *how* it happens.

The XS compiler (xsubpp) uses a lookup table called a *typemap* to work out what to do with each variable type it encounters. Perl comes with a file called typemap that contains the common variable types; this file is installed as part of Perl. On many Unix systems, it can be found in /usr/lib/perl5/5.6.0/ExtUtils/typemap.[5] Here is a subset of that file:

```
# basic C types
int               T_IV
unsigned int      T_UV
long              T_IV
unsigned long     T_UV
char              T_CHAR
unsigned char     T_U_CHAR
char *            T_PV
unsigned char *   T_PV
size_t            T_UV
STRLEN            T_UV
time_t            T_NV
double            T_DOUBLE

#############################################
INPUT
T_UV
        $var = ($type)SvUV($arg)
T_IV
```

---

[5] The location of the file on your system can be determined using Perl's `Config` module:

```
% perl -MConfig -MFile::Spec::Functions \
 -le 'print catfile($Config{installprivlib},"ExtUtils","typemap")'
/usr/lib/perl5/5.6.0/ExtUtils/typemap
```

```
        $var = ($type)SvIV($arg)
T_CHAR
        $var = (char)*SvPV($arg,PL_na)
T_U_CHAR
        $var = (unsigned char)SvUV($arg)
T_NV
        $var = ($type)SvNV($arg)
T_DOUBLE
        $var = (double)SvNV($arg)
T_PV
        $var = ($type)SvPV($arg,PL_na)
#############################################
OUTPUT
T_IV
        sv_setiv($arg, (IV)$var);
T_UV
        sv_setuv($arg, (UV)$var);
T_CHAR
        sv_setpvn($arg, (char *)&$var, 1);
T_U_CHAR
        sv_setuv($arg, (UV)$var);
T_NV
        sv_setnv($arg, (double)$var);
T_DOUBLE
        sv_setnv($arg, (double)$var);
T_PV
        sv_setpv((SV*)$arg, $var);
```

The first section contains a list of all the C types of interest (the actual file contains many more) along with a string describing the type of variable. As you can see, this list provides a many-to-one translation, because many different C variable types can have the same fundamental representation via the use of typedefs (see section 1.6.2). For example, both `size_t` and `STRLEN` are fundamentally integer types and can be represented by a `T_UV` in the typemap.

The second section is called `INPUT`; it provides the code required to translate a Perl variable to the corresponding C type. The third section is called `OUTPUT`, and it does the reverse: it provides code to translate C variables to Perl variables. Each label matches one of those defined in the first section, and the functions are simply those described in "SvIV and friends," page 112. For example, the typemap entry to translate an `SV` to an integer (`T_IV`) uses `SvIV` to retrieve the integer from the `SV` and `sv_setiv` to set the integer part of an `SV`.

The typemap file may look strange, because it includes Perl-style variables in C-type code. The variables $arg, $var, and $type (and for more complex entries, $ntype, $Package, $func_name, and $argoff) have a special meaning in typemaps:

- *$arg*—The name of the Perl `SV` in the Perl argument list.
- *$var*—The name of the C variable that is either receiving the value from the `SV` or setting the value in the `SV`.

- $type—The type of the C variable. It will be one of the types listed at the top of the typemap file.
- $ntype—The type of the C variable, with all asterisks replaced with the string *Ptr*. A char * would therefore set $ntype to charPtr. This variable is sometimes used for setting classnames or referencing helper functions.
- $Package—The Perl package associated with this variable. It is the same as the value assigned to the PACKAGE directive in the XS file.
- $func_name—The name of the XS function.
- $argoff—The position of the argument in the argument list. It begins counting at zero.

In many cases, you will need to add extra typemap entries when creating XS interfaces. Rather than add to the standard typemap, all you need to do is create a file called typemap in your module directory and add entries in the same format used in the default typemap shown earlier. The make file generated from Makefile.PL will automatically include this typemap file in the XS processing.

A description of each of the standard Perl typemaps can be found in appendix A.

6.4 THE ARGUMENT STACK

In Perl, arguments are passed into and out of subroutines as lists. The list is called an *argument stack*: arguments are pushed onto the stack by the caller and shifted off the stack by the subroutine. The following Perl program demonstrates this behavior:

```
my ($sum, $diff) = sumdiff( 5, 3 );

sub sumdiff {
  my $arg1 = shift; # implicitly shifts off @_
  my $arg2 = shift;

  return ( $arg1 + $arg2, $arg1 - $arg2 );
}
```

Perl keeps track of the number of arguments on the stack that are meant for the current subroutine (the size of @_). XS routines use the same technique when passing arguments from Perl to the XS layer. In our discussion so far, this step has happened automatically, and the arguments from the stack have been processed using the provided typemap. Perl provides the ST macro to retrieve the SV on the stack. ST(0) is equivalent to $_[0], ST(1) is equivalent to $_[1], and so forth. In the typemap definitions described in the previous section, $arg is replaced by ST() macros corresponding to the required stack position. More details on this replacement can be found in section 6.11 (if you want to know the details of how the Perl stacks work, skip forward to "The argument stack," page 291).

So far, we have only looked at XS functions that either modify input arguments (ultimately using the ST macros) and/or return a single value. You can also write XS functions that take full control of the argument stack; this chapter contains examples of how to do so using PPCODE (see "Returning a list," page 181).

6.5 C STRUCTURES

C structures (section 3.4) are used in many libraries to pass around related blocks of data. This section shows how you can handle C structures in XS. The choice you make depends entirely on the way the structure will be used.

6.5.1 C structures as black boxes

If you don't want to look inside the structure (or you aren't allowed to), then one approach to structures is simply to return the pointer to the structure and store it in a Perl scalar. Usually, the pointer is then used as an argument for other library routines. As a simple example, we will provide an XS interface to some of the POSIX functions that deal with time. They are as follows:

```
struct tm * gmtime(const time_t *clock);
```

This function returns a tm structure (using Universal Time) for a given time (for example, the output from the Perl time function supplied in a variable of type time_t). This routine is used for the Perl gmtime built-in.

```
time_t timegm(struct tm * tm);
```

This function converts a tm structure to a time_t time.

```
size_t strftime(char * s, size_t maxsize,
                char * format, struct tm * tm);
```

This function converts a tm structure to a formatted string.

In other words, to use these functions, you don't need to know the contents of the tm structure. For the purposes of this example, we will place the XS routines into a Perl module called Time. The first step is to create the module infrastructure:

```
% h2xs -A -n Time
Writing Time/Time.pm
Writing Time/Time.xs
Writing Time/Makefile.PL
Writing Time/test.pl
Writing Time/Changes
Writing Time/MANIFEST
```

We first implement the gmtime function, because it returns the base structure. Here is a first attempt at the XS code (after a #include <time.h> near the top of Time.xs):

```
struct tm *
gmtime( clock )
  time_t &clock
```

The ampersand indicates that we wish to pass a pointer to the gmtime function. Perl copies the argument into the variable clock and then passes the pointer to the function. Without the ampersand, the default behavior would be to pass the value to the function.

If we attempt to build this module (after running perl Makefile.PL), we get the following error:

```
Error: 'struct tm *' not in typemap in Time.xs, line 11
Please specify prototyping behavior for Time.xs (see perlxs manual)
make: *** [Time.c] Error 1
```

The problem is that Perl does not now how to deal with a pointer to a tm structure, because a struct tm * is not present in the default typemap file. To fix this error, we must create a typemap file (called typemap) and place it in the build directory. Because we are interested only in the pointer (not the contents), the typemap just needs to contain

```
struct tm *              T_PTR
```

where the variable type and the typemap name are separated by a tab. T_PTR tells Perl to store the pointer address directly into a scalar variable. After we save this file, the module builds successfully. We can test it with the following:

```
% perl -Mblib -MTime -le 'print Time::gmtime(time)'
1075295360
```

Your result will vary, because this is a memory address.

Now that we have a pointer, we can pass it to a function. timegm looks like this

```
time_t
timegm( tm )
  struct tm * tm
```

and can be used as follows:

```
use Time;
$tm = Time::gmtime( time() );
$time = Time::timegm( $tm );
```

The default implementation of strftime looks like this:

```
size_t
strftime( s, maxsize, format, tm )
  char * s
  size_t maxsize
  char * format
  struct tm * tm
 OUTPUT:
  s
```

Unfortunately, although this function works, there are serious problems with the interface to strftime as implemented. To use it, we must presize the output string and provide the length of the output buffer (including the C-specific terminating null character)—two things people are used to in C but that are unacceptable in a Perl interface:

```
use Time;
$tm = Time::gmtime( time() );
$s = "             ";  # presize output buffer
$maxsize = length($s)+1; # length must account for the null
$format = "%D";
$len = Time::strftime($s, $maxsize, $format, $tm);
print "length=$len output=$s\n";
```

A much better Perl interface would be something like

```
$s = strftime($tm, $format);
```

where we have removed the input buffer requirement and rearranged the argument order to place the tm structure at the start of the list. One way of implementing this interface is to write a pure Perl wrapper (placed in the .pm file) that deals with the presized buffer and then calls the XS code. Although this approach is sometimes easier to implement (especially if you are using Perl functionality), often it is more efficient to rewrite the XS layer using CODE: blocks:

```
char *
strftime( tm, format )
  struct tm * tm
  char * format
 PREINIT:
  char tmpbuf[128];
  size_t len;
 CODE:
  len = strftime( tmpbuf, sizeof(tmpbuf), format, tm);
  if (len > 0 && len < sizeof(tmpbuf)) {
     RETVAL = tmpbuf;
  } else {
     XSRETURN_UNDEF;
  }
 OUTPUT:
  RETVAL
```

This code is much better but still not perfect. The problem now is that we don't know the required size of the output buffer before calling strftime. In this example, we simply allocate 128 characters and hope that is enough. It will be enough in most cases, but if a large format is supplied, this function will currently return undef. We can overcome this problem by checking the return value of strftime and increasing the buffer size until it is large enough—this is the way POSIX::strftime is implemented in standard Perl.[6]

---

[6] See ext/POSIX/POSIX.xs in the Perl source tree for details of the implementation of POSIX::strftime.

The example so far has demonstrated how to pass a structure pointer from and to a C library, but the interface we've implemented has some remaining issues. In the following sections, we address some of these problems.

T_PTR versus T_PTRREF

Using a scalar to store a memory address is dangerous because it is possible that the Perl program may inadvertently change the value of an existing pointer (maybe by treating it as a normal number) or pass an undefined value (0) to the timegm or strftime function. If any of these things occurs, the program will crash with a memory error because the value will no longer point to a valid memory location. The best way to deal with this problem is to use an object interface (see section 6.5.2); but, failing that, another option is to return a reference to a scalar containing the pointer value rather than the scalar itself. The T_PTRREF typemap designation does just that:

```
T_PTR
        sv_setiv($arg, (IV)$var);
T_PTRREF
        sv_setref_pv($arg, Nullch, (void*)$var);
```

This approach offers an advantage: the function will not run unless a scalar reference is passed in (which is difficult to do by mistake).

Default arguments

Rather than always force the time to be supplied, a cleaner approach assumes the current time if no arguments are present. This technique matches the behavior of the built-in gmtime:[7]

```
struct tm *
gmtime ( ... )        ❶
  PREINIT:  <──────────┐  No required arguments, so
   time_t clock;       │  explicitly declares the clock variable
  CODE:
   if (items > 1)        ❷
      Perl_croak(aTHX_ "Usage: Time::gmtime( [time] )");        ❸
   else if (items == 1)
      clock = (time_t)SvNV(ST(0));        ❹
   else
      clock = time( NULL );        ❺

   RETVAL = gmtime( &clock );  <──┐  Runs gmtime using the value
  OUTPUT:                          │  stored in clock and stores
   RETVAL                          │  the pointer in RETVAL
```

---

[7] gmtime is implemented in Perl in the file pp_sys.c.

❶ The ellipsis (. . .) indicates to the XS compiler that the number of input arguments is not known. This example has no required arguments; a signature of gmtime(clock, . . .) could be used to indicate that there will be at least one argument.

❷ The items variable is supplied by the XS system and contains the number of input arguments waiting on the stack. Here we check to see if more than one argument has been supplied.

❸ If more than one argument has been supplied, we stop the program with Perl_croak. It provides similar functionality to the croak provided by the Carp module.

> **NOTE**   *Perl context*—aTHX_ is an example of a *Perl context-passing* function. It stands for "argument threads," and the trailing underscore implies a comma; it is matched by pTHX_ in a function's prototype. If threads support is enabled, this macro will expand to register PerlInterpreter *my_perl,; it will be empty if threads support is disabled. In addition, aTHX and pTHX are provided for functions that take no arguments other than the context.

❹ The ellipsis implies that we must do our own argument processing. If there is a single argument, the numeric value is retrieved from the first argument on the stack (ST(0)). This code is identical to that found in the standard typemap file (see section 6.3).

❺ If there are no arguments, the current time is obtained using the system time function. The NULL macro is used to indicate that we are only interested in a return value.

Static memory

A more worrisome problem is associated with the gmtime function itself. This function always uses the same structure (and therefore returns the same memory address), so each time it is called, it overwrites the answer from a previous call. This behavior is evident in the following example:

```
use Time;
$tm1 = Time::gmtime( time() );
print "First time: ",Time::timegm( $tm1 ), "\n";
$tm2 = Time::gmtime( time() + 100 );

print "First time (again): ",Time::timegm( $tm1 ), "\n";
print "Second time: ",Time::timegm( $tm2 ), "\n";
```

This code prints

```
First time: 983692014
First time (again): 983692114
Second time: 983692114
```

This result may cause confusion unless it's carefully documented (not everyone is an expert C programmer used to these oddities). On systems where it is available, one solution is to use gmtime_r (the reentrant [thread-safe] version of this function), because it takes the address of the structure as an argument:

```
struct tm *
gmtime( clock );
  time_t clock;
 PREINIT:
  struct tm * tmbuf;
 CODE:
  New( 0, tmbuf, 1, struct tm );
  RETVAL = gmtime_r( &clock, tmbuf );
 OUTPUT:
  RETVAL
```

A more general (but not thread-safe) solution is to copy the result from gmtime into a new structure each time:

```
struct tm *
gmtime_cp( clock );
  time_t clock;
 PREINIT:
  struct tm * tmbuf;
  struct tm * result;
 CODE:
  result = gmtime( &clock );
  New( 0, tmbuf, 1, struct tm );
  StructCopy( result, tmbuf, struct tm);
  RETVAL = tmbuf;
 OUTPUT:
  RETVAL
```

Both these techniques overcome the problem with gmtime, but they both introduce a memory leak because the memory allocated for the new structure (using the New function) is never given back to the system. The Perl scalar containing the memory address attaches no special meaning to it; if the variable goes out of scope, the SV is freed without freeing the memory. The C way to deal with this problem is to provide a function that can be called when the structure is no longer needed (an XS function that simply calls Safefree).

The more Perl-like way to handle the problem is to turn the structure into an object such that Perl automatically frees the memory when the variable goes out of scope. This approach is discussed in section 6.5.2. Alternatively, if the structure is fairly simple (and does not contain pointers to other variables), you can either copy the memory contents directly into a Perl variable by using the T_OPAQUEPTR typemap entry (see section A.2.27 for an example) or copy the contents into a Perl hash (partially discussed in section 6.5.3). These approaches both have the advantage of letting Perl—rather than the programmer—keep track of memory management. Both approaches let the caller modify the contents of the hash between calls; it is no longer a black box, and the hash approach requires more work from the XS programmer.

6.5.2   C structures as objects

You can think of an object as some data associated with a set of subroutines (methods). In many libraries, C structures take on the same role as objects, and Perl can treat them as such. An object-oriented (OO) interface to the time functions described earlier may look something like this (the use of new as a constructor is purely convention):

```
use Time;

$tm = new Time( time() );
$time = $tm->timegm;
$s = $tm->strftime( $format );
```

The changes required to the existing Time module to get this behavior are not extensive. In this section, we will modify the Time module so that it matches this interface.

The most important change is to modify the typemap entry to use T_PTROBJ instead of T_PTR or T_PTRREF. T_PTROBJ is similar to T_PTTREF, except that the reference is blessed into a class. Here is the OUTPUT entry in the standard Perl typemap file:

```
T_PTROBJ
        sv_setref_pv($arg, \"${ntype}\", (void*)$var);
```

By default, the reference will be blessed into class $ntype, which translates to struct tmPtr! A class containing a space is not helpful, because the XS compiler does not know how to handle it. We can get around this problem two ways. First, we can create a new OUTPUT entry (and corresponding INPUT entry) that uses a hard-wired package name:

```
struct tm *     T_TMPTROBJ

INPUT:
T_TMPTROBJ
        if (sv_derived_from($arg, \"TimePtr\")) {
            IV tmp = SvIV((SV*)SvRV($arg));
            $var = INT2PTR($type,tmp);
        }
        else
            Perl_croak(aTHX_ \"$var is not of type TimePtr\")
OUTPUT:
T_TMPTROBJ
        sv_setref_pv($arg, \"TimePtr\", (void*)$var);
```

Second, we can create a new variable type and associate it with T_PTROBJ. We will adopt the latter technique because it is more robust against changes to the behavior of typemap entries. We need to add the following line before the MODULE line in the XS file to generate a new type Time as an alias for struct tm:

```
typedef struct tm Time;
```

We must also modify the typemap file to include

```
Time *      T_PTROBJ
```

Now, wherever we used `struct tm`, we can use `Time`. Here is the new constructor (including all the changes suggested earlier):

```
Time *   ◁─────────────────┐       The return value is now a
new( class, ... );      ❶          pointer to Time rather than
  char * class                     a pointer to struct tm
 PREINIT:
  time_t clock;
  Time * tmbuf;
  Time * result;
 CODE:
  if (items > 2)
     Perl_croak(aTHX_ "Usage: new Time( [time] )");
  else if (items == 2)
     clock = (time_t)SvNV(ST(1));   ◁─┐  The time is now the second
  else                                 │  argument (ST(1)) rather
     clock = time( NULL );             │  than the first
  result = gmtime( &clock );
  New( 0, tmbuf, 1, Time );
  StructCopy( result, tmbuf, Time);
  RETVAL = tmbuf;
 OUTPUT:
  RETVAL
```

❶ The function name has changed to `new`, and now there is one required argument (the class name) as well as the optional second argument. This argument ordering is no different than any other Perl method.

The changes are minor compared to the previous non-OO version and are caused entirely by the extra argument.[8] When we build this module, we can check the result of the constructor:

```
% perl -Mblib -MTime -le 'print new Time()'
TimePtr=SCALAR(0x80f87b8)
```

As expected, it returns an object blessed into class `TimePtr`. The complication now is that the `timegm` and `strftime` methods must be put into the `TimePtr`

---

[8] If you are happy to have a non-OO style constructor, simply changing the typemap entry will be enough. The calling style would then remain

```
$object = Time::gmtime();
```

but it would return an object.

package and not the default Time namespace. We do so by adding an additional MODULE directive after the constructor and then adding the methods:

```
MODULE = Time          PACKAGE = TimePtr

time_t
timegm( tm )
  Time * tm

char *
strftime( tm, format )
  Time * tm
  char * format
 PREINIT:
  char tmpbuf[128];
  size_t len;
 CODE:
  len = strftime( tmpbuf, sizeof(tmpbuf), format, tm);
  if (len > 0 && len < sizeof(tmpbuf)) {
     RETVAL = tmpbuf;
  } else {
     XSRETURN_UNDEF;
  }
 OUTPUT:
  RETVAL
```

Other than the extra package declaration, these definitions are *exactly* the same as those used previously. Perl automatically finds these functions and passes the structure pointer (the object) as the first argument.

There are at least two reasons to prefer the OO interface over storing the plain pointer:[9]

- *Type safety*—The INPUT typemap entry for T_PTROBJ includes a check for the class of the input variable. This check guarantees that the object is of the correct type. Unless a programmer tries hard, it will prevent strange values (with even stranger memory addresses) from being passed to the C layer and causing segmentation faults.

- *Destructors*—As with any Perl class, when the object goes out of scope and is freed, Perl will call a DESTROY method. XS implementations of Perl classes behave the same way. Recall that in the previous implementation, the gmtime function generated a memory leak because it was not possible to automatically free the memory allocated to the structure. As written, the current object implementation also has this problem; but it can be fixed simply by adding a DESTROY function to the TimePtr class:

```
void
DESTROY( tm )
```

---

[9] Ignoring any preference in the syntax of Time::timegm($tm) versus $tm->timegm

```
       Time * tm
     CODE:
       printf("Calling TimePtr destructor\n");
       Safefree( tm );
```

Now, whenever a `TimePtr` object is freed, the destructor will be called and the memory will be freed.

6.5.3   C structures as hashes

If the main reason for the structure is to group return values that are of interest, then you should consider unpacking the structure into either a Perl hash or a list that can be converted into a hash. We will demonstrate both these techniques by extending our `Time` module so that it uses a Perl hash rather than a structure pointer. For clarity, the examples will not include support for defaulting of the time.

Returning a hash reference

One way of returning a hash is to return the reference to a hash:

```
$hash = Time::gmtime_as_href( time );
print "Day is ", $hash->{"mday"}, "\n";
```

The XS code required is as follows:

```
HV *                           ①      Calls function gmtime_as_href to distinguish
gmtime_as_href( clock )                it from the normal gmtime function
  time_t clock                         Passes in the time in seconds
 PREINIT:           ②                  rather than providing a means for
 HV * hash;                            defaulting to the current time
  struct tm * tmbuf;
 CODE:
  /* Run gmtime */                     Calls gmtime with the
  tmbuf = gmtime( &clock );            pointer to the current time

  hash = newHV();                      Creates a new hash and
                                       stores the pointer in hash
  /* Copy struct contents into hash */
  hv_store(hash, "sec",  3, newSViv(tmbuf->tm_sec), 0);      ③
  hv_store(hash, "min",  3, newSViv(tmbuf->tm_min), 0);
  hv_store(hash, "hour", 4, newSViv(tmbuf->tm_hour), 0);
  hv_store(hash, "mday", 4, newSViv(tmbuf->tm_mday), 0);
  hv_store(hash, "mon",  3, newSViv(tmbuf->tm_mon), 0);
  hv_store(hash, "year", 4, newSViv(tmbuf->tm_year), 0);
  hv_store(hash, "wday", 4, newSViv(tmbuf->tm_wday), 0);
  hv_store(hash, "yday", 4, newSViv(tmbuf->tm_yday), 0);

  RETVAL = hash;          The hash has been populated, so we can
 OUTPUT:                  copy the pointer to the RETVAL variable
  RETVAL
```

① Here we set the return value of our function to be a pointer to a hash. Remember that the argument stack can only contain scalar types, so the typemap will automatically convert this value to a hash reference when it is placed on the stack.

② This block declares the additional variables that will be required. `hash` is a pointer to an HV, and `tmbuf` is declared as a pointer to the `struct` that will contain the result from the `gmtime` call. Because the hash will also be returned, we could have used `RETVAL` throughout rather than creating an extra variable; however, the explicit use of a variable name is sometimes clearer.

③ These lines store the contents of the structure into the hash. The first argument is a pointer to the HV, the second argument is the key, and the third is the length of the key. The fourth argument must be an SV; therefore, an SV is created using the integer from each struct entry. The final argument is the hash number; because we don't know the value, we pass in 0 and ask Perl to calculate the value for us. Note that `hv_store` does not affect the reference count of the SV that is being stored; thus each SV stored in the hash will automatically have a `refcount` of 1.

This XS code does work and returns a reference to a hash containing the `gmtime` results, but it contains a subtle bug that is illustrated in the following output:

```
% perl -Mblib -MTime -MDevel::Peek \
      -le '$h=Time::gmtime_as_href(time);Dump($h)'
SV = RV(0x81109b4) at 0x815bd54
  REFCNT = 1
  FLAGS = (ROK)
  RV = 0x80f86e0
  SV = PVHV(0x81429a8) at 0x80f86e0
    REFCNT = 2
    ...
```

The reference count to the HV is 2. The variable $h has one of the references, but no other variables know about the reference. This situation constitutes a memory leak. If $h is later undefined or goes out of scope, the reference count on the HV will drop to 1, but it can't go any lower. Because it never goes to 0, the HV will not be freed until the program exits. This is the case because when the HV is created using newHV, its reference count is set to 1 as expected. The output typemap entry for an HV is

```
T_HVREF
   $arg = newRV_inc((SV*)$var);
```

which increments the reference count when the reference is taken. At this point there is an SV containing a reference to the hash on the stack, the `hash` variable contains the HV, and the reference count is, correctly, 2. Unfortunately when the XS function exits, the `hash` variable simply disappears without decrementing the reference count.

Perl overcomes such problems by introducing the concept of *mortality*. If an SV is marked as mortal, the reference count will automatically be decremented at some point later in time. For XS functions, mortal variables' reference counts are decremented on exit from the function. The previous code can be fixed to avoid the memory leak by marking `hash` as mortal. To do so, we replace

```
hash = newHV();
```

with

```
hash = (HV*)sv_2mortal((SV*)newHV());
```

The new sequence now becomes:

1 Create a new HV and increment the reference count. Reference count = 1.

2 Mark the HV as mortal. Reference count = 1.

3 Take a reference to the HV and store it on the argument stack. Reference count = 2.

4 Exit the XS function and automatically decrement the reference count. Reference count = 1.

NOTE You don't need to know exactly when a mortal variable's reference count is decremented. Suffice to say that all variables marked as mortal in your XS code will have their reference counts decremented some time after exiting your XS function and before returning control to the calling Perl code.

If we make this change, the test program now reports the correct reference count for $h:

```
% perl -Mblib -MTime -MDevel::Peek \
      -le '$h=Time::gmtime_as_href(time);Dump($h)'
SV = RV(0x81109b4) at 0x815bd54
  REFCNT = 1
  FLAGS = (ROK)
  RV = 0x80f86e0
  SV = PVHV(0x81429a8) at 0x80f86e0
    REFCNT = 1
    ...
```

Returning a list

An alternative way of returning a hash is to return a list with alternating keys and values:

```
%hash = Time::gmtime_as_list( time );
print "Day is ", $hash{"mday"}, "\n";
```

The XS code must push the keys and the values onto the argument stack just as if it were a normal Perl routine:

```
void         ❶
gmtime_as_list( clock )
  time_t clock
 PREINIT:
  struct tm * tmbuf;
 PPCODE:      ❷
  tmbuf = gmtime( &clock );
```

```
EXTEND(SP, 16);   ❸

PUSHs( sv_2mortal( newSVpv("sec", 3) ));    ❹
PUSHs( sv_2mortal( newSViv(tmbuf->tm_sec) ));
PUSHs( sv_2mortal( newSVpv("min", 3) ));
PUSHs( sv_2mortal( newSViv(tmbuf->tm_min) ));
PUSHs( sv_2mortal( newSVpv("hour", 4) ));
PUSHs( sv_2mortal( newSViv(tmbuf->tm_hour) ));
PUSHs( sv_2mortal( newSVpv("mday", 4) ));
PUSHs( sv_2mortal( newSViv(tmbuf->tm_mday) ));
PUSHs( sv_2mortal( newSVpv("mon", 3) ));
PUSHs( sv_2mortal( newSViv(tmbuf->tm_mon) ));
PUSHs( sv_2mortal( newSVpv("year", 4) ));
PUSHs( sv_2mortal( newSViv(tmbuf->tm_year) ));
PUSHs( sv_2mortal( newSVpv("wday", 4) ));
PUSHs( sv_2mortal( newSViv(tmbuf->tm_wday) ));
PUSHs( sv_2mortal( newSVpv("yday", 4) ));
PUSHs( sv_2mortal( newSViv(tmbuf->tm_yday) ));
```

❶ We use void as a return value for the function because the return values will be handled directly by the routine rather than by the XS compiler.

❷ We use PPCODE rather than CODE to indicate to the XS compiler that we are handling the return values ourselves. Doing so does not affect the processing of input arguments but does imply that OUTPUT cannot be used.

❸ The EXTEND macro makes sure the argument stack is large enough to contain the requested number of arguments. Because we know we will need to hold 16 items (8 keys and 8 values), we presize the stack for efficiency. Doing so is similar to using $#array = 15 in Perl. SP is the stack pointer (pointing to the current position in the stack) and is initialized for us automatically on entry to the routine.

❹ We need to start pushing arguments onto the stack. For XS programmers, the only approved ways of pushing arguments onto the stack are the PUSHs and XPUSHs macros. They push an SV onto the argument stack. The difference is that XPUSHs extends the size of the stack by one so that it is guaranteed to have room for the incoming SV. In this example, we could have used XPUSHs instead of PUSHs and removed the EXTEND call. Because we can only push SVs onto the stack, each argument (string key or integer value) is first converted to an SV and then marked as mortal. All SVs pushed onto the stack must be marked as mortal so they can be freed after assignment, because a copy of the SV is assigned to a Perl variable and not the original SV. If this were not the case, $a = $b would alias $a to $b!

If you scan the internals documentation, it may be tempting to use the PUSHi, PUSHp, and PUSHn functions (and the related XPUSH variants) to push plain integers, strings, and floats onto the stack in XS routines. Unfortunately, they are not part of the XS API. These routines are intended for use by the internals and can only be used to return a single value onto the stack. They use a single SV (that must be declared using the dTARG macro), and if five values are pushed onto the stack with these functions, they will all receive the value of the last thing pushed on—because it is the pointer to the same SV that is stored on the stack.

Passing the hash back into C

Both techniques we just described (returning a list or returning a hash reference) overcome the memory leak problem described earlier, because the information is copied to a Perl data structure and not kept inside a C structure. Perl knows nothing about the C structure, so it can only free its memory via an object destructor. When you use hashes to store the information, Perl can free the memory directly. Unfortunately, this behavior comes at a price when it is time to pass the information back to C. If the information is only required for use in Perl (such as the data returned from a call to stat), then this is not a problem; but if the data will be passed back into C (for example, to the timegm function), then more work is required—the data must be converted from the hash to a C structure. Even worse, you can no longer rely on the integrity of the data structure, because the contents of the hash can be changed arbitrarily before they are passed back to C. If structure integrity is a problem, then you should probably use objects.

6.6 ARRAYS

In some cases, a C routine wants to receive an array of numbers or strings. To handle this situation, you must convert the Perl array or list into a C array before calling the C function. Doing so usually involves the following steps:

1 Allocate some memory to hold the array.
2 Copy each element from the list/array to the C array.
3 After the C function has run, free the memory.

6.6.1 Passing numeric arrays from Perl to C

The ability to pass arrays of numbers to and from C is a common requirement, especially in the scientific community. This section will describe how to deal with one-dimensional arrays; the next section will discuss multidimensional arrays. We will also provide some benchmarking examples to provide a guide for the most efficient handling of arrays and lists.

Note that this section deals with converting lists and arrays to C arrays, not simply manipulating a Perl array as-is. The easiest way to handle a Perl array in C is simply to pass in the array reference and manipulate the AV* in C code.

We will illustrate how to pass Perl numeric arrays to C by providing an XS interface to a function that will sum the elements of the array and return the answer to Perl. The signature of the C function is

```
int sum(int count, intArray * array);
```

intArray is typedef'd to an int for two reasons: so that XS can distinguish a pointer to an integer from a pointer to an array of integers (they can both be written as int * in C) when it is looking up the correct typemap entry, and so that XS can determine whether the array contains integers.

NOTE For some typemap entries, xsubpp determines the type of element stored in the array by looking at the type used to specify the array. It does so by removing *Array* and *Ptr* from the type name. In this case, the type is intArray*, and the internal name of this type is intArrayPtr; therefore, the subtype (the xsubpp name for the elements in the array) is determined to be int. We use this ability in the next section when we use T_ARRAY to return a list from XS.

For this example, the module will be called Arrays. Here is the top of the XS file, including the sum function:

```
#include "EXTERN.h"
#include "perl.h"
#include "XSUB.h"

typedef int intArray;

/* Add up everything in an int array */
/* Args: the number of things to add, pointer to array */

int sum ( int num, intArray * array ) {
  int thesum = 0;
  int count;
  for (count = 0; count < num; count++) {
    thesum += array[count];
  }
  return thesum;
}

MODULE = Arrays          PACKAGE = Arrays
```

Passing a numeric array from Perl to C as a list

One of the simplest ways to pass an array into XS (and into other Perl subroutines) is to pass in a list:

```
$sum = Arrays::sum_as_list( @values);
```

Each element of the array @values is pushed onto the argument stack; so, in XS, each argument must be retrieved from the stack and copied into a C array. Perl provides the T_ARRAY typemap entry to handle this situation:

```
int
sum_as_list( array, ...)
  intArray * array
 CODE:
  /* ix_array is the total number of elements */
  RETVAL = sum( ix_array, array );
 OUTPUT:
  RETVAL
 CLEANUP:
  Safefree( array );
```

This code looks straightforward, but many things are going on behind the scenes:

- T_ARRAY is unique in the standard typemap file because it is designed to work on multiple input arguments. The ellipsis (. . .) indicates that an unknown number of arguments are expected, but they are all processed as part of the typemap entry.

- T_ARRAY is greedy. Only a single XS argument can be associated with T_ARRAY, and it must be the last argument in the list. This requirement should not be surprising, because the typemap is doing the C equivalent of @args = @_;. There can be arguments before the final list.

- T_ARRAY creates a variable called ix_${var} (in our example, ix_array) that contains the number of elements processed by T_ARRAY.

- Memory must be allocated in which to store the new integer array. T_ARRAY assumes that there is a memory allocation function called $ntype (in this case, intArrayPtr) that will return a pointer to some memory. It is passed a single argument containing the number of elements in the array. Of course, this memory must be freed at the end of the XS function.

- The XS compiler works out how to copy elements from the Perl list into the C array by guessing the C type of the variables from the type of the array. It does so by removing any mention of *Array* and *Ptr* from the $ntype variable and then looking in the standard typemap entry for the resulting string. In this example, $ntype is intArrayPtr, so each element is copied using the int typemap entry.

As it stands, this code will not compile, because xsubpp does not know that variables of type intArray * need to be processed using the T_ARRAY typemap entry. To tell xsubpp how to handle such variables, we need to create a file called typemap in the build directory and put in one line:

```
intArray *          T_ARRAY
```

For completeness, here is the typemap entry for T_ARRAY from Perl's default typemap file:

```
U32 ix_$var = $argoff;        ❶
$var = $ntype(items -= $argoff);       ❷
```

```
while (items--) {   ③
    DO_ARRAY_ELEM;    ④
    ix_$var++;
}
/* this is the number of elements in the array */
ix_$var -= $argoff    ⑤
```

■

① We declare a new variable and set it initially to the position of the first element in the list. This declaration causes problems if previous arguments have used complicated typemaps, because C does not like variable declarations partway through a block. This issue is discussed further in section 6.11.

② This line allocates memory using the function $ntype. The requested number of elements is calculated by using (and modifying) items. XS automatically sets this variable to the total number of XS arguments.

③ We loop over each element until no more remain. items is decremented until it hits 0, and ix_$var is incremented to provide an index into the argument list.

④ DO_ARRAY_ELEM is the magic string used by the XS compiler to indicate that an element must be copied from the stack to $var. It uses ix_$var to index into the stack and derives the type of the element from the type of the array.

⑤ Finally, we reset the value of ix_$var so that it reflects the number of elements in the C array.

So far, we have not said much about the memory allocation function in the current example. The default allocator (implied by the use of the Safefree function in the example) could look something like this:

```
intArray * intArrayPtr ( int num ) {
  intArray * array;

  New(0,array, num, intArray );
  return array;
}
```

We simply use the New macro to allocate num integers and return the pointer. Although this code will work, we still must make sure the memory is freed when we're finished with it. In most cases, this step just involves the use of a CLEANUP block in the XS definition, because we usually don't want to keep the memory. Because laziness is sometimes a virtue, another approach to memory allocation obviates the need for the CLEANUP block. During the discussion of structure handling (see section 6.5.3), we introduced the concept of mortality. Perl uses mortal variables to make sure variables are automatically freed when a Perl scope is exited. We can use this fact by allocating memory in a Perl scalar, marking it as mortal, and then letting Perl free the memory when the XS function is completed. The memory allocation function then becomes

```
void * intArrayPtr ( int num ) {
  SV * mortal;
  mortal = sv_2mortal( NEWSV(0, num * sizeof(intArray) ) );
  return SvPVX(mortal);
}
```

This function creates a new SV and makes sure the PV part of the SV is large enough to hold the required number of integers (the sizeof function determines how many bytes are required for each integer). This SV is marked as mortal, and the pointer to the PV part is returned using the SvPVX macro (it differs from SvPV in that it returns the pointer without looking at flags to see whether the SV contains a valid string). If we use this function, then we can remove the CLEANUP section of array_as_list.

When we place this memory allocation function before the XS code, remove the CLEANUP section, and build this example, the code will sum up all elements in an array:

```
% perl -Mblib -MArrays -le 'print Arrays::sum_as_list(5,6,7)'
18
```

NOTE   If this seems like too much magic, feel free to use CLEANUP blocks. Mortal memory allocators are extremely useful in typemaps, because a single typemap can be used by many XS functions—the allocators save you from having to remember to use a CLEANUP section in every function. Additionally, if you are using someone else's typemap, you may not be aware that you should free memory on exit. Using a mortal allocator can save you from worrying about causing a memory leak.

Passing a numeric array from Perl to C as an array reference

Just as when programming in Perl, an alternative to passing in a list is to pass in a reference to an array:

```
$sum = Arrays::sum_as_ref( \@values );
```

The main advantage of this technique is that multiple arrays can be passed to a function. The XS code is as follows:

```
int
sum_as_ref( avref )
  AV * avref;      ❶
 PREINIT:
  int len;
  int i;
  SV ** elem;      ⟵  Declares elem as a pointer to a
  intArray * array;     pointer to an SV. This type of
                        variable is returned by av_fetch
 CODE:
  len = av_len( avref ) + 1;   ⟵  This line finds out how many
  array = intArrayPtr( len );  ❷   elements are in the array
```

```
/* copy numbers from Perl array */        Loops over each element in the
for (i=0; i<len; i++) {          ⟵         AV, copying it to the C array
  elem = av_fetch( avref, i, 0);   ⟵       This line retrieves the ith
  if (elem == NULL) {      ❸                element from the array
    array[i] = 0;
  } else {
    array[i] = SvIV( *elem );    ❹
  }
}                                          Finally, we run the
RETVAL = sum( len, array );     ⟵          sum function
OUTPUT:
  RETVAL
```

❶ The argument is a pointer to an AV. The default typemap entry will make sure we have an array reference and will exit the program if we don't get one.

❷ We allocate some memory for the C array using the same function we used for sum_as_list.

❸ A complication here is that av_fetch can return NULL for the requested element. Thus we have to check that the pointer is valid before dereferencing it.

❹ We copy the integer part of the SV to the C array. Because SvIV expects a pointer to an SV, we must dereference elem.

Once built, this code produces the same answer as the previous example; but this time, an array reference is used:

```
% perl -Mblib -MArrays -le 'print Arrays::sum_as_ref([5,6,7])'
18
```

Passing a numeric array from Perl to C as a packed string

NOTE   In XS, the sense of pack/unpack and input/output is very different than expected by a Perl programmer. INPUT is used in XS to indicate data passing into C (and out of Perl), and OUTPUT indicates data passing out of C and into Perl. More confusing is that occasionally the term *pack* is used to indicate conversion of a C array to a Perl array, and *unpack* is used to indicate conversion of a Perl array to a C array. This terminology is completely different than the Perl use of the pack and unpack functions (we use the Perl sense in this chapter). Thus a C array is a packed form of a Perl array. This makes sense, because a C array uses less memory than a Perl array. These confusions arise because XS exists so that Perl data can be handled by the Perl internals, and therefore the internals are seen as the primary consumer of the data.

The third way to pass an array into C is to pack the Perl array into a byte string and then pass that string into C, where it will be treated as a C array. From Perl, this technique would look like the following:

```
$packed = pack("i*", @values);
$sum = Arrays::sum_as_packed( $packed );
```

In XS, we could implement it as follows:

```
int
sum_as_packed( packed )        Interrogates the SV directly
  SV * packed                  rather than extracting a specific
                               piece of information
 PREINIT:
  int len;
  intArray * array;
                                       Retrieves a pointer to the
 CODE:                                 byte array from the SV
  array = (intArray *)SvPV_nolen( packed );
  len = SvCUR( packed ) / sizeof(intArray);   ❶
  RETVAL = sum( len, array );
 OUTPUT:
  RETVAL
```

❶ We calculate the number of elements in the array by asking the SV for the total number of bytes and then dividing by the number of bytes used to represent an integer.

The main point is that we are using the SV directly rather than asking XS to translate it for us. This approach is useful because the SV knows how many bytes it is holding. If this information is not required, or if you can pass in the number of elements of the array as an argument,[10] this XS code can be simplified:

```
int
sum_as_packed2( len, packed )    The length of the array is
  int len                        included as an argument
  char * packed   ❶
 CODE:
  RETVAL = sum( len, (intArray *)packed );   ❷
 OUTPUT:
  RETVAL
```

❶ We use char * to indicate that we are interested in the PV part of the SV. Alternatively, we could have associated intArray * with T_PV in the typemap file.

❷ Because we have a pointer to a char, we have to cast the pointer to type intArray before passing it to the sum function.

---

[10] Only if you're using an intermediary wrapper function. Do not ask people to provide information that Perl already knows!

6.6.2 Passing numeric arrays from C to Perl

An array can be returned to Perl either as a list pushed onto the stack or by creating a Perl array and returning the reference. You saw in section 6.5.3 how to return a hash reference and a list; the only difference for arrays is the use of av_ functions rather than hv_ functions.

This section will highlight some additional methods for returning (numeric) arrays that may be useful. We included these techniques for completeness, because they are used in existing code, but they are probably not the best approach for new code (explicit use of PPCODE or a Perl array is usually better).

Passing a numeric array from C to Perl as a list without PPCODE

We used the T_ARRAY typemap entry in "Passing a numeric array from Perl to C as a list," page 184, to pass a list into C. It can, in principle, also be used to return a list from C without worrying about looping and using the PUSHs macro (see section 6.5.3 for details about pushing elements onto the return stack).

The main problem is that this approach only works with XS CODE blocks (because OUTPUT typemap entries are used only when the OUTPUT keyword is used in XS), but the XS compiler always forces a single return value. In general, it is safer to ignore T_ARRAY for output and use PPCODE instead.

If you do want to use T_ARRAY to return an array, then the easiest trick is to co-opt the CLEANUP section and make explicit use of the XSRETURN function. Here is an example of how to use T_ARRAY to return an array of integers:

```
intArray *                              ❶
test_t_array()
 PREINIT:                               ┐ Creates a test array in C that
  intArray test[2];       ◄──┘ contains two elements
  U32 size_RETVAL;        ❷
 CODE:                                  ┐ For this example, we simply copy
  test[0] = 1; test[1] = 2;   ◄──┘ two numbers into the array
  size_RETVAL = 2;    ◄─── This line stores the size of the array
  RETVAL = test;      ◄─┐ RETVAL now points to the first
 OUTPUT:                │ element of our test array
  RETVAL   ◄─── Marks RETVAL for output
 CLEANUP:
  XSRETURN(size_RETVAL);   ❸
```

❶ The return type is a pointer to an array. This example uses the same typemap we have used for the previous array examples.

❷ T_ARRAY requires the declaration of this variable (technically declared as size_$var in the typemap file, but this variable will almost always be associated with RETVAL). The typemap uses it to determine how many elements in the array are to be copied to the stack.

❸ This macro will exit the XS routine just before the normal exit provided by xsubpp. The argument indicates how many items have been placed on the return stack.

Passing a numeric array from C to Perl as a packed string

Just as you can pass to XS a byte array generated by the Perl pack function (see "Passing a numeric array from Perl to C as a packed string," page 188), you can also return a byte array that can be unpacked with the Perl unpack function. If you know how many elements are to be stored in the array at compile time, XS provides a way of returning the packed string to Perl. This example returns three integers as a packed string:

```
array(int, 3)
return_packed()
 PREINIT:
  intArray test[3];
 CODE:
  test[0] = 1; test[1] = 2; test[2] = 3;
  RETVAL = test;
 OUTPUT:
  RETVAL
```

When compiled, this code copies 3 x sizeof(int) bytes from RETVAL. They can be unpacked in Perl with unpack("i*",$retval).

If the size of the return array is not known at compile-time, we must copy the bytes to the Perl variable using a modified form of the T_OPAQUEPTR typemap entry:

```
intArray *
return_npacked()
 PREINIT:
  U32 size_RETVAL;
  intArray test[3];
 CODE:
  test[0] = 1; test[1] = 2; test[2] = 3;
  size_RETVAL = 3;
  RETVAL = test;
 OUTPUT:
  RETVAL
```

The corresponding typemap entry is

```
intArray *       T_OPAQUEARRAY

OUTPUT
T_OPAQUEARRAY
        sv_setpvn($arg, (char *)$var, size_$var * sizeof(*$var));
```

We associate intArray * with T_OPAQUEARRAY. The only difference between this and T_OPAQUEPTR is that we have used the size_$var variable to indicate how many elements to copy.

In general, if packed strings are returned and the bytes are not required directly, it is better to provide a Perl wrapper to the XS function so the bytes are hidden from the caller.

NOTE When looking through the typemap file, you will see entries called T_PACKED and T_PACKEDARRAY. They are not designed for dealing with packed strings! They are generic entries for converting to and from C data, but they require you to supply explicit pack/unpack routines. These entries are discussed in appendix A.

6.6.3 The Perl Data Language

If you are dealing with large or multidimensional arrays, the techniques described so far will probably prove inadequate. You should seriously consider changing your approach and using the Perl Data Language (PDL; http://pdl.perl.org/). PDL was developed as a means to handle multidimensional arrays in Perl compactly and efficiently. These issues are extremely important in scientific computing and image processing for the following reasons:

- *Multidimensionality*—Perl has no real concept of multidimensional arrays. In C, a multidimensional array is simply a contiguous block of memory containing objects of identical type (see section 3.1 for an example). A Perl array can have references to other arrays in order to simulate additional dimensions, but nothing in the language forces the same number of elements in each row or column (this is much closer to the C implementation of string arrays). When the dimensionality is greater than two, the Perl approach becomes unwieldy; it is very time consuming to check the dimensionality of the data. The following code shows how Perl emulates 1-, 2-, and 3-d arrays:

```
@oned   = ( 1, 2 );
@twod   = ( [1,2], [3,4] );
@threed = ( [ [1,2], [3,4] ],   [ [5,6],[7,8] ] );
```

- *Compactness*—When the number of elements in an array is large, the representation of that array can have an enormous effect on the memory requirements of the program. In section 4.4, you saw that both Perl arrays and Perl scalars have a significant memory overhead compared to that required for single numbers. This overhead is accepted because of the enormous gain in functionality. In situations where you are dealing with blocks of numbers, this flexibility is not required. As an example, the previous 3-d array requires seven Perl arrays, eight integer scalars, and six references. On a 32-bit Linux system, this requirement totals about 128 bytes for just 8 numbers (assuming 12 bytes for an sv_any, 16 bytes for an xpviv, and 44 bytes for an xpvav). A C representation requires just 32 bytes (8 elements of 4 bytes each). Clearly, for arrays of a million pixels, the closer the representation is to pure C the more significant the memory savings will be.

- *Speed*—So far in this section, we have shown that passing arrays into and out of Perl requires loops to pack and unpack the array each time. When a large data array is being passed continually to and from C, the time overhead will be enormous. Additionally, for N-dimensional data arrays, the large number of dereferences required to return the data values will be significant.

It is therefore not surprising that PDL was developed by scientists[11] as an attempt to solve these problems without having to use expensive proprietary packages or a language other than Perl.

PDL deals with the problems of dimensionality, speed, and compactness by using a PDL object (known as a *piddle*[12]) to store the data and information such as the dimensionality and data type. In reality, a piddle is a C struct for efficiency, and the data is stored as a normal C array.[13] We will not attempt to provide a complete guide to PDL; we'll stay within the scope of this book and show you how to interact with PDL from within XS.

A PDL primer

PDL provides a shell for interactive use (called perldl) that can be useful for general Perl experimentation as well as for PDL. Here are some examples that will provide a taste; you can type them in at the perldl shell or in a program in conjunction with use PDL;:

```
$a = pdl([0,1,2],[3,4,5]);
```

This command creates a 3x2 piddle.

```
$a = sequence(3,2);
```

This command creates the same piddle using the sequence command. It is effectively an N-dimensional version of the .. Perl operator.

```
print $a;
```

This command prints a stringified form of the piddle. It works for reasonably sized piddles. The output is

---

[11] The primary developers of PDL are Karl Glazebrook (an astronomer), Tuomas Lukka (a computer scientist/physical chemist), and Christian Soeller (a bio-physicist).

[12] It is possible that only English readers will see the double meaning of this name!

[13] Version 1 of PDL stored the data as a packed string in an SV exactly as shown "Passing a numeric array from Perl to C as a packed string," page 188. Version 2 made the object more opaque.

```
[
 [0 1 2]
 [3 4 5]
]
```

The following command multiplies each element in the piddle by 2:

```
$a *= 2;
```

`$a` is now

```
[
 [ 0  2  4]
 [ 6  8 10]
]
```

In PDL, the standard operators (+, -, *, /, and so forth) are overloaded so that piddles act like normal Perl variables. By default, PDL does not do matrix operations on piddles (but it can be made to).

```
$b = $a->slice("1,");
```

This command extracts a slice from `$a`. Here we use object notation to invoke the `slice` method. In this case, we are extracting column 1 (column indexes are zero-based, as in Perl and C):

```
[
 [2]
 [8]
]
```

The following command creates a two-element piddle (`[10 20]`) and adds it to `$b`:

```
$c = pdl(10,20); $b += $c;
```

`$b` becomes

```
[
 [32]
 [38]
]
```

More important, `$a` now becomes

```
[
 [ 0 32  4]
 [ 6 38 10]
]
```

because `$b` is a slice from `$a`, and any changes to the elements of a slice are reflected in the related elements of the original piddle. This is one of the most powerful features of PDL.

PDL is a powerful tool for manipulating array data; you should consider it seriously for any project dealing with arrays and Perl.

PDL and XS

Now that we have shown the utility of PDL when using arrays, we will demonstrate how to use PDL from XS. When viewed from Perl, a piddle is seen as an object; but from within C, a piddle is represented as a structure (denoted by a `pdl *`). In general, you should use PDL with XS only if you want direct access to the structure. PDL provides easier methods of passing data to C routines with the `PDL::PP` (section 7.4) and `PDL::CallExt` modules.

The PDL infrastructure provides typemap entries to handle the conversion from and to the PDL structure:

```
pdl *                   T_PDL

INPUT

T_PDL
        $var = PDL->SvPDLV($arg)

OUTPUT

T_PDL
        PDL->SetSV_PDL($arg,$var);
```

These typemap entries use the programming interface (API) provided by the PDL core to translate Perl objects to the PDL structures.

This raises the issue of how to use C functions that are provided by a separate Perl module in your XS code. For external C libraries, you simply make sure you link against the library when the XS module is built. The PDL shared library[14] is installed somewhere in the Perl site library tree in PDL/Core/Core.so (on many Unix systems). A number of difficulties are associated with attempting to use this library directly from other XS modules. In order to link your PDL XS code against it, you would first need to locate the library file (using the `Config` module) and then convince `MakeMaker` that the file should be included, even though it does not look like a standard library. You can do this by fooling `MakeMaker` into thinking Core.so is an object file, but is not recommended.

Rather than link against the PDL library as part of the module build (no PDL modules do this), PDL provides a method to simplify access to the PDL API: storing pointers to the public functions in a C structure. A pointer to this structure is then stored in a Perl variable in the PDL namespace. To use a PDL function, all you need to do is retrieve this pointer from the Perl variable. This approach is also taken by the Perl/Tk module. XS provides a means of doing this at load time using the `BOOT:` section, and PDL developers recommend the following code:

NOTE   `BOOT:` is the XS equivalent of a `BEGIN` block.

---

[14] Assuming your Perl can support dynamic loading of libraries

```
#include "pdl.h"              ❶    We declare a pointer to a Core.
#include "pdlcore.h"                A Core is typedef'd to struct
static Core * PDL;    ◄──────        Core in pdlcore.h

SV* CoreSV;   ◄───  This pointer to an SV is used to store the
                    SV retrieved from the PDL namespace
MODULE = Arrays   PACKAGE = Arrays
                                              This line gets the variable
BOOT:                                              $PDL::SHARE
  /* Get pointer to structure of core shared C routines */
  CoreSV = perl_get_sv("PDL::SHARE",FALSE);  /* SV* value */   ◄──
  if (CoreSV==NULL)  ❷
    Perl_croak(aTHX_
                "This module requires use of PDL::Core first");
  PDL = INT2PTR(Core*, SvIV( CoreSV ));  /* Core* value */   ❸
```

❶ These are standard include files for PDL. They declare the PDL constants and the function structure.

❷ We must load the PDL::Core module before attempting to load this module, or $PDL::SHARE will not be defined. We can do so most easily by making sure our Perl module loads PDL::Core before calling the bootstrap method.

❸ We retrieve the integer part of the SV, cast it to type Core* using INT2PTR (see section 5.5.3), and store it in a C variable called PDL. The standard PDL typemap entries described earlier assume that we have done this, because they use the variable PDL as a pointer to a structure in order to run the conversion methods. Now we can use any public PDL function simply by using this variable.

With this groundwork in place, we can write a PDL version of our routine to sum the elements in an array using the sum function presented earlier.[15] Here is the XS snippet:

```
int
sum_as_pdl( in )
  pdl * in   ❶
 CODE:
  PDL->converttype( &in, PDL_L, 1);   ❷
  RETVAL = sum( in->nvals, (intArray *)in->data);   ❸
 OUTPUT:
  RETVAL
```

❶ We assume we have a PDL argument. If an array is passed in, it will be rejected by the SvPDLV function included from the typemap file.

❷ A PDL is typed (by default, all PDLs are double precision), and this line is responsible for converting it to an integer type so that it can be summed by our function. This

---

[15] Of course, we can just use the PDL sum method directly!

example is slightly naughty, because it converts the input PDL to integer format. In a real application, you should either make a copy so the input piddle is not modified, or write a sum function for each data type.

③ Here we find the number of elements in the PDL using the nvals part of the structure and retrieve the values using the data part.

To compile this XS code, we need to generate a Perl module wrapper that will load PDL and a Makefile.PL that will correctly locate the PDL include files and typemap file from the installed tree. Here is a suitable pm file:

```
package Arrays;

use PDL::Core;
use base qw/ DynaLoader /;

our $VERSION;

$VERSION = '1.00';

bootstrap Arrays;
```

The corresponding Makefile.PL is as follows:

```
use ExtUtils::MakeMaker;
use File::Spec;
use Config;

my $pdlroot =  File::Spec->catdir($Config{'installsitearch'},
                             "PDL", "Core");      ①
my $pdltypemap = File::Spec->catfile($pdlroot, "typemap.pdl");

# Write the makefile
WriteMakefile(
           'NAME'=> 'Arrays',
           'VERSION_FROM' => 'Arrays.pm', # finds $VERSION
           'PREREQ_PM' => { 'PDL' => '2.0'},     ②
           'INC'       => "-I$pdlroot",
           'TYPEMAPS'   => [ $pdltypemap ],     ③
           );
```

> The PDL typemap file is in the same directory as the include files

① The PDL-specific include files (pdl.h and pdlcore.h) are installed as part of PDL into the Perl installsitearch directory. This line uses the Config module to determine that location and File::Spec to append the PDL directory to that location.

② The PDL internals were completely rewritten for version 2.0. This line instructs MakeMaker to check the version of the installed PDL and to complain if the version number is less than 2.0.

③ The TYPEMAPS option allows us to specify additional typemap files. It is required because MakeMaker does not look in the PDL install directory by default.

6.6.4   Benchmarks

So far, we have shown four ways of passing numeric data into C for processing and the associated ways of returning arrays back to Perl. These methods can be summarized as follows:

- Using a list
- Using a reference to an array
- Using a packed string
- Using a PDL object

To finish this section about arrays, we will write a simple benchmark to compare the efficiency of these techniques using the summing code described earlier. The only exception is that we will use the native PDL sum function. Here's the code:

```
use Benchmark;
use Arrays;
use PDL;
use strict;

my @array = (0..100);
my $pdl   = sequence(long,101);

timethese(-3, {
    'PDL' => sub { sum($pdl); },
    'List'=> sub { Arrays::sum_as_list(@array) },
    'Ref' => sub { Arrays::sum_as_ref(\@array) },
    'Pack'=> sub { Arrays::sum_as_packed( pack("i*", @array) ); },
})
```

This benchmark runs for at least three seconds and gives the following output:

```
Benchmark: running List, PDL, Pack, Ref, each for at least 3 CPU
seconds...
      List:   3 wallclock secs ( 3.28 usr +  0.00 sys =  3.28 CPU)
              @ 110633.84/s (n=362879)
       Ref:   2 wallclock secs ( 3.01 usr +  0.00 sys =  3.01 CPU)
              @ 77112.62/s (n=232109)
      Pack:   4 wallclock secs ( 3.34 usr +  0.00 sys =  3.34 CPU)
              @ 52336.53/s (n=174804)
       PDL:   4 wallclock secs ( 3.08 usr +  0.00 sys =  3.08 CPU)
              @ 10284.09/s (n=31675)
```

Because we are asking Benchmark to run for a specific amount of time, the important information is the number of times the subroutine was executed per second. You can see that for a small array (in this case, 101 elements), a list is 10 times faster than a PDL, twice as fast as using pack, and one-and-a-half times faster than using a reference. The PDL solution is surprisingly slow in this case; this result is in part due to the additional overhead present in the PDL system that is not being used by our example. The packed string is expected to be slow because it calls an additional Perl function each time. The reference is slower than a list due to the overhead of taking the reference. If we now increase the size of the array by two orders of magnitude to 10,000 elements, we get a different result:

```
Benchmark: running List, PDL, Pack, Ref, each for at least 3 CPU
seconds...
       List:  3 wallclock secs ( 3.20 usr +  0.02 sys =  3.22 CPU)
              @ 1495.65/s (n=4816)
        PDL:  4 wallclock secs ( 3.20 usr +  0.00 sys =  3.20 CPU)
              @ 4372.81/s (n=13993)
       Pack:  3 wallclock secs ( 3.14 usr +  0.00 sys =  3.14 CPU)
              @ 448.09/s (n=1407)
        Ref:  3 wallclock secs ( 3.08 usr +  0.00 sys =  3.08 CPU)
              @ 917.21/s (n=2825)
```

Now PDL is much faster than the rest; the overhead due to the PDL infrastructure becomes insignificant when compared to the cost of converting large arrays into C data structures.

Of course, specific benchmarks cannot tell the whole story, and your final choice will depend on many factors. For example, if you require multiple array arguments, then you cannot use a simple list; if you want maximal distribution, you may not want to insist on the user's installing PDL.

6.6.5   Character strings

You saw in section 3.3.1 that an array of strings is represented in C as an array of pointers that point to the memory location of the start of each string; a string is a NUL-terminated array of characters, and a string array is an array of pointers. In general for XS, you can create and populate the char** like any other array; however, you must take care if the new array is to persist after the call to the XS function—in the simple case, you copy the pointers from the SVs and use them, but once you return to Perl, there is no guarantee that the SV will still be around. In that case, you will have to take copies of the entire string rather than just storing the pointer.

Converting a char** to a Perl array is simply a case of stepping through the C array and copying the contents to the Perl array.

The following XS code demonstrates both techniques by copying an input array to a char** and then copying that char** back onto the output stack. Variants involving output references or input lists will be very similar. Note that this example does not have complete error checking:

```
void
copy_char_arr( avref )
   AV * avref;    ❶
  PREINIT:
   char ** array;
   int len;
   SV ** elem;
   int i;
  PPCODE:
   len = av_len( avref ) + 1;
```

```
    /* First allocate some memory for the pointers */
    array = get_mortalspace( len * sizeof( *array ));    ❷

    /* Loop over each element copying pointers to the new array */
    for (i=0; i<len; i++) {
      elem = av_fetch( avref, i, 0 );
      array[i] = SvPV( *elem, PL_na );    ❸
    }

    /* Now copy it back onto the stack */
    for (i=0; i<len; i++) {
      XPUSHs( sv_2mortal( newSVpv( array[i], 0) ) );    ❹
    }
```

❶ In this example, the input is expected to be a reference to an array, and the output is a list:

```
@copy = copy_char_arr(\@src);
```

❷ We get some temporary storage to hold the array of pointers. The get_mortalspace function is identical to the intArrayPtr function shown earlier, except that it takes the number of bytes as an argument rather than the number of integers.

❸ This line retrieves the pointer from the SV (converting it to a PV if required) and then stores it in the array. If we needed to copy the string first, we would also need to allocate some memory for it here.

❹ We copy each string from the string array back into a new SV and push it onto the argument stack.

If you've been reading the typemap file, you may have noticed that char** already has an explicit entry. Our example ignores this entry because in this case, it is simpler to use the array reference directly. The char** typemap entry uses T_PACKEDARRAY.[16] This typemap requires the user to supply packing and unpacking routines with an INPUT entry of

```
$var = XS_unpack_$ntype($arg)
```

and an OTPUT entry of

```
XS_pack_$ntype($arg, $var, count_$ntype);
```

So, for char**, the routines will be called XS_unpack_charPtrPtr and XS_pack_charPtrPtr. The behavior of these particular functions is well defined for a string array (either converting an SV* to a char** or vice versa), but you still have to provide your own. The previous example becomes the following code if we use the standard typemaps (with minimal error checking in this example):

---

[16] As of Perl 5.8.0. In earlier versions of Perl it used T_PACKED.

```
char ** XS_unpack_charPtrPtr( SV * arg ) {
  AV * avref;
  char ** array;
  int len;
  SV ** elem;
  int i;

  avref = (AV*)SvRV(arg);
  len = av_len( avref ) + 1;
  /* First allocate some memory for the pointers
     plus one for the end */
  array = get_mortalspace( (len+1) * sizeof( *array ));

  /* Loop over each element copying pointers to the array */
  for (i=0; i<len; i++) {
    elem = av_fetch( avref, i, 0);
    array[i] = SvPV_nolen( *elem );
  }
  /* add a null */
  array[len] = NULL;

  return array;
}

void XS_pack_charPtrPtr( SV * arg, char ** array, int count) {
  int i;
  AV * avref;

  avref = (AV*)sv_2mortal((SV*)newAV());
  for (i=0; i<count; i++) {
    av_push(avref, newSVpv(array[i], strlen(array[i])));
  }
  SvSetSV( arg, newRV((SV*)avref));
}

MODULE = Example          PACKAGE = Example

char **
copy_char_arr( array )
  char ** array
 PREINIT:
  int count_charPtrPtr;
  int i;
 CODE:
  RETVAL = array;
  /* decide how many elements to return */
  i = 0;
  while ( array[i] != NULL ) {
    i++;
  }
  /* loop exits with count */
  count_charPtrPtr = i;
 OUTPUT:
  RETVAL
```

This code is *significantly* longer than the first version, even though much of it is identical. Of course, if you are processing many string arrays the same way you can move the packing/unpacking code into a library and leave just the XS code, which is much cleaner.

6.7   CALLBACKS

A *callback* is a user-supplied function that is called by another function. The classic example of the use of callbacks in Perl is the Tk module. Whenever a Tk event occurs (for example, a button is clicked on the GUI), Tk determines whether a Perl subroutine should be called to process the event. The code in listing 6.1 shows how you can set up a Tk callback.

Listing 6.1   A simple Tk callback

```
use Tk;
use strict;

my $MW = new MainWindow;
my $button = $MW->Button( -text => "Exit",
                          -command => sub { exit; } );

$button->pack();
MainLoop;
```

When we run this program, it displays a window containing a single button. When we click the button, the callback associated with the button (configured using the -command option) is executed and the program exits. The callback is not called directly by user code; it is called from the event loop from C code.

The main difficulty with handling callbacks in XS is that Perl stores subroutines in a CV (section 4.9), whereas C callbacks are implemented as pointers to a C function (section 3.2.2). In order for C to call a Perl subroutine, you must insert an intermediate function that knows about Perl. This indirection leads to all the complications associated with using callbacks from Perl.

There are usually three types of callbacks that must be handled:

- A callback used for a single command, with control passing back to Perl once the callback has been used. This type is common in the qsort function and the standard search functions (such as bsearch).

- A single callback registered at one point in the program and then executed some time later (for example, an error handler).

- Multiple subroutines registered as callbacks that can be called at any time (for example, event-driven programs).

We will discuss each of these types in turn.

6.7.1 Immediate callbacks

The simplest type of callback is one in which the C function executes given the supplied callback and then completes before returning from XS. The C qsort function provides an excellent example. You can use this function to sort arrays; Perl used to use it to implement the Perl sort routine. The calling signature is

```
void qsort(void *base, size_t nel, size_t width,
           int (*compar)(const void *, const void *));
```

where *base* is a pointer to the start of the array, *nel* is the number of elements in the array, *width* is the number of bytes used to represent each element, and *compar* is a pointer to a function that is used to compare individual elements of the array. The compar function holds the C callback.

Obviously, the Perl interface to this function should behave like the standard sort function:

```
@sorted = qsorti &compar, @unsorted;
```

We are calling the function qsorti to indicate that this sort function can only be used to sort arrays of integers. (This limitation simplifies the example code and allows us to focus on the implementation of the callback rather than the complication of handling all data types.) For this example, we will use a module called CallBack. The XS code in listing 6.2 implements the qsorti function.

Listing 6.2 Implementing the qsort function with a callback

```
#include "EXTERN.h"
#include "perl.h"
#include "XSUB.h"
#include <stdlib.h>                    Creates a new type based on
                                       int so that we can associate
typedef int intArray;      ◄───────   it with the T_ARRAY typemap

/* Static memory for qsort callback */
static SV * qsortsv;     ❶

/* Routine to allocate memory for integer array */
/* Allocate the memory as a mortal SV so that it is
   freed automatically */
intArray * intArrayPtr ( int num ) {     ❷
  SV * mortal;
  mortal = sv_2mortal( NEWSV(0, num * sizeof(intArray) ) );
  return (intArray *)SvPVX(mortal);
}

/* The callback for qsort */                   This C function is
int qsorti_cb( const void *a, const void *b) {  ◄──┘ called by qsort

  dSP;   ❸
  int count;
  int answer;
```

```
ENTER;
SAVETMPS;                    ❹
PUSHMARK(SP);

/* Push some SVs onto the stack with the values of a and b */
XPUSHs(sv_2mortal(newSViv(*(int *)a)));    ⟵┐ Pushes the arguments supplied
XPUSHs(sv_2mortal(newSViv(*(int *)b)));    ⟵┤ by qsort onto the stack so that
                                            │ our Perl callback can access them
PUTBACK;   ❺

count = call_sv(qsortsv, G_SCALAR );   ❻

SPAGAIN;   ❼

if (count != 1)   ❽
  croak("callback returned more than 1 value\n");

answer = POPi;   ⟵┐ Reads the answer (as an
                  │ integer) off the stack
FREETMPS;   ❾
LEAVE;

return answer;   ⟵ Returns the answer to qsort
}
MODULE = CallBack        PACKAGE = CallBack   ⟵ The XS code begins
void
qsorti(cb, array, ...)   ❿
  SV * cb   ⓫
  intArray * array   ┐ Specifies a prototype for
 PREINIT:            │ the XS function. This
  U32 i;             │ prototype matches that
 PROTOTYPE: &@   ⟵──┘ of the Perl sort function
 PPCODE:                      ┌ Stores the code reference
  qsortsv = cb;   ⟵──────────┤ in a static variable for later
                              └ retrieval by our C callback
  qsort( array, ix_array, sizeof(int), qsorti_cb);   ⓬

  /* now need to push the elements back onto the stack */
  for ( i =0; i < ix_array; i++) {   ⟵┐ Finally, unpacks the integer
    XPUSHs(sv_2mortal(newSViv(array[i])));   │ array and pushes it onto the
  }                                          └ return argument stack
```

❶ This is some static memory that is used to store the code reference. It is required because our C callback must have access to the Perl code reference.

❷ This is called automatically as part of the T_ARRAY typemap entry. It is used to dynamically allocate memory for the C integer array. It uses a mortal SV to allocate the memory rather than the New macro. Doing so saves us from worrying about freeing the memory, because Perl will do it automatically when the XS function returns.

❸ Now we declare variables that we need. dSP is just a macro that gives us access to Perl's argument stack.

4 ENTER, SAVETMPS, and PUSHMARK are always used on entry to a callback to allow Perl to store the current status of the stack. They are paired with PUTBACK, FREETMPS, and LEAVE.

5 This line indicates that we have finished configuring the stack for our Perl function. It forms the end bracket for the PUSHMARK.

6 This line calls the Perl code block contained in qsortsv and returns the number of arguments that were placed onto the stack by the subroutine. The G_SCALAR flag indicates that we are calling the code block in a scalar context.

7 Because the stack no longer reflects the state it was in on entry (because the Perl subroutine we just called has messed with it), we use SPAGAIN to retrieve the current stack information.

8 In the unlikely event that more than one argument was returned from the Perl subroutine, we shut down the program. This should not happen because we forced scalar context.

9 This line frees any temporary SVs that were created (for example, the two we pushed onto the stack) and leaves the current context.

10 Our XS function is called qsorti, and it takes a code reference and variable-length list as arguments. The list will be processed using the T_ARRAY typemap entry.

11 We use a simple SV as an argument, because the call_sv function can automatically deal with an SV containing a reference to a CV.

12 We run the normal C qsort function using our array and the C callback that we defined at the top of the file. The ix_array variable is defined and set by the T_ARRAY typemap.

We also need a private typemap to indicate that an intArray * should be processed using the T_ARRAY typemap entry:

```
intArray *      T_ARRAY
```

Once we compile this module, we can do the following:

```
use strict;
use CallBack;

my @unsorted = (20,4,6,5,10,1);

my @sorted =  CallBack::qsorti { $_[0] <=> $_[1] } @unsorted;
print join("-",@sorted);
```

This module differs from the normal sort function in only two ways: it only sorts integer arrays, and there is no special use of $a and $b. Thus @_ must be used to obtain the sort arguments.

To summarize, we had to do the following to use the callback:

1 Write a C function that can be used as the callback and then use this function to configure the stack and call the Perl subroutine

2 Store the code reference (as an SV*) in some static memory for later retrieval

3 Call the C function (in this case, qsort) using our intermediary C function as the callback

6.7.2 Deferred callbacks

A *deferred callback* is registered with one command but called from another later in the program. A common example is an error handler. The error handler is registered early in the program but is called only when an error occurs.

To demonstrate this usage, we will use our existing qsort example but change the Perl calling interface to

```
register_qsort_cb(\&callback);
@sorted = qsorti_cb(@unsorted);
```

The obvious implementation is to simply split the existing XSUB entry into two parts:

```
void
register_qsort_cb( cb )
  SV * cb
 CODE:
  qsortsv = (SV *) cb;

void
qsorti_cb(array, ...)
  intArray * array
 PREINIT:
  U32 i;
 PPCODE:
  qsort( array, ix_array, sizeof(int), qsorti_cb);

  /* now need to push the elements back onto the stack */
  for ( i =0; i < ix_array; i++) {
    XPUSHs(sv_2mortal(newSViv(array[i])));
  }
```

The corresponding modified test program is as follows:

```
use strict;
use CallBack;

CallBack::register_qsort_cb( sub {$_[0] <=> $_[1] } );
my @unsorted = (20,4,6,5,10,1);
my @sorted = CallBack::qsorti_cb( @unsorted );
print join("-",@sorted);
```

If we run this program, we get the following

```
Undefined subroutine &main::20 called at ./cbtest line 6
```

(or something similar, depending on your system). The problem is that the SV stored in qsortsv has been reallocated by Perl between the time it's registered and used. Specifically, in this case, the SV now seems to be holding the first element of the new array. Because we are only storing a pointer to an SV that is meant to contain a reference to a subroutine (or a name of a sub), we are sensitive to the SV's changing. To overcome this problem, we can either copy the contents of the SV to a new SV when storing the callback or extract the CV that is referenced by the SV and store a pointer to that instead. Changing register_qsort_cb to

```
void
register_qsort_cb( cb )
  CV * cb
 CODE:
  qsortsv = (SV *) cb;
```

fixes the problem, because the CV * typemap entry retrieves the reference from the SV. One issue is that this approach will work only with code references (rather than sub names), but usually that is not a problem. A bigger problem is that technically, the reference count on the CV should be incremented when it is stored to indicate to Perl that another part of the system is interested in the CV. The reference count should also be decremented on the old CV whenever a new callback is registered. For simple systems, this step is usually not worth bothering with (in most cases, some other part of the system is sure to keep the CV alive). The better solution is to simply copy the SV on entry, because the SvSetSV function (newSVsv also calls it) automatically takes care of reference counting (both incrementing the reference count of the new value and decrementing the reference count of the variable being replaced):

```
void
register_qsort_cb( cb )
  SV * cb
 CODE:
  if (qsortsv == (SV*)NULL) {
      /* This is first time in so create an SV */
      qsortsv = newSVsv(cb) ;
  } else {
      /* overwrite since we have already stored something */
      SvSetSV(qsortsv, cb) ;
  }
```

This technique relies on knowing whether the function has been called before. To make this fact explicit, we can modify the declaration of qsortsv slightly:

```
static SV * qsortsv = (SV*)NULL;
```

6.7.3 Multiple callbacks

So far, we have only registered a single callback at any one time, and that callback has been stored in a static variable. In more complex situations, such as event-driven programs, you'll need to store many callbacks; so, you must use a different scheme.

Currently, each time a callback is registered, the previous callback is lost. You can use a number of approaches in this situation, and the choice depends mainly on how the underlying library is implemented.

If the calling interface provides a means for storing extra information along with the C callback (for example, a C struct is used that can contain a pointer to user-supplied data), then you can store a copy of the SV there and retrieve it when the callback occurs. The Tk module takes this approach.

If there is no provision for user-supplied data but the callback is associated with a specific data structure (such as a filehandle), then you can store the Perl callback in a static hash associated with the data structure and retrieve the relevant SV from the hash as required. For the particular example of a filehandle, you could use an array indexed by the file descriptor.

If the callback is passed arguments that do not identify the source (such as a text string from a file), then your only option is to write a number of callback functions in C and associate each with a specific Perl callback. The disadvantage of this approach is that the number of callbacks is limited to a fixed number.

The Tk module is an interesting example, because it allows you to provide many more ways of specifying a callback than simply providing a code reference or subroutine name. Some examples are as follows:

```
sub { }, \&somesub
```

This is a standard subroutine reference; it's used in listing 6.1.

```
[ \&somesub, $arg1, $arg2 ]
```

This code invokes a subroutine with arguments. The arguments are grouped in an anonymous array.

```
[ "method", $object ]
```

Here we invoke a method on an object. The arguments are grouped in an anonymous array.

The module achieves this flexibility by, in effect, storing the callback information in an object (in class Tk::Callback) and then invoking the Call method to run the callback.[17] If necessary, you can use this approach to simplify the C part of the callback code, because you can create the callback object in Perl (to contain whatever you want it to) and then pass it to C; the C callback code can invoke the Perl Call method on the object.

---

[17] The Call method in Tk::Callback is the Perl interface, but the methods are coded in C for efficiency. See the file Event/pTkCallback.c in the Tk source distribution for details.

6.8 OTHER LANGUAGES

We have been focusing on how to pass information between Perl and C, because Perl is written in C and large numbers of libraries are also written in C. Because Perl is written in C, it can communicate with other languages that can be accessed from C. This section describes how to link Perl to two other languages (C++ and Fortran) and touches on a third language (Java). If you have no interest in these languages, feel free to skip this section and rejoin us at section 6.9.

6.8.1 Linking Perl to C++

C++ is an evolution of C (the name indicates that this language is a developed C language) with the addition of a true object-oriented framework. In general, C++ compilers can compile C code as well as C++ code (although they don't have to); when the OO framework is stripped away, the core language is clearly based on C. However, contrary to popular belief and despite many similarities, C++ is not simply a superset of C—there are legal constructs in both languages that are illegal in the other.

To provide interfaces to C++ libraries, you can use XS as before—but this time in a C++ style. Because C compilers do not understand C++ and will not include the correct C++ infrastructure libraries, you can no longer use the C compiler that was used to build Perl. The first step in building a C++ interface is therefore to fix the Makefile.PL file so that it uses your C++ compiler. You can do so simply by using the CC key to WriteMakefile:

```
use ExtUtils::MakeMaker;

WriteMakefile(
      NAME => 'Coordinate',
      VERSION_FROM => 'Coordinate.pm',
      LD     => 'g++',
      CC     => 'g++',
);
```

This program can be used to configure a module called Coordinate (presented in a moment), and we replace the linker and the compiler command with g++. For compatibility with other operating systems, you can either guess the compiler name at this stage (for example, CC on Solaris; we take this approach later with Fortran) or simply ask for it from the command line.

The second change you have to deal with is found at the top of the XS file. In the XS files we have used so far, the beginning looks something like

```
#include "EXTERN.h"    /* std perl include */
#include "perl.h"      /* std perl include */
#include "XSUB.h"      /* XSUB include */
```

These are C include files rather than C++ include files, so we must alert the C++ compiler. We do so by adding some conditional code to the file that is included only when the routine is compiled as C++:

```
#ifdef __cplusplus
extern "C" {
#endif
#include "EXTERN.h"    /* std perl include */
#include "perl.h"      /* std perl include */
#include "XSUB.h"      /* XSUB include */
#ifdef __cplusplus
}
#endif
```

If this code is processed by a C++ compiler, the include files will be enclosed in an extern "C" block to indicate that the enclosed code is C rather than C++. If you want to be safe, you can use this approach for all your XS modules, because it will trigger only if a C++ compiler is building the module.

We will demonstrate some of the issues with C++ and Perl by writing a Perl interface to the simple C++ class in listing 6.3 (as hinted from the Makefile.PL example, we'll call the Perl module Coordinate).

Listing 6.3   C++ Coordinate class

```
class Coordinate {
    int _x, _y;
  public:
    Coordinate() {
      _x = _y = 0;
    }
    Coordinate(const int xval, const int yval) {
      _x = xval;
      _y = yval;
    }
    Coordinate(const Coordinate &from) {
      _x = from._x;
      _y = from._y;
    }

    void setX(const int val);
    void setY(const int val);
    int getX() { return _x; }
    int getY() { return _y; }

    int distance( const Coordinate &from);
    int distance( const int x, const int y);
  };

void Coordinate::setX(const int val) {
    _x = val;
}

void Coordinate::setY(const int val) {
    _y = val;
}
```

```cpp
int Coordinate::distance( const int x, const int y) {
  int xdiff, ydiff, sumsq;

  xdiff = x - _x;
  ydiff = y - _y;
  sumsq = (xdiff * xdiff) + (ydiff * ydiff);

  return int( sqrt( sumsq ));
}
int Coordinate::distance( const Coordinate &from ) {
  return this->distance( from._x, from._y );
}
```

This simple class stores X and Y coordinates. It has accessor methods for getting and setting the values and includes a method for finding the distance between these coordinates and some other position. If you are more comfortable in Perl than C++, listing 6.4 is an equivalent implementation in Perl (lacking a lot of error checking and comments).

Listing 6.4   Perl Coordinate class

```perl
package Coordinate;

sub new {
  my $proto = shift;
  my $class = ref($proto) || $proto;

  my ($x, $y) = (0,0);
  if (scalar(@_) == 1) {
    $x = $_[0]->getX;
    $y = $_[0]->getY;
  } elsif (scalar(@_) == 2) {
    $x = shift;
    $y = shift;
  }
  return bless { _x => $x, _y => $y }, $class;
}
sub setX { $_[0]->{_x} = $_[1] };
sub setY { $_[0]->{_y} = $_[1] };
sub getX { $_[0]->{_x} };
sub getY { $_[0]->{_y} };

sub distance {
  my ($self, $x, $y) = @_;
  if (UNIVERSAL::isa($x, "Coordinate")) {
    $y = $x->getX;
    $x = $x->getY;
  }
  my $xdiff = $x - $self->getX;
  my $ydiff = $y - $self->getY;
  my $sumsq = ($xdiff * $xdiff) + ($ydiff*$ydiff);
```

```
    return int( sqrt( $sumsq ) );
}

1;
```

<hr/>

We expect the Perl interface to be used in the following manner

```
$c1 = new Coordinate();
$c2 = new Coordinate( 3, 4);

$distance = $c1->distance( $c2 );
```

and we would like as much of that as possible to happen in XS. Here is the XS code for the simple part of the interface that includes a constructor that takes zero arguments, the accessor methods, and a version of the distance method that takes X and Y coordinates as arguments:[18]

```
MODULE = Coordinate   PACKAGE = Coordinate

Coordinate *
Coordinate::new()

MODULE = Coordinate PACKAGE = CoordinatePtr

int
Coordinate::getX()

int
Coordinate::getY()

void
Coordinate::setY( y )
  int y

void
Coordinate::setX( x )
  int x

int
Coordinate::distance( x, y )
  int x
  int y
```

As you can see, this XS code is just as simple as any code written for a C interface. The main difference is that we specify the C++ class name as well as the method, and we write a new method even though the C++ class does not explicitly have one. These hints are used by xsubpp to decide whether you are interfacing to a C++ library or a C library. All Perl methods require that the object be passed in as the first argument. This still happens; but rather than explicitly add the instance variable to the

<hr/>

[18] Because this example code is not from an external library, you can place it at the top of the XS file as you would for normal C code (make sure you put it before the MODULE line).

argument list (as would be required for a C library you were treating as an object-oriented library), xsubpp adds the required code automatically. Additionally, when xsubpp sees a function that looks like a C++ constructor, it automatically adds the C++ code required to instantiate an object, returning a pointer to it. Finally, the object itself is returned as a pointer to the C++ object; because we are using the T_PTROBJ typemap, the objects created by the constructor are blessed into the Perl class CoordinatePtr rather than simply Coordinate. If this bothers you, you can supply a new typemap OUTPUT entry that will ignore the pointer.

With the following minimalist Perl module

```
package Coordinate;

use base qw/ DynaLoader /;
use vars qw/ $VERSION /;

$VERSION = '0.01';

bootstrap Coordinate $VERSION;

1;
```

and a local typemap file declaring a Coordinate* as a Perl object

```
Coordinate *        T_PTROBJ
```

we can build this module. On a Gnu-based system, you might get something similar to the following:

```
% make
/usr/bin/perl -I/usr/lib/perl5/5.6.0/i386-linux
    -I/usr/lib/perl5/5.6.0
    /usr/lib/perl5/5.6.0/ExtUtils/xsubpp
     -typemap /usr/lib/perl5/5.6.0/ExtUtils/typemap
     Coordinate.xs > Coordinate.xsc &&
              mv Coordinate.xsc Coordinate.c
Please specify prototyping behavior for Coordinate.xs
g++ -c  -fno-strict-aliasing -O2 -DVERSION=\"0.01\"
    -DXS_VERSION=\"0.01\" -fPIC
    -I/usr/lib/perl5/5.6.0/i386-linux/CORE
    Coordinate.c
LD_RUN_PATH="" g++ -o blib/arch/auto/Coordinate/Coordinate.so
    -shared -L/usr/local/lib Coordinate.o
chmod 755 blib/arch/auto/Coordinate/Coordinate.so
```

We can test it with the following test program (either called test.pl or placed in the t directory):

```
# Test Coordinate class
use Test;
BEGIN { plan tests => 3 }

use Coordinate;

$c = new Coordinate();
```

```
ok( $c->getX(), 0);
ok( $c->getY(), 0);

$d = $c->distance( 3, 4 );
ok( $d, 5);
```

If everything is working, we get three oks when we run make test.

So far, we have shown that providing an interface to a simple C++ class is essentially as simple as providing an interface for a C library. Unfortunately, C++ allows multiple functions to be defined with the same name; the compiler decides which one to use on the basis of the arguments. Because Perl is not strongly typed, this kind of interface is difficult to implement. In general, there are two ways to deal with the issue of method overloading from Perl:

- Provide an XS method for each overloaded C++ method and give each one a different name. You can then either use those methods directly in your public Perl interface or, more likely, write some Perl code that will decide which C++ method to use on the basis of the Perl arguments.

- Provide a single XS method, using the items variable to determine how many arguments were provided and, if the argument count is ambiguous, determining the types (IV, NV, or PV) of the supplied Perl variables.

Because this is a book about XS, we will adopt the second approach to finish the example; but if you are more proficient programming in Perl, never be afraid to use the first option (the Perl code will be simpler, if nothing else). Listing 6.5 gives the XS code required to make full use of the C++ method overloading.

Listing 6.5   XS code using C++ method overloading

```
MODULE = Coordinate   PACKAGE = Coordinate

Coordinate *
Coordinate::new( ... )
 PREINIT:
  int x;
  int y;
  Coordinate * from;
 CODE:
  if (items == 1) {
    RETVAL = new Coordinate();
  } else if (items == 2) {
    if (sv_derived_from(ST(1), "CoordinatePtr")) {
        IV tmp = SvIV((SV*)SvRV(ST(1)));
        from = INT2PTR(Coordinate *,tmp);
    }
    else
        croak("from is not of type CoordinatePtr");
    RETVAL = new Coordinate( *from );
  } else if (items == 3) {
    x = (int)SvIV(ST(1));
```

```
      y = (int)SvIV(ST(2));
      RETVAL = new Coordinate(x, y );
    } else {
      croak("Too many arguments to distance");
    }
  OUTPUT:
   RETVAL


MODULE = Coordinate PACKAGE = CoordinatePtr

int
Coordinate::getX()

int
Coordinate::getY()

void
Coordinate::setY( y )
   int y

void
Coordinate::setX( x )
   int x

int
Coordinate::distance( ... )
 PREINIT:
  int x;
  int y;
  Coordinate * from;
 CODE:
  if (items == 2) {
    if (sv_derived_from(ST(1), "CoordinatePtr")) {
        IV tmp = SvIV((SV*)SvRV(ST(1)));
        from = INT2PTR(Coordinate *,tmp);
    }
    else
        croak("from is not of type CoordinatePtr");
    RETVAL = THIS->distance( *from );
  } else if (items == 3) {
    x = (int)SvIV(ST(1));
    y = (int)SvIV(ST(2));
    RETVAL = THIS->distance(x, y );
  } else {
    croak("Too many arguments to distance");
  }
  OUTPUT:
   RETVAL
```

This is a special variable created automatically by xsubpp. It is the C++ version of the Perl object

Because none of the overloaded methods have the same argument counts, the method switching is done entirely on the value of the items variable. The major complicating factor is that because we have a variable number of arguments (indicated by the

. . .), xsubpp can no longer extract the variable we want from the arguments stack using the typemap entries. All the work to process the argument stack must be done in the XS code! We have simply copied the typemap entries by hand. For the long typemaps (such as those for CoordinatePtr objects) it is best to extract the typemap code into a helper function, because it will be reused many times for a normal module.

We hope this whirlwind tour of using C++ with Perl and XS has shown you the possibilities and the difficulties involved with a C++ interface. In the next section, we will step back in time to cover Fortran.

6.8.2 Linking Perl to Fortran

Although Fortran has been around since the 1960s and its popularity is fading, enormous numbers of scientific libraries are available in this language; you might want to use them from Perl. Most Fortran implementations allow the object code and libraries to be included in C programs, but you must deal with the following issues when doing so:

- *Passing by reference*—All arguments are passed to Fortran subroutines as pointers, and it is not possible to pass by value.[19]

- *Types*—The variable types in Fortran are similar (there are integers, floating-point numbers, and strings), but you must be aware of the differences in representation. For example, it is possible that the number of bytes used to represent an INTEGER in Fortran is different than the default int in C. Usually this difference is not an issue.

- *Strings*—Fortran requires you to specify the lengths of all strings. Rather than using a null as a string terminator, the compiler automatically passes a length argument to subroutines in addition to the pointer to the string itself. When you're passing strings between C and Fortran, additional arguments are required because the C compiler will not add them automatically. The position of these arguments depends on the compiler. The most popular approach in Unix systems is to add all the lengths in order to the end of the calling list (the approach taken with g77, Sun Fortran, and Digital Unix Fortran), but you can also add the lengths into the argument list immediately following the string in question (as with Microsoft Visual C++ and Fortran). When you're sending a C string to a Fortran subroutine, the string should be padded with blanks (if it is bigger than the current contents); when returning a string from Fortran, you should add the null.

- *Packing order*—Perhaps the largest difference between C and Fortran is the order in which multidimensional arrays are stored in memory. Fortran arranges

---

[19] Modern Fortran implementations provide the %VAL function to let you pass pointers by value from integers.

arrays in column-major order (the column index is incremented before the row index in memory), whereas C arranges arrays in row-major order (the row index is incremented before the column index). Figure 6.1 shows this difference when using a 3-by-2 array containing the numbers 1 through 6. The top diagram shows the order of the elements in memory, the middle diagram shows how C would arrange these elements, and the lower diagram shows how Fortran would arrange them. Thus element [1][1] in C is not the same as element (2,2) in Fortran (additionally, C begins counting at zero, whereas Fortran begins counting from one). If you wish to pass a multidimensional array between C and Fortran, it will have to be translated into the correct order.

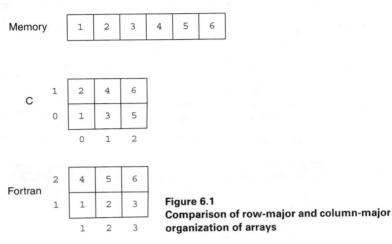

Figure 6.1
Comparison of row-major and column-major organization of arrays

- *String arrays*—Because strings in Fortran are of a specified length, arrays of strings in Fortran are simply contiguous blocks of memory rather than arrays of pointers. For strings of length 20, this memory layout is equivalent to the Perl code $packed = pack("a20",@array);. Thus it's easy to pass string arrays from Perl to Fortran.

- *Linker names*—Some compilers (especially on Unix) append an underscore (_) to the end of the subroutine name when the object code is generated. For example, a Fortran subroutine called MYSUB would be stored in the object file as mysub_. You need to know whether this happens on your platform. If you don't know, the easiest approach is to compile a Fortran program and examine the symbols.[20]

- *Linking*—When you link a Fortran library with a C program, you will also need to link with the Fortran runtime library. This library is included automatically

---

[20] Use the nm command on Unix systems.

when you use a Fortran compiler for the link, but you must specify it explicitly when linking from a C compiler.

Now that we have described the issues involved in calling Fortran subroutine libraries from C, we will provide a quick example (no arrays) of how to do this from XS. Our example provides some glue to talk to the PGPLOT Fortran library.[21] We will use the following simple subroutines from this library:

```
PGEND();
PGSCR(INTEGER CI, REAL CR, REAL CG, REAL CB);
INTEGER PGBEG(INTEGER UNIT, CHARACTER*(*) FILE,
              INTEGER NXSUB, INTEGER NYSUB);
PGQINF(CHARACTER*(*) ITEM, CHARACTER*(*) VALUE, INTEGER LENGTH);
```

On Linux with g77, this would translate to the following C code:

```
void pgend_();
void pgscr_(int *ci, float *cr, float *cg, float *cb);
int pgbeg_(int *unit, char *file, int *nxsub,
           int *nysub, int len_file);
void pgqinf_(char *item, char *value, int *length,
             int len_item, int len_value);
```

Once we know this translation, the XS code becomes straightforward (see listing 6.6).

Listing 6.6   Calling Fortran subroutine libraries from XS

```
#include "EXTERN.h"
#include "perl.h"
#include "XSUB.h"

#define F77BUFFER  256        ❶

#define pgend pgend_          ❷
#define pgscr pgscr_

MODULE = PGPLOT    PACKAGE = PGPLOT

void
pgend()                       ❸

void
pgscr(ci, cr, cg, cb)         ❹
  int &ci
  int &cr
  int &cg
  int &cb

int
```

---

[21] Tim Pearson's PGPLOT library is available from Caltech (http://www.astro.caltech.edu/~tjp/pgplot/) and can be used to generate scientific plots. The PGPLOT Perl module by Karl Glazebrook, using the C binding to this library, is available from the Comprehensive Perl Archive Network (CPAN; http://www.cpan.org/).

```
pgbeg(unit, file, nxsub, nysub)     ◁─┐  This function is not as simple.
   int &unit                           │  It takes four input arguments,
   char * file                         │  but one is a string
   int &nxsub
   int &nysub
 CODE:
  RETVAL = pgbeg_(&unit, file, &nxsub, &nysub, strlen(file));    ❺
 OUTPUT:
  RETVAL

void
pgqinf(item, value, length)    ❻
   char * item
   char * value = NO_INIT
   int length = NO_INIT
 PREINIT:        ❼
  char buff[F77BUFFER + 1];
 CODE:
  value = buff;
  pgqinf_(item, value, &length, strlen(item), F77BUFFER);    ❽
  value[length+1] = '\0';    ❾
 OUTPUT:
  value
  length
```

❶ We use this definition to specify the maximum size of static buffers required to receive strings from Fortran subroutines.

❷ We can set up preprocessor symbols that will let us use the expected names in our XS code but will tell the C compiler to look for the Fortran names. In principle, we could define all the functions this way. For this example, it is only convenient to do this for simple functions (those not using character strings, arrays, or multiple return values) that the XS compiler can deal with automatically without CODE blocks. Note that the function will look OK from Perl because the C code generated from the XS code registers the function using the XS name rather than subjecting it to the C preprocessor.

❸ pgend is simple because the XS compiler assumes it can call a C function pgend even though the C preprocessor will translate that text to pgend_. Without the definition at the top of the file, the XS name will be different than the function name, so a CODE block will be required.

❹ The pgscr function takes four integer arguments but must pass them to the Fortran subroutine using pointers. The XS compiler does this automatically because the variables are declared with an ampersand as a prefix.

❺ The integer arguments are passed in as pointers; the length of the string is added as an extra argument to the C routine. We do not have to convert this string to Fortran format because we know the length in C and can inform the Fortran compiler of that length directly.

6 This function has one input string and two output values. The NO_INIT tag indicates that the input values for those variables are irrelevant.

7 We declare a string buffer that can receive the output string. We declare it to be one character larger than we pass to the Fortran layer so there is space for the NUL character.

8 Because there are two string arguments, two lengths are appended to the argument list: the length of the input string and the length of the output string. In principle, we should pad the output string with blanks before sending it to Fortran (we've omitted that step for clarity).

9 The string that comes back from Fortran will not be NUL-terminated. Before we send it back to Perl, the string must be made compatible with C. In this example, we know the length of the string returned to us, so we can simply append the terminator. In general, we would need to step back through the string one character at a time until we found a non-blank character.

Once the XS code is written, the final issue is linking. All Fortran libraries require the Fortran runtime library to be included in the build. To simplify the task of keeping track of the runtime libraries required on different systems, you can use the ExtUtils::F77 module (note that it is not part of the standard Perl distribution and must be installed from CPAN). This module attempts to determine the libraries required to link Fortran programs on your system with the relevant Fortran compiler. A Makefile.PL file for the previous XS code that utilizes this module would look like the following:

```
use ExtUtils::MakeMaker;
use ExtUtils::F77;   <— Loads the ExtUtils::F77 module

# See lib/ExtUtils/MakeMaker.pm for details of how to influence
# the contents of the Makefile that is written.
WriteMakefile(                                      The PGPLOT
    'NAME'            => 'PGPLOT',                   library requires
    'VERSION_FROM'    => 'PGPLOT.pm', # finds $VERSION   X libraries for
    'PREREQ_PM'       => {}, # e.g., Module::Name => 1.1   some devices
    'LIBS'            => [ "-L/usr/local/lib -lpgplot " .
                          "-L/usr/X11R6/lib -lX11 "   <—
                          ExtUtils::F77->runtime ],  <—
);        Runtime libraries can be returned using the runtime class method
```

Now, when we run this program, we get the following output (with g77):

```
Loaded ExtUtils::F77 version 1.14
Found compiler g77
ExtUtils::F77: Using system=Linux compiler=G77
Runtime: -L/usr/lib/gcc-lib/i386-redhat-linux/2.96 -L/usr/lib -lg2c
         -lm -L/usr/lib/gcc-lib/i386-redhat-linux/2.96 -lgcc
```

```
ExtUtils::F77: Validating -L/usr/lib/gcc-lib/i386-redhat-linux/2.96
          -L/usr/lib -lg2c -lm
          -L/usr/lib/gcc-lib/i386-redhat-linux/2.96 -lgcc    [ok]
ExtUtils::F77: Compiler: g77
ExtUtils::F77: Cflags: -O
Writing Makefile for PGPLOT
```

ExtUtils::F77 has determined that we will be using the g77 compiler and that we need the g2c runtime library.

Fortran interface libraries and portability

The issue of portability depends on the particular circumstances of your module. For example, if you just want to use it on Solaris and Linux, where the Fortran implementations are compatible, you can write XS as described earlier. On the other hand, if you intend your module to be adopted widely, you will need to consider other operating systems and Fortran compilers. The ExtUtils::F77 library helps in this regard, because it can work out the libraries for many different compiler and OS combinations. Additionally, you can use it to determine whether a trailing underscore is required on function names (this ability can be used to set a C preprocessor macro).

A number of packages are available to simplify the writing of portable interface code. One of the most extensive is the CNF package[22] written by Starlink.[23] CNF provides a large set of C preprocessor macros for dealing with variable types and calling conventions. There is also a support library you can use to convert types (for example, strings and arrays) between the languages. Finally, CNF comes with detailed documentation about the issues associated with mixed programming as well as the use of CNF itself.

To demonstrate this alternative approach, here is the XS code for pgqinf rewritten to use CNF:

```
void
fpgqinf(item, value, length)
  char * item
  char * value = NO_INIT
  int length = NO_INIT
 PREINIT:
  DECLARE_CHARACTER(fitem, F77BUFFER);
  DECLARE_CHARACTER(fvalue, F77BUFFER);
  DECLARE_INTEGER(flength);
  char buff[F77BUFFER];
 CODE:
```

---

[22] The CNF package currently uses the Starlink Software Licence. This license allows for redistribution of source code but currently restricts the library to non-commercial use. Moves are currently underway to open up the license.

[23] Starlink (http://www.starlink.rl.ac.uk/) is a research organization in the United Kingdom. It provides data processing and analysis software for research astronomers in the UK.

```
  cnfExprt(item, fitem, fitem_length);
  F77_CALL(pgqinf) ( CHARACTER_ARG(fitem),
                     CHARACTER_ARG(fvalue),
                     INTEGER_ARG(&flength)
                     TRAIL_ARG(fitem)
                     TRAIL_ARG(fvalue) );
 length = (int)flength;
 value  = (char *)buff;
 cnfImprt( fvalue, length, value );
OUTPUT:
 value
 length
```

The extra verbosity inherent in this approach is immediately obvious; and, in order to guarantee that the correct types are used for the Fortran layer, a certain amount of copying is involved to go from the C to Fortran. This example also uses the translation functions cnfExprt and cnfImprt to export and import strings. Just to prove that CNF is doing the *right* thing, here is the same code block with the macros expanded (using g77):

```
char fitem[256]; const int fitem_length = 256;
char fvalue[256]; const int fvalue_length = 256;
int flength;
char buff[256];
cnfExprt(item, fitem, fitem_length);
pgqinf_ ( fitem,
          fvalue,
          &flength
          ,fitem_length
          ,fvalue_length );
length = (int)flength;
value = (char *)buff;
cnfImprt( fvalue, length, value );
```

It is clear that in this case, portability is counterbalanced by a decrease in speed in the resulting code, because there is so much more of it! For maximum performance, you should make some assumptions about your target platform.

Fortran interface considerations

The interface provided in this Fortran example is not very *Perl-y*. As described in section 2.5, you should address the needs of a particular library on a case-by-case basis. The PGPLOT library has a well-defined API that has been in use for many years, and there are some benefits to following that interface. When you're migrating from C or Fortran applications, it might be easier—both for the author of the module (less documentation to write, no complications with PPCODE blocks) and for the user (no need to learn a new interface)—if the Perl port of the library looks as much as possible like that implemented in other languages. This approach is taken with the PGPLOT module on CPAN.

For the routines described earlier, the most likely candidate for change is `pgqinf`. This routine has one input argument and two return arguments. One of these arguments is the length of the string and is not required by Perl. A much better approach from Perl's viewpoint is

```
$value = pgqinf($item);
```

The Perl Data Language goes a step further. The PGPLOT interface in PDL is completely divorced from the underlying library API by using an object-oriented layer to implement plotting. This abstraction simplifies the work of PDL users because they can use different plotting engines with only minimal changes to their code.

6.8.3 Linking Perl to Java

In 1998, Java was coming into its own as a programming language. This popularity led O'Reilly & Associates, Inc. to fund Larry Wall's work to provide a means for a Perl interpreter to be embedded inside a Java Virtual Machine, and for a Java Virtual Machine to be embedded in a Perl interpreter. This work led to the release of the Java Perl Lingo (JPL). Although it did work after a fashion, it was never really adopted by the Perl community, and the JPL code has not been updated to support newer versions of Java.[24]

From the point of view of this section, the key part of JPL is the `JNI` module. This code lets you call Java methods from Perl using XS. It may or may not work for you in its current form. If you want to call Java methods from Perl, the best idea is to use the `Inline::Java` module (available on CPAN). It works with current versions of Java and is actively supported. A short description of `Inline` (albeit the C version rather than the Java version) can be found in section 7.3.

6.9 INTERFACE DESIGN: PART 2

In section 2.5, we covered the basic interface issues you should think about before writing even the simplest XS module. Now that you have a more thorough grounding in XS, we will summarize the design issues we've brought up in this chapter:

- Look at the functions in the external library. Is the C library using objects in disguise? If it is repeatedly using an internal opaque structure, then you should use that structure as an object in Perl.

- Multiple return arguments should be returned as proper return arguments rather than as input arguments that are modified. Use PPCODE to adjust the return stack to suit.

- If a status variable can have only two states, consider translating the C value to a Perl `true` or `false` rather than matching the interface provided by the

---

[24] An article on JPL by Brian Jepson appeared in the Winter 1997 issue of the *Perl Journal* (http://www.samag.com/tpj/issues/vol2_4/).

external calling convention. Alternatively, if the function returns useful information only when the status is good, do not return the status value. Return the value if everything is OK and an empty list or `undef` otherwise. The `XSRETURN_*` functions are provided for this purpose. Using our example from section 2.5, we can change a signature of

```
int compute(int factor, double *result);
```

to

```
$result = compute( factor);
```

using the following XS code:

```
double
compute( factor )
  int factor
 PREINIT:
  int status;
 CODE:
  status = compute( factor, &RETVAL);
 OUTPUT:
  RETVAL
 CLEANUP:
   if (status == -1)
     XSRETURN_UNDEF;
```

- C++ context-based method overloading provides a particular headache for interface design. If you can determine the correct method from the argument stack (for example, by counting the number of arguments), then you can have a single Perl method that calls the required C++ method. If the distinction is simply by type, then you may need to have either distinct Perl methods (one for each type) or a single Perl method that uses a relevant Perl type (because Perl does not care about the difference between integers, doubles, and strings). This issue is discussed in section 6.8.1.

- Don't be scared of using Perl. Many of these examples can be simplified by using a Perl intermediary layer (for example, using `pack/unpack` to handle arrays). If you feel stronger in Perl than in C, this is a valid approach. If you feel that you need the extra speed, you can recode in C without changing the external interface to the module. The important thing is to have a clean public interface.

6.10 OLDER PERLS

As Perl 5 has developed, the API has evolved from one release to the next. Although an attempt is made to minimize API changes, occasional backward-incompatible API changes are unavoidable.

The most obvious example was the change at version 5.005. Prior to this version, many Perl functions and constants were not clearly Perl functions and constants. For example, na was a constant that people used in SvPV when they had no need to tell Perl how long the string should be; it doesn't look particularly Perl-ish! To minimize this namespace pollution (thus simplifying embedding enormously), the public constants were modified to include a PL_ prefix, and a Perl_ prefix was added to ambiguous functions. Thus, for example, na was now PL_na, sv_undef was now PL_sv_undef, and croak was now Perl_croak. Of course, this change caused havoc for many modules on CPAN. (Because the Perl developers were aware of the problem, both the old and the new APIs were available in Perl 5.005 to allow CPAN authors to modify their modules. Unsurprisingly, many modules were left unmodified until the old API was removed in Perl 5.6.0, thereby deferring the havoc until a year or two after the fact.)

The main problem with backward-incompatible changes is that they make it difficult for modules written with the new API to work in older version of Perl. For a while, everyone added C preprocessor directives to their modules, trying to work out which version was available and thus which corresponding API was available (Perl defines PERL_REVISION, PERL_VERSION, and PERL_SUBVERSION for this purpose). In general, this situation led to a lot of repetition.

Eventually, Kenneth Albanowski came to the rescue with his Devel::PPPort[25] module (this module is a standard part of Perl as of version 5.8.0). This module generates an include file that you can use in your XS code. Simply copy the ppport.h file generated by that module (it was installed with the other Perl include files when you built the module) to your module directory, add

```
#include "ppport.h"
```

to the top of your .xs file, and then use the modern API. You no longer need to worry about someone building your module using an older version of Perl. If more backward-incompatible changes are made to the API, you will need to obtain a newer version of ppport.h and modify your module to use the newer API; but at least you don't need to keep all the versions around.

6.11 WHAT'S REALLY GOING ON?

Up to this point, we have created XS files, typed make, and watched while lots of interesting things scrolled off the screen. In this section, we will take a closer look at what is really happening to these XS files and how XSUB interfaces to the Perl internals.

The XS interface exists to simplify the way user-supplied C code can be called from within Perl by being one layer above the Perl internals. In principle, you can write the C code directly without going through the XS layer. However, this approach is not recommended because it is more complex than is required for simple interfacing, it is repetitive and error prone when providing an interface to many external functions, and it may suffer compatibility problems if the internals are changed.

---

[25] In case you are wondering, PPPort stands for Perl/Pollution/Portability.

6.11.1　What does xsubpp generate?

By now, you know that the first step in creating an XS module is for the `xsubpp`
command to process the XS file in conjunction with a typemap file, and from these
files generate a C file that can be compiled. In this section we will revisit some of the
XS examples from section 2.3, but this time we will look at the .c output files. To
refresh your memory, listing 6.7 shows the XS file we will be experimenting with.

Listing 6.7　An interface to the example treble and strconcat functions

```
#include "EXTERN.h"
#include "perl.h"
#include "XSUB.h"

#include <stdio.h>
#include <string.h>


size_t strconcat (char* str1, char* str2, char* outstr) {
    strcpy( outstr, (const char*)str1 );
    strcat( outstr, (const char*)str2 );
    return strlen( outstr );
}

MODULE = Example          PACKAGE = Example

int
treble ( x )
  int x
 CODE:
   RETVAL = 3*x;
 OUTPUT:
  RETVAL

size_t
strconcat( str1, str2, outstr )
  char* str1
  char* str2
  char* outstr = NO_INIT
 PREINIT:
  size_t length;
 CODE:
  length = strlen( str1 ) + strlen( str2 ) + 1;
  New(0, outstr, length, char );
  RETVAL = strconcat( str1, str2, outstr );
 OUTPUT:
  outstr
  RETVAL
 CLEANUP:
  Safefree( outstr );
```

When we build this module, we find a C file called Example.c in the working directory. This file contains something like listing 6.8.

Listing 6.8   Example C code generated by xsubpp

```
/*
 * This file was generated automatically by xsubpp version 1.9507
 * from the contents of Example.xs.
 * Do not edit this file, edit Example.xs instead.
 *
 *ANY CHANGES MADE HERE WILL BE LOST!
 *
 */

#line 1 "Example.xs"
#include "EXTERN.h"
#include "perl.h"
#include "XSUB.h"

#include <stdio.h>
#include <string.h>


size_t strconcat (char* str1, char* str2, char* outstr) {
    strcpy( outstr, (const char*)str1 );
    strcat( outstr, (const char*)str2 );
    return strlen( outstr );
}

#line 25 "Example.c"
XS(XS_Example_treble)
{
    dXSARGS;
    if (items != 1)
        Perl_croak(aTHX_ "Usage: Example::treble(x)");
    {
        int     x = (int)SvIV(ST(0));
        int     RETVAL;
        dXSTARG;
#line 21 "Example.xs"
    RETVAL = 3*x;
#line 37 "Example.c"
XSprePUSH; PUSHi((IV)RETVAL);
    }
    XSRETURN(1);
}

XS(XS_Example_strconcat)
{
    dXSARGS;
    if (items != 3)
      Perl_croak(aTHX_
                 "Usage: Example::strconcat(str1, str2, outstr)");
    {
```

```
          char*    str1 = (char *)SvPV(ST(0),PL_na);
          char*    str2 = (char *)SvPV(ST(1),PL_na);
          char*    outstr;
#line 31 "Example.xs"
  size_t length;
#line 54 "Example.c"
        size_t   RETVAL;
        dXSTARG;
#line 33 "Example.xs"
  length = strlen( str1 ) + strlen( str2 ) + 1;
  New(0, outstr, length, char );
  RETVAL = strconcat( str1, str2, outstr );
#line 61 "Example.c"
        sv_setpv((SV*)ST(2), outstr);
        SvSETMAGIC(ST(2));
        XSprePUSH; PUSHi((IV)RETVAL);
#line 40 "Example.xs"
  Safefree( outstr );
#line 67 "Example.c"
    }
    XSRETURN(1);
}

#ifdef __cplusplus
extern "C"
#endif
XS(boot_Example)
{
    dXSARGS;
    char* file = __FILE__;

    XS_VERSION_BOOTCHECK ;

        newXS("Example::treble", XS_Example_treble, file);
        newXS("Example::strconcat", XS_Example_strconcat, file);
    XSRETURN_YES;
}
```

The global concepts to get from this file are the following:

- The C code that appears in the XS file before the MODULE keyword is passed through unchanged.

- Each XS function appears as a real C function, but with a modified name. The name is derived by concatenating the fixed prefix XS_, a C-ified form of the current PACKAGE (as defined by the PACKAGE keyword in the XS file), and the function name. If a PREFIX is defined, then it is removed from the function name before concatenation. For example, if the function name is slaMap, with the prefix *sla* and the package name Astro::SLA, the internal function name will be XS_Astro__SLA_Map. Here the colons have been replaced with underscores.

- If there is a fixed number of arguments, code has been inserted to check whether the correct number is on the stack and to issue an error message if necessary.

- Whenever there is a shift from original code to autogenerated code, the line numbering is changed to indicate the source of the code. This is achieved using the #line special directive.[26] Thus if an error occurs in an XS line, any compiler error messages will point to the correct line and filename rather than to the line in the translated C code. This simplifies debugging enormously.

- The final section is completely autogenerated. The boot function is responsible for registering the XS functions with Perl and is called automatically by Dyna-Loader when the module is loaded.

Now that you have a global overview of the file contents, let's examine the relationship between the XS definition of a function and the final C code. The XS sections are propagated to the C translation without changing the inherent order. Arguments are declared first; then come additional variable definitions (PREINIT), CODE blocks, the handling of output variables, and CLEANUP code to tidy things up. Of course, there are many other types of XS declarations, and they are included by xsubpp the same way. Most of these steps simply entail the addition of some standard stack-handling code or the insertion verbatim of the code supplied by the module author. The main complications involve variable input and output, which relate to the stack handling and variable declarations.

Let's take a closer look at the strconcat function shown earlier. The XS declaration and corresponding C code are

```
char* str1
char* str2
char* outstr = NO_INIT
```

and

```
char*    str1 = (char *)SvPV(ST(0),PL_na);
char*    str2 = (char *)SvPV(ST(1),PL_na);
char*    outstr;
```

xsubpp does the following to generate this code:

1 It looks up char* in the typemap file(s).

2 It looks up T_PV in the INPUT section.

3 It sees whether the INPUT entry matches /\t\$var =/.

4 If it matches, then the typemap entry is assumed to be a single statement, and the variable can be declared and assigned at the same time. This is the case with T_PV, which has a typemap entry of

```
<tab>$var = ($type)SvPV($arg,PL_na)
```

---

[26] It's identical to the #line special comment supported by Perl and described in the perlsyn man page.

5 If it does not match (for example, because the variable is to be type-checked before copying, as is the case with T_AVREF), the variable is simply declared, and the typemap code is deferred until after the other variable declarations (after the remaining arguments are declared and after PREINIT blocks). This step is necessary because C does not allow variables to be declared midway through a code block.

6 It replaces all the Perl variables in the typemap entry with the corresponding values and prints them to the C file. Recall that ST(n) refers to an SV on the argument stack (see section 6.4). In this example, positions 0 and 1 are relevant, and nothing is copied from position 2.

7 Return variables are dealt with in a similar way unless a PPCODE block is used. In our strconcat function, the output code for outstr is simply the typemap entry with variable substitutions. The RETVAL return variable is dealt with in the same manner, but xsubpp recognizes the standard variable types and translates them into the corresponding PUSH commands rather than use the OUTPUT typemap entry.

6.12 FURTHER READING

- *perlxstut*—This man page's XS tutorial comes with Perl and provides several XS examples.
- *perlxs*—This man page contains detailed information on XS.
- *perlcall*—This man page from the standard distribution contains a lot of detailed information about setting up callbacks.
- XS::Typemap—Starting with Perl 5.7.1, the source distribution includes the XS::Typemap module, which is used to test that the typemap entries behave as expected. This module is not installed, but the source code contains examples for most of the typemap entries. See also appendix A.
- *Astro::SLA, PGPLOT*—The Astro::SLA and PGPLOT modules on CPAN both contain helper code that you can use to pack and unpack arrays with the minimum of effort. The code in the arrays.c file from these distributions is useful for providing a prepackaged solution that deals with arrays without going to the expense of using PDL.

6.13 SUMMARY

In this chapter, you have extended your knowledge of XS to cover files, hashes, arrays, and callbacks, and you have seen how the XS code and typemap files translate into code suitable for use by the Perl internals. You have also learned how write XS code suitable for interfacing Perl to libraries written in Fortran and C++.

In chapter 7, we will step further away from the internals and see what systems are available to simplify the linking of Perl to external libraries.

C H A P T E R   7

Alternatives to XS

So far, we have created all of our Perl interfaces to C using XS and have demonstrated just how powerful and complex XS can be. In this chapter, we will take a step above XS and show how you can create an interface to C without using XS or reading page after page of documentation.

We will begin by looking at one of the earliest XS code generators and then proceed to the current front-runner for XS simplification. On the way, we will address the special demands of the Perl Data Language (PDL); we'll finish by briefly covering some of the less useful alternatives to XS that have been developed. We will use the examples from previous chapters to demonstrate the differences between and similarities of these approaches.

Nearly *all* the schemes described in this chapter are implemented as an abstraction layer above XS, either by generating .xs files to be passed to xsubpp or generating the code equivalent to the output of xsubpp that interfaces directly to Perl's internal XS system. This approach has the key advantage that a change to the XS system will only require a fix to the software that processes these definition files; all code that uses these systems will not require modification.

7.1 THE H2XS PROGRAM

By far the oldest attempt to provide simplified access to XS is the h2xs program that comes with Perl. We have already used this command in chapter 2 to generate a basic framework for Perl and XS-based modules, but it can be used to automatically generate XS wrapper code for simple libraries. As the name of the program suggests, it can take a C header file as input and generate an .xs file as output. We will not spend much time describing this program in detail; but, as an example, let's see what happens when we run it on a header file containing prototypes for the print_hello and treble examples used in section 2.2. We'll call this file example.h:

```
void print_hello ();
int treble (int x);
```

You can run h2xs with the -x option to force it to scan the header file looking for function prototypes (for this to work, you will need to download the C::Scan module from CPAN and use at least Perl version 5.8.0). Without this option, h2xs will attempt to read the include file, but it will only be able to extract #defines rather than full XS entries. We get the following output:

```
% h2xs -x -c -A example.h
Scanning typemaps...
 Scanning /usr/lib/perl5/5.7.2/ExtUtils/typemap
Scanning example.h for functions...
Scanning example.h for typedefs...
Writing Example/Example.pm
Writing Example/Example.xs
Writing Example/Makefile.PL
Writing Example/README
Writing Example/t/1.t
Writing Example/Changes
Writing Example/MANIFEST
```

The additional options turn off the code for handling constants (-c), because this module won't use any, and remove mention of the AutoLoader (-A). The output file Example.xs contains the following:

```
#include "EXTERN.h"
#include "perl.h"
#include "XSUB.h"

#include <example.h>


MODULE = Example            PACKAGE = Example


void
print_hello ()

int
treble(x)
        int        x
```

The output looks identical to that from section 2.2, except that the actual code for the functions is missing (you would have to put it after the `include` directives or else create a library to link against).

In general, h2xs is fine for handling simple interfaces using scalar arguments, but it rapidly runs out of steam. Even with a seemingly simple function such as strcon-cat from section 6.1, h2xs gets the wrong answer:

```
STRLEN
strconcat(str1, str2, outstr)
        char *   str1
        char *   str2
        char *   outstr
```

It assumes that all arguments are for input; additionally, the C interface requires that memory is allocated for the output string before use—something h2xs cannot possibly guess.

If you intend to use h2xs for anything but the simplest interface, be prepared to do a lot of work on the file that is automatically generated for you.

7.2 *SWIG*

SWIG (Simplified Wrapper and Interface Generator) was developed in 1995 by David Beazley at Los Alamos to simplify the writing of interface code between scripting languages and C/C++ libraries. The first supported language was proprietary but in 1996, SWIG was extended to cover Tcl, Perl, and Guile. Since then, it has been developed to cover many more languages, including Java. One of the major advantages of SWIG over XS is that it allows you to write a single interface specification and use it for all the languages supported by SWIG.

Let's begin our investigation of SWIG by seeing how to provide a Perl interface to the sinh math function (this interface already exists in the POSIX module) and a related constant. All SWIG interfaces begin with the generic interface definition. For sinh, the definition looks something like this:

```
%module Simple

double sinh ( double ang );
#define PI 3.141592654
```

All SWIG files begin by declaring the module name (if it is not defined here, it must be specified on the command line). SWIG commands always begin with a percent sign (%).

The second line is simply the C prototype for the function we are trying to call. SWIG can be used to parse a C include file and generate a language interface directly. In general, this approach is not recommended, because C include files tend to include many functions and data structures that are not required for the interface.

The C preprocessor define will be treated as a constant variable. Constants can also be defined using the %constant command.

If we save this description to a file `simple.swg` (`simple.i` is a common alternative), we can run SWIG on the file and generate the code required to interface the target language to the library function:

```
% swig -perl5 simple.swg
```

Here we use the `perl5` option to generate code for Perl rather than another language. Once executed, this command writes a `simple_wrap.c` file containing all the code necessary to call our function from Perl, and a small Perl wrapper module called `Simple.pm`. With version 1.3.11 of SWIG,[1] this C output file is approximately 14KB—impressively large for a two-line interface description file.

The important thing to realize is that the output code is C that can be compiled and linked as a module directly, because xsubpp is not required here. To convince yourself this is the case, look in `simple_wrap.c`. You will find the following XS code (or something similar) for `sinh`:

```
XS(_wrap_sinh) {
    double arg1 ;
    int argvi = 0;
    double result ;
    dXSARGS;

    if ((items < 1) || (items > 1))
    croak("Usage: sinh(ang);");
    arg1 = (double )SvNV(ST(0));
    result = (double )sinh(arg1);
    ST(argvi) = sv_newmortal();
    sv_setnv(ST(argvi++), (double) result);
    XSRETURN(argvi);
}
```

Unsurprisingly, this is very similar to the code generated by xsubpp (for example, see section 6.11). Once we have this C code, the next step is to compile it and link it as a shared library such that it can be used as a module. Rather than doing this manually, we can use MakeMaker as we would for any other module. Here is the `Makefile.PL` file:

```
use ExtUtils::MakeMaker;

WriteMakefile(
            'NAME'      => 'Simple',
            'VERSION'   => '0.01',
            'OBJECT'    => 'simple_wrap.o',);
```

The key difference between an XS module and a SWIG module is that we don't need to run xsubpp, and MakeMaker just needs to compile a C file. We do so by using the

---

[1] SWIG underwent a major rewrite between 1999 and 2001. Version 1.3.6 was the first stable version released since February 1998 (when version 1.1p5 was released). Our examples all use version 1.3.11. If you use a different version you may get slightly different output.

OBJECT hash key to tell `MakeMaker` the names of the object files we wish to use to form the module. The make file will automatically add the code for compiling the corresponding C files to object files. We can now build the module as we would any other XS module:

```
% perl Makefile.PL
Writing Makefile for Simple
% make
cp Simple.pm blib/lib/Simple.pm
cc -c   -fno-strict-aliasing -I/usr/local/include
 -D_LARGEFILE_SOURCE
 -D_FILE_OFFSET_BITS=64 -O2 -DVERSION=\"0.01\" -DXS_VERSION=\"0.01\"
 -fpic -I/usr/lib/perl5/5.6.1/i686-linux/CORE simple_wrap.c
Running Mkbootstrap for Simple ()
chmod 644 Simple.bs
rm -f blib/arch/auto/Simple/Simple.so
LD_RUN_PATH="" cc  -shared -L/usr/local/lib simple_wrap.o
    -o blib/arch/auto/Simple/Simple.so
chmod 755 blib/arch/auto/Simple/Simple.so
cp Simple.bs blib/arch/auto/Simple/Simple.bs
chmod 644 blib/arch/auto/Simple/Simple.bs
```

You could include a make-file dependency for the SWIG input file (running SWIG on it when it is modified). However, you probably shouldn't add a SWIG dependency to a distribution that will be put on CPAN, because doing so might limit its appeal (many sites don't have SWIG installed, and you will not be able to guarantee a particular version of SWIG). We can now run our simple module to see if it does what we expect:

```
% perl -Mblib -MSimple -le 'print Simple::sinh(3)'
10.0178749274099
% perl -Mblib -MSimple -le 'print $Simple::PI'
3.141592654
```

As an ever-so-slightly more complicated example, let's look at how to write an interface file for the `treble` function from section 2.2:

```
%module Treble

%{

int treble(int x)
{
   x *= 3;
   return x;
}

%}

int treble (int x);
```

The difference here is that C code has been inserted into the definition. The code between `%{` and `%}` is copied directly from the definition file to the output C code.

This is where you can load include files as well as C code. This module can be built in the same way as the `Simple` module.

7.2.1 Data structures

As we already mentioned, one thing that distinguishes SWIG from other approaches such as XS or `Inline` is its language-agnostic approach. In many cases this approach is beneficial; but when you're dealing with complicated data structures, it usually leads to modules that do not fit in well with the language philosophy. In SWIG, all complex data types (that is, pointer types) are treated as opaque objects. So, arrays and structures are always treated as pointers. In most cases this treatment is fine, because many libraries already use structures as opaque entities and simply pass the pointer from function to function. Additionally, if the components of the structure are defined, SWIG will generate accessor methods to enable access to the individual structure components.

In this section, we'll examine the use of structures from SWIG by looking at `gmtime` and related functions we used for the examples in section 6.5. Here is a simple SWIG interface to `gmtime`, `asctime`, and `mktime`:

```
%module Time

%{
#include <time.h>      ❶
%}

typedef int time_t;     ❷

%typemap(perl5, in) time_t * (time_t temp) {     ❸
  temp = SvIV( $input );     ❹
  $1 = &temp;     ❺
}

struct tm *gmtime(time_t * timep);
char * asctime( const struct tm *timeptr);
time_t mktime( struct tm *timeptr);
```

❶ This C code makes sure the C declarations are available when the module is built (the `include` directive is passed straight to the output C code).

❷ We tell SWIG that a `time_t` is an integer. This is true on Unix but may not be true in general. An alternative solution is to use

```
%include "time.h"
```

but doing so would have the side effect of providing SWIG declarations for all definitions in the include file.

❸ We declare a new input typemap for variables of type `time_t *` specifically for use with Perl5 (to use this SWIG file for other languages, you will need to define different typemaps in the same file). This typemap also declares an additional variable similar to PREINIT in XS.

4 We retrieve the integer associated with the input scalar and store it in a temporary variable.

5 Finally, we store the pointer of the temporary variable in the target variable (in some earlier versions of SWIG this variable is named $target rather than $1).

This code looks straightforward, except for the complication of the typemap definition (the typedef is there simply to tell SWIG that a time_t can be treated as an integer). The problem is that gmtime expects a pointer to a time_t variable rather than a simple variable of type time_t. We could write a wrapper C routine that allocates memory and populates the value, returning a pointer to Perl that can be passed to this function; but it is much simpler from the Perl perspective to write a typemap that will convert a simple integer (usually the output of the Perl time function) to a pointer. If we build this module and run, we see the following:

```
% perl -Mblib -MTime -le 'print Time::gmtime(time)'
_p_tm=SCALAR(0x8107cc8)
% perl -Mblib -MTime \
    -le '$t=Time::gmtime(time); print Time::asctime($t)'
Sat May 25 20:53:02 2002
```

SWIG has provided us with an interface even though it doesn't know what the contents of a tm structure are. All we get is a blessed scalar of an unhelpful class (in this case _p_tm, because this is a pointer to a tm), which SWIG can use for internal type-consistency checking. If we want to be able to look inside the structure, we tell SWIG what it contains:

```
%module Time

%{
#include <time.h>
%}

typedef int time_t;

%typemap(perl5, in) time_t * (time_t temp) {
  temp = SvIV( $input );
  $1 = &temp;
}

struct tm
{
  int tm_sec;      /* Seconds.       [0-60] (1 leap second) */
  int tm_min;      /* Minutes.       [0-59] */
  int tm_hour;     /* Hours.         [0-23] */
  int tm_mday;     /* Day.           [1-31] */
  int tm_mon;      /* Month.         [0-11] */
  int tm_year;     /* Year - 1900.   */
  int tm_wday;     /* Day of week.   [0-6] */
  int tm_yday;     /* Days in year.  [0-365] */
  int tm_isdst;    /* DST.           [-1/0/1] */
};
```

```
struct tm *gmtime(time_t * timep);
char * asctime( const struct tm *timeptr);
time_t mktime( struct tm *timeptr);
```

Now, if we use this module, we can find out the time from the structure:

```
% perl -Mblib -MTime \
    -le '$t=Time::gmtime(time); print Time::tm_tm_year_get($t)'
102
```

SWIG automatically creates accessor functions (there is a corresponding set method). In this case, the function is an accessor for the tm_year field in the struct tm, so the name is a bit repetitive. Because this approach clearly won't win any fans with users of your class, SWIG provides an option for handling structures as true Perl objects. If we use SWIG's -shadow option, the interface looks much more agreeable:

```
% swig -perl5 -shadow time.swg
% make
...
% perl -Mblib -MTime -le '$t=Time::gmtime(time); print $t'
Time::tm=HASH(0x8144648)
% perl -Mblib -MTime -le '$t=Time::gmtime(time); print $t->mktime;'
1022396126
% perl -Mblib -MTime \
    -le '$t=Time::gmtime(time); print $t->{tm_year}'
102
```

This example shows that the structure is converted to an object in class Module-name::structname and can be used to invoke methods (in this case, mktime) and to access object instance data via a tied hash interface.

7.3   THE INLINE MODULE

The Inline modules were first developed in 2000 by Brian Ingerson in order to simplify the XS learning curve. The family of Inline modules allows you to write non-Perl code within the body of your Perl program with the expectation that Perl will know what to do with it. We'll demonstrate this ability by showing the Inline version of our first XS examples from section 2.2:

> **NOTE**   Inline is not distributed as part of Perl. You will need to download it and its dependencies (such as the Parse::RecDescent module) from CPAN before you can run these examples.

```
use Inline "C";

print treble(5),"\n";
&print_hello;

__END__
__C__
void print_hello ()
{
```

```
    printf("hello, world\n");
}

int treble(int x)
{
    x *= 3;
    return x;
}
```

When we run this program, it does exactly what we expect. No need to create a module and work out the XS syntax—it just works. We get the following output:

```
15
hello,world
```

The first time you run the program, it will probably take a few seconds to execute. The second time it will run as fast as you would expect the XS version to run.

Inline is not limited to C. Modules exist for writing and calling C++, Python, and Java code from Perl. As an introduction to the techniques of using Inline, we will limit our description to the C implementation; however, if you are interested in other languages, CPAN has them all covered!

7.3.1 What is going on?

Before we rush headlong into more examples, we'll explain what is happening here.[2] When you write a Perl program using Inline, unsurprisingly, a lot of work is going on behind the scenes. In outline, the following is occurring:

1 The module reads the code from the appropriate place (usually below the DATA handle).

2 An MD5 checksum is calculated for the code in question.

3 This checksum and associated information (such as the operating system and Perl version number) are compared with those of any modules that were automatically generated on previous occasions (this all happens in the _Inline or $HOME/.inline directory unless specified otherwise). If the code does not match any existing checksum or configuration, it is analyzed to determine the function names and calling arguments (perhaps using a parser module such as Parse::RecDescent).

4 An XS module is generated based on the functions and arguments in the inlined code. Its name is derived from the checksum. (If no name is specified, the module's name will be the name of the file containing the original code with punctuation removed, plus the first few letters of the checksum.)

---

2 At least, we'll explain what is happening with version 0.43 of Inline. Development of this module is fairly rapid, so things may have changed to some extent by the time you read this.

5 The module is built and installed into a local directory.

6 Alternatively, if the checksum matches with a checksum calculated during a previous run of the program, the module is loaded directly without being compiled.

In essence, this process is straightforward. A module is built automatically if required; otherwise it is loaded like any other module. This explains why an inlined program takes a while to run the first time through but is then almost as fast as a normal module on subsequent runs. The main complication is the parsing of the C code to generate the XS specification. The relationship between `Inline` and the approaches of SWIG and XS is shown in figure 7.1.

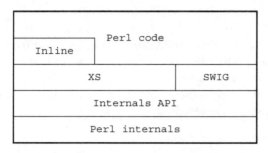

Figure 7.1
Conceptual relationship between
`Inline`, `SWIG`, and `XS`

This diagram shows the conceptual relationship between the three most popular ways to integrate C with Perl. You can see that `Inline` goes through an XS layer, whereas SWIG cuts out the middle man and goes straight to the low-level API.

By default, `Inline` removes the build tree if the build completed successfully (if the build fails, `Inline` leaves the build tree for you to debug). All we need to do to retain the build tree is add

```
use Inline Config => CLEAN_AFTER_BUILD => 0;
```

to the top of our program. You can now play with the XS code; doing so is an excellent way to find out what is really going on when you write `Inline` modules.

7.3.2 Additional Inline examples

Now that you have seen the magic and have an idea what is happening, let's look at some more serious examples. Anything that simply passes in some scalar arguments and gets a return value should look like a normal C function. In this section, we'll discuss memory allocation issues, lists, and multiple return arguments, because these are the most likely sources of confusion.

Strings and things

If your function returns a string (essentially a memory buffer) that has been created in your function, then you will probably have to worry about memory allocation. We can examine this issue by using the string concatenation example from section 6.1.

This function took two strings and returned the concatenated string. In that example we used New and Safefree for the memory allocation. This approach was OK, but it relied on the CLEANUP section of the XS code running after the memory buffer had been copied back onto the argument stack. With Inline we cannot get away with this, because the function is called by the XS routine; if it returns a char*, we have no way to free it after it has been returned. To overcome this problem, we have two choices: we can return an SV rather than a char*, or create a new SV with the result and push it onto the stack.

Returning an SV containing the result rather than returning a char* lets us free the memory before returning from our function, because the string is copied into an SV and so becomes Perl's responsibility:

```
SV * strconcat( char * str1, char * str2 ) {      Marks this function as
  char * outstr;                                   returning an SV*
  SV* outsv;
  int len = strlen(str1) + strlen(str2) +1;        Allocates a string buffer
  New(0, outstr, len, char);                       of the right size

  strcpy( outstr, (const char*)str1 );        ❶
  strcat( outstr, (const char*)str2 );             Creates a new SV and copies the
                                                   contents of the string buffer into it
  outsv = newSVpv(outstr, len);
  Safefree(outstr);        Frees the buffer because we
  return outsv;    ❷      don't need it any longer
}
```

❶ These two lines are the core of the strconcat function described in earlier chapters. They represent a real-world call to an external library.

❷ We return the SV*. It is automatically marked as mortal by XS before being put onto the return stack.

This process is a little inefficient, because we end up allocating two string buffers: once for the string buffer we are using and once when we create the SV. In fact, because we are going to the trouble of using an SV, we may as well use the SV's buffer directly:

```
SV * strconcat( char * str1, char * str2 ) {
  SV* outsv;                                       Creates a new SV with a string
  int len = strlen(str1) + strlen(str2) +1;        buffer of the correct size
  outsv = NEWSV(0, len);

                                                   Uses the SvPVX macro to
  strcpy( SvPVX(outstr), (const char*)str1 );      obtain the char* pointing
  strcat( SvPVX(outstr), (const char*)str2 );      to the start of the buffer

  SvPOK_on(outsv);        ❶
  SvCUR_set(outsv, len-1);
  return outsv;
}
```

❶ Now that we have populated the string, we need to tell Perl that the string component is valid and what its useful length is.

This approach has an added inconvenience: we must mark the SV as a valid string (SvPOK) and specify its length (SvCUR), but we allocate only one buffer. Of course, for this example we can use the Perl API directly, without referring to any external functions:

```
SV * strconcat ( char * str1, char * str2 ) {
  SV * outsv;
  outsv = newSVpv( str1, 0 );
  sv_catpv( outsv, str2 );
  return outsv;
}
```

Our second solution to the problem of returning a char* is to do what XS does and simply create a new SV with the result and push it onto the stack ourselves. Doing so is identical to returning an SV* to Inline but cuts out the middle man. We'll describe how to manipulate the argument stack from Inline in the next section.

If we need to allocate a buffer and return it as a non-SV, then we must use a memory allocator that uses mortal SVs:

```
static void * get_mortalspace ( size_t nbytes ) {    ❶
  SV * mortal;
  mortal = sv_2mortal( NEWSV(0, nbytes ) );
  return (void *)SvPVX(mortal
}

char * strconcat ( char * str1, char * str2 ) {
  char* outstr;
  int len = strlen(str1) + strlen(str2) + 1;
  outstr = get_mortalspace( len ); );    ◁─┐ Allocates some
  strcpy( outstr, (const char*)str1 );      │ memory for the
  strcat( outstr, (const char*)str2 );      │ buffer

  return outstr;
}
```

❶ This is the memory allocator described in sections 6.6.1 and 6.6.5. We put it here explicitly rather than in an external file purely for convenience. To prevent Inline from creating a Perl interface to this function, we declare it as static. Inline knows that static functions are not externally accessible, and therefore it ignores them.
The XS code will receive the char pointer, put it into an SV, and push it onto the argument stack. Once the SV is read from the stack, the memory associated with it will be freed automatically.

Summing an array

In section 6.6.1, we covered in detail how to handle Perl an array with XS in the form of a list, a reference, and a packed string. Here we will show you how to use `Inline` to deal with lists and an array reference.

Let's begin with a reference.[3] Because a reference is a scalar and a corresponding typemap entry exists, it is fairly easy to handle with `Inline`:

```
use Inline "C";

print sum_as_ref([1..10]);

__END__
__C__
int sum_as_ref(AV* avref)
{
  int len;
  int i;
  int sum = 0;
  SV ** elem;

  len = av_len(avref) + 1;

  for (i=0; i<len; i++) {
    elem = av_fetch(avref, i, 0);
    if (elem != NULL)
        sum += SvIV( *elem );
  }
  return sum;
}
```

This code is almost identical to the example using XS (for clarity, we are doing the sum in place rather than calling the external C routine); there is nothing new in it.

When you're processing lists, things get more interesting. `Inline` generates the XS code for your function and then calls the function. Thus you can no longer rely on XS to provide all the stack-handling facilities you are familiar with. `Inline` overcomes this problem by providing some simple macros of its own for initializing the stack variables and manipulating the stack. The following code demonstrates (with the Perl code removed, because it is nearly identical to the previous example):

```
int sum_as_list( SV* arg1, ... )    ❶
{
  int i;
  int len;
  int sum = 0;
  SV* elem;
  Inline_Stack_Vars;    ❷          Counts the number
                                   of arguments on
  len = Inline_Stack_Items;   ◄─┘  the stack
```

---

3 As in chapter 6, this example requires Perl 5.8 because the typemap in earlier Perl versions does not deal correctly with array references.

```
    for (i=0; i<len; i++) {
        elem = Inline_Stack_Item(i);        ◄──┐  Retrieves the ith SV
        sum += SvIV( elem );        ❸          │  from the stack
    }
    return sum;
}
```

❶ An ellipsis (...) indicates to Inline that multiple arguments will be used. At least one argument must be declared even though we may be retrieving all the stack variables using the macros. In this case, we declare arg1, but it is not used in the function directly (it is used via Inline_Stack_Item(0)).

❷ We initialize the stack-related variables used by the other stack macros. This code must always be placed in the variable declaration section of the function.

❸ Now that we have the SV* from the stack, we retrieve the associated integer and add it to the sum.

Rather than use the T_ARRAY typemap entry (which would require us to provide a memory allocator as well as lose information about the size of the array), we have written this code using Inline's stack macros. Because the set of macros is limited, the macros are designed to be simple and easy to understand—you don't have to face the daunting contents of the Perl internals documentation. Using them has the additional advantage that you are not tied to the Perl XS macros—if XS is changed or replaced, then your Inline module probably will continue working without any problems.

Multiple return arguments

Just as you can read multiple arguments off the stack, you can also push return arguments onto the stack using Inline macros. Here is how we would implement the function to return the current time in a hash, which was described in "Returning a list," page 181:

```
#include <time.h>
                                        ┌─ As for XS, we use a void return type when we
void gmtime_as_list( time_t clock )  ◄──┘  push arguments onto the stack ourselves
{
    struct tm * tmbuf;
    Inline_Stack_Vars;   ◄────────┐
    Inline_Stack_Reset;   ❶       │ Initializes the stack
                                  │ variables used by the            ┌─ Pushes an SV onto
    tmbuf = gmtime( &clock );     │ other macros                     │  the stack. This code
                                                                     │  is equivalent to
    Inline_Stack_Push( sv_2mortal( newSVpv("sec", 3) ) );  ◄─────────┘  XPUSHs
    Inline_Stack_Push( sv_2mortal( newSViv(tmbuf->tm_sec) ) );
    Inline_Stack_Push( sv_2mortal( newSVpv("min", 3) ) );
    Inline_Stack_Push( sv_2mortal( newSViv(tmbuf->tm_min) ) );
    Inline_Stack_Push( sv_2mortal( newSVpv("hour", 4) ) );
    Inline_Stack_Push( sv_2mortal( newSViv(tmbuf->tm_hour) ) );
    Inline_Stack_Push( sv_2mortal( newSVpv("mday", 4) ) );
```

```
        Inline_Stack_Push( sv_2mortal( newSViv(tmbuf->tm_mday) ));
        Inline_Stack_Push( sv_2mortal( newSVpv("mon", 3) ));
        Inline_Stack_Push( sv_2mortal( newSViv(tmbuf->tm_mon) ));
        Inline_Stack_Push( sv_2mortal( newSVpv("year", 4) ));
        Inline_Stack_Push( sv_2mortal( newSViv(tmbuf->tm_year) ));
        Inline_Stack_Push( sv_2mortal( newSVpv("wday", 4) ));
        Inline_Stack_Push( sv_2mortal( newSViv(tmbuf->tm_wday) ));
        Inline_Stack_Push( sv_2mortal( newSVpv("yday", 4) ));
        Inline_Stack_Push( sv_2mortal( newSViv(tmbuf->tm_yday) ));

        Inline_Stack_Done;    ❷
}
```

❶ This statement must be used before any variables are pushed onto the stack. It resets the stack pointer to the beginning of the stack (rather than the end of the input arguments).

❷ We use this macro to indicate when all the necessary variables have been pushed onto the stack.

All we have done here is replace XPUSHs with Inline_Stack_Push. It's as simple as that!

7.3.3   Inline and CPAN

Once you have a working interface, what happens if you want to put it onto CPAN for other people to use? In general, you can package your module as is and put it onto CPAN. Doing so will require a dependency on Inline (don't forget to use the PREREQ_PM option to MakeMaker to formalize this dependency), which might not be convenient for everybody. Additionally, some sites do not want the added risk of a module building itself dynamically, or the support overhead of explaining to users that the program will run faster the second time they use it!

One solution is to configure Inline so that it doesn't remove the build tree:

```
use Inline Config => CLEAN_AFTER_BUILD => 0;
```

You can then edit the build files and construct a distribution. This process is a little tedious, but it is the only solution if you do not want the people installing your module to have a dependency on Inline. If you know that Inline is available and the only issue is to make sure it is not compiled dynamically, then Inline provides you with a solution. A replacement for ExtUtils::MakeMaker is distributed with Inline; it will make sure a precompiled version of the module is installed. Here is an example of a simple module that shows how to use this technique:

```
package Trig;

use strict;
use vars qw/ $VERSION /;

$VERSION = '0.10';
```

```
use Inline C => 'DATA', VERSION => '0.10', NAME => 'Trig';

__DATA__
__C__
double sine ( double ang ) {
    return sin( ang );
}
```

The only thing to note here is that the name and version number of the module must be supplied to `Inline`. The real magic occurs in the `Makefile.PL` file:

```
use Inline::MakeMaker;

WriteInlineMakefile( NAME => 'Trig',
                     VERSION_FROM => 'Trig.pm');
```

Rather than using `ExtUtils::MakeMaker` and the `WriteMakefile` function, we use `Inline::MakeMaker` and `WriteInlineMakefile`. If we now build the module, it behaves slightly differently than normal:

```
% perl Makefile.PL
Checking if your kit is complete...
Looks good
Writing Makefile for Trig
% make
mkdir blib
mkdir blib/lib
mkdir blib/arch
mkdir blib/arch/auto
mkdir blib/arch/auto/Trig
mkdir blib/lib/auto
mkdir blib/lib/auto/Trig
cp Trig.pm blib/lib/Trig.pm
/usr/bin/perl -Mblib -MInline=_INSTALL_ -MTrig -e1 0.10 blib/arch
```

When we look in the build directory, the module has been built and is ready to be installed.

7.3.4   Inline module summary

`Inline` is a powerful addition to your armory. With only a small loss in overall flexibility (much of which you won't miss), you can mix Perl and C code without having to worry about make files and XS syntax. All you need is a knowledge of the variable manipulation API and possibly typemaps. The main things to be aware of are as follows:

- You cannot have input arguments that are also return arguments. If you need this functionality, use the `SV*` as an argument and modify it directly. For example,

```
void modify_inplace( SV* sv ) {
  sv_setiv(sv, 5);
}
```

If we call this function via `Inline`, then the scalar argument will be set to 5 on completion. Also, as mentioned in section 2.5, in many cases the design of the interface is better if an alternative approach is adopted.

- Be careful with memory allocation. You will not be able to explicitly free memory when you return from your `Inline` function (especially if you have allocated memory for a string buffer that is to be returned), so either use an `SV` directly (either by pushing it onto the stack or by returning it) or allocate memory using mortal SVs (`sv_2mortal(NEWSV(..))` and return the buffer pointer with `SvPVX`) rather than with `New`.

We cannot cover all of `Inline` here, but this section has given you a taste of what is possible.

7.4 THE PDL::PP MODULE

You saw in "PDL and XS," page 195 that creating interfaces from the Perl Data Language to external libraries using XS is quite complex. In addition to the native complexity of PDL, four issues further complicate PDL/XS interfaces:

- *Data typing*—Many libraries have different routines for different data types. Writing XS interfaces that are identical except for the data type of the piddle is time consuming and error prone.

- *Slicing*—When a subsection of a piddle is used, PDL does not make a copy (data can be modified "in place"). If a slice is passed to XS, the pointer will not be referring to the start of the slice but to the start of the parent piddle!

- *PDL threading*—One nice feature of PDL is its ability to automatically *thread* over additional dimensions.[4] This functionality must be implemented in C for speed, but it is essentially impossible to get right if you code it by hand.

- *Changes in API*—If the internal API for either PDL or Perl is modified, it is highly likely that the XS code will have to be fixed. Writing XS code that works for multiple versions of internals API is difficult and quickly leads to an `ifdef` forest of C preprocessor directives.

To solve these issues, a PDL preprocessor language was written to abstract out the numeric interface from the XS implementation. These interface definitions (using the file `suffix.pd`) are automatically processed by the `PDL::PP` module to generate the required XS code. `PDL::PP` automatically generates code for multiple data types, keeps track of slicing, and implements threading. If the API is changed, all that needs to be modified is `PDL::PP`—PDL itself can be rebuilt with minimal changes.

---

4 This is the PDL term for automatic iteration over redundant dimensions. On a multithreaded system, it will happen by starting multiple processor threads. On a single-threaded system, the dimensions will be processed one at a time.

The primary goal of PDL::PP is to let you write numerical code in a C-like language (for speed) without having to worry about XS. Support for external libraries is a side effect of this goal. PDL::PP is an extremely complicated module, and we'll make no attempt to describe all its features. However, we will show you how to write a PDL::PP interface to the sum function described in chapter 6.

7.4.1 The .pd file

Instead of using an .xs file, PDL::PP code is written to a .pd file. In this example, we'll create a file called sum.pd to hold the definitions. This file is a Perl program that is run as part of the make process (the next section shows how). This program creates the normal XS infrastructure: the XS file and the associated Perl module. For this example, the first thing we need to do is to supply the code for sum. We do this using pp_addhdr. This function places additional C code at the top of the output XS file (before the MODULE line). That C code is supplied as an argument:

```
pp_addhdr('

int sum ( int num, int * array ) {
  int thesum = 0;
  int count;
  for (count = 0; count < num; count++) {
    thesum += array[count];
  }
  return thesum;
}

');
```

Now that the C function is present, we can supply the PP code for the PDL interface. We do this using the pp_def function:

```
pp_def( 'ppsum',        ❶
        Pars => 'a(n); [o]b()',      ❷
        GenericTypes => [L],    ❸
        Code => '$b() = sum( $SIZE(n), $P(a));',      ❹
);

pp_done();      ❺
```

❶ The first argument to pp_def is the name of the routine being generated. We use ppsum because a PDL sum function already exists.[5]

❷ This is the calling signature of the PDL routine. Here we are saying that the first argument is a one-dimensional vector of dimension n with an output argument (that can

---

[5] PDL always imports PP functions into the main namespace. This is done so that the interactive perldl shell will always work as expected even though it sometimes results in namespace clashes.

also be a second input argument treated as a buffer) that is a simple scalar piddle (no dimensions are specified).

❸ GenericTypes indicates to PP that only specific data types are supported by the routine. In this case, only type long int is supported by our C function.

❹ This is the actual implementation of the PP routine. $SIZE(n) retrieves the size of dimensions labeled n. $P(a) retrieves the pointer to the piddle $a. These two arguments are passed to the C sum function, and the result is stored in the scalar variable $b.

❺ We have to inform PDL::PP that we are done, and there are no more definitions to read, so that it can write out the XS and PM files.

This code looks fairly strange at first, but there is logic to it—and it has successfully formed a layer between you and XS (the XS file generated from this example PP file is 30KB!). This definition on its own is useless, so the next step is to convert the file to XS code.[6]

7.4.2   The Makefile.PL file

We now have a file called sum.pd rather than the file Sum.xs expected by ExtUtils::MakeMaker. So, in order to generate a normal XS file, we must add some PDL helper routines to Makefile.PL, to make sure the PP definition file is processed. We do so by adding a new make-file target and retrieving PDL-specific build options from the module PDL::Core::Dev:

```
# Use this as a template for the Makefile.PL for
# any external PDL module.

use ExtUtils::MakeMaker;
use PDL::Core::Dev qw/ pdlpp_stdargs pdlpp_postamble/;      ❶

$pack = [qw/ sum.pd Sum PDL::Sum /];   ❷
%hash = pdlpp_stdargs($pack);   ❸

WriteMakefile(%hash);

sub MY::postamble {   ❹
        pdlpp_postamble($::pack);   ❺
}   # Add genpp rule
```

❶ The PDL::Core::Dev module contains some helper routines designed specifically for generating make files for PDL::PP extensions.

❷ $pack contains a reference to an array specifying the name of the source file, the name of the resulting module (.pm and .xs) files, and the namespace of the module.

---

6   An Inline::PDLPP module is under development at this time. It will allow PP definitions to be placed in Perl programs directly, as described in section 7.3 for the C language.

❸ pdlpp_stdargs returns a hash containing the MakeMaker arguments required to build a PDL::PP-based module.

❹ The postamble method overrides the default version in the MY class (as set up by MakeMaker) and is invoked automatically by MakeMaker to place additional dependencies in the output Makefile.

❺ The pdlpp_postamble function generates the PDL-specific make file dependencies from the single argument. The argument is specified as $::pack to indicate that the variable is from the main namespace and not from the MY namespace.

Now, when we build this module, we get the following output (on Linux):

```
% perl Makefile.PL
Writing Makefile for PDL::Sum
% make
/usr/local/bin/perl
    -I/usr/local/perl5/lib/site_perl/5.6.0/i686-linux/blib/lib
    -I/usr/local/perl5/lib/site_perl/5.6.0/i686-linux/blib/arch
    "-MPDL::PP qw/PDL::Sum PDL::Sum Sum/" sum.pd
cp Sum.pm blib/lib/PDL/Sum.pm
/usr/local/bin/perl -I/usr/local/perl-5.6/lib/5.6.0/i686-linux
  -I/usr/local/perl5/lib/5.6.0
    /usr/local/perl5/lib/5.6.0/ExtUtils/xsubpp
     -typemap /usr/local/perl5/lib/5.6.0/ExtUtils/typemap
      -typemap/usr/local/perl5/lib/site_perl/5.6.0/i686-linux/PDL/
Core/typemap.pdl
      Sum.xs > Sum.xsc && mv Sum.xsc Sum.c
gcc -c -I/usr/local/perl5/lib/site_perl/5.6.0/i686-linux/PDL/Core
    -fno-strict-aliasing -D_LARGEFILE_SOURCE -D_FILE_OFFSET_BITS=64
    -O2 -DVERSION=\"0.10\" -DXS_VERSION=\"0.10\" -fpic
    -I/usr/local/perl5/lib/5.6.0/i686-linux/CORE  Sum.c
Running Mkbootstrap for PDL::Sum ()
chmod 644 Sum.bs
LD_RUN_PATH="" gcc -o blib/arch/auto/PDL/Sum/Sum.so
    -shared -L/usr/local/lib Sum.o
chmod 755 blib/arch/auto/PDL/Sum/Sum.so
cp Sum.bs blib/arch/auto/PDL/Sum/Sum.bs
chmod 644 blib/arch/auto/PDL/Sum/Sum.bs
Manifying blib/man3/PDL::Sum.3
```

The first step in the build is now to run the .pd file through Perl before proceeding with a normal build (xsubpp followed by the C compiler). Once built we can see if it works (here using the interactive shell):

```
% perldl
perlDL shell v1.30
 PDL comes with ABSOLUTELY NO WARRANTY. For details, see the file
 'COPYING' in the PDL distribution. This is free software and you
 are welcome to redistribute it under certain conditions, see
 the same file for details.
```

```
ReadLines enabled
Reading PDL/default.perldlrc...
Type 'help' for online help
Type 'demo' for online demos
Loaded PDL v2.3.2
perldl> use blib; use PDL::Sum

perldl> $pdl = pdl(10,20,30)

perldl> print $pdl
[10 20 30]
perldl> print ppsum($pdl)
60
```

7.4.3 Pure PDL

Now that we have shown you how to call an external function using PDL::PP, it will be instructive to show the equivalent routine written using the PP language without referring to any external C code (this is the actual code used to implement the PDL sumover function):

```
pp_def(
        'sumover',
        Pars => 'a(n); [o]b();',        Initializes a new
        Code => 'double tmp=0;          double-precision        Loops over dimension
                                        variable                n using the built-in
                loop(n) %{       ◄                              loop() macro
                    tmp += $a();    ❶
                %}
                $b() = tmp;      ◄  Assigns the total
                '                   to the output
            );                      variable

    pp_done();
```

❶ This line adds the current value to the temporary placeholder. Note that no index is required. PDL::PP automatically works out what index we are referring to.

This code is still translated to C and built as an XS module, but now it works on all data types natively. This is the recommended approach for writing fast loops in PDL, and it is one of the reasons PDL can approach the speed of pure C.

7.5 EARLIER ALTERNATIVES

The modules and packages we've described are by no means an exhaustive list, but we've covered the techniques you would most likely want to pursue. There are other, less portable methods for calling functions in C shared libraries from Perl, but with the appearance of the Inline module most of these techniques can (and probably should) be safely ignored. For example, you can use the C::DynaLib module to call C functions directly from shared libraries, and it did have a use for prototyping simple systems without requiring XS. The following example (from the C::DynaLib documentation) shows how to use it to call a function from the standard math library:[7]

```
use C::DynaLib;
$libm = new C::DynaLib("-lm");
$sinh = $libm->DeclareSub("sinh", "d", "d");
print "The hyperbolic sine of 3 is ", &$sinh(3), "\n";
```

This code prints the expected answer: 10.018 (on supported architectures). With Inline, this code would be written as follows:

```
use Inline "C";

print "The hyperbolic sine of 3 is ", mysinh(3), "\n";

__END__
__C__
double mysinh (double ang) {
    return sinh(ang);
}
```

This version has two key advantages: it's simpler to write[8] and more portable. The PDL equivalent of C::DynaLib is PDL::CallExt, and it has also been superceded—this time by PDL::PP.

7.6   FURTHER READING

- *Inline*—The Inline Project (http://inline.perl.org/).
- *PDL::PP*—The documentation for PDL::PP is available as part of the PDL distribution. It is fairly complete but also fairly opaque.
- *SWIG*—Simplified Wrapper and Interface Generator (http://www.swig.org/).

---

[7] Current versions of this module do not seem to work on Linux, although this example works on Solaris. The module has not been updated since February 2000 and is not being actively supported.

[8] This code can be written in two lines, for those of you who prefer compactness:
```
    use Inline C => "double mysinh (double ang) { return sinh(ang); }";
    print "The hyperbolic sine of 3 is ", mysinh(3), "\n";
```

7.7   SUMMARY

In this chapter, you've learned how to use systems that do not require knowledge of XS in order to link Perl programs to C libraries. You've seen that SWIG takes a language-agnostic approach, whereas `Inline` generates XS code directly from C embedded in your Perl program. The decision about which system to use depends on your circumstances. If you are only interested in Perl, `Inline` is probably the best choice (you can even use it to learn about XS by looking at the intermediate files it generates). If you're interested in using the same C interface in a number of libraries, then you should choose SWIG. Finally, although SWIG and `Inline` are the main choices, other systems are available; if you are using large data arrays, you should consider using `PDL::PP`.

CHAPTER 8

Embedding Perl in C

In the first half of this book, we've looked at what it means to extend Perl with additional routines from C. Sometimes, however, you'll want to call a piece of Perl from inside a C program—this is called *embedding* Perl in C, because you link an entire Perl interpreter inside another C program.

8.1   WHEN TO EMBED

The best and most well-known example of embedding Perl in C is Apache's `mod_perl` module. It allows the user to interact with Perl at every level of the Apache web server—you can write configuration files in Perl, write Perl programs to handle HTTP requests with Perl objects, and so on. In short, it lets you use Perl to script and control the rest of the program.

More specific examples include the embedding of Perl into the Xchat IRC client to enable the user to script complex actions in Perl; the GIMP graphics editor, which allows graphical manipulations to be encoded in Perl; the `vim` text editor, which can be both configured and manipulated using Perl; and `gnumeric`, the GNOME spreadsheet, which exposes the data in the spreadsheet cells to Perl for additional manipulation.

All of these examples have common objectives:

- To make the application extensible through user-provided plug-in scripts
- To make configuration more flexible by involving a high-level language and the control structures it provides
- To help the user script common or complex sequences of actions

If an application you are working with could benefit from these features, you should contemplate embedding a Perl interpreter.

8.2 WHEN NOT TO EMBED

Embedding Perl into a program is not a panacea, and embedding Perl into an existing program is not a step to be taken lightly. We don't recommend embedded Perl as a cheap way of avoiding writing a configuration parser or extensible scripting system.

You should also be conscious that embedding Perl into an application will increase its size and memory usage, possibly introduce memory leaks or instabilities if you aren't careful, and occasionally slow the application. Nevertheless, the examples we have given show that, in a lot of cases, you can make a big gain by including Perl in your program.

8.3 THINGS TO THINK ABOUT

In chapter 9, we'll look in more detail at the decisions you need to make when embedding Perl into an application. Fundamentally, however, you must consider the degree to which Perl should have access to the guts of your program.

This consideration in turn influences details such as which data structures you will expose to Perl and how they will appear to the Perl programmer; which C functions in your API will be available, and, again, how they would be used from Perl; where your Perl programs will come from and at what point in the program they will be used; and so on.

Again, you'll see practical answers to these questions in chapter 9. Let's now look at an example of calling a Perl program from inside a C program.

8.4 "HELLO C" FROM PERL

The fundamentals of embedding are simple: you perform almost exactly the same function as the main body of the `perl` binary. That is, you construct and initialize an interpreter, use it to parse a string of code, and then execute that code. Here's a simple program that does so:

```
#include <EXTERN.h>    ❶
#include <perl.h>      ❷

static PerlInterpreter *my_perl;    ❸

int main(int argc, char **argv)
```

```
{
    char* command_line[] = {"", "-e",
                            "print \"Hello from C!\\n\";"};      ❹

    my_perl = perl_alloc();       ❺
    perl_construct(my_perl);        ❻
    perl_parse(my_perl, NULL, 3, command_line, (char **)NULL);     ❼
    perl_run(my_perl);       ❽
    perl_destruct(my_perl);       ❾
    perl_free(my_perl);
    return 0;
}
```

❶ This first header file sets up some macros to tell the main Perl header file that we're not really Perl, but an external application using the Perl API.

❷ We load the main Perl header, which provides the macros and prototypes for all the functions in the Perl API.

❸ It is possible to have multiple Perl interpreters in a program, because all the interpreter-global data is stored in a structure called, naturally, a `PerlInterpreter`. In this program we have one interpreter, which is stored in the pointer `my_perl`.

❹ Even when we're embedding Perl, we're dealing with the honest-to-goodness Perl interpreter, which expects to get arguments from the command line. Hence, we must provide a set of command-line arguments, just as we'd expect to find in `argv`. (And just like in `argv`, the first element of the array is the name of the command, rather than the first command-line argument; we're not bothered about the name of the command, so we leave it blank.)

❺ We need to allocate memory, just as we would for any other structure pointer; `perl_alloc` returns some memory for a Perl interpreter.

❻ Next, we set up the interpreter and all its associated data structures with `perl_construct`.

❼ Now we're in a position where we can parse the incoming Perl "script," which is specified in the `-e` argument to the faked command line.

❽ Perl is bytecode-compiled—first the code is parsed into an internal representation, and then it's run. `perl_run` starts the main loop running the code.

❾ We cleanly shut down the interpreter and release the memory that had been allocated for it.

It's interesting to compare this code with the source of the Perl interpreter; if you don't believe we're performing the same functions as the Perl interpreter, take a look at the guts of `miniperlmain.c` from Perl 5.6.1:

```
if (!PL_do_undump) {
    my_perl = perl_alloc();
    if (!my_perl)
        exit(1);
    perl_construct(my_perl);
    PL_perl_destruct_level = 0;
}

exitstatus = perl_parse(my_perl, xs_init, argc, argv,
                        (char **)NULL);
if (!exitstatus) {
    exitstatus = perl_run(my_perl);
}

perl_destruct(my_perl);
perl_free(my_perl);

PERL_SYS_TERM();

exit(exitstatus);
return exitstatus;
```

As you can see, this is much the same as our example, with a little more error checking.

8.4.1 Compiling embedded programs

Compiling programs that embed Perl is a little special; you must ensure that you're compiling the code with exactly the same options that were used to compile the Perl interpreter. Although you could get them from Config.pm, a module makes it easy for you: ExtUtils::Embed.

As you know from chapter 1, a program's compilation takes place in two stages: compilation proper and linking. ExtUtils::Embed provides two functions, ccopts and ldopts, to tell you the options for each stage. If you run these functions from the perl command line, they'll handily spit out the options to standard output, making the module ideal to use as part of your build process.

Let's compile and then link the previous example code, simple.c:

```
% cc -o simple.o -c simple.c `perl -MExtUtils::Embed -e ccopts`
% cc -o simple simple.o `perl -MExtUtils::Embed -e ldopts`
% ./simple
Hello from C!
```

Now you have a way to execute simple Perl programs from C, albeit if you specify them on the Perl command line. Let's make this approach a bit more powerful.

8.5 PASSING DATA

In a real embedded application, you need a way to share data between Perl and C. For instance, the Apache embedded Perl module, mod_perl, allows you to store configuration data in Perl variables.

As you saw on "get_sv," page 103, Perl provides a function called `get_sv` that lets you grab an SV from the Perl symbol table. Suppose we're writing a mail client (we'll call it Hermes) and we want our users to be able to set some of the configuration in Perl. First, we'll look at general settings that apply to the whole application; in the next section, we'll write some logic for settings that apply on a per-message basis.

Our sample configuration file looks like this:

```
package Hermes;

$save_outgoing = 1;

# Prefer vim, but use emacs if vim not available.
$editor = `which vim` || `which emacs`;

$quote_char = "> ";

$check_every = 10; # seconds
```

Inside our mail client, we'll have Perl parse and run this configuration; we also want to get at the results. We know how to do the first part—we allocate, make, and instantiate a Perl interpreter:

```
#include <EXTERN.h>
#include <perl.h>

static PerlInterpreter *my_perl;

int parse_config(char * config_file)
{
    char* command_line[2] = {"", NULL};
    command_line[1] = config_file;

    my_perl = perl_alloc();
    perl_construct(my_perl);
    if (perl_parse(my_perl, NULL, 2, command_line, (char **)NULL)) {
        return 0; /* Failed to parse */
    }

    perl_run(my_perl);
    if (SvTRUE(ERRSV)) {
        return 0; /* Failed to execute */
    }

    return 1;
}
```

This code is substantially the same as the previous code, except that the "command line" passed to Perl is determined at runtime when the name of the configuration file is passed in to `parse_config`. The other difference is that once we have run the Perl program, we check whether ERRSV is `true`; this is the C-side equivalent of checking $@. We also don't destroy the interpreter, because we'll be using it to get at Perl values and execute Perl code in the rest of our mailer.

Now we have executed the Perl program, and we should be able to determine the values of the configuration variables using the `get_sv` function. For instance, suppose it is time to edit an email message before sending it; we look up the location of the editor we're going to use:

```
int edit_message(char* filename) {
    char *editor;

    editor = SvPV_nolen(get_sv("Hermes::editor"));

    /* And now we execute the editor */
    ...
}
```

Similarly, we can set these SVs to values from our C code using `sv_setpv` or `sv_setiv` if we want to communicate information back to Perl. However, you'll usually pass values to Perl subroutines; let's see how to do this.

8.6 CALLING PERL ROUTINES

The techniques you saw in section 6.7.1 for calling Perl subroutines from XS are equally applicable to calling Perl subroutines from an embedded program. You still need to put parameters onto the stack, make a call out to Perl, and collect return values. Let's take a closer look at those techniques.

Perl has a number of different functions for calling routines, but the two we'll concentrate on are `call_sv` and `call_pv`. It's easy to decide which one to call: if you have an SV that refers to a subroutine—one that contains either a code reference or a subroutine's name (a symbolic reference)—then you use `call_sv`. Otherwise, if you only have the name as a string, you use `call_pv`. The typical embedded program will generally call subroutines by name using `call_pv`, although there are instances where `call_sv` is correct.

For example, suppose we want to allow users of our mailer to define a subroutine that is passed a mail message for preprocessing as the user replies to it. We could state in our program's embedding API that the configuration file must define a subroutine called `Hermes::reply_to_hook`, and we could use `call_pv` with the string `"Hermes::reply_to_hook"`; or, we could allow something like this:

```
package Hermes;
$reply_to_hook = sub {
    my @mail = @_;
    ...
}
```

In this case, we'd use `get_sv("Hermes::reply_to_hook", TRUE)` to return a code reference, which we'd then call with `call_sv`.

You'll see another example where `call_sv` is necessary when we look at callbacks later in this section. For now, we'll concentrate on `call_pv`.

Here's the simplest possible instance of calling a Perl routine from C; it has no parameters and no return value. One good example of this type of routine would be an exit handler—something that our mail program calls when it's about to quit, so that any state established by the Perl program can be cleared up.[1] This would be the Perl side of it:

```perl
package Hermes;
    sub atexit {
    # Close any open file handles
    ...
    #
    print "Thank you for using Hermes/Perl. Going away now.\n";
}
```

And here is the C side:

```c
/* Clean up Perl embedding */
void perl_stop(void) {      ❶
    dSP;       ◁

    PUSHMARK(SP);      ❷
    call_pv("Hermes::atexit", G_DISCARD | G_NOARGS);      ❸

    perl_destruct(my_perl);    ❹
    perl_free(my_perl);
}
```

As in section 6.7.1, dSP provides local access to Perl's argument stack

❶ This function is used before the mailer exits to shut down all elements of the Perl embedding—we'll call our exit handler routine Hermes::atexit, and then close down the Perl interpreter. It's a good idea when you're embedding to keep the number of functions that interact with the Perl interpreter to a minimum, and if possible, in their own separate file. Hence, we have a wrapper function that can be called anywhere in our mailer to shut down the Perl embedding.

❷ PUSHMARK pushes a *bookmark* onto the argument stack. In our example in chapter 6, we used a complicated prologue to call the callback, using ENTER/SAVETMPS/PUSHMARK and PUTBACK/FREETMPS/LEAVE; but we are not concerned about parameters and return values here, so we can do without most of these macros. We must still push a bookmark, because the argument stack is not always empty; if we're already inside a Perl expression, the stack will not be empty. However, when a callback receives parameters or returns values, it needs to know how many items from the top of the stack belong to it. For instance, there may already be four items on the stack before we call Hermes::atexit. Suppose we want to push another two items on as parameters. Perl needs some way to know that the four items previously on the

---

[1] Of course, this is what END blocks are for. If we used an END block in our Perl configuration file, then all these steps would be done automatically—but that would not make a good example.

stack are no concern of `atexit`, and so it pushes a bookmark to denote the bottom of the local stack.

❸ Now we call the routine. `call_pv` and `call_sv` take two parameters: the name or SV for the subroutine to be called, and a set of flags. In this instance, our flags are `G_DISCARD`, signifying that we're going to discard the return value of the call (and therefore that `Hermes::atexit` should be called in void context); and `G_NOARGS`, to state that we're not pushing in any arguments, so the subroutine doesn't need to look at the stack.

❹ We've called the routine, so we can shut down the interpreter and free the memory it used, in preparation for exiting the program.

8.6.1 Stack manipulation

So much for the easy case. Unfortunately, in most other examples, you must deal with both parameters and return values.

Parameters

You already know the basics of handling parameters from "Returning a list," page 181; you use `PUSHs` to put things on the stack. To be sure the values you put onto the stack are properly garbage collected, you need to make them temporary; doing so tells Perl that they should go away at the end of the scope. Thus you must declare a scope—and this is where the `ENTER/SAVETMPS/PUSHMARK` business comes in.

Let's take another example from our mythical mailer and pass a mail message to a Perl function for preprocessing. The message will come in as an array of strings, so we need to make them all into temporary SVs before pushing them onto the stack:

```
void preprocess_callout(char** message) {
    dSP;        ❶
    int i;

    ENTER;             ❷    Again, pushes a bookmark
    SAVETMPS;               to declare the local bottom
    PUSHMARK(SP);    ⏎      of the stack

    for (i=0; message[i]; i++)                        ❸
        XPUSHs(sv_2mortal(newSVpv(message[i], 0)));

    PUTBACK;    ❹

    call_pv("Hermes::preprocess", G_DISCARD);    ❺

    FREETMPS;          Finally, we clean up the temporaries
    LEAVE;             we created and close the scope

}
```

❶ As before, we need a copy of the stack pointer so we know where in memory we're putting our parameters.

❷ We begin by opening a new scope with ENTER and setting out a new scope for temporary values with SAVETMPS.

❸ We iterate over the array, creating a new SV for each line of the message (see "Creating SVs with values," page 106), making them temporary with sv_2mortal, and then pushing them onto the stack. If we knew in advance how many lines we had, we could use EXTEND(n) to pre-extend the stack and then use PUSHs instead of XPUSHs; but the approach we use here keeps things simple.

❹ PUTBACK sets Perl's copy of the stack pointer equal to the value of the local variable SP. Because we've put things onto the stack, our SP will have grown; but our changes to the local variable need to be reflected in the global stack pointer.

❺ Now we can call the function. This time we have some arguments, so we don't use G_NOARGS; but we're still discarding the return value.

Return values

It's not much good preprocessing a message if you don't get the message back after preprocessing it, so you have to deal with return values. Once again, you'll use many of the same principles you saw with respect to XS callbacks. We can modify our example slightly:

```
char** preprocess_callout(char** message) {
    dSP;
    int i;
    int count;
    char **newmessage;

    ENTER;
    SAVETMPS;
    PUSHMARK(SP);

    for (i=0; message[i]; i++)
        XPUSHs(sv_2mortal(newSVpv(message[i], 0)));

    PUTBACK;

    count = call_pv("Hermes::preprocess", G_ARRAY);      ❶

    SPAGAIN;      ❷

    newmessage = malloc((count + 1) * sizeof(char*));
    newmessage[count] = NULL;      i = count;

    while (i > 0)
        newmessage[--i] = savepv(SvPV_nolen(POPs));      ❸
```

```
    FREETMPS;
    LEAVE;

    return newmessage;
}
```

❶ This time we use G_ARRAY to specify that we're calling the function in array context. call_pv returns the number of values returned by the subroutine.

❷ Because the subroutine will have put more values on the stack, we need to refresh our local copy of the stack pointer—this is what SPAGAIN does. Again, this code is the same as in section 6.7.1.

❸ The way we fetch the values is slightly tricky. First, the values come off the stack in reverse order, so we put the first value to be popped at the end of the array. Second, the values on the stack are temporaries and will be swept away at the FREETMPS. Because we don't want to end up with an array of invalid pointers, we make a copy of each string with savepv.

We also need to remember that arrays are zero-based, so if count = 2, we should store the first value in newmessage[1]. This is why we say newmessage[--i].

8.6.2 Context

You've seen that you can use the G_... flags to affect the context of a call. For instance, you can force scalar context on a list function by passing the G_SCALAR flag. The perlcall documentation has a comprehensive list of what all the flag values do and how they affect the context of your call.

8.6.3 Trapping errors with eval

You may have noticed that if a fatal error is generated by the Perl subroutine, then the entire process gets shut down. You should guard against this occurrence in embedded situations, so you need to be aware of another G_... flag.

G_EVAL is the equivalent of wrapping the code to be executed in an eval { ... } block. Let's modify our example again to make sure it doesn't die:

```
char** preprocess_callout(char** message) {
    dSP;
    int i;
    int count;
    char **newmessage;

    ENTER;
    SAVETMPS;
    PUSHMARK(SP);
```

```
    for (i=0; message[i]; i++)
        XPUSHs(sv_2mortal(newSVpv(message[i], 0)));

    PUTBACK;

    count = call_pv("Hermes::preprocess", G_ARRAY | G_EVAL);    ❶

    SPAGAIN;

    if (SvTRUE(ERRSV)) {    ❷
        display_message(
          "An error occurred in the Perl preprocessor: %s",    ❸
          SvPV_nolen(ERRSV));
        return message; /* Go with the original */
    }

    newmessage = malloc((count + 1) * sizeof(char*));
    newmessage[count] = NULL;
    i = count;

    while (i > 0) {
        SV* line_sv = POPs;
        newmessage[--i] = savepv(SvPV_nolen(line_sv));
    }

    FREETMPS;
    LEAVE;

    return newmessage;
}
```

❶ Adding the G_EVAL flag is all we need to do to protect ourselves from a die in the Perl code.

❷ Once we've called the subroutine and restored the stack to normality, we check to see whether the error SV ($@) has a true value.

❸ Assuming we have a function for displaying formatted messages, we spit out the text of the error message and return the original array unmodified.

8.6.4   Calling Perl methods in C

As you know, there are two types of methods: object methods and class methods. They are both called using the call_method function from C code; the trick is that the object (in the case of an object method) or an SV representing the class name (in the case of a class method) must be placed on the stack before any parameters. Here's an example of calling an object method from C:

```
PUSHMARK(sp);
XPUSHs(object);
XPUSHs(param);
PUTBACK;

call_method("display", G_DISCARD);
```

8.6.5 Calling Perl statements

But isn't this approach a lot of work, just to run some Perl code? There should be a much easier way to run Perl code from C. Thankfully, Perl provides functions called `eval_pv` and `eval_sv`, which are essentially the equivalent of `eval "..."`. As with `eval`, you can do anything you can normally do in a Perl program, including load other modules.

For instance, we can use Perl to nicely format a C string, using the `Text::Autoformat` module:

```
char* tidy_string (char* input) {
    SV* result;

    setSVpv(DEFSV, input, 0);
    result = eval_pv("use Text::Autoformat; autoformat($_)", FALSE);
    if (SvTRUE(ERRSV))
        return NULL;
    else
        return SvPV_nolen(result);
}
```

Notice that we store the input string in `$_` (`DEFSV`) and that the second argument to `eval_pv` and `eval_sv` is a boolean denoting the behavior on error—if it is `TRUE`, then the process will exit if the Perl code `dies`.

In many cases, `eval_sv` and `eval_pv` are all you need to get a lot out of embedding Perl in your application. The `perlembed` man page contains a very good example of using Perl's regular expression functions from C with these functions.

8.7 USING C IN PERL IN C

In many cases when embedding Perl in C, you're providing the user with an alternative way of scripting the program's behavior. As a result, you often want to provide a way for the user's Perl to perform actions back in the original C program. For instance, the `mod_perl` Apache module allows Perl programs to control incoming HTTP requests; this control involves such things as finding out information about the request and sending an HTTP response back to the remote client via the Apache server. These things can't be done from Perl, and they must be implemented as calls to C functions inside Apache. Thus, in addition to an embedding framework, you need some XS modules to expose the C API of your programs back to the Perl scripts.

Let's assume we've written an XS module to do this. If we try the obvious solution

```
eval_pv("use Hermes;", TRUE);
```

then this happens:

```
Can't load module Hermes, dynamic loading not available in this perl.
(You may need to build a new perl executable which either supports
dynamic loading or has the Hermes module statically linked into it.)
```

The very basic Perl interpreter we created does not have support for dynamic loading of XS modules.[2]

Adding this support is easy, especially because `ExtUtils::Embed` can help us out again. The easiest way to get started is to use `ExtUtils::Embed`'s `xsinit` function:

```
% perl -MExtUtils::Embed -e xsinit -- Hermes
```

This command creates a file called `perlxsi.c`, which we can link into our program; it provides a function called `xs_init` that we can pass to `perl_parse`:

```
int main(int argc, char **argv)
{
    char* command_line[] = {"", "-e",
                            "print \"Hello from C!\\n\";"};

    my_perl = perl_alloc();
    perl_construct(my_perl);
    perl_parse(my_perl, xs_init, 3, command_line, (char **)NULL);
    perl_run(my_perl);
    perl_destruct(my_perl);
    perl_free(my_perl);
}
```

If you do this, you will also have to link the `Hermes.so` file generated by your XS module to your embedded executable.

A more flexible way to use XS modules is to allow dynamic linking by having `xs_init` load `DynaLoader` for you. You can do so by not passing any parameters to `xsinit`:

```
% perl -MExtUtils::Embed -e xsinit
```

Now your embedded code will be able to load any Perl module.

8.8   EMBEDDING WISDOM

Here are a few random pieces of advice for applications that embed Perl. These ideas have generally been discovered through bitter experience but left undocumented, so we've gathered them together to save you a little time in your own projects:

- Never call `perl_parse` more than once; you'll only leak memory.
- Setting the global variable `PL_destruct_level` to 1 may help if you're having problems with values not being freed properly.
- Avoid using Perl API macros as arguments to other Perl API macros (this advice is also relevant for XS programming).

---

[2]   This is the difference between `miniperlmain.c`, from which we took our first example, and `perlmain.c`, which is the main file used in building an ordinary `perl`.

8.9 SUMMARY

Embedding a Perl interpreter into an application is a great way to increase its flexibility, extensibility, and scriptability. Nevertheless, it comes at a price, in terms of possible memory leaks, a potential drop in speed, and the added complexity of coding the embedding.

We've shown you how to add a Perl interpreter to a program and how to generate build information for the resulting program; we've built a simple interpreter using the `alloc/construct/parse/run/destruct/free` cycle. Once you have an interpreter, you can get at Perl values using `get_sv` and also use any of the functions from the Perl API to communicate with Perl; these abilities include running Perl subroutines via the callback mechanism and examining the Perl stack.

We've also discussed using `eval_pv` as an easy way to execute Perl code and shown you the tricks necessary to allow an embedded interpreter to load XS modules. Finally, we've presented some collected wisdom on the implementation of an embedded application.

CHAPTER 9

Embedding case study

As we mentioned in chapter 8, we'll now apply what we've discussed about embedding Perl to a real application. For our case study, we'll use the mutt mail client, a relatively commonly used Unix mail reader.

The case study will be a no-holds-barred look at the process of embedding Perl into an existing application, including some of the problems we faced and how we worked around them.

9.1 GOALS

Let's begin by looking at what we're trying to achieve. Primarily, we want to give Perl control over the configuration of mutt—we want to rip out the muttrc configuration file parsing and options-checking code and replace it with Perl equivalents. Doing so will allow mutt users to use a Perl configuration file.

For our example, we won't completely rewrite mutt's option parsing. We'll deal with the easiest set of options and leave alone the hooks, address books, custom headers, aliases, and so on. In true textbook style, we leave these items as exercises for the reader.

9.2   PREPARING THE GROUND

We begin, fairly obviously, by getting a copy of the `mutt` sources to work from. At the time of writing, the current development version was 1.3.24, which we downloaded from the `mutt` FTP site (ftp://ftp.mutt.org/pub/mutt/mutt-1.3.24i.tar.gz). After unpacking a pristine copy of the sources, we made another copy called mutt-1.3.24i-perl for our working environment.

Let's look at how to get Perl compiled into the eventual binary. We must modify the configuration and Makefile. `mutt` uses the de facto standard `autoconf` system (http://www.gnu.org/software/autoconf/). We'll make Perl support a configure-time option, which defines the `USE_PERL` macro.

We do this with `autoconf` by declaring the macro in acconfig.h like so:

```
 #undef USE_SASL

+/* Do you want to use Perl for config file parsing?
+   (--with-perl) */
+#undef USE_PERL
+
 /* Do you want support for IMAP GSSAPI authentication?
    (--with-gss) */
 #undef USE_GSS
```

We also add an option in configure.in. We copy some of the code for linking in the SASL authentication library, because it also needs to define a macro and add libraries to the build path. As in chapter 8, we use `ExtUtils::Embed` as a handy, portable way of determining the compile and link options:

```
+dnl Perl config file support
+AC_ARG_WITH(perl,
+    [  --with-perl              Perl support for .muttrc parsing],
+        [
+        if test "$with_perl" != "no"
+        then
+          CFLAGS="$CFLAGS `perl -MExtUtils::Embed -e ccopts`"
+          MUTTLIBS = "$MUTTLIBS `perl -MextUtils::Embed -e ldopts`"
+          AC_DEFINE(USE_PERL)
+        fi
+        ])
+
```

(`AC_DEFINE` means "#define this macro.") Notice that because `configure` (the file generated from configure.in) is a shell script, the backticks are performed when `configure` is run; so, the options are determined when the Makefile is built.

Next, we rerun `autoconf` to regenerate the `configure` command. Testing it both with and without the new `--use-perl` option, we can make sure that `mutt` still compiles.

For completeness, we notice that, like `perl`, `mutt` will show all of its configuration options when given the appropriate command-line argument. So, we make the following change to main.c's `show_version` function:

```
 #ifdef DL_STANDALONE
     "+DL_STANDALONE  "
 #else
     "-DL_STANDALONE  "
 #endif

+#ifdef USE_PERL
+    "+USE_PERL  "
+#else
+    "-USE_PERL  "
+#endif
```

9.3   CONFIGURATION OPTIONS

Let's move on to thinking about how we'll replace the configuration file parsing. `mutt` has several kinds of options: binary options, string options, and quad-state options. After examining the sources, we find that these options are parsed in init.c; the main function is `source_rc`. Because we're going to provide our own facility for parsing `mutt` RC files, we can conditionalize these functions on `#ifndef USE_PERL`.

Our initial idea was to keep everything inside init.c and simply provide two versions of `source_rc`—one for the Perl-based parsing and one for the ordinary parsing. However, this approach turned out to be problematic; some of the macros and structures defined in the `mutt` header files conflicted with Perl's header files, and it would be messy to extricate `mutt`'s definitions from Perl's.

So, we decided to follow our own advice from chapter 8 and put all the embedding functionality in a single file: perl.c. Doing so requires another change to the `Makefile`, which must be specified in configure.in. This time, we need to add to the substituted variable `MUTT_LIB_OBJECTS` by editing configure.in again:

```
        MUTTLIBS="$MUTTLIBSS `perl -MExtUtils::Embed -e ldopts`"
+       MUTT_LIB_OBJECTS="$MUTT_LIB_OBJECTS perl.o"
        AC_DEFINE(USE_PERL)
```

Now we're set up to use perl.c. As an added advantage, we can make our Perl interpreter static to this file. We can write our replacement for `source_rc`, parsing the config file using Perl. Listing 9.1 shows our initial cut of perl.c.

Listing 9.1   Initial attempt at embedding a Perl interpreter inside mutt

```
#include "config.h"

#define REGEXP mutt_REGEXP
#include "mutt.h"
#undef REGEXP /* Don't want mutt's version of this */

#include <EXTERN.h>
```

```
#include <perl.h>

static PerlInterpreter *my_perl;

int source_rc (const char *rcfile, BUFFER *err)
{
  FILE *f;
  pid_t pid;
  struct stat file_stat;
  size_t rc_size;
  char* rc;

  if (stat(rcfile, &file_stat) ||
        ((f = mutt_open_read (rcfile, &pid)) == NULL))
  {
    snprintf (err->data, err->dsize, "%s: %s", rcfile, strerror
(errno));
    return (-1);
  }

  if (!my_perl)
  {
    char *embedding[] = { "", "-e", "0" };
    my_perl = perl_alloc();
    perl_construct(my_perl);
    perl_parse(my_perl, NULL, 3, embedding, NULL);
    perl_run(my_perl);
    /* OK, we now have a Perl up and running */
  }

  rc_size = file_stat.st_size;
  rc = malloc(rc_size);
  fread(rc, 1, rc_size, f);

  if (!rc)
  {
    snprintf (err->data, err->dsize, "%s: %s", rcfile, strerror
(errno));
    return (-1);
  }

  eval_pv(rc, FALSE);
  if (SvTRUE(ERRSV))
  {
    snprintf (err->data, err->dsize, "%s: %s", rcfile,
      SvPV_nolen(ERRSV));
    return (-1);
  }
return (0);
}
```

The bulk of this code is taken from the original `source_rc`. Notice that we've even kept the original code's brace and indentation style—a surprisingly important point when contributing to third-party projects.

The beginning few lines are necessary for the definition of BUFFER. We protect REGEXP by substituting it for mutt_REGEXP while the original header files do their thing and then removing the substitution once they're finished. Then come the familiar set-up lines for an embedded application—the Perl header files and our interpreter.

After testing that we can open the RC file, next comes the good stuff: we read the contents of the file into memory and evaluate it as a Perl string. Thus a Perl .muttrc of the form

```
package Mutt;
our $folder = "/home/simon/mail/";
our $copy = 1;
...
```

will set the appropriate variables. Of course, if there's an error, we need to tell the user about it.

Notice that we don't simply pass the RC file name to Perl on our faked command line, because it's possible that we could be sourcing more than one RC file. That's also why we test whether a Perl interpreter is already instantiated before we create one.

Because we've provided our own source_rc function, we must add a prototype into one of the header files to keep the compiler satisfied. We add the following to mutt.h:

```
#ifdef USE_PERL
int source_rc (const char *rcfile, BUFFER *err);
#endif
```

We'll also need to protect the original version with an #ifndef PERL.

Now our program won't do much, but it should compile and run the user's .muttrcs as Perl programs. However, we don't tidy up the Perl interpreter on exit; let's do that by adding a hook to mutt's mutt_exit in main.c:

```
 void mutt_exit (int code)
 {
   mutt_endwin (NULL);
+#ifdef USE_PERL
+  perl_stop();
+#endif
   exit (code);
 }
```

Once again, this code requires a prototype in mutt.h. Our perl_stop destructor is simply

```
void perl_stop(void)
{
  perl_destruct(my_perl);
  perl_free(my_perl);
}
```

We also need to also add a prototype for `perl_stop`. We'll do so in mutt.h, in the same spot where we declared `source_rc()`:

```
#ifdef USE_PERL
int source_rc (const char *rcfile, BUFFER *err);
void perl_stop(void);
#endif
```

9.4   TESTING OPTIONS

We need to replace the functions that set and test the options. We'll begin with the binary options, because they are the easiest to deal with.

9.4.1   Binary options

`mutt` uses four macros to get and set binary options:

```
#define set_option(x) mutt_bit_set(Options,x)
#define unset_option(x) mutt_bit_unset(Options,x)
#define toggle_option(x) mutt_bit_toggle(Options,x)
#define option(x) mutt_bit_isset(Options,x)
```

We'll use a trick similar to the one we used in the previous section and conditionally replace these macros with functions in perl.c. We fold all the conditional definitions together and end up with something like this:

```
#ifdef USE_PERL
void perl_set_option(int x);
void perl_unset_option(int x);
void perl_toggle_option(int x);
int perl_option(int x);

int source_rc (const char *rcfile, BUFFER *err);
void perl_stop(void);

#define set_option(x) perl_set_option(x)
#define unset_option(x) perl_unset_option(x)
#define toggle_option(x) perl_toggle_option(x)
#define option(x) perl_option(x)
#else
#define set_option(x) mutt_bit_set(Options,x)
#define unset_option(x) mutt_bit_unset(Options,x)
#define toggle_option(x) mutt_bit_toggle(Options,x)
#define option(x) mutt_bit_isset(Options,x)
#endif
```

Now we need to define these functions in perl.c. This is where things get tricky, because the `option` macros aren't passed the name of the option but rather an integer enumerator for the option. This enumerator is keyed to the actual option by the `MuttVars` structure in init.h. The `mutt_option_index` allows us to go from an option name to an enumerator, but we need the opposite. Let's use `mutt_option_index` as a template and write a function to get the name of a boolean value:

```
const char* mutt_option_name_bool(int o) {
  int i;

  for (i = 0; MuttVars[i].option; i++)
    if (MuttVars[i].type == DT_BOOL && MuttVars[i].data == o)
      return MuttVars[i].option;

  return NULL;
}
```

Because MuttVars is declared in the header file for init.c, our mutt_option_name_bool function needs to go there as well.

Now we can think about our functions to get options:

```
int perl_option(int o) {
  const char* optname = mutt_option_name_bool(o);
  char* varname;
  int   rv;

  if (!optname) /* unknown option */
    return 0;

  varname = malloc(strlen(optname) + 7);
  sprintf(varname, "Mutt::%s", optname);
  rv = SvTRUE(get_sv(varname, TRUE));
  free(varname);

  return rv;
}
```

We form our Perl variable name by adding Mutt:: to the front of the option name we derived from the previous step; then we use get_sv to get the Perl-side variable and SvTRUE to test its boolean value. The set functions can be implemented in a similar manner.

9.4.2   Quad-state options

With that under our belt, we can turn to mutt's quad-state options. Quad-state options can be "yes," "no," "ask but yes," or "ask but no." They are handled using a method similar to that of enumerated constants, this time with the OPT_ prefix. We need to redefine the quadoption, set_quadoption, and toggle_quad-option functions from init.c. We begin once again by going from the enumeration to the Perl variable name:

```
const char* mutt_option_name_quad(int o) {
  int i;

  for (i = 0; MuttVars[i].option; i++)
    if (MuttVars[i].type == DT_QUAD && MuttVars[i].data == o)
      return MuttVars[i].option;

  return NULL;
}
```

Now we create a `perl_quadoption` function in perl.c:

```
int perl_quadoption(int o) {
  const char* optname = mutt_option_name_quad(o);
  char* varname;
  SV* option;

  if (!optname) /* unknown option */
    return 0;

  varname = malloc(strlen(optname) + 7);
  sprintf(varname, "Mutt::%s", optname);
  option = get_sv(varname, TRUE);
  free(varname);
  if (strEQ(SvPV_nolen(option), "no"))
    return 0;
  else if (strEQ(SvPV_nolen(option), "yes"))
    return 1;
  else if (strEQ(SvPV_nolen(option), "ask-no"))
    return 2;
  else if (strEQ(SvPV_nolen(option), "ask-yes"))
    return 3;
  else /* invalid value */
    return 0;
}
```

9.4.3   String options

Finally, we turn to string options, which are the most difficult. They are a pain because they're keyed slightly differently from the other options. For instance, when the RC file parser comes across `attach_format`, it looks it up in the `MuttVars` structure and finds that it is attached to the global variable `AttachFormat`. Other parts of the code use this variable directly.

This is one of the points in embedding where we have to get our hands dirty and rip up the existing code. We replace every occurrence of string option variables with a function—hence `AttachFormat` now appears as:

```
mutt_string_option("attach_format")
```

The function has two definitions: one in init.c like this

```
char* mutt_string_option(char* o) {
  int i;

  for (i = 0; MuttVars[i].option; i++)
    if (mutt_strcmp (o, MuttVars[i].option) == 0)
      return *(MuttVars[i].data);

  return NULL;
}
```

and one in `perl.c` like this

```
char* string_option(char* o) {
```

```
    char * rv;
    char * varname = malloc(strlen(o) + 7);

    sprintf(varname, "Mutt::%s", o);
    rv = SvPV_nolen(get_sv(varname, TRUE));
    free(varname);
    return rv;
}
```

After all that, `mutt` should be able to read configuration files in Perl!

9.5   SUMMARY

We've shown you a simple, but real, example of what it means to embed Perl into an application, as well as some of the problems we've come across and how we've faced them. In most cases, it's surprisingly easy to add Perl support; unfortunately, there will always be some cases in which you have no option but to restructure the code of the host application.

If you are lucky, the application will be designed with embedding in mind. Apache's module support made it easy to embed Perl without disturbing much of the code around it. In our example, we had to start from scratch, planning how to get Perl into the application and the interface we would provide for it. Notice, however, that we kept the embedding completely optional; it's switchable by a single configuration option. You should aim to do this if possible, because it further minimizes the effect of your changes on the rest of the code base.

We could have done a lot more with `mutt`; for instance, we could have turned `mutt`'s built-in hook mechanism into a callback mechanism to call Perl subroutines. We also could have dealt with the list-based options, using Perl arrays to hold multiple values. And, finally, we could have tidied up our interface, using Perl hashes to store the `MuttVars` options structure, and eliminating some of the lookups. However, our example has given you a taste of how to approach the topic of embedding Perl in an existing application.

C H A P T E R   1 0

Introduction to Perl internals

You've seen how to extend Perl with C libraries and how to embed Perl in C applications; where next? To the internals of the `perl` interpreter, of course! This chapter provides an introduction to the workings of `perl`. By the end of the chapter, you should have a good idea of what happens to a Perl program as it is digested and executed.

10.1   THE SOURCE TREE

This section introduces the major parts of the Perl source tree with which you should be familiar.

10.1.1   The Perl library

The most approachable part of the source code, for Perl programmers, is the Perl library. It resides in lib/ and comprises all the standard, pure Perl modules and pragmata that ship with `perl`.

Both Perl5 modules and unmaintained Perl4 libraries are shipped for backward compatibility. In Perl 5.6.0, the Unicode tables are placed in lib/unicode, and in Perl 5.8.0 they have been moved to lib/unicore.

10.1.2 The XS library

You'll find the XS modules that ship with Perl in ext/. For instance, the Perl compiler B can be found here, as can the DBM interfaces. The most important XS module here is DynaLoader, the dynamic-loading interface that allows the runtime loading of every other XS module.

As a special exception, you'll find the XS code to the methods in the UNIVERSAL class in universal.c.[1]

10.1.3 The I/O subsystem

Recent versions of Perl (5.8.0 and later) come with a completely new standard I/O implementation: PerlIO. It allows several layers to be defined through which all I/O is filtered, similar to the line disciplines mechanism in sfio. These layers interact with modules such as PerlIO::Scalar, which is also in the ext/ directory.

The I/O subsystem is implemented in perlio.c and perlio.h. Declarations for defining the layers are in perliol.h, and documentation on how to create layers is in pod/perliol.pod.

You can compile Perl without PerlIO support, in which case a number of abstraction layers present a unified I/O interface to the Perl core. perlsdio.h aliases ordinary standard I/O functions to their PerlIO names, and perlsfio.h does the same thing for the alternate I/O library sfio.

The other abstraction layer is the *Perl host* scheme in iperlsys.h. This is confusing. The idea is to reduce process overhead on Win32 systems by having multiple Perl interpreters access all system calls through a shared Perl host abstraction object. You can find an explanation in perl.h, but it is best avoided.

10.1.4 The Regexp engine

Another area of the Perl source that's best avoided is the regular expression engine. It resides in reg*.*. The regular expression matching engine is, roughly speaking, a state machine generator. Your match pattern is turned into a state machine made up of various match nodes—you can see these nodes in regcomp.sym. The compilation phase is handled by regcomp.c, and the state machine's execution is performed in regexec.c.

10.1.5 The parser and tokenizer

The first stage in Perl's operation is to understand your program. It does so through a joint effort of the tokenizer and the parser. The tokenizer is found in toke.c and the parser in perly.c (although you're far better off looking at the Yacc[2] source in perly.y).

---

[1] That's right—ordinary C files can contain XS code. As you know, code written in the XS language is stored in files with the extension .xs and preprocessed by xsubpp into C code. The universal.c file contains preprocessed code such as would be generated by xsubpp; but all the same, it provides an interface between Perl functions and C code.

The job of the tokenizer is to split the input into meaningful chunks, or *tokens*, and also to determine what type of thing they represent—a Perl keyword, a variable, a subroutine name, and so on. The job of the parser is to take these tokens and turn them into *sentences*, understanding their relative meaning in context.

10.1.6   Variable handling

As you already know, Perl provides C-level implementations of scalars, arrays, and hashes. The code for handling arrays is in av.*, for hashes in hv.*, and for scalars in sv.*.

10.1.7   Runtime execution

The code for Perl's built-ins—`print`, `foreach`, and the like—resides in pp.*. Some of the functionality is shelled out to doop.c and doio.c for I/O functions.

The main loop of the interpreter is in run.c.

10.2   THE PARSER

Perl is a bytecode-compiled language, which means execution of a Perl program happens in two stages. First, the program is read, parsed, and compiled into an internal representation of the operations to be performed; after that, the interpreter takes over and traverses this internal representation, executing the operations in order. We'll first look at how Perl is parsed, before moving on to the internal representation of a program.

As we discussed earlier, the parser resides in perly.y. This code is in a language called Yacc, which is converted to C using the `byacc` command. In order to understand this language, you must understand how grammars and parsing work.

10.2.1   BNF and parsing

Computer programmers define a language by its grammar, which is a set of rules. They usually describe this grammar in a form called *Backhaus-Naur Form*[3] (BNF). BNF tells you how phrases fit together to make sentences. For instance, here's a simple BNF for English—obviously, it doesn't describe the whole of the English grammar, but it's a start:

```
sentence    : nounphrase verbphrase nounphrase;

verbphrase  : VERB;

nounphrase  : NOUN
```

---

[2]   *Yet Another Compiler Compiler*

[3]   Sometimes *Backhaus Normal Form*

```
|  ADJECTIVE   nounphrase
|  PRONOMINAL  nounphrase
|  ARTICLE     nounphrase;
```

The prime rule of BNF is as follows: you can make the thing on the left of the colon if you see all the things on the right in sequence. So, this grammar tells you that a sentence is made up of a noun phrase, a verb phrase, and then a noun phrase. The vertical bar does what it does in regular expressions: you can make a noun phrase if you have a noun, or an adjective plus another noun phrase, or a pronominal plus a noun phrase, or an article plus a noun phrase. Turning the things on the right into the thing on the left is called a *reduction*. The idea of parsing is to reduce all the input to the first thing in the grammar—a sentence.

Things that can't be broken down any further are in capitals—no rule tells you how to make a noun, for instance. Such things are fed to you by the lexer; they are called *terminal symbols*, and the things that aren't in capitals are called *non-terminal symbols*. To understand why, let's see what happens if we try to parse the sentence from figure 10.1 in this grammar:

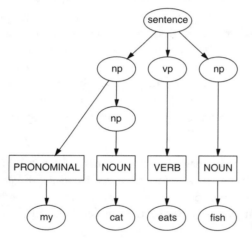

Figure 10.1
Parsing an English sentence

1 The text at the bottom—*my cat eats fish*—is what we get from the user. The tokenizer turns it into a series of tokens—PRONOMINAL NOUN VERB NOUN.

2 From the tokens, we can begin performing some reductions: we have a pronominal, so we're looking for a noun phrase to satisfy the nounphrase : PRONOMINAL nounphrase rule. We can make a noun phrase by reducing the NOUN (*cat*) into a nounphrase.

3 We can use PRONOMINAL nounphrase to make another nounphrase.

4 We have a nounphrase and a VERB. We can't do anything further with the nounphrase, so we'll switch to the VERB; the only thing we can do with it is turn it into a verbphrase.

CHAPTER 10   INTRODUCTION TO PERL INTERNALS

5 We can reduce the noun to a nounphrase, leaving us with nounphrase verbphrase nounphrase.

6 We can turn this result into a sentence, so we've parsed the text.

10.2.2 Parse actions and token values

It's important to note that the tree we constructed in the previous section—the *parse tree*—is only a device to help us understand the parsing process. It doesn't exist as a data structure anywhere in the parser. This is a little inconvenient, because the whole point of parsing a piece of Perl text is to come up with a data structure pretty much like this device.

Fortunately, Yacc lets you extend BNF by adding actions to rules. Every time the parser performs a reduction using a rule, it can trigger a piece of C code to be executed. Here's an extract from Perl's grammar in perly.y:

```
term    :    term ASSIGNOP term
             { $$ = newASSIGNOP(OPf_STACKED, $1, $2, $3); }
        |    term ADDOP term
             { $$ = newBINOP($2, 0, scalar($1), scalar($3)); }
```

The pieces of code in the curly braces ({ }) are actions to be performed. Here's the final piece of the puzzle: each symbol carries some additional information. For instance, in our *cat* example, the first NOUN had the value cat. You can get the value of a symbol from a Yacc variable that begins with a dollar sign: in the previous example, $1 is the value of the first symbol on the right of the colon (term), $2 is the value of the second symbol (either ASSIGNOP or ADDOP, depending on which line you're reading), and so on. $$ is the value of the symbol on the left. Hence information is propagated up the parse tree by manipulating the information on the right and assigning it to the symbol on the left.

10.2.3 Parsing some Perl

Let's see what happens if we parse the Perl code $a = $b + $c. We have to assume that $a, $b, and $c have already been parsed a little; they'll turn into term symbols. Each of these symbols will have a value, which will be an *op*. An op is a data structure representing an operation, and the operation to be represented will be that of retrieving the storage pointed to by the appropriate variable.

Let's start from the right[4] and deal with $b + $c. The lexer turns the + into the terminal symbol ADDOP. Now, just as lots of different nouns can all be tokenized to NOUN, there can be several different ADDOPs—concatenation is classified as an ADDOP, so $b . $c would look just the same to the parser. The difference, of course, is the value of the symbol—this ADDOP will have the value '+'.

---

[4] This is slightly disingenuous, because parsing is always done from left to right; but this simplification is easier than getting into the details of how Yacc grammars recognize the precedence of operators.

Hence, we have `term ADDOP term`. As a result, we can perform a reduction using the second rule in our snippet. When we do, we must perform the code in curly braces under the rule:

```
{ $$ = newBINOP($2, 0, scalar($1), scalar($3)); }
```

`newBINOP` is a function that creates a new binary op. The first argument is the type of binary operator, and we feed it the value of the second symbol. This symbol is `ADDOP`, and as we have just noted, it has the value `'+'`. So, although `'.'` and `'+'` look the same to the parser, they'll eventually be distinguished by the value of their symbol. The next argument of `newBINOP` contains the flags we wish to pass to the op. We don't want anything special, so we pass 0.

Next come our arguments to the binary operator. Obviously, these are the value of the symbol on the left and the value of the symbol on the right of the operator. As we mentioned earlier, these are both ops, to retrieve the values of `$b` and `$c`, respectively. We assign the new op created by `newBINOP` to be the value of the symbol we're propagating upward. Hence, we've taken two ops—the ones for `$b` and `$c`—plus an addition symbol, and turned them into a new op representing the combined action of fetching the values of `$b` and `$c` and then adding them together.

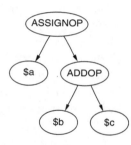

Figure 10.2
Parsing $a = $b + $c

Now we do the same thing with `$a = ($b+$c)`. We've put the right side in braces to show that we already have something that represents fetching `$b` and `$c` and adding them. `=` is turned into an `ASSIGNOP` by the tokenizer the same way we turned `+` into an `ADDOP`. And, in the same way, there are various types of assignment operators: `||=` and `&&=` are also passed as `ASSIGNOP`s. From here, it's easy: we take the `term` representing `$a`, plus the `ASSIGNOP`, plus the `term` we've just constructed, reduce them all to another `term`, and perform the action under the rule. We end up with a data structure a little like that shown in figure 10.2.

NOTE   You can find a hypertext version of the Perl grammar at http://simon-cozens.org/hacks/grammar.pdf.

10.3   THE TOKENIZER

The tokenizer in toke.c is one of the most difficult parts of the Perl core to understand, primarily because there is no roadmap to explain its operation. In this section, we'll show how the tokenizer is put together.

10.3.1   Basic tokenizing

The core of the tokenizer is the intimidatingly long `yylex` function. This function is called by the parser, `yyparse`, when it requests a new token of input.

Let's begin with some basics. When a token has been identified, it is placed in `PL_tokenbuf`. Input is read from the filehandle `PL_rsfp`. The current position in the input is stored in the variable `PL_bufptr`, which is a pointer into the `PV` of the `SV PL_linestr`. When scanning for a token, the variable `s` advances from the start of `PL_bufptr` toward the end of the buffer (`PL_bufend`) until it finds a token.

The parser tests whether the next thing in the input stream has already been identified as an identifier; when the tokenizer sees `'%'`, `'$'`, and the like as part of the input, it tests to see whether it introduces a variable. If so, it puts the variable name into the token buffer. It then returns the type sigil (`%`, `$`, and so forth) as a token and sets a flag (`PL_pending_ident`) so that the next time `yylex` is called, it can pull the variable name straight out of the token buffer. Hence, right at the top of `yylex`, you'll see code that tests `PL_pending_ident` and deals with the variable name.

Tokenizer state

Next, if there's no identifier in the token buffer, the tokenizer checks its state. It uses the variable `PL_lex_state` to store state information.

One important state is `LEX_KNOWNEXT`, which occurs when Perl has had to look ahead one token to identify something. If this happens, it has tokenized not just the next token, but the one after as well. Hence, it sets `LEX_KNOWNEXT` to say "we've already tokenized this token; simply return it."

The functions that set `LEX_KNOWNEXT` are `force_word`, which declares that the next token must be a word (for instance, after having seen an arrow in `$foo->bar`); `force_ident`, which makes the next token an identifier (for instance, if it sees a `*` when not expecting an operator, meaning this must be a glob); `force_version` (on seeing a number after `use`); and the general `force_next`.

Many of the other states have to do with interpolation of double-quoted strings; we'll look at those in more detail in the next section.

Looking ahead

After checking its state, it's time for the lexer to peek at the buffer and see what's waiting; this is the beginning of the giant `switch` statement in the middle of `yylex`, just after the label `retry`.

One of the first things we check for is character zero—it signifies either the start or the end of the file or the end of the line. If it's the end of the file, the tokenizer returns `0` and the game is won; at the beginning of the file, Perl has to process the code for command-line switches such as `-n` and `-p`. Otherwise, Perl calls `filter_gets` to get a new line from the file through the source filter system, and calls `incline` to increase the line number.

The next test is for comments and new lines, which Perl skips. After that are tests for individual special characters. For instance, the first test is for minus, which could be any of the following:

- Unary minus if followed by a number or identifier
- The binary minus operator if Perl is expecting an operator

- The arrow operator if followed by a >
- The start of a filetest operator if followed by an appropriate letter
- A quoting option such as (-foo => "bar")

Perl tests for each case and returns the token type using one of the uppercase token macros defined at the beginning of toke.c: OPERATOR, TERM, and so on.

If the next character isn't a symbol Perl knows about, it's an alphabetic character that might start a keyword: the tokenizer jumps to the label keylookup, where it checks for labels and things like CORE::function. It then calls keyword to test whether it is a valid built-in; if so, keyword turns it into a special constant (such as KEY_open), which can be fed into the switch statement. If it's not a keyword, Perl has to determine whether it's a bareword, a function call, an indirect object, or a method call.

Keywords

The final section of the switch statement deals with the KEY_ constants handed back from keyword; this section performs any actions necessary for using the built-ins. (For instance, given __DATA__, the tokenizer sets up the DATA filehandle.)

10.3.2 Sublexing

Sublexing refers to the fact that a different type of tokenization is required inside double-quoted strings and other interpolation contexts (regular expressions, for instance). This process is typically started after a call to scan_str, which is an exceptionally clever piece of code that extracts a string with balanced delimiters, placing it into the SV PL_lex_stuff. Then sublex_start is called; it sets up the data structures used for sublexing and changes the lexer's state to LEX_INTERPPUSH, which is essentially a scoping operator for sublexing.

To understand why sublexing needs scoping, consider something like "Foo\u\LB\uarBaz". This is tokenized as the equivalent of

```
"Foo" . ucfirst(lc("B" . ucfirst("arBaz")))
```

The push state (which makes a call to sublex_push) quite literally pushes an opening bracket onto the input stream, and then changes the state to LEX_INTERPCONCAT; the concatenation state uses scan_const to pull out constant strings and supplies the concatenation operator between them. If a variable to be interpolated is found, the state is changed to LEX_INTERPSTART: this means "foo$bar" is changed into "foo".$bar and "foo@bar" is turned into "foo".join($",@bar).

Sometimes the tokenizer is not sure when sublexing of an interpolated variable should end. In these cases, a function called intuit_more is called to make an educated guess about the likelihood of more interpolation.

Finally, once sublexing is finished, the state is set to LEX_INTERPEND, which puts any outstanding closing brackets into place.

10.3.3 Tokenizer summary

We've briefly examined how Perl turns Perl source input into a tree data structure suitable for executing. Next, we'll look more specifically at the nature of the nodes in that tree.

This operation has two stages:

1 The tokenizer, toke.c, chops up the incoming program and recognizes different token types.

2 The parser, perly.y, assembles these tokens into phrases and sentences.

In reality, the whole task is driven by the parser—Perl calls yyparse to parse a program, and when the parser needs to know about the next token, it calls yylex.

Although the parser is relatively straightforward, the tokenizer is trickier. The key to understanding it is to divide its operation into checking the tokenizer state, dealing with non-alphanumeric symbols in ordinary program code, dealing with alphanumerics, and dealing with double-quoted strings and other interpolation contexts.

Few people understand entirely how the tokenizer and parser work. However, this part of the chapter has given you a useful insight into how Perl understands program code and how you can locate the source of particular behavior inside the parsing system.

10.4 OP CODE TREES

You've seen that the job of the parsing stage is to reduce a program to a tree structure, and each node of the tree represents an operation. In this section, we'll look more closely at those operations: what they are, how they're coded, and how they fit together.

10.4.1 The basic op

Just as AVs and HVs are extensions of the basic SV structure, there are a number of different flavors of ops, built on a basic OP structure. You can find this structure defined as BASEOP in op.h:

```
OP*          op_next;
OP*          op_sibling;
OP*          (CPERLscope(*op_ppaddr))(pTHX);
PADOFFSET    op_targ;
OPCODE       op_type;
U16          op_seq;
U8           op_flags;
U8           op_private;
```

Some of these fields are easy to explain, so we'll deal with them now.

The op_next field is a pointer to the next op that needs to be executed. You'll see in section 10.4.4 how the thread of execution is derived from the tree.

op_ppaddr is the address of the C function that carries out this particular operation. It's stored here so that your main execution code can simply dereference the function pointer and jump to it, instead of having to perform a lookup.

Each unique operation has a different number; you can find it in the `enum` in opnames.h:

```
typedef enum opcode {
    OP_NULL,         /* 0 */
    OP_STUB,         /* 1 */
    OP_SCALAR,       /* 2 */
    OP_PUSHMARK,     /* 3 */
    OP_WANTARRAY,    /* 4 */
    OP_CONST,        /* 5 */

    ...
    OP_SETSTATE,     /* 349 */
    OP_METHOD_NAMED, /* 350 */
    OP_CUSTOM,       /* 351 */
    OP_max
};
```

The number of the operation to perform is stored in the `op_type` field. We'll examine some of the more interesting operations in section 10.4.4.

`op_flags` is a set of flags generic to all ops; `op_private` stores flags specific to the type of op. For instance, the `repeat` op, which implements the x operator, has the flag `OPpREPEAT_DOLIST` set when it's repeating a list rather than a string. This flag makes sense only for that particular operation, so it's stored in `op_private`. Private flags have the `OPp` prefix, and public flags begin with `OPf`.

`op_seq` is a sequence number allocated by the optimizer. Among other things, it allows for correct scoping of lexical variables by storing the sequence numbers of the beginning and end of scope operations inside the pad.

We'll examine `op_sibling` in section 10.4.3 and `op_targ` in section 10.4.7.

10.4.2   The different operations

Perl currently has 351 different operations implementing all the built-in functions and operators, as well as the more structural operations required internally—entering and leaving a scope, compiling regular expressions, and so on. The array `PL_op_desc` in opcode.h describes each operation: it may be easier to follow the data from which this table is generated, at the end of opcode.pl. We'll take a closer look at that file later in section 10.4.3.

Many of the operators are familiar from Perl-space, such as `concat` and `splice`, but some are used purely internally: for instance, one of the most common, `gvsv`, fetches a scalar variable; `enter` and `leave` are block control operators; and so on.

10.4.3   Different flavors of ops

There are a number of different flavors of op structures related to the arguments of an operator and how it fits together with other ops in the op tree. For instance, `scalar` is a unary operator (UNOP). It extends the basic op structure shown earlier with a link to the argument:

```
struct unop {
    BASEOP
    OP *    op_first;
};
```

Binary operators, such as i_add (integer addition), have both a first and a last:

```
struct binop {
    BASEOP
    OP *    op_first;
    OP *    op_last;
};
```

List operators are more interesting; they have a first and a last, but they also have some ops in the middle. This is where op_sibling comes in; it connects sibling ops on the same level in a list. For instance, look at the following code and the graph of its op tree in figure 10.3:

```
open FILE, "foo";
print FILE "hi\n";
close FILE;
```

The dashed lines represent op_sibling connections. The root operator of every program is the list operator leave, and its children are the statements in the program, separated by nextstate (next statement) operators. open is also a list operator, as is print. The first child of print is pushmark, which puts a mark on the stack (see "The argument stack," page 291) so that Perl knows how many arguments on the stack belong to print. rv2gv turns a reference to the filehandle FILE into a GV, so that print can print to it; and the final child is the constant hi\n.

Some operators hold information about the program; these are code operators (COPs) . Their definition is in cop.h:

```
struct cop {
    BASEOP
    char *  cop_label;  /* label for this construct */
#ifdef USE_ITHREADS
```

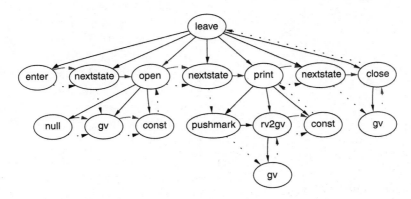

Figure 10.3   Sibling ops in an op tree

```
    char *   cop_stashpv;    /* package line was compiled in */
    char *   cop_file;    /* file name the following line # is from */
#else
    HV *     cop_stash;   /* package line was compiled in */
    GV *     cop_filegv; /* file the following line # is from */
#endif
    U32      cop_seq;      /* parse sequence number */
    I32      cop_arybase;    /* array base this line was
                                compiled with */
    line_t     cop_line;        /* line # of this command */
    SV *     cop_warnings;   /* lexical warnings bitmask */
    SV *     cop_io;        /* lexical IO defaults */
};
```

COPs are inserted between every statement; they contain the label (for goto, next, and so on) of the statement; the file name, package, and line number of the statement; and lexical hints such as the current value of $[, warnings, and I/O settings. Note that a COP doesn't contain the current CV or the padlist—these are kept on a special stack called the *context stack*.

The final type of op is the null op. Any op with type zero means a previous op has been optimized away (we'll look at how this is done in section 10.4.8); for now, you should skip the null op when you see it in an op tree.

10.4.4 Tying it all together

You've seen a little about how the op tree is connected together with op_first, op_last, op_sibling, and so on. Now we'll look at how the tree is manufactured and how it is executed.

Tree order

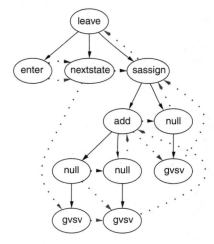

After our investigation of the parser in section 10.2, it should now be straightforward to see how the op tree is created. The parser calls routines in op.c that create the op structures, passing ops further down the parse tree as arguments. This process threads together a tree as shown in figure 10.3. For comparison, figure 10.4 shows what the example in that section ($a = $b + $c) looks like as an op tree.

Again, you can see the places where an op was optimized away and became a null op. This is not so different from the simplified version we gave earlier.

Figure 10.4
The op tree for $a = $b + $c

Execution order

The second thread through the op tree, indicated by the dotted line in our diagrams, is the execution order. This is the order in which Perl must perform the operations to run the program. The main loop of Perl is very simple, and you can see it in run.c:

```
while ((PL_op = CALL_FPTR(PL_op->op_ppaddr)(aTHX))) {
    PERL_ASYNC_CHECK();
}
```

That's all the Perl interpreter is. PL_op represents the op that's currently being executed. Perl calls the function pointer for that op and expects another op to be returned; this return value is then set to PL_op, which is executed in turn. Because everything apart from conditional operators (for obvious reasons) just return PL_op->op_next, you can find the execution order through a program by chasing the trail of op_next pointers from the start node to the root.

You can trace the execution order in several ways. If Perl is built with debugging (section 11.2.2), then we can say

```
perl -Dt -e 'open ...'
```

Alternatively, and perhaps more simply, the compiler module B::Terse has an -exec option to print the execution order. For instance, in our open-print-close example earlier, the execution order is

```
% perl -MO=Terse,-exec -e 'open FILE, "foo"; ...'
OP (0x8111510) enter               ❶
COP (0x81121c8) nextstate
OP (0x8186f30) pushmark      ❷  )
SVOP (0x8186fe0) gv  GV (0x8111bd8) *FILE        ❸
SVOP (0x8186f10) const  PV (0x810dd98) "foo"
LISTOP (0x810a170) open [1]
COP (0x81114d0) nextstate
OP (0x81114b0) pushmark              ❹
SVOP (0x8118318) gv  GV (0x8111bd8) *FILE
UNOP (0x8111468) rv2gv
SVOP (0x8111448) const  PV (0x8111bfc) "hi\n"
LISTOP (0x8111488) print  ❺
COP (0x8111fe0) nextstate
SVOP (0x8111fc0) gv  GV (0x8111bd8) *FILE        ❻
UNOP (0x8111fa0) close
LISTOP (0x8111420) leave [1]
```

❶ This program, like every other program, begins with the enter and nextstate ops to enter a scope and begin a new statement, respectively.

❷ Then a mark is placed on the argument stack: marks represent the start of a set of arguments, and a list operator can retrieve all the arguments by pushing values off the stack until it finds a mark. Hence, we're notifying Perl of the beginning of the arguments to the open operator.

❸ The arguments in this case are the filehandle to be opened and the filename; after operators put these two arguments on the stack, `open` can be called. This is the end of the first statement.

❹ Next, the arguments to `print` begin. This is trickier, because whereas `open` can only take a true filehandle, `print` can take any sort of reference. Hence, `gv` returns the GV, which is turned into the appropriate filehandle type by the `rv2gv` operator. After the filehandle come the arguments to be printed—in this case, a constant (`"hi\n"`).

❺ Now that all the arguments have been placed on the stack, `print` can be called. This is the end of the second statement.

❻ Finally, a filehandle is put on the stack and closed.

Note that at this point, the connections between the operators—unary, binary, and so forth—are not important; all manipulation of values comes not by looking at the children of the operators but by looking at the stack. The types of op are important for the construction of the tree in tree order, but the stack and the `op_next` pointers are the only important things for the execution of the tree in execution order.

> **NOTE** You may wonder how the execution order is determined. The function `linklist` in op.c takes care of threading the `op_next` pointers in prefix order. It does so by recursively applying the following rule: if there is a child for the current operator, visit the child first, then its siblings, and then the current op.
>
> Hence, the starting operator is always the first child of the root operator (always `enter`), the second op to be executed is its sibling (`nextstate`), and then the children of the next op are visited. Similarly, the root (`leave`) is always the last operator to be executed. Null operators are skipped during optimization.

10.4.5 PP Code

You know the order of execution of the operations and what some of them do. Now it's time to examine how they're implemented—the source code inside the interpreter that carries out `print`, `+`, and other operations.

The functions that implement operations are known as push pop code (PP code) because most of their work involves popping elements off a stack, performing some operation on them, and then pushing the result back. PP code can be found in several files:

- pp_hot.c contains frequently used code, put into a single object to encourage CPU caching.
- pp_ctl.c contains operations related to flow control.
- pp_sys.c contains system-specific operations such as file and network handling.
- pp_pack.c is a recent addition, containing the code for `pack` and `unpack`.
- pp.c contains everything else.

The argument stack

We've already talked a little about the argument stack. The Perl interpreter uses several stacks, but the argument stack is the main one.

The best way to see how the argument stack is used is to watch it in operation. With a debugging build of Perl, the -Ds command-line switch prints out the contents of the stack in symbolic format between operations. Here is a portion of the output of running $a=5; $b=10; print $a+$b; with the -Dst debug flags:

```
(-e:1)   nextstate        │  At the beginning of a statement,
   =>                     │  the stack is typically empty
(-e:1)   pushmark        ❶
   =>     *
(-e:1)   gvsv(main::a)        The values of $a and $b
   =>     *   IV(5)           are retrieved and
(-e:1)   gvsv(main::b)        pushed onto the stack
   =>     *   IV(5)   IV(10)
(-e:1)   add             ❷
   =>     *   IV(15)
(-e:1)   print           ❸
   =>     SV_YES
```

❶ Perl pushes a mark onto the stack to know when to stop pushing off arguments for print.

❷ The addition operator is a binary operator; hence, logically, it takes two values off the stack, adds them together, and puts the result back onto the stack.

❸ Finally, print takes all the values off the stack up to the previous bookmark and prints them out. Let's not forget that print itself has a return value—the true value SV_YES—which it pushes back onto the stack.

Stack manipulation

Let's now look at one of the PP functions: the integer addition function pp_i_add. The code may look formidable, but it's a good example of how the PP functions manipulate values on the stack:

```
PP(pp_i_add)    ❶
{
    dSP; dATARGET; tryAMAGICbin(add,opASSIGN);    ❷
    {
      dPOPTOPiirl_ul;    ❸
      SETi( left + right );    ❹
      RETURN;    ❺
    }
}
```

❶ In case you haven't guessed, everything in this function is a macro. This first line declares the function `pp_i_add` to be the appropriate type for a PP function.

❷ Because the following macros will need to manipulate the stack, we need a local copy of the stack pointer, `SP`. And because this is C, we need to declare it in advance: `dSP` declares a stack pointer. Then we need an `SV` to hold the return value, a *target*. It is declared with `dATARGET` (see section 10.4.7 for more about how targets work). Finally, there is a chance that the addition operator has been overloaded using the `overload` pragma. The `tryAMAGICbin` macro tests to see if it is appropriate to perform A (overload) magic on either of the scalars in a binary operation; if so, the macro does the addition using a magic method call.

❸ We will deal with two values, `left` and `right`. The `dPOPTOPiirl_ul` macro pops two SVs off the top of the stack, converts them to two integers (hence `ii`), and stores them into automatic variables `right` and `left` (hence `rl`).

> **NOTE** Wondering about the `_ul`? It makes sure the value on the stack that we're going to use for the "left" variable is a real `SV`, and defaults to zero if it isn't.

❹ We add the two values and set the integer value of the target to the result, pushing the target to the top of the stack.

❺ As mentioned earlier, operators are expected to return the next op to be executed, and in most cases this is simply the value of `op_next`. Hence `RETURN` performs a normal return, copying the local stack pointer `SP` we obtained back into the global stack pointer variable, and then returning the `op_next`.

As you might have guessed, there are a number of macros for controlling what happens to the stack; you'll find them in pp.h. The more common are as follows:

- *POPs*—Pops an `SV` off the stack and returns it.
- *POPpx*—Pops a string off the stack and returns it (requires a variable `STRLEN n_a` to be in scope).
- *POPn*—Pops an `NV` off the stack.
- *POPi*—Pops an `IV` off the stack.
- *TOPs*—Returns the top `SV` on the stack, but does not pop it (the macros `TOPpx`, `TOPn`, and so forth are analogous).
- *TOPm1s*—Returns the penultimate `SV` on the stack (there is no `TOPm1px`, and so on).
- *PUSHs*—Pushes the scalar onto the stack; you must ensure that the stack has enough space to accommodate it.
- *PUSHn*—Sets the `NV` of the target to the given value and pushes it onto the stack. `PUSHi` and so forth are analogous. In addition, `XPUSHn` and so on extend the stack if necessary.

- *SETs*—Sets the top element of the stack to the given SV. SETn and so forth are analogous.
- *dTOPss, dPOPss*—Declare a variable called sv and either return the top entry from the stack or pop an entry and set sv to it.
- *dTOPnv, dPOPnv*—Similar, but declare a variable called value of the appropriate type. dTOPiv and so on are analogous.

In some cases, the PP code is purely concerned with rearranging the stack, and the PP function will call out to another function in doop.c to perform the relevant operation.

10.4.6   The opcode table and opcodes.pl

The header files for the opcode tables are generated from a Perl program called opcode.pl. Here is a sample entry for an op:

```
index        index             ck_index isT@    S S S?
```

The entry is in five columns:

- The first column is the internal name of the operator. When opcode.pl is run, it will create an enum including the symbol OP_INDEX.
- The second column is the English description of the operator, which will be printed during error messages.
- The third column is the name of the check function that will be used to optimize this tree; see section 10.4.8.
- Then come additional flags plus a character that specifies the flavor of the op: in this case, index is a list op, because it can take more than two parameters, so it has the symbol @.
- Finally, the prototype for the function is given. S S S? translates to the Perl prototype $$;$, which is the prototype for CORE::index.

Although most people will never need to edit the op table, it is useful to understand how Perl knows what the ops look like. A full description of the format of the table, including details of the meanings of the flags, appears in opcodes.pl.

10.4.7   Scratchpads and targets

PP code is the guts of Perl execution and hence is highly optimized for speed. In time-critical areas, you don't want to create and destroy SVs, because allocating and freeing memory is a slow process. So, Perl allocates for each op a *target* SV that is created at compile time. You've seen earlier that PP code gets the target and uses the PUSH macros to push the target onto the stack.

Targets reside on the scratchpad, just like lexical variables. op_targ for an op is an offset in the current pad; it is the element number in the pad's array, which stores the SV that should be used as the target. Perl lets ops reuse the same target if they are not going to collide on the stack; similarly, it directly uses lexical variables on the pad as targets if appropriate instead of going through a padsv operation to extract them. (This is a standard compiler technique called *binding*.)

You can tell if an SV is a target by its flags: targets (also known as temporaries) have the TEMP flag set, and SVs bound to lexical variables on the pad have the PADMY flag set.

10.4.8   The optimizer

Between compiling the op tree and executing it, Perl goes through three stages of optimization. The first stage happens as the tree is being constructed. Once Perl creates an op, it passes it off to a check routine. You saw earlier how the check routines are assigned to operators in the op table; an index op is passed to ck_index. This routine can manipulate the op any way it pleases, including freeing it, replacing it with a different op, or adding new ops above or below it. The check routines are sometimes called in a chain: for instance, the check routine for index simply tests to see if the string being sought is a constant, and if so, performs a Fast Boyer-Moore string compilation to speed up the search at runtime; then it calls the general function-checking routine ck_fun.

Second, the constant folding routine fold_constants is called if appropriate. It tests to see whether all the descendents of the op are constants; if they are, it runs the operator as if it was a little program, collects the result, and replaces the op with a constant op reflecting that result. You can tell if constants have been folded by using the deparse compiler backend (see "The B::Deparse module," page 299):

```
% perl -MO=Deparse -e 'print (3+5+8+$foo)'
print 16 + $foo;
```

Here, the 3+5 has been constant-folded into 8, and then 8+8 is constant-folded to 16.

Third, the peephole optimizer peep is called. It examines each op in the tree in execution order and attempts to determine local optimizations by thinking ahead one or two ops and seeing whether multiple operations can be combined into one. It also checks for lexical issues such as the effect of use strict on bareword constants.

10.4.9   Op code trees summary

Perl's fundamental operations are represented by a series of structures, analogous to the structures that form Perl's internal values. These ops are threaded together in two ways: into an op tree during the parsing process, where each op dominates its arguments; and by a thread of execution that establishes the order in which Perl has to run the ops.

To run the ops, Perl uses the code in pp*.c, which is particularly macro-heavy. Most of the macros are concerned with manipulating the argument stack, which is the means by which Perl passes data between operations.

Once the op tree is constructed, it is optimized a number of ways—check routines; constant folding, which takes place after each op is created; and a peephole optimizer, which performs a dry run over the execution order.

10.5   EXECUTION

Once you have constructed an op code tree from a program, executing the code is a simple matter of following the chain of op_next pointers and executing the operations specified by each op. The code that does this is in run.c:

```
while ((PL_op = CALL_FPTR(PL_op->op_ppaddr)(aTHX))) {
    PERL_ASYNC_CHECK();
}
```

We begin with the first op, PL_op, and we call the function in its op_ppaddr slot. This will return another op, which we assign to PL_op, or a null pointer meaning the end of the program. In between executing ops, we perform the asynchronous check that dispatches signal handlers and other events that may occur between operations.

As you know from looking at XS programming, Perl keeps values between operations on the argument stack. The job of ops is to manipulate the arguments on the stack. For instance, the and operator is implemented like this (in pp_hot.c):

```
PP(pp_and)
{
    dSP;
    if (!SvTRUE(TOPs))
        RETURN;
    else {
        --SP;
        RETURNOP(cLOGOP->op_other);
    }
}
```

If the SV on the top of the argument stack does not have a true value, then the and cannot be true, so we simply return the next op in the sequence. We don't even need to look at the right side of the and. If it is true, however, we can discard it by popping the stack, and we need to execute the right side (stored in op_other) to determine whether it is true as well. Hence, we return the chain of operations starting at op_other; the op_next pointers of these operations will be arranged to meet up with the operation after and.

10.6   THE PERL COMPILER

We'll finish our tour of the Perl internals by discussing the oft-misunderstood Perl compiler.

10.6.1   What is the Perl compiler?

In 1996, Chip Salzenburg announced a challenge: the first person to write a compiler suite for Perl would win a laptop. Malcolm Beattie stepped up to the challenge and won the laptop with his B suite of modules. Many of these modules have now been brought into the Perl core as standard modules.

The Perl compiler is not just for compiling Perl code to a standalone executable; in fact, some would argue that it's not *at all* for compiling Perl code into a standalone executable. You've already seen the use of the B::Terse and B::Tree modules to help you visualize the Perl op tree, and this should give you a hint about what the Perl compiler is all about.

The compiler comes in three parts:

- A front-end module, O, which does little more than turn on Perl's -c (compile only, do not run) flag and load a backend module
- The backend module, such as B::Terse, which performs a specific compiler task
- The B module, which acts as a low-level driver

The B module at the heart of the compiler is a stunningly simple XS module that makes Perl's internal object-like structures—SVs, ops, and so on—into real Perl-space objects. It provides a degree of introspection: you can, for instance, write a backend module that traverses the op tree of a compiled program and dumps out its state to a file. (The B::Bytecode module does this.)

It's important to know what the Perl compiler is not. It's not something that will magically make your code go faster, or take up less space, or be more reliable. The backends that generate standalone code generally do exactly the opposite. Essentially, the compiler is a way of getting access to the op tree and doing something potentially interesting with it. The following sections describe some of these interesting things you can do with the op tree.

10.6.2   B:: modules

The compiler in the Perl core includes 12 backend modules, and many more are available on CPAN. Here we'll briefly examine those that are particularly interesting or helpful to internals hackers.

The B::Concise module

B::Concise was written recently by Stephen McCamant to provide a generic way of getting concise information about the op tree. It is highly customizable and can be used to emulate B::Terse and B::Debug.

Here's the basic output from B::Concise:

```
% perl -MO=Concise -e 'print $a+$b'
8  <@> leave[t1] vKP/REFC ->(end)
1     <0> enter ->2
2     <;> nextstate(main 1 -e:1) v ->3
7     <@> print vK ->8
3        <0> pushmark s ->4
6        <2> add[t1] sK/2 ->7
-           <1> ex-rv2sv sK/1 ->5
4              <$> gvsv(*a) s ->5
```

```
-              <1> ex-rv2sv sK/1 ->6
5                  <$> gvsv(*b) s ->6
```

Each line consists of five main parts:

- A number for each operator, stating its position in execution order.
- A type signifier (@ is a list operator—think arrays).
- The name of the op and its target, if any, plus any other information about it.
- The flags for this operator. Here, v signifies void context and K shows that this operator has children. The private flags are shown after the slash and are written out as an abbreviation longer than one character: REFC shows that this op is refcounted.
- The label for the next operator in the tree, if there is one.

Note also that, for instance, ops that have been optimized away to a null operation are left as ex-.... The exact meanings of the flags and the op classes are given in the B::Concise documentation:

```
=head2 OP flags abbreviations

    v     OPf_WANT_VOID     Want nothing (void context)
    s     OPf_WANT_SCALAR   Want single value (scalar context)
    l     OPf_WANT_LIST     Want list of any length (list context)
    K     OPf_KIDS          There is a firstborn child.
    P     OPf_PARENS        This operator was parenthesized.
                             (Or block needs explicit scope entry.)
    R     OPf_REF           Certified reference.
                             (Return container, not containee).
    M     OPf_MOD           Will modify (lvalue).
    S     OPf_STACKED       Some arg is arriving on the stack.
    *     OPf_SPECIAL       Do something weird for this op (see op.h)

=head2 OP class abbreviations

    0     OP (aka BASEOP)   An OP with no children
    1     UNOP              An OP with one child
    2     BINOP             An OP with two children
    |     LOGOP             A control branch OP
    @     LISTOP            An OP that could have lots of children
    /     PMOP              An OP with a regular expression
    $     SVOP              An OP with an SV
    "     PVOP              An OP with a string
    {     LOOP              An OP that holds pointers for a loop
    ;     COP               An OP that marks the start of a statement
```

As with many of the debugging B:: modules, you can use the -exec flag to walk the op tree in execution order, following the chain of op_next's from the start of the tree:

```
% perl -MO=Concise,-exec -e 'print $a+$b'
1k <0> enter
1l <;> nextstate(main 7 -e:1) v
```

```
1m <0> pushmark s
1n <$> gvsv(*a) s
1o <$> gvsv(*b) s
1p <2> add[t1] sK/2
1q <@> print vK
1r <@> leave[t1] vKP/REFC
-e syntax OK
```

Among other options (again, see the documentation), B::Concise supports a
-tree option for tree-like ASCII art graphs, and the curious but fun -linenoise
option. (Try it...)

The B::Debug module

B::Debug dumps out *all* the information in the op tree; for anything bigger than a
trivial program, it gives way too much information. Hence, to sensibly make use of it,
it's a good idea to go through with B::Terse or B::Concise first and determine
which ops you're interested in, and then grep for them.

Some output from B::Debug looks like this:

```
LISTOP (0x81121a8)
        op_next         0x0
        op_sibling      0x0
        op_ppaddr       PL_ppaddr[OP_LEAVE]
        op_targ         1
        op_type         178
        op_seq          6433
        op_flags        13
        op_private      64
        op_first        0x81121d0
        op_last         0x8190498
        op_children     3
OP (0x81121d0)
        op_next         0x81904c0
        op_sibling      0x81904c0
        op_ppaddr       PL_ppaddr[OP_ENTER]
        op_targ         0
        op_type         177
        op_seq          6426
        op_flags        0
        op_private      0
```

As you know from section 10.4, this is all the information contained in the op structure: the type of op and its address, the ops related to it, the C function pointer
implementing the PP function, the target on the scratchpad this op uses, its type, its
sequence number, and public and private flags. The module also does similar dumps
for SVs. You may find the B::Flags module useful for turning the flags—which are
usually specified as integers—into human-readable strings.

The B::Deparse module

`B::Deparse` takes a Perl program and turns it into a Perl program. This doesn't sound very impressive, but it does so by decompiling the op tree back into Perl. Although this module has interesting uses for things like serializing subroutines, it's particularly interesting for internals hackers because it shows how Perl understands certain constructs. For instance, we can see that logical operators and binary `if` are equivalent:

```
% perl -MO=Deparse -e '$a and do {$b}'
if ($a) {
    do {
        $b;
    };
}
-e syntax OK
```

We can also see, for instance, how the magic added by command-line switches goes into the op tree:

```
% perl -MO=Deparse -ane 'print'
LINE: while (defined($_ = <ARGV>)) {
    @F = split(" ", $_, 0);
    print $_;
}
-e syntax OK
```

10.6.3   What B and O provide

To see how you can build compilers and introspective modules with `B`, you need to understand what `B` and the compiler front-end `O` give you. We'll begin with `O`, because it's simpler.

The O module

The guts of the `O` module are very small—only 48 lines of code—because all it does is set up the environment for a backend module. The backends are expected to provide a subroutine called `compile` that processes the options passed to it and then returns a subroutine reference which does the actual compilation. `O` then calls this subroutine reference in a `CHECK` block.

`CHECK` blocks were specifically designed for the compiler—they're called after Perl has finished constructing the op tree and before it begins running the code. `O` calls the `B` subroutine `minus_c`, which, as its name implies, is equivalent to the command-line `-c` flag to Perl: it means to compile but not execute the code. `O` ensures that any `BEGIN` blocks are accessible to the backend modules, and then calls `compile` from the backend processor with any options from the command line.

The B module

As we have mentioned, the B module allows Perl-level access to ops and internal variables. There are two key ways to get this access: from the op tree or from a user-specified variable or code reference.

To get at the op tree, B provides the `main_root` and `main_start` functions. They return B::OP-derived objects representing the root of the op tree and the start of the tree in execution order, respectively:

```
% perl -MB -le 'print B::main_root; print B::main_start'
B::LISTOP=SCALAR(0x8104180)
B::OP=SCALAR(0x8104180)
```

For everything else, you can use the `svref_2object` function, which turns some kind of reference into the appropriate B::SV-derived object:

```
% perl -MB -l
a = 5; print B::svref_2object(\$a);
@a=(1,2,3); print B::svref_2object(\@a);
__END__
B::IV=SCALAR(0x811f9b8)
B::AV=SCALAR(0x811f9b8)
```

(Yes, it's normal for the objects to have the same addresses.)

In the next section, we'll concentrate on the op-derived classes, because they're the most useful feature of B for compiler construction. The SV classes are much simpler and analogous.

10.6.4 Using B for simple tasks

Now that you have the objects, what can you do with them? B provides accessor methods similar to the fields of the structures in `op.h` and `sv.h`. For instance, we can find out the type of the root op like this:

```
$op=B::main_root; print $op->type;
178
```

Oops: `op_type` is an enum, so we can't get much from looking at it directly; however, B also gives us the `name` method, which is a little friendlier:

```
$op=B::main_root; print $op->name;
leave
```

You can also use `flags`, `private`, `targ`, and so on—in fact, everything you saw prefixed by `op_` in the B::Debug example earlier.

To traverse the op tree, `first`, `sibling`, `next`, and friends return the B::OP object for the related op. Thus we can follow the op tree in execution order by doing something like this:

```
#!/usr/bin/perl -cl
use B;
CHECK {
```

```
    $op=B::main_start;
    print $op->name while $op=$op->next;
}

print $a+$b;
...
```

However, when we get to the last op in the sequence, the "enter" operation at the root of the tree, op_next will be a null pointer. B represents a null pointer with the B::NULL object, which has no methods. This has the handy property that if $op is a B::NULL, then $$op will be zero. So, we can print the name of each op in execution order by saying

```
$op=B::main_start;
print $op->name while $op=$op->next and $$op;
```

Walking the tree in normal order is trickier, because we have to make the right moves appropriate for each type of op: we need to look at both first and last links from binary ops, for instance, but only the first from a unary op. Thankfully, B provides a function that does this for us: walkoptree_slow. It arranges to call a user-specified method on each op in turn. Of course, to make it useful, we have to define the method:

```
#!/usr/bin/perl -cl
use B;
CHECK {
    B::walkoptree_slow(B::main_root, "print_it", 0);
    sub B::OP::print_it { my $self = shift; print $self->name }
}

print $a+$b;
...
```

Because all ops inherit from B::OP, this duly produces

```
leave
enter
nextstate
print
pushmark
add
null
gvsv
null
gvsv
```

We can also use the knowledge that walkoptree_slow passes the recursion level as a parameter to the callback method, and make the tree a little prettier, like this:

```
        sub B::OP::print_it {
            my ($self,$level)=@_;
            print "    "x$level, $self->name
        }

leave
    enter
    nextstate
    print
        pushmark
        add
            null
                gvsv
            null
                gvsv
```

See how we're beginning to approximate B::Terse? Actually, B::Terse uses the
B::peekop function, a little like this:

```
        sub B::OP::print_it {
            my ($self,$level)=@_;
            print "    "x$level, B::peekop($self), "\n";
        }
```

```
LISTOP (0x81142c8) leave
    OP (0x81142f0) enter
    COP (0x8114288) nextstate
    LISTOP (0x8114240) print
        OP (0x8114268) pushmark
        BINOP (0x811d920) add
            UNOP (0x8115840) null
                SVOP (0x8143158) gvsv
            UNOP (0x811d900) null
                SVOP (0x8115860) gvsv
```

B::Terse provides slightly more information based on each different type of op,
and we can easily do this by putting methods in the individual op classes: B::LIS-
TOP, B::UNOP, and so on.

Let's finish our little compiler—we'll call it B::Simple—by turning it into a
module that can be used from the O front-end. This is easy enough to do in our case,
once we remember that compile must return a callback subroutine reference:

```
package B::Simple;
use B qw(main_root peekop walkoptree_slow);

sub B::OP::print_it {
    my ($self,$level)=@_;
    print "    "x$level, peekop($self), "\n";
}
```

CHAPTER 10 INTRODUCTION TO PERL INTERNALS

```
sub compile {
    return sub { walkoptree_slow(main_root, "print_it", 0); }
}

1;
```

We can save this code as B/Simple.pm and run it on our own programs with

```
perl -MO=Simple ...
```

We now have a backend compiler module!

10.7 FURTHER READING

- *perlguts*—If you want to dive into the deep end, `perlguts` in the Perl documentation tells you far more than you needed to know about Perl's internals.

- *perlhack*—For a gentler introduction to the Perl internals, look at the `perlhack` documentation that comes with Perl or the extended Perl Internals tutorial (http://www.netthink.co.uk/downloads/internals/book.html).

10.8 SUMMARY

In our whirlwind tour of the Perl internals, we've looked at where to find things in the Perl source tree, the outline of the process Perl goes through to execute a program, how the parser and tokenizer work, and the way Perl's fundamental operations are coded. We've also examined the Perl compiler: how to use it to debug Perl programs, and how to write compiler modules. We've given you enough information about the Perl internals that if you want to investigate Perl's behavior, you'll have some idea where to begin digging into the source.

C H A P T E R   1 1

Hacking Perl

Just like any other piece of software, Perl is not a finished product; it's still being developed and has a lively development community. Both the authors are regular contributors to Perl, and we'd like to encourage you to think about getting involved with Perl's continued maintenance and development. This chapter will tell you what you need to know to begin.

11.1 THE DEVELOPMENT PROCESS

Perl is developed in several "strands"—not least, the new development of Perl 6 (see section 11.4), which is occurring separately from the ongoing maintenance of Perl 5. Here we concentrate on the current development of Perl 5.

11.1.1 Perl versioning

Perl has two types of version number: versions before 5.6.0 used a number of the form x.yyy_zz; x was the major version number (Perl 4, Perl 5), y was the minor release number, and z was the patchlevel. Major releases represented, for instance, either a complete rewrite or a major upheaval of the internals; minor releases sometimes added non-essential functionality, and releases changing the patchlevel were primarily to fix bugs. Releases where z was 50 or more were unstable developers' releases working toward the next minor release.

Since 5.6.0, Perl uses the more standard open source version numbering system—version numbers are of the form x.y.z; releases where y is even are stable releases, and releases where it is odd are part of the *development track*.

11.1.2 The development tracks

Perl development has four major aims: extending portability, fixing bugs, adding optimizations, and creating new language features. Patches to Perl are usually made against the latest copy of the development release; the very latest copy, stored in the Perl repository (see section 11.1.5), is usually called the *bleadperl*.

The bleadperl eventually becomes the new minor release, but patches are also picked up by the maintainer of the stable release for inclusion. There are no hard and fast rules, and everything is left to the discretion of the maintainer, but in general, patches that are bug fixes or that address portability concerns (which include taking advantage of new features in some platforms, such as large file support or 64-bit integers) are merged into the stable release as well, whereas new language features tend to be left until the next minor release. Optimizations may or may not be included, depending on their impact on the source.

11.1.3 The perl5-porters mailing list

All Perl development happens on the `perl5-porters` (P5P) mailing list; if you plan to get involved, a subscription to this list is essential.

You can subscribe by sending an email to perl5-porters-subscribe@perl.org; you'll be asked to send an email to confirm, and then you should begin receiving mail from the list. To send mail to the list, address the mail to perl5-porters@perl.org; you don't have to be subscribed to post, and the list is not moderated. If, for whatever reason, you decide to unsubscribe, simply mail perl5-porters-unsubscribe@perl.org.

The list usually receives between 200 and 400 emails per week. If this is too much mail for you, you can subscribe instead to a daily digest service by emailing perl5-porters-digest-subscribe@perl.org.

There is also a `perl5-porters` FAQ (http://simon-cozens.org/writings/p5p.faq) that explains a lot of this information, plus more about how to behave on P5P and how to submit patches to Perl.

11.1.4 Pumpkins and pumpkings

Development is very loosely organized around the release managers of the stable and development tracks; these are the two *pumpkings*.

Perl development can also be divided into several smaller subsystems: the regular expression engine, the configuration process, the documentation, and so on. Responsibility for each of these areas is known as a *pumpkin*, and hence those who semiofficially take responsibility for them are called pumpkings.

You're probably wondering about the silly names. They stem from the days before Perl was kept under version control; to avoid conflicts, people had to manually check out a chunk of the Perl source by announcing their intentions to the mailing list. While the list was discussing what this process should be called, one of Chip Salzenburg's co-workers told him about a system they used for preventing two people from using a tape drive at once: there was a stuffed pumpkin in the office, and nobody could use the drive unless they had the pumpkin.

11.1.5 The Perl repository

Now Perl is kept in a version control system called Perforce (http://www.perforce.com/), which is hosted by ActiveState, Inc. There is no public access to the system, but various methods have been devised to allow developers near-realtime access:

- *Archive of Perl Changes*—This FTP site (ftp://ftp.linux.activestate.com/pub/staff/gsar/APC/) contains both the current state of all the maintained Perl versions and a directory of changes made to the repository.

- *rsync*—Because it's a little inconvenient to keep up to date using FTP, the directories are also available via the software synchronization protocol rsync (http://rsync.samba.org/). If you have rsync installed, you can synchronize your working directory with bleadperl by issuing the command

```
% rsync -avz rsync://ftp.linux.activestate.com/perl-current/
```

  If you use this route, you should periodically add the --delete option to rsync to clean out any files that have been deleted from the repository. Once, a proposed feature and its test were both removed from Perl, and those following bleadperl by rsync reported test failures for a test that no longer existed.

- *Periodic snapshots*—The development pumpking releases periodic snapshots of bleadperl, particularly when an important change happens. These are usually available from a variety of URLs, and always from ftp://ftp.funet.fi/pub/languages/perl/snap/.

11.2 DEBUGGING AIDS

A number of tools are available to developers to help you find and examine bugs in Perl; these tools are, of course, also useful if you're creating XS extensions and applications with embedded Perl. There are four major categories:

- Perl modules such as Devel::Peek, which allow you to get information about Perl's operation
- perl's own debugging mode
- Convenience functions built into perl that you can call to get debugging information
- External applications

11.2.1 Debugging modules

You saw in chapter 4 how the `Devel::Peek` module can dump information about SVs; you've also learned about the `B::Terse` module for dumping the op tree. The op tree diagrams in chapter 10 were produced using the CPAN module `B::Tree`. You can use other modules to get similar information.

Compiler modules

Due to the way the compiler works, you can use it to get a lot of information about the op tree. The most extensive information can be found using the `B::Debug` module, which dumps all the fields of all OPs and SVs in the op tree.

Another useful module is `B::Graph`, which produces the same information as `B::Debug` but does so in the form of a graph.

Other modules

The core module `re` has a debugging mode, `use re 'debug';`, which traces the execution of regular expressions. You can use it, for instance, to examine the regular expression engine's backtracking behavior:

```
% perl -e 'use re "debug"; "aaa" =~/\w+\d/;'
Compiling REx `\w+\d'
size 4 first at 2
   1: PLUS(3)
   2:    ALNUM(0)
   3: DIGIT(4)
   4: END(0)
stclass `ALNUM' plus minlen 2
Matching REx `\w+\d' against `aaa'
  Setting an EVAL scope, savestack=3
   0 <> <aaa>              | 1:  PLUS
                             ALNUM can match 3 times out of 32767...
  Setting an EVAL scope, savestack=3
   3 <aaa> <>             | 3:     DIGIT
                              failed...
   2 <aa> <a>             | 3:     DIGIT
                              failed...
   1 <a> <aa>             | 3:     DIGIT
                              failed...
                            failed...
Freeing REx: `\w+\d'
```

Turning to CPAN, you can use the `Devel::Leak` module to detect and trace memory leaks in `perl`, and `Devel::Symdump` is useful for dumping and examining the symbol table.

11.2.2 The built-in debugger: perl -D

If you configure Perl passing the flag `-Doptimize='-g'` to `Configure`, it will do two things: it will tell the C compiler to add special debugging information to the object files it produces (you'll see how that's used in a moment), and it will define the preprocessor macro DEBUGGING, which turns on some special debugging options.

NOTE　　If you're running Configure interactively, you can turn on debugging as follows.

By default, Perl 5 compiles with the -O flag to use the optimizer. Alternately, you might want to use the symbolic debugger, which uses the -g flag (on traditional Unix systems). Either flag can be specified here. To use neither flag, specify the word none.

You should use the optimizer/debugger flag [-O2] -g.

Compiling perl like this allows you to use the -D flag on the perl command line to select the level of debugging you require. The most useful debugging options are as follows (see the perlrun documentation for a full list).

The -Ds option

This option turns on stack snapshots, printing a summary of what's on the argument stack each time an operation is performed. It is not too useful on its own, but is highly recommended when combined with the -Dt switch. Here you can see how Perl builds up lists by putting successive values onto the stack, and performs array assignments:

```
% perl -Ds -e '@a = (1,2,3)'

EXECUTING...

    =>
    =>
    =>
    =>   *
    =>   *   IV(1)          ❶
    =>   *   IV(1)   IV(2)
    =>   *   IV(1)   IV(2)   IV(3)
    =>   *   IV(1)   IV(2)   IV(3)   *   ❷
    =>   *   IV(1)   IV(2)   IV(3)   *   GV()   ◁
    =>   *   IV(1)   IV(2)   IV(3)   *   AV()   ◁
    =>   ❸
```

The array is first placed on the stack as a glob—an entry into the symbol table

The rv2av operator resolves the glob into an AV

❶ Perl pushes each of the values of the list onto the argument stack. The asterisk before the list represents an entry in the mark stack.

❷ Once the list has been built up, Perl places another mark between the right side of an assignment and the left side, so it knows how many elements are due for assignment.

❸ Once the assignment has been made, everything from the first mark is popped off the stack.

The -Dt option

This option traces each individual op as it is executed. Let's see the previous code again, but this time with a listing of the ops:

```
% perl -Dst -e '@a = (1,2,3)'

EXECUTING...

    =>
(-e:0)  enter
    =>
(-e:0)  nextstate
    =>
(-e:1)  pushmark
    =>  *
(-e:1)  const(IV(1))
    =>  *  IV(1)
(-e:1)  const(IV(2))
    =>  *  IV(1)  IV(2)
(-e:1)  const(IV(3))
    =>  *  IV(1)  IV(2)  IV(3)
(-e:1)  pushmark
    =>  *  IV(1)  IV(2)  IV(3)  *
(-e:1)  gv(main::a)
    =>  *  IV(1)  IV(2)  IV(3)  *  GV()
(-e:1)  rv2av
    =>  *  IV(1)  IV(2)  IV(3)  *  AV()
(-e:1)  aassign
    =>
(-e:1)  leave
```

The -Dr option

The -Dr flag is identical to the use re 'debug'; module discussed earlier.

The -Dl option

This option reports when perl reaches an ENTER or LEAVE statement, and reports on which line and in which file the statement occurred.

The -Dx option

This option is roughly equivalent to B::Terse. It produces a dump of the op tree using the op_dump function described later. It's a handy compromise between B::Terse and B::Debug.

The -Do option

This option turns on reporting of method resolution—that is, what happens when Perl calls a method on an object or class. For instance, it tells you when DESTROY methods are called, as well as what happens during inheritance lookups.

11.2.3 Debugging functions

The Perl core defines a number of functions to aid in debugging its internal goings-on. You can call them either from debugging sections of your own C or XS code or from a source-level debugger.

The sv_dump function

```
void sv_dump(SV* sv);
```

This function is roughly equivalent to the `Devel::Peek` module—it allows you to inspect any of Perl's data types. The principle differences between this function and `Devel::Peek` is that it is not recursive—for instance, a reference will be dumped like this

```
SV = RV(0x814fd10) at 0x814ec80
  REFCNT = 1
  FLAGS = (ROK)
  RV = 0x814ec5c
```

and its referent is not automatically dumped. However, it does let you get at values that are not attached to a variable, such as arrays and scalars used to hold data internal to `perl`.

The op_dump function

```
void op_dump(OP* op);
```

The `-Dx` debugging option is implemented, essentially, by calling `op_dump(PL_mainroot)`. It takes an op; lists the op's type, flags, and important additional fields; and recursively calls itself on the op's children.

The dump_sub function

```
void dump_sub(GV* gv);
```

This function extracts the CV from a glob and runs `op_dump` on the root of its op tree.

11.2.4 External debuggers

There's another way to debug your code, which is often more useful when you're fiddling around in C. A *source level debugger* allows you to step through your C code line by line or function by function and execute C code on the fly, just as you'd do with the built-in Perl debugger.

Source-level debuggers come in many shapes and sizes: if you're working in a graphical environment such as Microsoft Visual Studio, a debugging mode may be built into it. Just as with compilers, there are also command-line versions. In this section we'll look at another free tool, the GNU Debugger (gdb); much of what we say is applicable to other similar debuggers, such as Solaris's dbx.

Compiling for debugging

Unfortunately, before you can use the debugger on a C program, you must compile it with special options. As you've seen, the debugging option (usually `-g` on command-line compilers) embeds information into the binary detailing the file name and line number for each operation, so that the debugger can, for instance, stop at a specific line in a C source file.

So, before using the debugger, you must recompile Perl with the `-Doptimize='-g'` option to `Configure`, as shown in section 11.2.2.

Invoking the debugger

We'll assume you're using `gdb` and you've compiled Perl with the `-g` flag. If we type `gdb perl` in the directory in which you built Perl, we see the following:

```
% gdb perl
GNU gdb 5.0
Copyright 2000 Free Software Foundation, Inc.
GDB is free software, covered by the GNU General Public License, and
you are welcome to change it and/or distribute copies of it under
certain conditions.
Type "show copying" to see the conditions.
There is absolutely no warranty for GDB.  Type "show warranty" for
details.
This GDB was configured as "i686-pc-linux-gnu"...
(gdb)
```

If, however, you see the words "`(no debugging symbols found)`", you're either in the wrong place or you didn't compile Perl with debugging support.

You can type `help` at any time to get a summary of the commands, or type `quit` (or just press Ctrl-D) to leave the debugger.

You can run `perl` without any intervention from the debugger by simply typing `run`; doing so is equivalent to executing `perl` with no command-line options and means it will take a program from standard input.

To pass command-line options to `perl`, put them after the `run` command, like this:

```
(gdb) run -Ilib -MDevel::Peek -e '$a="X"; $a++; Dump($a)'
Starting program: /home/simon/patchbay/perl/perl -Ilib -MDevel::Peek
-e '$a="X"; $a++; Dump($a)'
SV = PV(0x8146fdc) at 0x8150a18
  REFCNT = 1
  FLAGS = (POK,pPOK)
  PV = 0x8154620 "Y"\0
  CUR = 1
  LEN = 2

Program exited normally
```

Setting breakpoints

Running through a program normally isn't very exciting. The most important thing to do is choose a place to freeze execution of the program, so you can examine further what's going on at that point.

The `break` command sets a *breakpoint*—a point in the program at which the debugger will halt execution and bring you back to the (gdb) prompt. You can give `break` either the name of a function or a location in the source code of the form `filename.c:lineno`. For instance, in the version of Perl installed here,[1] the main op dispatch code is at `run.c:53`:

```
(gdb) break run.c:53
Breakpoint 1 at 0x80ba331: file run.c, line 53.
```

This code sets breakpoint number 1, which will be triggered when execution gets to line 53 of run.c.

> **NOTE** *Setting breakpoints*—Blank lines, or lines containing comments or preprocessor directives, will never be executed; but if you set a breakpoint on them, the debugger should stop at the next line containing code. This also applies to sections of code that are #ifdef'd out.
>
> If you give `break` a function name, be sure to give the name in the `Perl_` namespace: that is, `Perl_runops_debug` instead of `runops_debug`.

When you use `run`, execution will halt when it gets to the specified place. gdb will display the number of the breakpoint that was triggered and the line of code in question:

```
(gdb) run -e1
Starting program: /home/simon/patchbay/perl/perl -e1

Breakpoint 1, Perl_runops_debug () at run.c:53
53              } while ((PL_op = CALL_FPTR(PL_op->op_ppaddr)(aTHX)));
```

You can now use the backtrace command, `bt`, to examine the call stack and find out how you got there (`where` is also available as a synonym for `bt`):

```
(gdb) bt
#0  Perl_runops_debug () at run.c:53
#1  0x805dc9f in S_run_body (oldscope=1) at perl.c:1458
#2  0x805d871 in perl_run (my_perl=0x8146b98) at perl.c:1380
#3  0x805a4d5 in main (argc=2, argv=0xbffff8cc, env=0xbffff8d8)
    at perlmain.c:52
#4  0x40076dcc in __libc_start_main () from /lib/libc.so.6
```

This result tells us that we're currently in `Perl_runops_debug`, after being called by `S_run_body` on line 1380 of `perl.c`. gdb also displays the value of the

---

[1] 5.6.0. Don't worry if you get slightly different line numbers in your version.

arguments to each function, although many of them (those given as hexadecimal numbers) are pointers.

You can restart execution by typing `continue`; if the code containing a breakpoint is executed again, the debugger will halt once more. If not, the program will run until termination.

You can set multiple breakpoints simply by issuing more `break` commands. If multiple breakpoints are set, the debugger will stop each time execution reaches any of the breakpoints in force.

Unwanted breakpoints can be deleted using the `delete` command; on its own, `delete` will delete all breakpoints. To delete a given breakpoint, use `delete n`, where *n* is the number of the breakpoint.

To temporarily turn off a breakpoint, use the `disable` and `enable` commands.

Good breakpoints to choose when debugging `perl` include the main op dispatch code shown earlier, `main`, `S_parse_body`, `perl_construct`, `perl_destruct`, and `Perl_yyparse` (not for the faint of heart, because it places you right in the middle of the Yacc parser).

Stepping through a program

Although it's possible to work out the flow of execution just by using breakpoints, it's a lot easier to watch the statements as they are executed. The key commands to do this are `step`, `next`, and `finish`.

The `step` command traces the flow of execution step by step. Let's see what happens when we break at the main op dispatch loop and step through execution:

```
(gdb) run -e1
Starting program: /home/simon/patchbay/perl/perl -e1

Breakpoint 1, Perl_runops_debug () at run.c:53
53              } while ((PL_op = CALL_FPTR(PL_op->op_ppaddr)(aTHX)));
(gdb) step

Perl_pp_enter () at pp_hot.c:1587
1587            djSP;
(gdb) step
1589            I32 gimme = OP_GIMME(PL_op, -1);
(gdb)
1591            if (gimme == -1) {
(gdb)
1592                if (cxstack_ix >= 0)
(gdb)
1595                    gimme = G_SCALAR;
```

TIP   Pressing Return repeats the last command.

As we `stepped` into the first op, `enter`, `gdb` loaded up pp_hot.c and entered the `Perl_pp_enter` function. The function in question begins like this:

```
1585  PP(pp_enter)
1586  {
1587      djSP;
1588      register PERL_CONTEXT *cx;
1589      I32 gimme = OP_GIMME(PL_op, -1);
1590
1591      if (gimme == -1) {
1592          if (cxstack_ix >= 0)
1593              gimme = cxstack[cxstack_ix].blk_gimme;
1594          else
1595              gimme = G_SCALAR;
1596      }
1597  ...
```

gdb first stopped at line 1587, which is the first line in the function. The first three lines of the function are, as you might expect, variable definitions. gdb does not normally stop on variable definitions unless they are also assignments. djSP happens to be a macro that expands to

```
register SV **sp = PL_stack_sp
```

declaring a local copy of the stack pointer. The next line, however, is not an assignment, which is why step causes gdb to move on to line 1589. gdb also skips blank space, so the next line it stops on is 1591.

Because the program enters the if statement, we know the gimme (the context in which this piece of Perl is being executed) is -1, signifying "not yet known." Next we go from the inner if statement to the else branch, meaning that cx_stack_ix, the index into the context stack, is less than zero. Hence gimme is set to G_SCALAR.

In Perl terms, this means the context stack holds the context for each block; when you call a sub in list context, an entry is popped onto the context stack signifying this event. This entry allows the code that implements return to determine which context is expected. Because we are in the outermost block of the program, there are no entries on the context stack at the moment. The code we have just executed sets the context of the outer block to scalar context. (Unfortunately, wantarray is useful only inside a subroutine, so the usual way of demonstrating the context won't work. You'll have to take our word for it.)

Sometimes step is too slow, and you don't want to descend into a certain function and execute every line in it. For instance, you'll notice after a while that ENTER and SAVETMPS often appear next to each other and cause Perl_push_scope and Perl_save_int to be executed. If you're not interested in debugging those functions, you can skip them using the next command. They will still be executed, but the debugger will not trace their execution:

```
Breakpoint 2, Perl_pp_enter () at pp_hot.c:1598
1598            ENTER;
(gdb) next
1600            SAVETMPS;
(gdb)
1601            PUSHBLOCK(cx, CXt_BLOCK, SP);
(gdb)
1603            RETURN;
(gdb)
```

Alternatively, you can run the current function to its conclusion without tracing it by using the finish command:

```
(gdb) step
Perl_runops_debug () at run.c:42
42              PERL_ASYNC_CHECK();
(gdb)
43                  if (PL_debug) {
(gdb)
53                  } while ((PL_op = CALL_FPTR(PL_op->op_ppaddr)(aTHX)));
(gdb)
Perl_pp_nextstate () at pp_hot.c:37
37                  PL_curcop = (COP*)PL_op;
(gdb) finish
Run till exit from #0  Perl_pp_nextstate () at pp_hot.c:37
0x80ba64b in Perl_runops_debug () at run.c:53
53                  } while ((PL_op = CALL_FPTR(PL_op->op_ppaddr)(aTHX)));
Value returned is $1 = (OP *) 0x814cb68
```

Here we step over the main op dispatch loop until Perl_pp_nextstate is called. Because we're not particularly interested in that function, we call finish to let it run. The debugger then confirms that it's running Perl_pp_nextstate until the function exits and displays where it has returned to and the value returned from the function.

> **TIP**
>
> *Emacs makes it easy*—If you're a user of the Emacs editor, you might find gdb major mode to be extremely helpful; it automatically opens any source files gdb refers to and can trace the flow of control in the source buffers. Thus it's easy for you to see what's going on around the source that's currently being executed.
>
> *Alternatives to gdb*—If you're not a fan of command-line debugging, you may wish to investigate alternatives to gdb. For Windows users, Microsoft Visual C can't be beaten; for Unix users, Tim recommends ddd (Data Display Debugger), which is a graphical front-end to gdb. ddd extends the usual source-navigation functions of a debugger with an interactive graphical display of data, including arrays and structures.

Evaluating expressions

You can now perform most of the debugging you need with ease, but one more feature of gdb makes it even easier. The `print` command allows you to execute C expressions on the fly and display their results.

Unfortunately, there is one drawback: gdb doesn't know about preprocessor macros, so you must expand the macros yourself. For instance, to find the reference count of an SV, we can't say

```
(gdb) print SvREFCNT(sv)
No symbol "SvREFCNT" in current context.
```

Instead, we have to say

```
(gdb) print sv->sv_refcnt
$1=1
```

Or, to look at the contents of the SV,

```
(gdb) print *sv
$2 = {sv_any = 0x8147a10, sv_refcnt = 1, sv_flags = 536870923}
```

You can also use `print` to call C functions, such as the debugging functions mentioned earlier:

```
(gdb) print Perl_sv_dump(sv)
SV = PV(0x8146d14) at 0x8150824
  REFCNT = 1
  FLAGS = (POK,READONLY,pPOK)
  PV = 0x8151968 "hello"\0
  CUR = 5
  LEN = 6
$9 = void
```

Using these functions in conjunction with the execution-tracing commands of gdb should allow you to examine almost every area of Perl's internals.

Debugging XS code

There are a couple of little wrinkles when it comes to debugging XS modules. With XS, modules are usually dynamically loaded into memory; thus when `perl` starts, the functions aren't loaded—and when gdb starts, it can't find them.

The solution is to choose a breakpoint after the XS module has been dynamically loaded. A good place is `S_run_body`—here the BEGIN blocks have been processed and hence all use'd modules have been loaded. This is just before the main part of the script is executed. If this is too late for your debugging, another good place to stop is inside the dynamic loading module, DynaLoader. `XS_DynaLoader_dl_load_file` is called for each module that needs to be dynamically loaded.

NOTE   Don't forget that to effectively debug an XS module, you must recompile it with the debugging flag, -g. The official way to do this is to run Makefile.PL as follows:

```
% perl Makefile.PL OPTIMIZE=-g
```

However, it's also possible to hack the OPTIMIZE= line in the Makefile itself (but don't tell anyone we said that).

The next small problem is that the names of XS functions are mangled from the names you give them in the .xs file. You should look at the .c file produced by xsubpp to determine the real function names. For instance, the XS function sdbm_TIEHASH in the XS code for the SDBM_File becomes XS_SDBM_File_TIEHASH.

The rules for this mangling are regular (section 6.11):

1 The PREFIX given in the XS file is removed from the function name. Hence, sdbm_ is stripped off to leave TIEHASH.

2 The PACKAGE name (SDBM_File) undergoes "C-ification" (any package separators, ::, are converted to underscores) and is added to the beginning of the name: SDBM_File_TIEHASH.

3 XS_ is prefixed to the name to give XS_SDBM_File_TIEHASH.

11.3   CREATING A PATCH

Suppose you've noticed a problem and debugged it. Now what? If possible, you should fix it; then, if you want fame and immortality, you should submit that patch back to perl5-porters. Let's explore this process.

11.3.1   How to solve problems

You should keep in mind a few standard design goals when you're considering how to approach a Perl patch; quite a lot of unwritten folklore explains why certain patches feel better than others. Here is an incomplete list of some of the more important principles we've picked up over the years:

- The most important rule is that you may not break old code. Perl 5 can happily run some ancient code, even dating back to Perl 1 days; we pride ourselves on backward compatibility. Hence, nothing you do should break that compatibility. This rule has a few direct implications: adding new syntax is tricky. Adding new operators is basically impossible; if you wanted to introduce a chip operator that took a character off the beginning of a string, it would break any code that defined a chip subroutine itself.

- Solve problems as generally as possible. Platform-specific ifdefs are frowned upon unless absolutely and obviously necessary. Try to avoid repetition of code. If you have a good, general routine that can be used in other places of the Perl core, move it out to a separate function and change the rest of the core to use it. For instance, we needed a way for Perl to perform arbitrary transformations on incoming data—for example, to mark it as UTF-8 encoded, or convert it between different character encodings. The initial idea was to extend the source filter mechanism to apply not just to the source file input, but also to any file-handle. However, the more general solution was an extension of the Perl I/O abstraction to a layered model where transformation functions could be applied to various layers; then source filters could be re-implemented in terms of this new I/O system.

- Change as *little* as possible to get the job done, especially when you're not well known as a solid porter. Sweeping changes scare people, whether or not they're correct. It's a lot easier to check a 10-line patch for potential bugs than a 100-line patch.

- Don't do it in the core unless it needs to be done in the core. If you can do it in a Perl module or an XS module, it's unlikely that you need to do it in the core. As an example, DBM capability was moved out of the core into a bunch of XS modules; this approach also had the advantage that you could switch between different DBM libraries at runtime, and you had the extensibility of the tie system that could be used for things other than DBMs.

- Try to avoid introducing restrictions, even on things you haven't thought of yet. Always leave the door open for more interesting work along the same lines. A good example is lvalue subroutines, which were introduced in Perl 5.6.0. Once you have lvalue subroutines, why not lvalue method calls or even lvalue over-loaded operators?

Some of the goals are just ideas you have to pick up in time. They may depend on the outlook of the pumpking and any major work going on at the time. For instance, during the reorganization of the I/O system mentioned earlier, any file-handling patches were carefully scrutinized to make sure they wouldn't have to be rewritten once the new system was in place. Hence, it's not really possible to give hard-and-fast design goals; but if you stick to the list we've just provided, you won't go far wrong.

11.3.2   Autogenerated files

A number of files should not be patched directly, because they are generated from other (usually Perl) programs. Most of these files are clearly marked, but the most important of these deserves a special note: if you add a new function to the core, you *must* add an entry to the table at the end of embed.pl. Doing so ensures that a correct function prototype is generated and placed in protos.h, that any documentation for that function is automatically extracted, and that the namespace for the function is automatically handled. (See the following note.) The syntax for entries in the table is explained in the documentation file perlguts.pod.

NOTE   Perl's internal functions are carefully named so that when Perl is embedded in another C program, they do not override any functions the C program defines. Hence, all internal functions should be named `Perl_something` (apart from static functions, which are by convention named `S_something`). `embed.h` uses a complicated system of automatically generated `#define`s to allow you to call your function as *something()* inside the core and in XSUBs, but `Perl_something` must be used by embedders.

You must remember to rerun `embed.pl` after adding this entry. The Make target `regen_headers` will call all the Perl programs that generate other files.

A special exception is perly.c, which is generated by running `byacc` on perly.y and then being fixed with a patch. In the *extraordinarily* unlikely event that you need to fiddle with the Perl grammar in perly.y, you can run the Make target `run_byacc` to call `byacc` and then fix the resulting C file; if you are changing perly.y, it's polite to drop the VMS porters mailing list (vmsperl@perl.org) a copy of the patch, because they use a different process to generate perly.c.

For changes that involve autogenerated files, such as adding a function to the core or changing a function's prototype, you only need to provide a patch for the generating program and leave a note to the effect that `regen_headers` should be run. You should not include, for instance, a patch to protos.h.

11.3.3 The patch itself

Patching styles vary, but the recommended style for Perl is a unified `diff`. If you're changing a small number of files, copy, say, sv.c to sv.c~, make your changes, and then run

```
% diff -u sv.c~ sv.c > /tmp/patch
% diff -u sv.h~ sv.h >> /tmp/patch
```

and so on for each file you change.

If you are doing this, remember to run `diff` from the root of the Perl source directory. Hence, if we're patching XS files in `ext/`, we say

```
% diff -u ext/Devel/Peek/Peek.xs~ ext/Devel/Peek/Peek.xs
    >> /tmp/patch
```

For larger patches, you may find it easier to do something like this:

```
/home/me/work % rsync -avz
rsync://ftp.linux.activestate.com/perl-current/ bleadperl
/home/me/work % cp -R bleadperl myperl
/home/me/work % cd myperl
/home/me/work/myperl % Make your changes...
/home/me/work/myperl % cd ..
/home/me/work % diff -ruN bleadperl myperl > /tmp/patch
```

This code will create a patch that turns the current bleadperl into your personal Perl source tree. If you do this, please remember to prune your patch for autogenerated files and also items that do not belong in the source distribution (any test data you have used, or messages about binary files).

NOTE   *Makepatch*—An alternative tool that can make patching easier is Johan Vromans' `makepatch`, available from `$CPAN/authors/id/JV/`. It automates many of the steps we've described. Some swear by it, but some of us are stuck in our ways and do things the old way…

11.3.4   Documentation

If you change a feature of Perl that is visible to the user, you must, must, must update the documentation. Patches are not complete if they do not contain documentation.

Remember that if you introduce a new warning or error, you need to document it in pod/perldiag.pod.

Perl 5.6.0 introduced a system for providing documentation for internal functions, similar to Java's javadoc. This apidoc is extracted by embed.pl and ends up in two files: pod/perlapi.pod contains documentation for functions that are deemed suitable for XS authors,[2] and pod/perlintern.pod contains the documentation for all other functions (internal functions).

apidoc is simply POD embedded in C comments; you should be able to pick up how it is used by looking around the various C files. If you add apidoc to a function, you should turn on the d flag in that function's embed.pl entry.

11.3.5   Testing

The t/ directory in the Perl source tree contains many (294, at last count) regression test scripts that ensure Perl is behaving as it should. When you change something, you should make sure your changes have not caused any of the scripts to break—they have been specially designed to try as many unexpected interactions as possible.

You should also add tests to the suite if you change a feature, so that your changes aren't disturbed by future patching activity. Tests are in the ordinary style used for modules, so remember to update the `1..n` line at the top of the test.

11.3.6   Submitting your patch

Once you've put together a patch that includes documentation and new tests, it's time to submit it to P5P. Your subject line should include the tag `[PATCH]`, with optionally a version number or name, or the name of the file you're patching: for example, `[PATCH bleadperl]` or `[PATCH sv.c]`. This line lets the pumpking easily distinguish possible patches to be integrated from the usual list discussion. You

---

[2]   Chapter 5 of this book was developed by starting from `pod/perlapi.pod`, and, in fact, we contributed back some pieces of chapter 5 as apidoc.

should also put a brief description of what you're solving on the subject line: for instance, [PATCH blead] Fix B::Terse indentation.

The body of your email should be a brief discussion of the problem (some Perl code that demonstrates the problem is adequate) and how you've solved it. Then insert your patch directly into the body of the email—try to avoid sending it as an attachment. Also, be careful with cutting-and-pasting your patch in, because doing so may corrupt line wrapping or convert tabs to spaces.

Once you're ready, take a deep breath and hit Send!

11.4   PERL 6: THE FUTURE OF PERL

While we were busily preparing this book, something significant happened—Perl 6 was announced. Let's look at what led up to this announcement, and where the Perl 6 effort has gotten since then.

11.4.1   A history

At the Perl Conference in July 2000, Chip Salzenburg called a brainstorming session meeting of some eminent members of the Perl community to discuss the state of Perl. Chip wanted some form of "Perl Constitution" to resolve perceived problems in Perl 5 development; however, Jon Orwant suggested (in a particularly vivid and colorful way) that there were deeper problems in the state of Perl and the Perl community that should be fixed by a completely new version of Perl.

The majority consensus was that this was a good idea, and Larry Wall picked up on it. It was presented to the main perl5-porters meeting the same afternoon, and various people offered to take roles in the development team. Larry announced the start of Perl 6 development in his keynote "State of the Onion" address the following day.

We then experienced a period of feeling around for the best way to organize the development structure of Perl 6. The single-mailing-list model of Perl 5 was prone to infighting; in addition, the pumpking system was problematic because Perl was beginning to get too big for a single person to maintain, and cases of pumpking burnout were too common.

The consensus was that design should be split between a number of working groups, each of which would have a chair. The first two working groups were perl6-language and perl6-internals, for language design proposals and implementation design, respectively. The busier working groups spawned subgroups for discussion of more focused topics, and developers were encouraged to express their desires for language change in formal Requests for Changes (RFCs).

The comments stage ended on October 1, 2000, after 361 RFCs were submitted. These went to Larry, who sat down to the grueling task of reading each one to assess its merits. Larry then responded by unfolding the language design in a series of articles called *Apocalypses*. Damian Conway, who through generous sponsorship has been working full-time for the Perl community, has been assisting Larry, and has also produced explanatory articles called *Exegeses*. This process will continue well into 2002.

On the other side, the Perl 6 internals working group started an almost independent subproject: to write a generic interpreter that could be used for Perl 6, Perl 5, and perhaps other dynamic languages as well. Dan Sugalski volunteered to be the internals designer for this interpreter (codenamed Parrot, after a particularly pervasive April Fool's joke by one of the authors of this book...) and explained his decisions in a series of Parrot Design Documents.

When enough of the design was ready, Simon stepped up to be the release manager in another futile attempt to put off finishing this book. The first public release of Parrot happened on Monday, September 10, 2001.

At the time of this writing, Parrot has support for pluggable data types, both simple and aggregate; it can compile and execute four mini-languages, (mini-Scheme, mini-Perl, and two languages specially written for Parrot: Jako and Cola); it has working and efficient garbage collections; and it has the beginnings of an x86 just-in-time compiler.

You can get the latest release of Parrot from CPAN in Simon's home directory (http://www.cpan.org/authors/id/S/SI/SIMON/) or by CVS from the perl.org CVS server (http://cvs.perl.org/).

11.4.2   Design and implementation

Dan has been keeping one thing in mind while designing Parrot: speed. The Parrot interpreter will run Perl 6 very fast, and most of the other elements of the design filter down from there. However, we're not forgetting the lessons learned from the Perl 5 internals, and the guts of Parrot are designed to be clearly understandable and easily maintainable.

Parrot deviates from the normal techniques used in building a virtual machine by choosing a register rather than a stack architecture. Although a register-based machine is slightly more difficult to compile for, it has several advantages: first, it lets you use standard compiler optimization techniques tailored for ordinary register-based CPUs; second, it eliminates many of the stack-manipulation operations that take up much of the time of a VM such as Perl 5's; finally, by more closely resembling the underlying hardware, it should be more straightforward to compile down to native code.

Parrot's data abstraction is done via a system of Parrot Magic Cookies (PMCs). These are the equivalent of SVs, but are much more sophisticated. Instead of calling a function on an SV, the PMC carries around with it a vtable (a structure of function pointers) full of the functions it can perform. In a sense, it is an object on which you can call methods. In fact, the PMC abstraction acts as an abstract virtual class, with each language providing vtables that implement the interface; for instance, Perl classes have an addition function that will do the right thing on a Perl value, and Python classes may provide a function that does something different. In this way, the core of Parrot can be language-agnostic, with individual users of Parrot providing data types to fit the needs of their language.

Finally, Parrot has the ability to add in, on a lexically scoped basis, custom ops in addition to its core set. Thus even if a language does certain things wildly differently than Parrot expects, the language will still be able to use the interpreter.

11.4.3 What happens next

Parrot and the design of Perl 6 are developing in parallel; Larry will continue to produce Apocalypses explaining the design, whereas the Parrot hackers are nearing the point where it's worth thinking about compiling real languages onto the VM.

The immediate goals for Parrot at time of writing are to add subroutine and symbol table support, which should be everything needed for a sensible interpreter. By the time the language design firms up, we'll be able to switch emphasis towards writing a compiler from Perl 6 down to Parrot assembler.

11.4.4 The future for Perl 5

If Perl 6 is coming and it's going to be so cool, why have we just written a book about Perl 5? For starters, Perl 6 won't be completed for quite a while—writing a Perl interpreter from scratch is an ambitious exercise! It will also take a long time to become generally accepted.

Perl 5 will continue to be developed up until the release of version 5.8.0, and even then maintenance will continue throughout the lifespan of Perl 6. Perl 5 won't become unsupported.

In short, Perl 5 isn't going away anytime soon. Remember how long it took to get rid of all the Perl 4 interpreters and code? That was when we *wanted* to get rid of it; because Perl 6 is likely to be non-compatible with Perl 5, you can expect uptake to be even slower. There's an awful lot of working Perl 5 code, so people won't want to break it all by upgrading to Perl 6.

11.5 FURTHER READING

More thoughts on patching Perl can be found in the `perl5-porters` FAQ at http://simon-cozens.org/writings/p5p.faq, Simon's "So You Want to Be a Perl Porter?" (http://simon-cozens.org/writings/perlhacktut.html), and in pod/perlhack.pod, Porting/patching.pod, and Porting/pumpking.pod in the Perl distribution.

11.6 SUMMARY

This chapter looked at how to develop `perl` itself, the development process, and the `perl5-porters` mailing list. In addition to discussing some of the tools available to help you develop, such as `perl`'s debugging mode and the GNU debugger, we also looked at the less technical parts of being a Perl porter—how to approach Perl maintenance, and how to submit patches and get them integrated to the Perl core.

We also discussed Perl 6 and gave you a glimpse of how Perl may look in the future.

Perl's typemaps

We have made significant use of the different typemaps throughout this book, but we have not covered all of them. This appendix is a reference that describes all the typemap entries you are likely to encounter, along with simple examples.

A.1 QUICK REFRESHER

As you'll recall from section 6.3, the typemap file consists of three sections:

- A section that defines all the C variable types supported by the typemap along with the corresponding typemap name
- The INPUT section, which describes how a Perl variable is converted to the required C type
- The OUTPUT section, which describes how a C variable is converted to the required Perl variable

The INPUT and OUTPUT entries are a mixture of C code and Perl-style variables. The Perl-style variables have the following meaning:

- *$arg*—The name of the Perl SV in the Perl argument list.
- *$var*—The name of the C variable that is either receiving the value from the SV or setting the value in the SV.
- *$type*—The type of the C variable. This will be one of the types listed at the top of the typemap file.

- $ntype—The type of the C variable, with all asterisks replaced with the string Ptr. A char * would therefore set $ntype to charPtr. This variable is sometimes used for setting classnames or for referencing helper functions.
- *$Package*—The Perl package associated with this variable. This is the same as the value assigned to the PACKAGE directive in the XS file.
- *$func_name*—The name of the XS function.
- *$argoff*—The position of the argument in the argument list. The value begins counting at 0.

A.2 THE TYPEMAPS

In this section we will describe each typemap entry,[1] first showing the INPUT and OUTPUT entries and then showing a (usually contrived) usage. The examples are from the XS::Typemap module that comes as standard with Perl as of version 5.8.0. This module exists purely to make sure the typemap entries have not been broken during the development of Perl, but it provides a simple introduction to all the usual XS types. The typemap entries discussed here come from the typemap file distributed with Perl 5.8.0. In the interests of writing code that will work on older versions of Perl, typemap entries that are broken in Perl 5.6 are noted when applicable.

A.2.1 T_SV

This typemap simply passes the C representation of the Perl variable (an SV*) in and out of the XS layer. You can use it if the C code wants to deal directly with the Perl variable.

T_SV INPUT

```
T_SV
        $var = $arg
```

This is the simplest typemap entry. It makes a simple copy of the pointer (in this case, a pointer to an SV).

T_SV OUTPUT

```
T_SV
        $arg = $var;
```

Similarly, this typemap simply copies the pointer from the XS variable to the argument stack.

---

[1] We'll ignore a handful that no one can remember anything about but that sneaked into the standard typemap file a few years ago!

T_SV example

```
SV *
T_SV( sv )
  SV * sv
 CODE:
  RETVAL = sv_mortalcopy( sv );
  SvREFCNT_inc(RETVAL);
 OUTPUT:
  RETVAL
```

In this example, we need to copy the input variable to the output. In order to do this, we use sv_mortalcopy to make a copy of the variable. Unsurprisingly, it is a mortal copy. The final thing we do is increment the reference count (which would leave sv with a reference count of 2, even though we have only one variable). This code may look a bit strange, due to an assumption made by xsubpp. Because in many cases a new SV is created by the OUTPUT typemap entry, xsubpp tries to be helpful and automatically adds a sv_2mortal(ST(0)) before returning (you know from chapter 6 that mortal SVs should be pushed onto the argument stack). In our example, we have the choice of making sv a mortal SV (knowing that its reference count will be reduced twice because it has been marked as a mortal twice), using a non-mortal SV, or using PP code and pushing the mortal SV onto the stack ourselves. We chose the first option because the sv_mortalcopy function is convenient and using PP code would result in the OUTPUT typemap entry not being used.

A.2.2 T_SVREF

Fixed in Perl 5.8.0. This typemap is used to pass in and return a reference to an SV.

T_SVREF INPUT

```
T_SVREF
        if (SvROK($arg))
            $var = (SV*)SvRV($arg);
        else
            Perl_croak(aTHX_ \"$var is not a reference\")
```

This entry is more complicated than that for a simple scalar because some sanity checking is applied. If the argument is a reference, then the SV* being referenced is retrieved; otherwise Perl complains.

T_SVREF OUTPUT

```
T_SVREF
        $arg = newRV((SV*)$var);
```

This typemap uses newRV to create a new reference to the output scalar. Doing so will increment the reference count on the argument.

T_SVREF example

```
SVREF
T_SVREF( svref )
  SVREF svref
 CODE:
  RETVAL = svref;
 OUTPUT:
  RETVAL
```

In this example, we have used a type of SVREF to indicate that we are providing a reference to a scalar. Even though xsubpp knows how to deal with a type of SVREF, C doesn't; so, we must add a typedef to the top of our XS file as follows:

```
typedef SV * SVREF; /* T_SVREF */
```

A.2.3   T_AVREF

Fixed in Perl 5.8.0. This typemap is used to pass an array reference into and out of C.

T_AVREF INPUT

```
T_AVREF
        if (SvROK($arg) && SvTYPE(SvRV($arg))==SVt_PVAV)
            $var = (AV*)SvRV($arg);
        else
            Perl_croak(aTHX_ \"$var is not an array reference\")
```

This entry is similar to that for T_SVREF except here we are even more explicit and do an additional check to make sure we have an array reference rather than any other type.

T_AVREF OUTPUT

```
T_AVREF
        $arg = newRV((SV*)$var);
```

T_AVREF example

```
AV *
T_AVREF( av )
  AV * av
 CODE:
  RETVAL = av;
 OUTPUT:
  RETVAL
```

A.2.4   T_HVREF

Fixed in Perl 5.8.0. This typemap is used to pass a hash reference into and out of C.

T_HVREF INPUT

```
T_HVREF
        if (SvROK($arg) && SvTYPE(SvRV($arg))==SVt_PVHV)
            $var = (HV*)SvRV($arg);
        else
            Perl_croak(aTHX_ \"$var is not a hash reference\")
```

This entry is similar to that for T_AVREF, except here we check to make sure we have a hash reference rather than any other type.

T_HVREF OUTPUT

```
T_HVREF
        $arg = newRV((SV*)$var);
```

T_HVREF example

```
HV *
T_HVREF( hv )
  HV * hv
 CODE:
  RETVAL = hv;
 OUTPUT:
  RETVAL
```

A.2.5   T_CVREF

Fixed in Perl 5.8.0. This typemap is used to pass a reference to a Perl subroutine into and out of C.

T_CVREF INPUT

```
T_CVREF
        if (SvROK($arg) && SvTYPE(SvRV($arg))==SVt_PVCV)
            $var = (CV*)SvRV($arg);
        else
            Perl_croak(aTHX_ \"$var is not a code reference\")
```

This entry is similar to that for T_AVREF, except here we check to make sure we have a code reference rather than any other type.

T_CVREF OUTPUT

```
T_CVREF
        $arg = newRV((SV*)$var);
```

T_CVREF example

```
CV *
T_CVREF( cv )
  CV * cv
 CODE:
```

```
     RETVAL = cv;
  OUTPUT:
   RETVAL
```

A.2.6   T_SYSRET

The `T_SYSRET` typemap is used to process return values from system calls. It is meaningful only when you're passing values from C to Perl (there is no concept of passing a system return value from Perl to C).

System calls return -1 on error (setting `errno` with the reason) and (usually) 0 on success. If the return value is -1, this typemap returns `undef`. If the return value is not -1, this typemap translates a 0 (Perl false) to "0 but true" (which is treated as a `true` value in Perl) or returns the value itself, to indicate that the command succeeded.

The `POSIX` module makes extensive use of this type.

T_SYSRET INPUT

An `INPUT` entry is not relevant for this typemap.

T_SYSRET OUTPUT

```
T_SYSRET
        if ($var != -1) {
            if ($var == 0)
                sv_setpvn($arg, "0 but true", 10);
            else
                sv_setiv($arg, (IV)$var);
        }
```

T_SYSRET example

```
# A successful return

SysRet
T_SYSRET_pass()
 CODE:
  RETVAL = 0;
 OUTPUT:
  RETVAL

# A failure

SysRet
T_SYSRET_fail()
 CODE:
  RETVAL = -1;
 OUTPUT:
  RETVAL
```

This example requires that the `SysRet` type is declared using a typedef as

```
typedef int SysRet; /* T_SYSRET */
```

A.2.7 T_UV

This typemap is for an unsigned integer. It is cast to the required unsigned integer type when passed to C and converted to a UV when passed back to Perl.

T_UV INPUT

```
T_UV
        $var = ($type)SvUV($arg)
```

T_UV OUTPUT

```
T_UV
        sv_setuv($arg, (UV)$var);
```

T_UV example

```
unsigned int
T_UV( uv )
  unsigned int uv
 CODE:
  RETVAL = uv;
 OUTPUT:
  RETVAL
```

A.2.8 T_IV

This typemap is for a signed integer. It is cast to the required integer type when passed to C and converted to an IV when passed back to Perl.

T_IV INPUT

```
T_IV
        $var = ($type)SvIV($arg)
```

T_IV OUTPUT

```
T_IV
        sv_setiv($arg, (IV)$var);
```

T_IV example

```
long
T_IV( iv )
  long iv
 CODE:
  RETVAL = iv;
 OUTPUT:
  RETVAL
```

A.2.9 T_INT

This typemap is for a signed integer. It converts the Perl value to a native integer type (the int type on the current platform). When the value is returned to Perl, it is processed the same way as for T_IV.

This typemap's behavior is identical to using an int type in XS with T_IV.

T_INT INPUT

```
T_INT
        $var = (int)SvIV($arg)
```

T_INT OUTPUT

```
T_INT
        sv_setiv($arg, (IV)$var);
```

T_INT example

See T_IV.

A.2.10 T_ENUM

This typemap is for an enum value. It's used to transfer an enum component from C. There is usually no reason to pass an enum value to C because it will always be stored as an IV inside the SV, but the facility is provided.

T_ENUM INPUT

```
T_ENUM
        $var = ($type)SvIV($arg)
```

T_ENUM OUTPUT

```
T_ENUM
        sv_setiv($arg, (IV)$var);
```

T_ENUM example

```
svtype
T_ENUM()
 CODE:
  RETVAL = SVt_PVHV;
 OUTPUT:
  RETVAL
```

The svtype enum is defined in the include file sv.h that comes with the standard Perl distribution (SVt_PVHV is part of that enum). Because the default typemap does not know that svtype should be processed using T_ENUM, this example would require a local typemap file containing the line

```
svtype        T_ENUM
```

A.2.11 T_BOOL

This typemap is for a boolean type. It can be used to pass true and false values to and from C.

T_BOOL INPUT

```
T_BOOL
        $var = (bool)SvTRUE($arg)
```

T_BOOL OUTPUT

```
T_BOOL
        $arg = boolSV($var);
```

T_BOOL example

```
bool
T_BOOL( in )
  bool in
 CODE:
  RETVAL = in;
 OUTPUT:
  RETVAL
```

A.2.12 T_U_INT

This typemap is for unsigned integers. It is equivalent to using T_UV but explicitly casts the variable to type unsigned int. Ironically, the default type for unsigned int itself is T_UV.

T_U_INT INPUT

```
T_U_INT
        $var = (unsigned int)SvUV($arg)
```

T_U_INT OUTPUT

```
T_U_INT
        sv_setuv($arg, (UV)$var);
```

T_U_INT example

See T_UV.

A.2.13 T_SHORT

This typemap is for short integers. It is equivalent to T_IV but explicitly casts the return to type short. The default typemap for short is T_IV.

T_SHORT INPUT

```
T_SHORT
        $var = (short)SvIV($arg)
```

T_SHORT OUTPUT

```
T_SHORT
        sv_setiv($arg, (IV)$var);
```

T_SHORT example

See T_IV.

A.2.14 T_U_SHORT

This typemap is for unsigned short integers. It is equivalent to T_UV but explicitly casts the return to type unsigned short. The default typemap for unsigned short is T_UV, but T_U_SHORT is used for type U16 in the standard typemap.

T_U_SHORT INPUT

```
T_U_SHORT
        $var = (unsigned short)SvUV($arg)
```

T_U_SHORT OUTPUT

```
T_U_SHORT
        sv_setuv($arg, (UV)$var);
```

T_U_SHORT example

```
U16
T_U_SHORT( in )
  U16 in
 CODE:
  RETVAL = in;
 OUTPUT:
  RETVAL
```

A.2.15 T_LONG

This typemap is for long integers. It is equivalent to T_IV but explicitly casts the return to type long. The default typemap for long is T_IV.

T_LONG INPUT

```
T_LONG
        $var = (long)SvIV($arg)
```

T_LONG OUTPUT

```
T_LONG
        sv_setiv($arg, (IV)$var);
```

T_LONG example

See T_IV.

A.2.16 T_U_LONG

This typemap is for unsigned long integers. It is equivalent to T_UV but explicitly casts the return to type unsigned long. The default typemap for unsigned long is T_UV, but T_U_LONG is used for type U32 in the standard typemap.

T_U_LONG INPUT

```
T_U_LONG
        $var = (unsigned long)SvUV($arg)
```

T_U_LONG OUTPUT

```
T_U_LONG
        sv_setuv($arg, (UV)$var);
```

T_U_LONG example

```
U32
T_U_LONG( in )
  U32 in
 CODE:
  RETVAL = in;
 OUTPUT:
  RETVAL
```

A.2.17 T_CHAR

This typemap is used for single 8-bit characters (it differs from T_U_CHAR because it returns characters rather than bytes).

T_CHAR INPUT

```
T_CHAR
        $var = (char)*SvPV_nolen($arg)
```

T_CHAR OUTPUT

```
T_CHAR
        sv_setpvn($arg, (char *)&$var, 1);
```

T_CHAR example

```
char
T_CHAR( in );
  char in
 CODE:
  RETVAL = in;
 OUTPUT:
  RETVAL
```

A.2.18 T_U_CHAR

This typemap is used for an unsigned byte.

T_U_CHAR INPUT

```
T_U_CHAR
        $var = (unsigned char)SvUV($arg)
```

T_U_CHAR OUTPUT

```
T_U_CHAR
        sv_setuv($arg, (UV)$var);
```

T_U_CHAR example

```
unsigned char
T_U_CHAR( in );
  unsigned char in
 CODE:
  RETVAL = in;
 OUTPUT:
  RETVAL
```

A.2.19 T_FLOAT

This typemap is used for a floating-point number. It guarantees to return a variable cast to a `float`.

T_FLOAT INPUT

```
T_FLOAT
        $var = (float)SvNV($arg)
```

T_FLOAT OUTPUT

```
T_FLOAT
        sv_setnv($arg, (double)$var);
```

T_FLOAT example

```
float
T_FLOAT( in )
  float in
 CODE:
  RETVAL = in;
 OUTPUT:
  RETVAL
```

A.2.20 T_NV

This typemap is used for a Perl floating-point number. It's similar to T_IV and T_UV in that the return type is cast to the requested numeric type rather than to a specific type.

T_NV INPUT

```
T_NV
        $var = ($type)SvNV($arg)
```

T_NV OUTPUT

```
T_NV
        sv_setnv($arg, (NV)$var);
```

T_NV example

```
NV
T_NV( in )
  NV in
 CODE:
  RETVAL = in;
 OUTPUT:
  RETVAL
```

A.2.21 T_DOUBLE

This typemap is used for a double-precision floating-point number. It guarantees to return a variable cast to a double.

T_DOUBLE INPUT

```
T_DOUBLE
        $var = (double)SvNV($arg)
```

T_DOUBLE OUTPUT

```
T_DOUBLE
        sv_setnv($arg, (double)$var);
```

T_DOUBLE example

```
double
T_DOUBLE( in )
  double in
 CODE:
  RETVAL = in;
 OUTPUT:
  RETVAL
```

A.2.22   T_PV

This typemap is used for a string.

T_PV INPUT

```
T_PV
        $var = ($type) SvPV_nolen($arg)
```

T_PV OUTPUT

```
T_PV
        sv_setpv((SV*)$arg, $var);
```

T_PV example

```
char *
T_PV( in )
  char * in
 CODE:
  RETVAL = in;
 OUTPUT:
  RETVAL
```

A.2.23   T_PTR

This typemap is used for a pointer. It's typically associated with a void * type.

T_PTR INPUT

```
T_PTR
        $var = INT2PTR($type,SvIV($arg))
```

T_PTR OUTPUT

```
T_PTR
        sv_setiv($arg, PTR2IV($var));
```

T_PTR example

```
# Change the value using the input value and return the pointer

void *
T_PTR_OUT( in )
  int in;
 CODE:
  xst_anint = in;
  RETVAL = &xst_anint;
 OUTPUT:
  RETVAL

# Pass in the pointer and return the value

int
```

```
T_PTR_IN( ptr )
  void * ptr
 CODE:
  RETVAL = *(int *)ptr;
 OUTPUT:
  RETVAL
```

This example provides one function that returns a pointer to a static integer and another that reads that pointer and returns the value of the integer it points to. This example requires that the variable xst_anint has been declared as an integer at the top of the XS file.

A.2.24   T_PTRREF

This typemap is similar to T_PTR, except that the pointer is stored in a scalar and the reference to that scalar is returned to the caller. It can be used to hide the actual pointer value from the programmer, because it is usually not required directly from within Perl.

T_PTRREF INPUT

```
T_PTRREF
        if (SvROK($arg)) {
                IV tmp = SvIV((SV*)SvRV($arg));
                $var = INT2PTR($type,tmp);
        }
        else
                Perl_croak(aTHX_ \"$var is not a reference\")
```

The typemap checks that a scalar reference is passed from Perl to XS.

T_PTRREF OUTPUT

```
T_PTRREF
        sv_setref_pv($arg, Nullch, (void*)$var);
```

T_PTRREF example

```
# Set the static variable using the supplied number and return
# a pointer.

intRef *
T_PTRREF_OUT( in )
  intRef in;
 CODE:
  xst_anint = in;
  RETVAL = &xst_anint;
 OUTPUT:
  RETVAL

# pass in the pointer and return the value

intRef
```

```
T_PTRREF_IN( ptr )
  intRef * ptr
 CODE:
  RETVAL = *ptr;
 OUTPUT:
  RETVAL
```

This example is similar to that provided for T_PTR, except that here we use a type of intRef* rather than a void*, making sure the local typemap file declares that an intRef* is to be processed using T_PTRREF. intRef is typedef'd to an integer.

A.2.25 T_PTROBJ

This typemap is similar to T_PTRREF except that the reference is blessed into a class, allowing the pointer to be used as an object. It's commonly used to deal with C structs. The typemap checks that the Perl object passed into the XS routine is of the correct class (or part of a subclass).

The pointer is blessed into a class that is derived from the name of the pointer's type, but with all asterisks in the name replaced with Ptr.

T_PTROBJ INPUT

```
T_PTROBJ
        if (sv_derived_from($arg, \"${ntype}\")) {
            IV tmp = SvIV((SV*)SvRV($arg));
            $var = INT2PTR($type,tmp);
        }
        else
            Perl_croak(aTHX_ \"$var is not of type ${ntype}\")
```

T_PTROBJ OUTPUT

```
T_PTROBJ
        sv_setref_pv($arg, \"${ntype}\", (void*)$var);
```

T_PTROBJ example

```
# Pass in a value and return the pointer as an object

MODULE = XS::Typemap   PACKAGE = XS::Typemap

intObj *
T_PTROBJ_OUT( in )
  intObj in;
 CODE:
  xst_anint = in;
  RETVAL = &xst_anint;
 OUTPUT:
  RETVAL

# pass in the pointer and return the value

MODULE = XS::Typemap   PACKAGE = intObjPtr
```

```
intObj
T_PTROBJ_IN( ptr )
  intObj * ptr
 CODE:
  RETVAL = *ptr;
 OUTPUT:
  RETVAL
```

This example is essentially the same as that for T_PTRREF, except that here intObj* is assumed to be associated with type T_PTROBJ in the local typemap file (intObj is a typedef to an integer). In addition, the function T_PTROBJ_IN is placed into package intObjPtr, because that is the class in which the T_PTROBJ typemap will bless the return value. These functions could be used as follows:

```
$object = T_PTROBJ_OUT( $in );
$out = $object->T_PTROBJ_IN;
```

This is how they are used in the tests for XS::Typemap.

A.2.26   T_REF_IV_PTR

This typemap is similar to T_PTROBJ in that the pointer is blessed into a scalar object. The difference is that when the object is passed back into XS, it must be of the correct type (inheritance is not supported).

The pointer is blessed into a class that is derived from the name of the pointer's type, but with all asterisks in the name replaced with Ptr.

T_REF_IV_PTR INPUT

```
T_REF_IV_PTR
        if (sv_isa($arg, \"${ntype}\")) {
            IV tmp = SvIV((SV*)SvRV($arg));
            $var = INT2PTR($type, tmp);
        }
        else
            Perl_croak(aTHX_ \"$var is not of type ${ntype}\")
```

T_REF_IV_PTR OUTPUT

```
T_REF_IV_PTR
        sv_setref_pv($arg, \"${ntype}\", (void*)$var);
```

T_REF_IV_PTR example

See the example for T_PTROBJ, except that inheritance will be disabled.

A.2.27   T_OPAQUEPTR

You can use this typemap to store bytes in the string component of the SV. Here the representation of the data is irrelevant to Perl, and the bytes themselves are stored in the SV. It is assumed that the C variable is a pointer (the bytes are copied from that memory location). If the pointer is pointing to something that is represented by 8 bytes, then those 8 bytes are stored in the SV (and length() will report a value of 8).

In principle, you can use the unpack command to convert the bytes back to a number (if the underlying type is known to be a number).

This typemap can also be used to store a C structure[2] (the number of bytes to be copied is calculated using the C sizeof function) and can be used as an alternative to T_PTRREF without having to worry about a memory leak (because the byte representation of the struct will be in a Perl variable stored in the SV rather than simply storing a pointer in the SV).

T_OPAQUEPTR INPUT

```
T_OPAQUEPTR
        $var = ($type) SvPV_nolen($arg)
```

T_OPAQUEPTR OUTPUT

```
T_OPAQUEPTR
        sv_setpvn($arg, (char *)$var, sizeof(*$var));
```

T_OPAQUEPTR example

```
astruct *
T_OPAQUEPTR_IN_struct( a,b,c )
  int a
  int b
  double c
 PREINIT:
  astruct test;
 CODE:
  test.a = a;
  test.b = b;
  test.c = c;
  RETVAL = &test;
 OUTPUT:
  RETVAL

void
T_OPAQUEPTR_OUT_struct( test )
  astruct * test
 PPCODE:
  XPUSHs(sv_2mortal(newSViv(test->a)));
  XPUSHs(sv_2mortal(newSViv(test->b)));
  XPUSHs(sv_2mortal(newSVnv(test->c)));
```

In this example, the first function takes three arguments, puts them into a structure declared in the PREINIT block, and on output copies the contents to the Perl string

---

[2] Assuming the structure itself does not contain pointers

buffer. When that buffer is passed to the second function, the bytes are unpacked and a pointer to that buffer is stored in the `test` variable. The values are then extracted from the structure and pushed onto the argument stack. In this example, a struct has been declared at the top of the XS file as

```
struct t_opaqueptr {
  int a;
  int b;
  double c;
};
```

```
typedef struct t_opaqueptr astruct;
```

A.2.28   T_OPAQUE

This typemap is almost identical to `T_OPAQUEPTR`, but it works on non-pointer types. Whereas `T_OPAQUEPTR` would read the bytes from, say, an `int*`, this typemap would extract the bytes from an `int`. For example, if an integer is imported into Perl using `T_OPAQUE` rather than `T_IV`, the underlying bytes representing the integer will be stored in the `SV` but the actual integer value will not be available. The data is opaque to Perl and can be retrieved only using the `unpack` function.

T_OPAQUE INPUT

```
T_OPAQUE
        $var = *($type *)SvPV_nolen($arg)
```

T_OPAQUE OUTPUT

```
T_OPAQUE
        sv_setpvn($arg, (char *)&$var, sizeof($var));
```

T_OPAQUE example

```
shortOPQ
T_OPAQUE_IN( val )
  int val
 CODE:
  RETVAL = (shortOPQ)val;
 OUTPUT:
  RETVAL

IV
T_OPAQUE_OUT( val )
  shortOPQ val
 CODE:
  RETVAL = (IV)val;
 OUTPUT:
  RETVAL
```

In this example, an integer is given to the first function, the integer is cast to a `short`, and the bytes are stored in the return value. Those bytes are then read into the second function, converted back to a `short`, and cast as an `int` for return.

A.2.29 T_PACKED

This typemap is used to exchange data between Perl and C in a generic manner outside the typemap file. You must write helper functions to convert between the Perl and C datatypes, and these are called from the typemap system. The names of these functions depend on the C type.

T_PACKED INPUT

```
T_PACKED
        $var = XS_unpack_$ntype($arg)
```

T_PACKED OUTPUT

```
T_PACKED
        XS_pack_$ntype($arg, $var);
```

T_OPAQUE example

See `T_PACKEDARRAY`.

A.2.30 T_PACKEDARRAY

This typemap is used to exchange array data between Perl and C in a generic manner outside the typemap file. You must write helper functions to convert between the Perl and C datatypes, and these are called from the typemap system. The names of these functions depend on the C type. The input typemap is identical to that for `T_PACKED`. The difference between `T_PACKED` and `T_PACKEDARRAY` is that the output typemap has an extra argument indicating the number of array elements to return. The XS writer must define and set the variable `count_$ntype`.

T_PACKEDARRAY INPUT

```
T_PACKEDARRAY
        $var = XS_unpack_$ntype($arg)
```

T_PACKEDARRAY OUTPUT

```
T_PACKEDARRAY
        XS_pack_$ntype($arg, $var, count_$ntype);
```

T_PACKEDARRAY example

The usual example for this typemap entry is string arrays. Functions named `XS_unpack_charPtrPtr` and `XS_pack_charPtrPtr` must be supplied to import/export string arrays. An example can be found in section 6.6.5.

A.2.31 T_ARRAY

Fixed in Perl 5.8.0. This typemap is used to convert the Perl argument list to a C array and to push the contents of a C array onto the Perl argument stack (if you don't want to go to the trouble of using a PPCODE block).

The usual calling signature is

```
@out = array_func( @in );
```

Any number of arguments can occur in the list before the array, but the input and output arrays must be the last elements in the list.

When this typemap is used to pass a Perl list to C, the XS writer must provide a function or a macro (named after the array type but with Ptr substituted for each asterisk) to allocate the memory required to hold the list. A pointer should be returned. It is up to the XS writer to free the memory on exit from the function or to use a memory allocator that uses mortal space (for example, get_mortalspace, described in "Strings and things," page 240[3]). The variable ix_$var is set to the number of elements in the new array (of course, the value of $var will depend on the array name).

When returning a C array to Perl, the XS writer must provide an integer variable called size_$var containing the number of elements in the array. It is used to determine how many elements should be pushed onto the return argument stack. This value is not required on input because Perl knows how many arguments are on the stack when the routine is called. Ordinarily this variable is called size_RETVAL.

Additionally, the type of each element is determined from the type of the array. If the array uses type intArray *, xsubpp will automatically determine that it contains variables of type int and use that typemap entry to perform the copy of each element (this information is encoded in the DO_ARRAY_ELEM part of the typemap entry). All pointer (*) and Array tags are removed from the name to determine the subtype.

T_ARRAY INPUT

```
T_ARRAY
        U32 ix_$var = $argoff;
        $var = $ntype(items -= $argoff);
        while (items--) {
            DO_ARRAY_ELEM;
            ix_$var++;
        }
        /* this is the number of elements in the array */
        ix_$var -= $argoff
```

---

[3] You can use a generic memory allocator such as get_mortalspace in conjunction with the T_ARRAY typemap by using macros. For example the allocator for an intArray* could be defined as a macro with

```
#define intArrayPtr(n) get_mortalspace((n) * sizeof(intArray))
```

T_ARRAY OUTPUT

```
T_ARRAY
      {
          U32 ix_$var;
          EXTEND(SP,size_$var);
          for (ix_$var = 0; ix_$var < size_$var; ix_$var++) {
              ST(ix_$var) = sv_newmortal();
              DO_ARRAY_ELEM
          }
      }
```

T_ARRAY example

```
intArray *       ❶
T_ARRAY( array, ... )    ❷
  intArray * array
 PREINIT:
  U32 size_RETVAL;       ❸
 CODE:
  size_RETVAL = ix_array;    ❹
  RETVAL = array;        ❺
 OUTPUT:
  RETVAL     ❻
 CLEANUP:
  Safefree(array);       ❼
  XSRETURN(size_RETVAL);     ❽
```

❶ Somewhere we need to typedef `intArray` to an integer and tell xsubpp (via a local typemap file) that an `intArray*` should be processed using `T_ARRAY`.

❷ We are expecting many input arguments, so we use the ellipsis to indicate that we don't know how many arguments are coming.

❸ This variable contains the number of elements we wish to return to Perl. The name of the variable is chosen for us, because the typemap entry must obtain this information using this variable.

❹ The number of input arguments supplied is stored in `ix_array` by the INPUT typemap, so we simply copy this value to `size_RETVAL` for use in the OUTPUT typemap.

❺ Because we are just copying the input array to the output, we copy the pointer to `RETVAL`.

❻ If we don't mention this, xsubpp will not return anything!

❼ If the memory used for the array was not mortal, it must be freed here (the CLEANUP functions are called after the values are copied to the argument stack).

8 Because xsubpp was only expecting us to return a single value (after all, we are not using a PPCODE section), the C code generated from this XS code finishes with XSRETURN(1). If this function is used, Perl will think that only one value has been returned. If we use an explicit XSRETURN in the CLEANUP block, we can subvert this behavior and return from XS earlier than expected (the CLEANUP block is good because we know it's called after the values are copied onto the argument stack).

A.2.32 T_STDIO

New in Perl 5.8.0. This typemap is used for passing Perl filehandles to and from C using standard I/O FILE* structures. T_INOUT should be used if a PerlIO* is required.

T_STDIO INPUT

```
T_STDIO
        $var = PerlIO_findFILE(IoIFP(sv_2io($arg)))
```

T_STDIO OUTPUT

```
T_STDIO
        {
            GV *gv = newGVgen("$Package");
            PerlIO *fp = PerlIO_importFILE($var,0);
            if ( fp && do_open(gv, "+<&", 3, FALSE, 0, 0, fp) )
                sv_setsv($arg, sv_bless(newRV((SV*)gv),
                        gv_stashpv("$Package",1)
            else
                $arg = &PL_sv_undef;
        }
```

T_STDIO example

```
FILE *
T_STDIO_open( file )
  const char * file
 CODE:
  RETVAL = fopen( file, "w" );
 OUTPUT:
  RETVAL

int
T_STDIO_print( stream, string )
  FILE * stream
  const char * string
 CODE:
  RETVAL = fprintf( stream, string );
 OUTPUT:
  RETVAL
```

A.2.33 T_INOUT

This typemap is used for passing Perl filehandles to and from C using the Perl I/O subsystem (via `PerlIO*` structures). If you are using `FILE*` streams, you should use `T_STDIO`.

T_INOUT INPUT

```
T_INOUT
        $var = IoIFP(sv_2io($arg))
```

T_INOUT OUTPUT

```
T_INOUT
        {
            GV *gv = newGVgen("$Package");
            if ( do_open(gv, "+<&", 3, FALSE, 0, 0, $var) )
                sv_setsv($arg, sv_bless(newRV((SV*)gv),
                           gv_stashpv("$Package",1)));
            else
                $arg = &PL_sv_undef;
        }}
```

T_INOUT example

```
PerlIO *
T_INOUT_open( file )
  const char * file
 CODE:
  RETVAL = PerlIO_open( file, "w" );
 OUTPUT:
  RETVAL

int
T_INOUT_print( f, string )
  PerlIO * f
  const char * string
 CODE:
  RETVAL = PerlIO_printf( f, string );
 OUTPUT:
  RETVAL
```

APPENDIX B

Further reading

As we mentioned back in the preface, we've tried to make this book as definitive as possible. However, we can't possibly explain everything, and you may find many other references useful in the course of your work integrating Perl and C.

PERL

Conway, Damian. *Object Oriented Perl.* Manning Publications, 1999, 18844777791.

NetThink Perl 5 Internals tutorial: http://www.netthink.co.uk/downloads/internals/.

NetThink Perl and Unicode tutorial: http://www.netthink.co.uk/downloads/unicode.pdf.

Parrot: http://www.parrotcode.org/.

Perl 6 development site: http://dev.perl.org/.

Perl documentation: `perlxs`, `perlxstut`, `perlapi`, `perlguts`, `perlcall`, `perlembed`, `XS::Typemap`.

"PerlGuts Illustrated": http://gisle.aas.no/perl/illguts.

Srinivasan, Sriram. *Advanced Perl Programming.* O'Reilly and Associates, 1997, 1565922204.

Wall, Larry, Tom Christiansen, and Jon Orwant. *Programming Perl.* 3d ed. O'Reilly and Associates, 2000, 0596000278.

C

comp.lang.c FAQ: http://www.eskimo.com/~scs/C-faq/top.html.

Darwin, Ian, and Geoff Collyer, "Can't Happen or /* NOTREACHED */ or Ral Programs Dump Core," USENIX Association Winter Conference, Dallas 1985 Proceedings (http://www.cs.umd.edu/users/cml/cstyle/cant.pdf).

Harbison, Samuel, and Guy Steele. *C: A Reference Manual.* 5th ed. Prentice Hall, 2002, 013089592X.

Kernighan, Brian, and Dennis Ritchie. *The C Programming Language.* 2d ed. Prentice Hall, 1988, 0131103628.

Kelley, Al, and Ira Pohl, *A Book on C*, 4th. ed., Addison-Wesley, 1998, 0201183994.

"Programming in C": http://www.lysator.liu.se/c/.

APPENDIX C

Perl API index

Chapter 5 detailed and provided examples for many of the functions in the Perl API. However, the API is the means through which C programmers interact with Perl, and as such it pervades this book. This index draws together all the references to the Perl API functions we've used throughout the book.

G_NOARGS 261
G_NODEBUG 133, 159
G_SCALAR 159–160, 203, 263
G_VOID 160
get_av 132–133, 140, 145, 159
get_cv 133, 145, 159
get_hv 145, 159
get_sv 103–104, 113, 125–126,
　　145, 159, 258–259, 274–276
GIMME 160
GIMME_V 160
gv_stashpv 132, 346–347
GvCV 134
GvHV 147, 149
HeVAL 148
hv_clear 146
hv_delete 146–147
hv_delete_ent 146–147
hv_exists_ent 147
hv_fetch 145, 147–148, 159
hv_fetch_ent 147
hv_iterinit 141, 149
hv_iterkeysv 141, 150
hv_iternext 141
hv_iternextsv 149
hv_store 145–146, 148–149,
　　158, 179
hv_store_ent 148
hv_undef 146
HvKEYS 130
INT2PTR 131, 158–159, 176,
　　196, 337–340
IoIFP 346–347
is_utf8_char 156
is_utf8_string 156
isALNUM 161
isALPHA 161
isDIGIT 161
isLOWER 161
isSPACE 161
isUPPER 161
LEAVE 102, 133, 204, 260–
　　261, 263–264
Move 151–152
n_a 292

New 68, 150, 153–154, 165,
　　175, 186, 227, 241, 247
newAV 107, 133–134, 138,
　　141, 143, 201
Newc 150
newGVgen 346–347
newHV 129, 132, 145–146,
　　179
newRV 102, 124, 129–130,
　　145, 326–328, 346–347
newRV_noinc 102, 129, 132
NEWSV 104–105, 107, 154,
　　187, 203, 241–242, 247
newSV 102, 104, 108
newSViv 106, 158, 179, 182,
　　203, 244, 341
newSVnv 106, 341
newSVpv 106, 122, 135, 140,
　　146, 160, 182, 241–242, 244,
　　261–262, 264
newSVpvf 108–109, 122, 127
newSVpvn 106, 120, 155
newSvpvn 106
newSVsv 107–108, 138, 207
newSVuv 106
newXS 228
Newz 150, 154
Nullch 126, 338
op_dump 310
perl_alloc 256–258, 266, 271
PERL_ASYNC_CHECK 289
perl_construct 256–258, 266,
　　271
Perl_croak 110, 118, 131, 159,
　　174, 176, 225, 227, 326–328,
　　338–340
perl_destruct 256–257, 260,
　　266, 272
perl_free 256–257, 260, 266,
　　272
perl_get_av 132
perl_get_cv 145
perl_get_hv 145
perl_get_sv 104
perl_module2file 147

perl_parse 256–258, 266, 271
PERL_REVISION 225
perl_run 256–258, 266, 271
PERL_SUBVERSION 225
Perl_sv_cmp 141–142
Perl_sv_cmp_locale 141–142
Perl_sv_upgrade 75
PERL_SYS_TERM 257
Perl_utf8_length 156
PERL_VERSION 225
PerlIO_close 102
PerlIO_findFILE 346
PerlIO_importFILE 346
PerlIO_open 102, 347
PerlIO_printf 130, 347
PerlIO_stdoutf 104
PL_destruct_level 266
PL_do_undump 257
PL_na 108, 111, 113, 167, 199,
　　225, 227
PL_op 286, 289, 295
PL_patchlevel 125
PL_perl_destruct_level 257
PL_res 102
PL_strtab 89
PL_sv_no 103, 138
PL_sv_undef 101–103, 109,
　　133, 139, 225, 346–347
PL_sv_yes 103, 138, 141
PL_tainting 112
POPi 292
POPn 292
POPpx 292
POPs 139, 262, 264, 292
pTHX 174
pTHX_ 105, 152, 174
PTR2IV 158, 337
PTR2NV 158
PTR2UV 158
PUSHi 109, 183, 227, 292
PUSHMARK 159, 203, 260,
　　263–264
PUSHn 183
PUSHp 183
PUSHs 103, 109, 120, 139,
　　182, 190, 261, 292

index

formats 108
Fortran 58, 63, 223
   arrays 216
   Makefile.PL 220
   portability 221
Free Software Foundation 2
fundamental operations 285

G

g++ 209
g77 216, 220
GCC 2
gcc 34
gdb 310–316
get_mortalspace 200, 242, 344
gethostbyname 122
getppid 153
GIMP 254
Glazebrook, Karl 193, 218
globs 91
Gnome 47, 254
gnumeric 254
grammar 282

H

h2xs 29–31, 40, 42, 45, 170, 232
Harbison, Samuel 69
hashes
   API 144–150
   efficiency 90
   implementation 87
   number 88
   reference 179
   value 147
header files 3
HTTP 254, 265

I

I/O
   buffered 62
   descriptor 63
include files 3

inet_aton 122
Ingerson, Brian 238
Inline 238
   arrays 243
   CPAN 245
   internals 239
   return arguments 244
   stack manipulation 243
   strings 240
Inline API
   Inline_Stack_Push 244
   Inline_Stack_Reset 244
   Inline_Stack_Vars 244
INT_MAX 12, 17
INT_MIN 12
interpolation 284

J

jako 322
Java 65, 118, 223, 239
javadoc 320
Jepson, Brian 223
JPL 223

K

Kernighan, Brian 1, 69
Keywords 284

L

lexical variables
   implementation 95
limits.h 12
linked list 88
Linux 221
Lukka, Tuomas 193
lvalue 97, 136

M

macros 21–22
magic 81
make 27, 33, 35, 50, 68
Makefile.PL 27, 44, 47, 234, 246, 249

MakeMaker 28
   CC 209
   DEFINE 45, 47
   INC 45, 47
   LD 209
   LIBS 45, 47
   MODULE 44
   NAME 45, 47, 209, 234
   OBJECT 235
   PACKAGE 44
   PREREQ_PM 28, 45, 47, 245
   TYPEMAPS 197
   VERSION 234
   VERSION_FROM 28, 45, 47, 209
   WriteMakefile 28, 44–45, 47
makepatch 320
MANIFEST 28, 33
mantissa 14
McCamant, Stephen 296
memory
   allocation 64
   leak 64, 105, 175, 180
   management 150, 165, 199
   mortal 203, 242
methods 309
Microsoft Visual C++ 216
Microsoft Visual Studio 2
module
   Apache 113
   Apache::SubRequest 140
   Apache::Table 160
   Apache::Util 122
   Astro::SLA 228, 230
   AutoLoader 40, 232
   B 114, 289
   B::Bytecode 296
   B::Concise 298
   B::Debug 298, 307
   B::Flags 299
   B::Graph 307
   B::Terse 296, 298, 307
   C::DynaLib 251
   C::Scan 232